Y0-DCA-026

Probing the Frontiers
of Biblical Studies

Princeton Theological Monograph Series

K. C. Hanson, Charles M. Collier, and D. Christopher Spinks,
Series Editors

Recent volumes in the series:

Lowell K. Handy
Psalm 29 Through Time and Tradition

D. Seipl and Frederick W. Weidmann, editors
Enigmas and Powers

Stanley D. Walters
Go Figure!

Mark W. Hamilton et al., editors
Renewing Tradition

Scott A. Ellington
Risking Truth

David A. Ackerman
Lo, I Tell You a Mystery

Lloyd Kim
Polemic in the Book of Hebrews

Probing the Frontiers
of Biblical Studies

EDITED BY
J. HAROLD ELLENS *and*
JOHN T. GREENE

PICKWICK *Publications* · Eugene, Oregon

BS
600.3
.P76
2009

PROBING THE FRONTIERS OF BIBLICAL STUDIES

Princeton Theological Monograph Series 111

Copyright © 2009 Wipf and Stock Publishers. All rights reserved. Except for brief quotations in critical publications or reviews, no part of this book may be reproduced in any manner without prior written permission from the publisher. Write: Permissions, Wipf and Stock Publishers, 199 W. 8th Ave., Suite 3, Eugene, OR 97401.

Pickwick Publications
A Division of Wipf and Stock Publishers
199 W. 8th Ave., Suite 3
Eugene, OR 97401

www.wipfandstock.com

ISBN 13: 978-1-60608-460-1

Cataloging-in-Publication data:

Probing the frontiers of biblical studies / edited by J. Harold Ellens and John T. Greene.

xii + 304 p. ; 23 cm. Includes indexes.

Princeton Theological Monograph Series 111

ISBN 13: 978-1-60608-460-1

1. Bible. O.T.—Criticism, interpretation, etc. 2. Bible. O.T. Pentateuch—Criticism, interpretation, etc. 3. J document (Biblical criticisim). 4. Bible. O.T. Job—Criticism, interpretation, etc. 5. Balaam (Biblical figure). I. Ellens, J. Harold, 1932–. II. John T. Greene. III. Clines, David J. A. IV. Title. V. Series.

BS1171.3 P75 2009

Manufactured in the U.S.A.

Dedicated to David J. A. Clines,
consummate Old Testament scholar
with an irrepressible sense of humor.
While consistently producing the most serious academic work,
he persists in the good sense
of not taking the Academy too seriously.
He seems to esteem all humankind gracefully,
but none of us overmuch!

Contents

Abbreviations

AB	Anchor Bible
ANET	*Ancient Near Eastern Texts Relating to the Old Testament.* 3rd ed. Edited by James B. Pritchard. Princeton: Princeton University Press, 1969
AOTC	Abingdon Old Testament Commentaries
ATM	Altes Testament und Moderne
BA	*Biblical Archaeologist*
BAR	*Biblical Archaeology Review*
BASOR	*Bulletin of the American Schools of Oriental Research*
BASORSup	Bulletin of the American Schools of Oriental Research Supplements
BHS	Biblia Hebraica Stuttgartensia
BibIntSer	Biblical Interpretation Series
BJS	Brown Judaic Studies
BWANT	Beiträge zur Wissenschaft vom Alten und Neuen Testament
BZAW	Beihefte zur Zeitschrift für die alttestamentliche Wissenschaft
CBET	Contributions to Biblical Exegesis and Theology
CBQ	*Catholic Biblical Quarterly*
CC	Continental Commentary
EQ	*Evangelical Quarterly*
EvTh	*Evangelische Theologie*
FCBS	Fortress Classics in Biblical Studies
FOTL	Forms of the Old Testament Literature
FRLANT	Forschungen zur Religion und Literatur des Alten und Neuen Testaments
HAR	*Hebrew Annual Review*

HKAT	Handkommentar zum Alten Testament
HSM	Harvard Semitic Monographs
HSS	Harvard Semitic Studies
IBC	Interpretation: A Bible Commentary for Teaching and Preaching
IBT	Interpreting Biblical Texts
ICC	International Critical Commentary
IDBS	*Interpreter's Dictionary of the Bible, Supplementary Volume*
IEJ	*Israel Exploration Journal*
Int	*Interpretation*
ITC	International Theological Commentary
JBL	*Journal of Biblical Literature*
JBQ	*Jewish Biblical Quarterly*
JDT	*Jahrbuch für deutsche Theologie*
JNSL	*Journal of Northwest Semitic Languages*
JPSTC	JPS Torah Commentary
JSOT	*Journal for the Study of the Old Testament*
JSOTSup	Journal for the Study of the Old Testament Supplements
JTS	*Journal of Theological Studies*
LCBI	Literary Currents in Biblical Interpretation
LHBOTS	Library of Hebrew Bible/Old Testament Studies
LXX	Septuagint
MT	Masoretic Text
NCBC	New Century Bible Commentary
NICOT	New International Commentary on the Old Testament
NRT	*La nouvelle revue théologique*
NT	New Testament
OT	Old Testament
OTL	Old Testament Library
OTR	Old Testament Readings

OTS	Old Testament Studies
1QM	*Milḥamah* (War Scroll)
1QS	*Serek ha-Yaḥad* (Rule of the Community)
RB	*Revue biblique*
RQ	*Revue de Qumran*
SBLSymSer	Society of Biblical Literature Symposium Series
SBT	Studies in Biblical Theology
SJOT	*Scandinavian Journal of the Old Testament*
ST	*Studia Theologica*
TDOT	*Theological Dictionary of the Old Testament.* 14 vols. Edited by G. Johannes Botterweck, Helmer Ringgren, and Heinz-Josef Fabry. Grand Rapids: Eerdmans, 1974–
ThBü	Theologische Bücherei
VT	*Vetus Testamentum*
VTSup	Vetus Testamentum Supplements
WBC	Word Biblical Commentary
WMANT	Wissenschaftliche Monographien zum Alten und Neuen Testament
ZAW	*Zeitschrift für die alttestamentliche Wissenschaf*
ZRGG	*Zeitschrift für Religions-und Geistesgeschichte*

PART ONE

Pastoral Perspectives

1

Introduction

Hebrew Bible and New Testament as Scholarly Vocation

J. Harold Ellens

THE HEBREW BIBLE OR TANAK IS PARADIGMATIC FOR THE ENTIRE Western World, and has been for 2,000 years. Its configuration as Old Testament, in Christian Scriptures, is somewhat different from the standard order of its component elements, the books of the Bible, in the Tanak. However, the content of both canons is similar, and it is clear that devout Jews and Christians have always valued the Hebrew Bible or Old Testament with a similar high level of intensity, since soon after the time of Philo, Josephus, and Jesus Christ.

However, when I claim that the Hebrew Bible is paradigmatic for the entire Western World, I am not referring primarily to the function of the Tanak as religious text in shaping personal piety or communal liturgies. It has been important in those regards, of course, throughout the entire 2,000 year history of its existence as a canon of sacred scripture. Moreover, it promises to be of towering permanent value in that regard, as long as humanity lasts. However, its literary, philosophical, and psychological influences have been widely pervasive throughout all the layers of the fabric of Western Culture, as well.

It is impossible, for example, to read with any coherent understanding or aesthetic appreciation, the literature of the New Testament, Chaucer, Schiller, Goethe, Donne, Shakespeare, Marlowe, Bunyan, Blake, Mann, Updike, DeVries, Percy, or O'Conner without a deep awareness of the metaphors and archetypes that shape the cadences, characters, and claims of the Hebrew Bible. All the classics of literature, the principles of political theory, the ideals and conundrums of philosophy, and the enigmas of ethics and aesthetics in the West are rooted and grounded in the Tanak.

There are some positive values that we derive from that. First, it is the ethical claims of the Hebrew Bible that shape Western religions as action religions. The three major faiths, which may be called the Abrahamic faiths, Judaism, Christianity, and Islam, derive their core systems from the ancient Israelite religion described in the Hebrew Bible. These Western faith systems are distinguishable from Eastern religions mainly by the fact that Western religions externalize their ethical claims and thus become action religions which tend and intend to build structures in societies that reach for ideal states of being, structures, and institutions in the culture. Eastern religions, in contrast, tend to be interior and not conscious and intentional builders of idealized external social cultures.

Western societies tend to build good sewers and medical systems, for example; while Eastern religions tend to be religions of withdrawal instead of externalized cultural action, and in what they do accomplish in beneficial infrastructure is simply emulate the West. Eastern religions value interiority and personal spirituality as a mode and method toward transcendence of material reality and the achievement of Nirvana. They, consequently, tend to have bad sewers and medical systems. It is interesting that the exception to this has always been Confucianism; however, it is not a religion but an ethical philosophy. It has no inherent theism, as religions do by general definition. Good sewers, for example, are the product of the Hebrew Bible and its emphasis upon responsible culture building, social idealism, and care of the community as a divine requirement. The Hebrew Bible moves from the image of the ideal farm or garden to sacral space, ideal city, and sacred community.

Another strongly positive value that the Tanak has contributed to the shape of things in the Western World, indeed the entire world these days, is the hopeful sense of optimism inherent in the remarkable theology of grace. That is the main stream of the ideology of the Hebrew Bible. The history of world religions is the history of humans cowering before the face of divine threat and devising strategies for placating monstrous gods. There is much of that in the Hebrew Bible also. However, its mainstream flows from Abraham's incredible insight that God might just happen to be on our side, a God of good will and unconditional grace, acceptance, and forgiveness. It is the only religious good news ever sounded on this planet. Out of that sense of things came the positive and optimistic side of the Psalms, the prophets, the religion of Jesus Christ, and the idealizing theology of St. Paul.

The prophet Micah put it all together in his remarkable words that should be carved in stone somewhere so nobody can miss them. "Who is a God like our God, he pardons iniquity, passes over transgressions, delights in steadfast love, will not be perpetually angry, is faithful to us when we are unfaithful to him, tramples all our iniquities under his feet, and casts all our sins into the depths of the sea. Moreover, he guaranteed this to us all before we were born" (Mic 7:18–20). So there it is, theological and psychological metaphors under which a person cannot lose. This is a win-win world.

However, the hell of it is that it is not that set of metaphors, symbols, and archetypes from the Hebrew Bible that tend to stick with us and dominate our culture today. We seem much more inclined by nature to relish and remember the negative ones. Of those there are far too many in the Tanak. Playing around the edges of the mainstream of grace ideology throughout the Hebrew Bible is a large set of very destructive metaphors that form and inform our inherent psychological archetypes with content that can kill.[1]

Bishop Oxnam of the Methodist Church remarked in 1900 that the God of the OT is a big bully and in no sense the God whom we see in the face, person, and ministry of Jesus of Nazareth. Well, this is not a very good comment on the OT, but it is a telling indicator about the bishop. He was like a lot of folks. He could not keep in focus the mainstream of grace in the Hebrew Bible and kept sliding into preoccupation with the destructive scenes and stories he found there. He did not know how to read the OT for his own good. However, there is plenty there to make a person and a culture sick and hopeless.

For example, one of the things that most readers and non-readers of the OT have stuck in their minds is the image of God as the Warrior.

---

1. J. Harold Ellens, "Introduction: The Destructive Power of Religion," 1:1–10, and "Religious Metaphors Can Kill," 1:255–74, in J. Harold Ellens, ed., *The Destructive Power of Religion: Violence in Judaism, Christianity, and Islam*, 4 vols. (Westport, CT: Praeger, 2004). See also the one-volume edition, *The Destructive Power of Religion: Violence in Judaism, Christianity, and Islam, Condensed and Updated*, 1–7, 44–58, 97–104, 139–60, 200–18, 229–38.

He seems to be awfully busy in the Tanak fighting enemies and stirring up the Israelites to fight their enemies, and to create enemies even where there were not any. In fact, when God ran out of enemies he turned on the Israelites themselves and beat the living daylights out of them a number of times. It seemed like God was so bloody ticked off about something or other that he just could not get his head screwed back on right until he found an excuse to kill somebody: Egyptians, Canaanites, Philistines, Israelites, you, me, or his own unique son, Jesus.

What is that all about, and why does it appeal to us so much that it is the message that sticks in our minds, rather than the word of grace? There is an answer to that question. The answer is that in the Hebrew Bible, behind the Warrior God metaphor is a far more dangerous set of word pictures. The Tanak starts to paint this picture already in the third chapter. It is the picture of a cosmic conflict being waged between God and the forces of evil. These forces take on the shape of an alternative God. So the Hebrew Bible creates the assumption that the God of grace is up against an equivalent evil god and that the warfare between them takes place on the battleground of history and the human heart. Moreover, it remains to be seen who will win.

Consequently, it is the imperative spelled out in the Tanak that we are all called to fight God's fight so as to insure that evil does not win. That is what the Israelites thought they were doing when they exterminated the Canaanites in their ancient story about 1,200 years before Christ. That is what the Christians thought they were doing when they mounted the crusades against the "infidel Turks" about 1,200 years after Christ. That is what the Muslim Jihadists think they are doing today.

Of course, it is all based upon a lie. There is no cosmic evil force. There is no opposing evil God. God is not a Warrior. There is no cosmic conflict, no war of the worlds. There is not a shred of empirical evidence in all of human experience that such an evil force or warfare exists, and there is no basis in the sacred scriptures for taking those horrible metaphors seriously. It is all a lie. However, unfortunately that has not stopped those evil metaphors from the Hebrew Bible from infecting our Western psychology.

Clearly, if God solves all of his cosmic problems by immediate resorts to ultimate violence, why should we not do the same? If God solves all his disappointments, grievances, and daily confusion by killing somebody, how can we expect our own worlds to work well in any other way? If that is God's template, obviously that is how life and the world are wired! These ancient sick metaphors are stuck deeply into the unconscious archetypes of the proponents of Judaism, Christianity, and Islam. The heritage of the Hebrew Bible is paradigmatic for the entire Western World and one very prominent side of that influence is pervasively destructive, indeed, continuously disastrous. It breeds a psychology which unconsciously longs for catastrophe as the ultimate relief from the burden of the battle. Evangelical Zionism is a classic, practical example of this sick psychology.

Now, of course, good scholarship on the Hebrew Bible readily sorts out the garbage from the gospel in that amazing set of sacred scriptures that constitute the Tanak. It does not take much to discern that the stories of the Israelite extermination of the Canaanites was a case of gross confusion of Israelite self-aggrandizing foreign policy with the will of Yahweh. The Israelites got it wrong. One sometimes wonders how different their foreign policy is today, or ours. Their prophets, commanding them to genocide, were crazy. Samuel's command to Saul, the king, to exterminate the Amalekites, men, women, children, cats, dogs, cattle, and pet skunks, was evil. It was the kind of evil that humans constantly do to each other. Samuel, the prophet, was a monster in that action and in his undermining Saul's rather effective kingship. The only kind of evil that exists in this world is that which we do to each other. There is no cosmic evil. We have enough of our own. The only thing "out there" is the God of grace!

It does not take very long for sound biblical scholarship to see that the stories about Israel's ancient history were written or edited long after the fact and crafted to make their history heroic. The tragedy is that we are stuck, in the Western World, with that old Israelite Master Story, which has tragically infiltrated itself into all our Master Stories, psychologically, culturally, and spiritually. It has reinforced all our primal tendencies to violence in the exercise of our survival instincts as individuals and as societies and cultures. The pervasive paradigmatic prominence of the myths and metaphors of the Tanak have produced three millennia of tragedy. We must get rid of that sick heritage.

The only way that is possible is by making a thorough-going scholarly study of the Hebrew Bible that lifts up the other side of that ancient story, namely, the side which represents Yahweh as a God of unconditional, radical, and universal grace and goodness. Then we must apply that throughout Western culture, down on the ground where the rubber hits the road. For accomplishing that, we are greatly indebted to those who have made the Hebrew Bible their scholarly vocation, and given their lives to this enterprise. However, that enterprise will not bear fruit beyond the theoretical world of professional lectures and conference papers unless our scholars have the motive and the courage to speak their wisdom in the language of the people, with the urgency our great and long standing religious, cultural, and social tragedy deserves.

One of the productive scholars of Hebrew Bible who has called for that, and himself done that consistently, is David J. A. Clines. Some of his work is included in this volume that is also dedicated to honor his perspective and his productive practical scholarship. In this volume, interested colleagues have assembled to reflect together on some of the theoretical, academic, and practical problems of Hebrew Bible scholarship with an eye to the role the Tanak has in shaping our lives and cultures, individually and communally. We have taken our cue from the applied perspective for scholarship set by the trajectory of the work of David J. A. Clines over the years of his labor of love for the Hebrew Bible.[2]

2. David J. A. Clines, *Interested Parties: The Ideology of Writers and Readers of the Hebrew Bible*, JSOTSup 205 (Sheffield: Sheffield Academic, 1995); Clines, *The Theme of the Pentateuch*, 2nd ed., JSOTSup 10 (Sheffield: Sheffield Academic, 1997); Clines, *On the Way to the Postmodern, Old Testament Essays, 1967–1998*, 2 vols., JSOTSup 292, 293 (Sheffield: Sheffield Academic, 1998).

2

The Ways of God in the World

The Drama of 2 Kings 6:8–23

Christopher Dorn

IN HIS MAGISTERIAL WORK, *THE ART OF BIBLICAL NARRATIVE*, ROBERT
Alter writes that "the biblical tale might usefully be regarded as a narrative experiment in the possibilities of moral, spiritual, and historical
knowledge, undertaken through a process of studied contrasts between
the *variously limited knowledge* of the human characters and the *divine
omniscience* quietly but firmly represented by the narrator."[1] In this *divine omniscience* with which the narrator artfully tells the story in 2
Kings 6:8–23, the main character, the prophet Elisha, shares.

In the process of the studied contrasts between the other four
significant characters of this story, the king of Aram, his officer, the attendant of Elisha, and the king of Israel, the narrator constructs a lively
tale that instructs as it delights. In sum, he tells how the king of Aram
plots to capture Elisha, who has been frustrating Aramean raids by pre-
dicting where they will happen. He learns that Elisha is in Dothan, to
which he sends his army. Once there the soldiers are struck blind, and
then brought by the prophet to Samaria, where their sight is restored.
The king of Israel, on the advice of Elisha, does not kill the soldiers but
lavishes upon them a great feast, after which he sends them safely home.
The story ends with the report that no more Aramean raiders came into
the land of Israel.[2]

1. Robert Alter, *The Art of Biblical Narrative* (New York: Basic Books, 1981) 157
(emphasis added).

2. I have adapted this summary account from Robert LaBarbara, "The Man of War
and the Man of God: Social Satire in 2 Kings 6:8—7:20," *CBQ* 46 (1984) 639.

A more careful analysis of this narrative will reveal a sophisticated development of the plot in which the narrator employs such literary devices as irony, farce, and reversal to express his vision of the ways that God works in the world. To appreciate the narrator's art and purpose it will prove helpful to approach the narrative as drama. The structure of a drama can be divided into three constituent parts: complication (rising action), crisis (climax), and resolution (falling action). Following an analysis of these parts, we proceed to distill the themes that will have emerged in the unfolding of the dramatic action. In the concluding section, we will attempt to bring these themes to bear on the vexed question of the relationship between religion and violence.

Complication

In the world of drama, the term "complication" refers to all the activity that precipitates the crisis. In 2 Kings 6:8–23 the reader is introduced to enough background material for an understanding of the principal characters, their relationships, and the potential for action that becomes realized later in the drama.[3] The setting in this ancient Hebrew drama is introduced with a minimum of detail, a convention typical of biblical narrative generally.[4] The reader encounters first the king of Aram and his actions *in medias res*: he is at war with Israel. The initial scene opens on this king and his officers as they confer with one another to determine the most strategic location for an ambush site (v. 8). Now what is concealed from the king's knowledge is revealed to the reader in the next scene, in which a second character, identified only as "the man of God," is introduced. Somehow the man of God always knows where the king if Aram's army is going next and relays the information to the king of Israel, the third character now mentioned in the drama. This king sends warning to the place of which the man of God spoke, so that it goes on alert; and this happens more than once or twice (v. 10).

With a shift in scene, the narrator portrays the comic frustration of the king of Aram, foiled by the hidden opposition of the man of God. The dramatic irony gives the scene the intended comic effect: the king does not know that the man of God has been informing the king of

---

3. Jack A. Vaughan, *Drama A to Z: A Handbook* (New York: Ungar, 1978), 63.

4. See, e.g., Eric Auerbach, *Mimesis: The Representation of Reality in Western Literature* (Princeton: Princeton University Press, 1973) 3–23.

Israel about his plans and so can only suspect one of his own officers of betrayal. "Now tell me *who* among us sides with the king of Israel" (v. 11)? The further irony of the king's question will become apparent when it is answered by the situation in which his army finds itself at the conclusion of the drama, as guests of the king of Israel, at a great feast he prepares for them *all*. For now it serves to disclose to him the identity of the man of God, his antagonist.

One of the officers responds that the man of God who has been frustrating his plans is Elisha, the prophet of Israel (v. 12). How the prophet is able to do this the officer explains to the king. The omniscience of Elisha is underscored by the officer's remark that Elisha "tells the king of Israel the words that you [the king of Aram] speak in your bedchamber" (v. 12). Both combatants in the conflict are, at this stage in the drama, fully identified. Now the reader anticipates how the king's discovery will determine his subsequent course of action.

Crisis

The moment or incident, in which the potential for action that has been gradually building becomes realized, constitutes the crisis of the drama.[5] This moment transpires when the king of Aram decides to take on Elisha. Evidently the special knowledge the narrator grants to the king's officer of the nature of the opposition does not avail the king. He fails to recognize that by going up against Elisha, he is thereby going up against God. Presumably this has already been intimated to the reader by the king's officer in v. 12. Nonetheless, the king orders his officers to go and see where Elisha is, so that he may seize him (v. 13).

The irony here can hardly escape the reader. The king plots the capture of one who already knows his every move! However, the king somehow vainly imagines that he can overcome the clairvoyant powers of his opponent by sending a detachment of soldiers under the cover of darkness (v. 14). The absurdity of his thinking is amplified by the incongruity between his goal and the means by which he aims to achieve it. The king mobilizes "horses and chariots and a great army" to seize one man (v. 14)! The scene closes with the report that these forces are surrounding the city of Dothan, at which Elisha is presumed to be. The stage is set for the imminent confrontation.

5. Vaughan, *Drama A to Z*, 62–63.

The next scene introduces the attendant of Elisha as the last significant character in the drama. The attendant arises early in the morning to discover the forces of the king of Aram amassed outside the city.
Now the reaction of the attendant to the impressive spectacle of the
Aramaean army with horses and chariots heightens the dramatic tension in the scene: "Alas, master! What shall we do?" (v. 15). Elisha, however, does not react in the same way. He occupies the standpoint from
which God views the spectacle and so with relative calm can command
the attendant not to be afraid, "for there are more with us than there are
with them" (v. 16). Elisha then prays that the Lord grant to the attendant
the capacity to see, so that he may see what Elisha himself sees. The
reader does not know what Elisha sees until the narrator discloses it
through the eyes of the attendant: surrounding Elisha are chariots and
horses of fire (v. 17).

The chariots and horses of fire adumbrate a favorable outcome for
Elisha. But first the tension in the narrative reaches its highest pitch
when the Aramaean army comes down against him. The response of
Elisha is to pray to the Lord and the immediate answer to that prayer
relieves that tension; but the subsequent action does not proceed on
an expected course. The reader anticipates a second prayer from Elisha
similar to that offered on behalf of the attendant, for with a revelation of
the forces of heaven arrayed against them, the terror-stricken Aramean
army certainly would have fled, and Elisha and the God in whose name
he acts would have scored a dramatic victory.

Curiously, however, Elisha prays that the Lord strike them with
blindness (v. 18). When he receives again from the Lord what he asks,
Elisha goes down to meet them. The words with which he addresses
them are not without comic effect. They betray that Elisha, perhaps in
a moment of self-irony, misunderstands that the massive forces mar-
shaled against the city were intended to capture him! To paraphrase
him: "Oh, it seems that you are prepared for war; you must be looking
for the king of Israel (and his forces). You are on the wrong way and
have reached the wrong place. But let me help you out. I will lead you
to the one you seek" (v. 19). The story at this stage in its unexpected
development is dripping with irony. The very man who has occasioned
the original conflict by preventing the king of Aram from engaging the
king of Israel is now helping the army of the former to reach the latter!

Elisha brings the army to Samaria where the king of Israel is located. The sight of the intended captive leading the army captive into the hands of its enemy can only intensify the irony. But tension in the narrative is again created in the anticipation of what fate awaits the blinded and helpless Aramaeans within the confines of the city of the enemy. Perhaps the answer to the second prayer Elisha offers here will strike more terror in their hearts than if this prayer had otherwise been offered as the first one for them while in Dothan: "Lord, open the eyes of these men so that they may see," and "the Lord opened their eyes, and they saw that they were inside Samaria" (v. 20).

Resolution

In the resolution or falling action the outcome of the crisis is played out. In it is disclosed to the reader the point or meaning toward which all that has gone before has been tending.[6] Elisha's action in escorting the soldiers to Samaria facilitates the entrance of the king of Israel. Noteworthy is the deferential "father" with which he addresses Elisha, and the repetition of his request for permission (!) to strike the enemies Elisha has delivered over to him (v. 21). With this brief stroke, the narrator characterizes the king as an excited child who overreacts to his good fortune. Elisha has to scold him as a child. He points out that it was not with the sword and the bow that the king captured those whom he wants now to kill (v. 22).

Elisha's command to the king to set bread and water before them serves to chastise the king for his misconceived desire to kill them, and serves to humiliate the Aramaeans for their misconceived plan to mount an attack against him. The king prepares an extravagant feast for the captives before he sends them away so that they may return to their master (v. 23). The acquiescence of the king to Elisha in complying with this order reflects the stature of the prophet. He is a man to whom the king and the king's enemies must answer. Through all the events from the beginning of the drama until the end Elisha is a man in complete control. Through the intervention of this powerful prophet the threat to Israel by the marauding Aramaeans is neutralized. The narrative concludes with the report that they no longer came raiding into the land of Israel (v. 23).

6. Ibid., 64.

Themes

This essay began with Alter's observation that the biblical story is a *narrative experiment* in the possibility of the knowledge of truth, through the studied contrast between the variously limited knowledge of the characters within it and the divine omniscience of the narrator. It should now have become clear that in this story of the two kings and Elisha, the illusion (or lie) in the human realm, as embodied primarily in the character and actions of the two kings, is contrasted with the reality (or truth) in the divine realm, as revealed primarily through the character and actions of Elisha. The possibility of the *reader's knowledge* of truth is realized through the study of this contrast.

This contrast is developed, by the narrator, primarily through the motif of sight. Seeing and not seeing, or perhaps more precisely, perceiving and misperceiving, becomes the hinge on which the action unfolds in this drama. Elisha can perceive, and plays a role in helping others to perceive, such as his attendant and the Aramaean soldiers. The officer of the king of Aram can perceive, at least momentarily, and therefore is in a position to advise his king. This king of Aram, as well as the king of Israel, in contrast cannot perceive and, therefore, in the end they disqualify themselves as unfit to exercise authority.

The counsel of his officer to the contrary notwithstanding, the king of Aram is determined to resist the power of his enemy Elisha. But he is culpable because of his decision to send a reconnaissance to locate the position of his enemy. He has already been briefed by one of his officers, who knows what the narrator knows about the prophet Elisha. The king has willfully refused to factor this intelligence into his strategizing. That this ill-fated decision ultimately will cost this king his authority to command, the narrator proceeds to elaborate by means of the literary technique of repetition.

Alter observes that one of the most common features of biblical narrative is the purposeful repetition of certain key-words or word-roots. The repetition of a key-word or word-root qualifies it as a motif through its recurrence at different moments in the narrative. The associations that it accrues in varied contexts serve subtly to convey meaning which otherwise the narrator would be obliged to spell out directly.[7] The narrator introduces in verse 13 a pair of words that recur

7. Ibid., 92–93.

through the rest of the story. Here the king of Aram gives the order to "go and see" (*lĕkû ûrĕ'û*).

The king depends implicitly on the sight of his army to overcome the opposition of Elisha; but this sight in the end proves unreliable. The eyes of the soldiers do not prove effective as an organ to apprehend reality as it is, as it has been revealed to Elisha's attendant, who has been granted the ability to see (*wĕyir'eh*) as a result of Elisha's prayer (v. 17). When Elisha prays again, the soldiers are reduced to blindness (v. 18). In the two verses that follow, the words "go" and "see" recur, but it is noteworthy that the agent is no longer the king of Aram, but Elisha.

Just as the king of Aram had before him, the prophet now commands the soldiers to "go" (*lĕkû*), assuring them that he will "cause them to go" (*wĕ'ôlîkâ*), which he does in fact when he "causes them to go" (*wayyōlek*) to the city of Samaria. When they arrive at their destination, Elisha prays that they may see (*wĕyir'û*), and they do in fact see (*wayyir'û*), again through the mediation of the prophet (v. 20).[8] Thus the delegitimated authority of the king of Aram to command is ceded to the prophet Elisha, who through his own command proves to be the one to enable this king's army to fulfill the original command of their king to "go and see."

The king of Israel enters the stage in verse 20. Once again the verb "to see" appears, and the subject is in fact this king, who "in seeing them [the Aramaean soldiers]" (*kir'ōtōh*) turns to address Elisha. But the sight of the king of Israel is judged by the prophet to be just as defective as that of the soldiers, who perceived Elisha and his attendant only as enemies to be captured and destroyed. With these same soldiers now vulnerable before him, the king perceives them in the same manner, only as the enemy of Israel. He wants to seize the propitious opportunity afforded him to destroy them. The king's desire betrays his complicity with the king of Aram in what theologian John Milbank has called an "'ontology of violence,' a reading of the world which assumes the priority of force and tells how this force is best managed and confined by counter-force."[9]

However, this "reading of the world" is a mis-reading, according to the prophet Elisha. So this king, too, like his counterpart the king of

---

8. LaBarbara, "The Man of War and the Man of God," 643.

9. John Milbank, *Theology and Social Theory: Beyond Secular Reason* (Cambridge: Blackwell, 1990) 4.

Aram, disqualifies himself as one fit to command. From this moment in the narrative until the end, he is subject to the authority of the prophet, who commands him to spare the soldiers and to "set bread and water" before them so that they can be replenished for the safe journey home. Thus the character of Elisha emerges in contrast to that of the two kings: one malevolent king sends men to capture and perhaps kill a prophet; this same prophet now sends those men away unharmed from a second malevolent king who sees them vulnerable and wants to kill them.

So Elisha, in the end, emerges as the only one fit to exercise authority, because his "reading of the world" serves as the only legitimate basis for appropriate action in a world that, in the last analysis, cannot be constrained by the logic of violence. It is in fact providently guided and governed by an omnipotent God. God's ways are manifestly not the ways of men and women (cf. Isa 55:8). Through the prophet's perception of the reality of the divine realm, on which he bases his actions in the human realm, the reader is afforded the possibility of obtaining knowledge of theological truth. In other words, through attending to Elisha, the reader is given access to the ways of God in the world.

The knowledge that the reader obtains through attending to Elisha is that of the nature and purpose of God's power in the world. Through Elisha's sight, granted even to his attendant as a result of prayer, in verse 21, the reader learns that the power of God circumscribes and overrules human actions. The forces that the king of Aram musters against Elisha (God) surround or contain the city; but the king's forces are surrounded and contained by the forces of the Lord. God's action circumscribes the king's action and overrules it. However, this cannot be perceived through un-illuminated sight, which in this instance can only evoke fear. Elisha's response to his attendant serves as a reminder to the Israelite hearers and today's reader of the biblical confession: "Some trust in chariots, and some in horses, but we trust in the name of the Lord our God" (Ps 20:7).

Moreover, the reader learns that this power of God is life-preserving. That truth emerges in a meditation on the interesting uses to which the narrator puts the verb "to strike." The Aramaean soldiers are appropriately blinded by their illusion that human power can prevail over divine power. This happens when Elisha's prayer reduces them to powerlessness through the loss of their sight. However, the verb "to strike" that Elisha uses in his petition in verse 18 (hak-nāʾ) is a word that denotes most often "a deadly blow, an injury caused by a human agent that leads to the immediate or rapid death of the victim, usually another human being."[10] It is clearly in this sense that the verb is intended when it is later in the mouth of the king of Israel, who requests permission from father Elisha "to strike" (*ăkeh*) his captive enemies.

It is apparent that two contrasting attitudes towards power are concentrated in this verb. When the Lord "strikes" the enemies of Israel in answer to Elisha's prayer, it is not with the intent of dealing them a deadly blow. Rather it is to immobilize them temporarily so that they can be safely led to a place in which they may receive divine blessing and come to awareness of deeper truth. That is to say, the Lord does not bring them into the city under, the command of his prophet, to destroy them; but to show them undeserved favor, in spite of the fact that they are Israel's (and God's) enemies. This is God's "way" into the heavenly city, of which Samaria can be seen perhaps as a type. The "way" that Elisha indicated to the army at Dothan now reveals its theological significance as "God's way."

Once having arrived at the city of Samaria, Elisha invites the king to re-assess his own conception of power. Perhaps implicit in Elisha's words to him are a criticism of military power and its application generally. Directed against Israel it assumes the form of this question: "Did you in your own power reduce your enemies to guests in your own home?" (cf. v. 22). The message is clear: with the sword and the bow this is not possible; only divine power can accomplish this transformation. Against Aram it takes the form of this ironic question: "Are your predatory raids on my people necessary to resource you?"

The irony here is that the king of Aram uses the power of his army to acquire bread from Israel, which Israel ends up giving to the army in any case, by holding a great feast for it. God's "way" in the heavenly city is to provide freely by divine power that which human power seizes by violence. That the king of Israel did not recognize this indicates that the lesson applied as much to the Israelites as to their enemies. In the last analysis, the God of Israel, in whose name Elisha prophesies, is revealed in this drama not as a God who enlists human violence in the service of the divine cause in the world, but rather a God who calms fears, restores

---

10. J. Conrad, "*nkh*," in *TDOT*, 9:417.

sight, shows mercy, gives contentment, and liberates his people as well as their enemies.

Concluding Reflections

Religious scholars and critics of contemporary culture have decried, in recent years, the role that religion has played in violent conflict throughout the world.[11] The destructive impact on human societies of ideologies inspired by religion seems to be a constant in human history; nor does there appear to be an end to this deplorable trend in the foreseeable future. In fact, the turn of the twenty-first century has witnessed a recrudescence of religion and the violence which seems always to accompany it.

Ethnic and national communities are engaged in retrieving traditional sources of group identification in reaction to the disruptions of agricultural, industry, and post-industrial revolutions worldwide. We have seen emerging as a result a process by which competing ideologies and advanced technology combine with archaic modes of self-consciousness and collective identification to produce a world that is in danger of obliterating itself. It is not without reason that scholars with an increasing sense of urgency are subjecting the major religious traditions of the world to critical scrutiny in order to discern how they have served, and continue to serve, to defend, justify, and even promote acts of violence.

In this regard, the great monotheistic religions, Judaism, Christianity, and Islam, have been especially singled out. Religious faith, shaped and determined by an uncompromising devotion to the one true God, gives rise to intolerance and hatred toward others who do not adhere to the faith.[12] By definition these others are God's enemies,

11. See, e.g. Hector Avalos, *Fighting Words: The Origins of Religious Violence* (Amherst, NY: Prometheus, 2005); J. Harold Ellens, ed., *The Destructive Power of Religion: Violence in Judaism, Christianity, and Islam,* 4 vols. (Westport, CT: Praeger, 2004, updated and condensed single volume edition, 2006); Sam Harris, *The End of Faith: Religion, Terror, and the Future of Reason* (New York: Norton, 2004); R. Joseph Hoffman, ed., *The Just War and Jihad: Violence in Judaism, Christianity, and Islam* (Amherst, NY: Prometheus, 2006); Jack Nelson-Pallmeyer, *Is Religion Killing Us? Violence in the Bible and Quran* (Harrisburg, PA: Trinity, 2003); Regina Schwarz, *The Curse of Cain: The Violent Legacy of Monotheism* (Chicago: University of Chicago Press, 1997).

12. Bahar Davary, "Violence in the Text, Violence through the Text," in *Just War and Jihad,* 122.

from whom the faithful must separate themselves or against whom they must wage war when the infidel poses a threat. Nor are God's own people ever entirely immune from religious violence; they can become God's enemies when they disobey the commandments or defect from the worship of the one true God.

Enacting God's vengeance on his enemies is commanded and even lauded in the sacred scriptures that constitute these monotheistic faiths. J. Harold Ellens has observed that the scriptures acknowledged by Jews and Christians contain "toxic texts that certify violence as a legitimate mode of pressing the claims of God and his kingdom in the world."[13] The problem for our world, according to Ellens, is that these "toxic texts" continue to furnish metaphors that give content to our "unconscious psychological archetypes," those deep sources of our motivations, which in the process are driven toward destructive solutions to our conflicts with the other.[14] It is for this reason that at least one scholar has regarded it as his vocation to show how "religion may contribute to the detriment of the well-being of humanity."[15]

But if there are toxic texts in these scriptures, there are also, in keeping with the metaphor, texts that provide an antidote, a fact that Ellens certainly would not deny. Religion scholars cannot neglect to examine these as they critically probe the historical and textual origins of the great monotheistic traditions. Regina Schwarz has identified both types of text in her reading of the scriptures of the Jews and the Christians. She observes that "two poles of representation of monotheism" can be found in the Bible. The one is marked by generosity. "God is depicted as infinitely charitable, infinitely giving, with blessings for all." She invokes the manna in the story of the Exodus (ch. 16) as a metaphor of the provident God who is an inexhaustible supply of resources to each according to his or her need.

13. J. Harold Ellens, "Biblical Metaphors as Psychological Agents that Legitimate Violence in Society," in *God's Word for our World: Theological and Cultural Studies in Honor of Simon John DeVries*, eds. J. Harold Ellens, Deborah L. Ellens, Rolf P. Knierim and Isaac Kalimi (London: T. & T. Clark, 2004) 2:236. See also J. Harold Ellens, ed., *The Destructive Power of Religion, Violence in Judaism, Christianity, and Islam*, 4 volumes (Westport, CT: Praeger, 2004).

14. Ibid., 238, 240, and 241.

15. Avalos, "Rethinking Religious Violence: Fighting over Nothing," in Hoffman, ed., *The Just War and Jihad*, 116.

The other pole is marked by exclusion and intolerance. God is depicted as "playing favorites," bestowing blessings on one at the expense of the other, as if those blessings are too few to be enough for both.[16] The paradigmatic stories here are those of Cain and Abel (Genesis 4) and Jacob and Esau (Genesis 27). In the first, the brothers come to present their offerings before God, who accepts the gift of Abel while rejecting that of Cain. Overcome with jealous rage, Cain murders his brother. In the second, Jacob steals from his elder brother Esau their father's blessing. When Esau learns what his brother has done, he implores his father with tears for another blessing, which Isaac denies to him.[17] So Esau, too, conceives a desire to murder his brother.

In a world divided between those privileged to enjoy the divine blessings and those excluded from them, there can only always be strife and violence. Schwarz challenges us to imagine an alternative world, in which people and land and resources are not objects to be possessed and hoarded, but rather "expressions of infinite giving."[18] In this world people can imitate the God represented by the monotheism of the first pole, a "monotheism of plenitude, of infinite giving, of love."[19] Schwarz claims to find this alternative world in the Bible from creation through the prophets. She certainly would find it in the drama of Elisha and the two kings as we have sought to present it. In this world blinded eyes are healed so that they are made to see a God who is present, protecting, and provident, to Israel as well as to her enemies, indeed, to all the people of God—all humanity. Ellens points out that this expression of universal grace is a mainstream throughout the Hebrew Bible and the New Testament. He especially points to Micah 7:18–20 which speaks of the infinite grace and forgiveness of God to all humankind. St. Paul thinks God is provident to all creation, and I dare say he is right!

16. Regina Schwarz, "Holy Terror," in ibid., 192–94.
17. Ibid., 193.
18. Ibid., 198.
19. Ibid., 200.

3

David and Jonathan in Iraq

Combat Trauma and the Forging of Friendship[1]

Nathan Solomon

"NOBODY BACK HOME CAN FUCKING UNDERSTAND. THEY SAY WE WERE like brothers, but that ain't the half of it."[2,3] These are the words of a combat veteran Marine regarding the death of a comrade at the battle for An Nasiriyia, Iraq in April 2003. Combat veterans have always been at risk for being misunderstood and rejected by those who have never shared a similar experience. Civilians never involved in combat operations have difficulty understanding the nature of the bond that arises between comrades in a kill-or-be-killed situation.[4] For most of human history, the psychological toll of war upon combatants has been largely ignored.

However, beginning with the extraordinary World War II studies of S. L. A. Marshall, clinical psychology started paying much closer attention to the effects of war upon combatants. This attention increased significantly during and after the Vietnam War in an attempt to treat and

---

1. The title for this essay is derived from Jonathan Shay's works on the *Iliad* and the *Odyssey* and combat trauma: *Achilles in Vietnam: Combat Trauma and the Undoing of Character* (New York: Simon & Schuster, 1995); and *Odysseus in America: Combat Trauma and the Trials of Homecoming* (New York: Scribner, 2004).

2. LCPL John Smith [pseud.], from the personal diary of Lt. Nathan Solomon, CHC, USNR, May-October 2003.

3. The identity of all Marines directly quoted has been obscured to maintain confidentiality. Permission to use these quotes was given by the individuals quoted at the time of the interview.

4. Hans van Wees, "Heroes, Knights and Nutters: Warrior Mentality in Homer," in *Battle in Antiquity*, A. Lloyd, ed., (Oakville, CT: Duckworth and David Brown, 1997) 18.

understand the vast numbers affected by involvement in combat. While the study of combat and its effects on humans is still in its infancy, the experiences of those counseling combat veterans has provided many insights that can help us understand the combat veteran, both modern and ancient.

Conflict and combat are often narrative elements of the Hebrew Bible and notable among biblical combat veterans and their experiences are David and Jonathan and their famous friendship. The question of whether their combat experience had anything to do with their friendship is what this chapter attempts to address.

The history of scholarship analyzing the friendship of David and Jonathan is long and varied. Scholarly opinions on the subject range the gamut from the cynical to the sublime.[5] However, no consensus has emerged on the foundations of the friendship. Some have described the friendship as one we would like to have but hardly deserve.[6] Still others assume some sort of sexual relationship between the two.[7] This second assumption is quite natural, considering the apparent intensity of the relationship between David and Jonathan. After all, the language used by the characters leaves little doubt that this was more than an ordinary friendship.

However, no existing study of the relationship between David and Jonathan takes seriously their combat experience as a key to the friendship.[8] There are two obstacles obscuring this view of David and Jonathan's friendship. The first is the academy's native unfamiliarity with the realities of warfare. The second is the inadequacy of language, both modern and ancient, to speak accurately about friendships forged in trauma. This chapter primarily deals with point one, the academy's native unfamiliarity with combat. Utilizing as an interpretive lens, the gains of clinical psychology in diagnosing and treating combat veter-

5. Kurt L. Noll, "Faces of David" (Ph.D. diss., Union Theological Seminary and Presbyterian School of Education, 1995).

6. Patricia K. Tull, "Jonathan's Gift of Friendship," *Int* 58 (2004) 131.

7. The relationship between David and Jonathan is not the first friendship in antiquity assumed to have a sexual dimension. Cf. van Wees, "Heroes," 1–86.

8. Walter Brueggemann is quite honest and correct when he notes that the friendship defies "interpretive words." Walter Brueggemann, *First and Second Samuel*, IBC (Louisville: Westminster John Knox, 1990) 217. S. Bakon comes closer still when he sees no surprise in the two warriors becoming friends but only sees warfare as something they have in common. Shimon Bakon, "Jonathan," *JBQ* 23 (1995) 145.

ans, I propose a new examination of the relationship between David and Jonathan as a soldier's friendship.

Though the second obstacle, the inadequacy of language, is not the focus of this essay, it is necessary to make a few remarks concerning it in order to understand why this friendship has been so enigmatic to interpreters. It is axiomatic that language encodes culture, naturally producing vocabulary and structure sufficient to verbalize those things which a given culture has need to communicate. Therefore, it is not a defect of language itself that it is not able to give voice to describe the intense friendships forged in traumatic situations; but rather a defect of a given culture when it fails to grant these friendships a status worthy of special vocabulary.

Friendship, of any type, exists mainly outside of cultural structures.[9] There are no rituals marking the beginning or the end of friendship. There is no legal status granted those who are *merely* friends.[10] Friendship, both today and in the ancient Near Eastern world, is an interstitial, quasi-institution, always in third place after marriage and kinship.[11]

In peace-time, the interstitial status of friendship largely works. It is in the chaos of combat and loss that friendships are forged that are unwieldy and intrusive in civilian life. The language used to describe friendships in the civilian world simply cannot carry the freight these relationships ask them to bear. Lacking the ability to verbalize the intensity with integrity, cultures default to language and categories with which they are familiar. The result is that the vocabulary of romance and kinship is often appropriated to describe what arises between comrades on the battlefield because no other suitable language or category exists.[12]

This "defaulting" of language to romantic and kinship vocabularies is evident in several ancient sources. A few brief examples of the most

9. David M. Halperin, *One Hundred Years of Homosexuality and Other Essays on Greek Love* (New York: Routledge, 1990) 25.

10. Dorothy Hammond and Alta Jablow, "Gilgamesh and the Sundance Kid: The Myth of Male Friendship," in *The Making of Masculinities: The New Men's Studies,* Harry Brod, ed. (Boston: Allen & Unwin, 1987) 242.

11. Hammond and Jablow, "Gilgamesh," 243.

12. Cooper, Jerrold S., "Buddies in Babylonia: Gilgamesh, Enkidu, and Babylonian Homosexuality," in *Riches Hidden in Secret Places: Ancient Near Eastern Studies in Memory of Thorkild Jacobsen,* Tzvi Abusch, ed. (Winona Lake, IN: Eisenbrauns, 2002), 81. As well as: Halperin, *One Hundred Years,* 85; Hammond and Jablow, "Gilgamesh," 242.

significant of these will illustrate the point.[13] In the *Epic of Gilgamesh*, the language used to describe the relationship between Gilgamesh and Enkidu is frequently described as brotherly (VI:154; VII:16–24). Furthermore, following the death of Enkidu, Gilgamesh is described as weeping for Enkidu as a "wailing woman" (VIII:ii:3), presumably in the sense of a woman who has lost someone close.[14] The friendship between the two is what drives the story, and yet it is clear that the relationship they share exceeds the common cultural understanding of friendship, driving language to describe it in both kinship and marital terms.

The account of the friendship between Achilles and Patroclus in *The Iliad* also appropriates romantic and kinship vocabulary to describe the extraordinary friendship between the two. Throughout the epic, Patroclus is described in roles that are reserved for a female spouse, and Achilles and Patroclus are described with language reminiscent of a married couple (9:216–17; 9:620–21, 658–59; 19:315).[15] Additionally, after the death of Patroclus, Apollo notes (24:44–52)[16] that Achilles' grief for Patroclus is out of order, exceeding the love of a father for a son or a man for his brother. Finally, it is interesting to note that Homer takes care to describe both men as having their own concubines with them before the walls of Troy. Indeed, it is Agamemnon's crime of taking Achilles' concubine that sparks Achilles' rage and drives the whole story.

The language used to describe the relationship between David and Jonathan also appropriates romantic and kinship vocabulary. In 1 Samuel 18:1, Jonathan's soul becomes "bound up" (*niqšĕrâ*) with David's. The root *qšr*, normally associated with political conspiracy, is notably employed in one other place for an intense kinship type of relationship, namely, in the Joseph narrative where it is used to describe Jacob's love for Benjamin (Gen 44:30). In 1 Samuel 20:41, David and Jonathan kiss and weep in each other's arms. Finally, and most famously, 2 Samuel 1:26:

13. Halperin, *One Hundred Years*, 76.
14. "The Epic of Gilgamesh," translated by E. A. Speiser (*ANET*, 85–88).
15. Halperin, *One Hundred Years*, 84.
16. Homer *Iliad* 9, 19, 24.

> I am grieved for you,
> My brother Jonathan
> You were greatly beloved to me.
> Wonderful was your love to me,
> Greater than the love of women.[17]

Here, both kinship and romantic language are used in the same sentence. Moreover, besides the established default vocabularies of romance and kinship, ancient Israel also possessed the language of covenant. It is interesting to note that this covenant language is also appropriated to describe the friendship. Using language that is most often reserved for the political arena, the two are described as entering into a covenant *(běrit)* on two different occasions (18:3; 23:18).[18]

Given the interstitial nature of friendship and language's consequent inability to articulate particularly intense instances of it, it is hardly surprising that the friendship of David and Jonathan would generate so many differing scholarly opinions. Therefore, I submit that the friendship of David and Jonathan might be fruitfully analyzed as an intense friendship of the type forged in trauma, for it is the trauma that seems, in large part, to create and cement the friendship.[19] Recent gains in understanding modern combat veterans, as well as my own experience as a chaplain counseling Marines returning from the Iraq war, provides a vehicle for coming to terms with the friendship of David and Jonathan.

The work of clinical psychologists and trained chaplains with combat veterans offers useful interpretational tools for understanding the effects of war upon combatants appearing in the Hebrew Bible. Warfare, as it appears in the Hebrew Bible, has generally been the purview of the historical critical method. Moreover, it has been concerned mostly with ascertaining the what, where, and how of various battles. The psychological impact of combat upon biblical characters has been largely ignored. At the very least, it has received short-shrift from the academic community. Ignoring the psychological impact of combat upon biblical characters is, I believe, largely due to the academy's failure to recognize that combat, particularly close-quarters combat, falls outside the pale of

17. Author's translation.

18. Tull, "Jonathan," 134.

19. Hammond and Jablow, "Gilgamesh," 248.

virtually all other human experience. Jonathan Shay, a Veterans Affairs psychologist, puts it this way: "We can never fathom the soldier's grief if we do not know the human attachment which battle nourishes and then amputates. As civilians we have no native understanding of the soldier's grief. Combat calls forth a passion of care among [people] who fight beside each other that is comparable to the earliest and most deeply felt family relationships."[20]

These recent psychological insights of the long-term effects of combat on the soldier are useful in understanding warfare and its effects upon characters of the Hebrew Bible. In addition, they also open the possibility that those who have experienced combat and are trying to live with its aftermath may find a resource in the text of the Hebrew Bible.

Using the relationship between David and Jonathan as a test case, it is worthwhile to examine the narrative describing their relationship in 1 and 2 Samuel, through the lens of combat experience. In the Hebrew Bible, David and Jonathan are both described, first and foremost, as combat veterans. Even before he is introduced as Saul's son, Jonathan is introduced as commander of a battalion-size force. The narrative moves very quickly to establish Jonathan's résumé as a soldier's soldier, crediting him with taking the Geba garrison while the rest of the army lies idle.[21]

Further, Jonathan is described as a veteran of heroic close-quarters combat. First Samuel 14:1–15 could almost be cast as a type of "valor scene" common in the modern era in citations for bravery. Notable in this "valor scene" is the apparent irrational behavior of Jonathan. From a tactical standpoint, he attacks an enemy that greatly outnumbers him in an elevated and fortified position without the element of surprise. As mentioned above, 1 Samuel 14:1–15 bears striking similarities to many citations for personal bravery during twentieth-century combat. Compare the narrative of Jonathan's raid with the following, typical, American Medal of Honor citation from the Vietnam War:

> Jonathan's Raid
>
> One day Jonathan the son of Saul said to the young man who bore his armor, "Come, let us go over to the Philistine garrison outpost on the other side of the Mishmash pass . . . It may be

20. Shay, *Achilles in Vietnam*, 39.
21. 1 Sam 13:2–4.

that the Lord will work for us . . . His sergeant said, "OK, let's roll!" . . . So both of them exposed themselves to the Philistine garrison and the Philistines hailed Jonathan . . . and said, "Come on up here and we will show you a thing or two." So Jonathan said to his sergeant, "Follow me up, for the Lord has given them into our hand." Then Jonathan climbed up to the garrison on his hands and feet, with his sergeant right behind him; and the two of them overcame the Philistines and took out twenty enemy soldiers within the first ten yards, so that the garrison panicked and fled, sending the entire enemy field force into disorganized retreat.

Medal of Honor Citation

On 18 March [1968] while advancing to contact [the enemy], the lead elements of the company became engaged in heavy automatic weapon, machine gun, RPG, Claymore mine, and small-arms fire of an estimated battalion-size force. Captain Bucha, with complete disregard for his safety, moved to the threatened area to direct the defense . . . seeing that his men were pinned down by heavy machine gun fire . . . Captain Bucha crawled through the hail of fire to single-handedly destroy the bunker with grenades.[22]

The similarities between 1 Samuel 14:1–15 and the above citation highlight Jonathan's raid as an act of extreme, even fool-hardy, bravery, and we would remember it graphically as an event of towering heroism, except for one thing. It is immediately overshadowed by the even more memorable Goliath narrative in 17:1–58 in which the shepherd boy, David, takes on the whole Philistine army in the person of the giant Goliath and kills him with a slung stone. Note that in the Goliath narrative, like Jonathan's raid and the above citation, David is at a similar tactical disadvantage and displays the same kind of extreme bravery.[23] Clearly, the writer means for us to understand both David and Jonathan as veterans of the most intense kind of personal close-combat.

There is also an aspect of David's character that is not present in Jonathan's recorded combat experience, and may be a factor in understanding their friendship, since the narrative includes no scenes of

22. J. Dean Coy, *Valor* (Mobile, AL: Evergreen, 1993) 43.

23. David conducts a "frontal assault" against an armored, more powerful enemy without the benefit of any cover for himself while using inferior weapons (1 Sam 17:28–49).

David and Jonathan actually fighting side-by-side. That is, David shows some evidence of berserk behavior. In psychological terms, a berserker is one who displays a wild frenzy for combat.[24] The berserker often takes reckless risks, puts others at risk, and behaves in ways that are outside the accepted norms for soldiers. Although both David and Jonathan take great risks and place others at risk, David exhibits berserker-like behavior by his willingness to mutilate the corpses of slain enemies. Not only does David slay Goliath (1 Sam 17:51), he cuts the head off the corpse and claims the armor of Goliath as a war trophy.

Later, when Saul (1 Sam 18:25) requests one hundred Philistine foreskins as a bride price, in giving his daughter to David as wife, David shows no resistance and does not hesitate to do the arbitrarily violent deed. Finally, upon hearing of the death of Jonathan and Saul in 2 Samuel 1, David orders the immediate execution of the messenger. Although the above examples are not conclusive evidence that David acted as a berserker (not to mention the possible differences regarding "normal" behavior for combatants across the centuries), these behaviors are characteristic of the state of a berserker. The possibility that David might have acted as a berserker is important for the current discussion in that often other, non-berserk, soldiers display a close attachment to the berserker.[25] Consider the following statement from a Marine returning from the Iraq War: "Everyone was tight with [Jones] after the first fire-fight. He was a stud when the shit hit the fan, fucking made of ice. I mean we'd be taking rounds and he's cool with it, returning fire like he'd been doing it his whole life."[26]

Whether motivated by the act of killing Goliath or David's enthusiasm for combat, it is notable that Jonathan first proclaims his love for David following the Goliath narrative. Whether David's berserker-like behavior was the key requires more investigation.

It is also important to recognize that these stories of individual bravery and cruelty fall into the overarching story of continuing conflict with the Philistines. The valor scenes of individual bravery concerning David and Jonathan are highlights within an ongoing war that threatened Israel's survival. Recent work by Dave Grossman, a U.S.

---

24. Shay, *Achilles in Vietnam*, 82.

25. Ibid., 90.

26. Pvt. John Smith [pseud.], Solomon Diary, May 2003.

Army psychiatrist, suggests that the psychological impact of combat is inversely proportional to the distance between combatants.[27] That is, the psychological trauma of killing occurs much less frequently in bomber crews than with infantry.

In close-quarters combat there is "a direct struggle of sinew, muscle, and spirit. If flesh was torn or bone broken [the soldier] felt it give way under his hand."[28] In such situations there can be no escaping the reality of killing other humans. Of course, in the ancient world *all* combat occurred at close quarters. At its most intimate, the killing occurred at sexual range, with one combatant literally on top of another, using some weapon to penetrate the body of the foe. At its most distant, the foe was no more than a fifty-meter bow shot away. Hand-to-hand killing was the ancient reality and the narrative does not shrink from telling us that both David and Jonathan literally have blood on their hands.

However, the point of the above is not to analyze the effects of combat upon David or Jonathan individually but to establish a *common base of experience*[29] from which their friendship might have sprung. When the common combat experience of David and Jonathan is recognized, new possibilities for understanding their relationship are presented.

Shay's clinical experience has demonstrated that friendships forged in combat are among the strongest relationships human beings may develop.[30] In conflicts where "winning" means continuing to live and "losing" means death or mutilation, the combatant's horizon shrinks to the point where only personal survival and the survival of one's fellow combatants matters.[31] Issues of force, country, and even family fall by the wayside in combat. A quote from another Marine involved in the Iraq War is instructive: "I didn't give a damn about anything. Home, my wife, my folks . . . nothing mattered but taking care of [Tim] cause he was *the only one* watching out for my ass."[32]

27. Dave Grossman, *On Killing: The Psychological Cost of Learning to Kill in War and Society* (New York: Back Bay, 1996) 97–98.

28. Ibid., 99.

29. Note that although the two are not spoken of as fighting side-by-side, they are both heroes of similar combat experiences who became friends during a war for national survival.

30. Shay, *Achilles in Vietnam*, 39.

31. Ibid., 28.

32. Sgt. John Smith [pseud.], Solomon Diary, May 2003.

This commitment to a fellow combat veteran extends even past the combat experience. Consider the following statement from the same Marine quoted above: "Yeah, when I got home the first time my wife didn't understand why I had to see [Tim] everyday. He's my bro and we're connected. Hard to explain, hell, no one here gets it."[33] Compare the above with 1 Samuel 18:3, following David's slaying of Goliath: "When David had finished speaking to Saul, the soul of Jonathan was bound to the soul of David, and Jonathan loved him as his own soul."

While this one biblical quotation is not enough to equate the veteran's experience with Jonathan's, it is instructive to note that the level of commitment expressed between David and Jonathan is similar to the level of commitment expressed by other, modern, combat veterans.

Like the Marine quoted above, Jonathan places his relationship with David on a higher plane than both his relationship with his father, Saul, and his own career concerns.[34] Again, like the veteran marine, Jonathan essentially states that his relationship with David is the most important thing in his life. This behavior of prioritizing the friendship of fellow veterans above family or career has been well documented among combat veterans of recent wars. Shay documents instances of veterans who have lost their jobs because they left work to aid another veteran. Many veterans have also alienated their spouses because they would leave home with no notice to go to the aid of fellow veterans.[35]

In my own experience with Marines returning from the Iraq War, I have also noted four separate instances when returning veterans have created marital discord by showing a greater loyalty to their fellow Marines than to their spouses and children.[36] In each of these instances the veterans have expressed a closer connection to their comrades of close-quarters combat than to their own family. Again, this similarity does not equate the experiences and relationships of recent combat veterans with the friendship of David and Jonathan, but one is compelled to recognize that both Jonathan and David *are* combat veterans *and* one of them, Jonathan, has put this relationship ahead of both family and career.

33. Ibid.

34. Cf. 1 Sam 20:1–42.

35. Shay, *Achilles in Vietnam,* 41.

36. N. Solomon, Solomon Diary, Sept. 2003.

David, in his own way, will also put his relationship with Jonathan above family and career concerns. After the death of Saul and Jonathan, and after his reign has been established, David will maintain a bond of loyalty to Jonathan. Through his kindness to Mephibosheth (2 Sam 9:1-13),[37] David fulfills the loyalty oath he made to Jonathan in their last meeting.[38] Although David is inconstant in many other things, in this instance he delivers on his promise despite both the cultural norms of the day and the best interests of protecting his dynasty.[39]

Such loyalty is consistent with modern clinical counseling experience; loyalty oaths made between soldiers in combat often have an unusually strong hold, especially if one of the comrades perishes.[40] The surviving veteran feels that he or she must "keep faith" with the dead. To forget the dead comrade is dishonorable both to the dead and to the living.[41] Like the primacy of the combat relationship itself, keeping faith with the dead can trump the family and career concerns of the living. Understood in this light, David's actions toward Mephibosheth are neither illogical nor unexpected, even though they seem out of character with the rest of David's ambitious and often selfish life.

The academy has widely speculated upon the exact nature of the relationship between Jonathan and David.[42] There are several reasons for this fascination. The descriptive terms each character uses to describe the relationship are much stronger than any other friendship language in the biblical text. The language is also stronger than language that we currently use to describe modern friendships. Considering the nature of the bonds often formed between soldiers in combat, I submit that the

37. Jonathan's wish is no small request. Tull, "Jonathan," 135.

38. 1 Sam. 20:14–15.

39. NB: David's future treatment of the case *Ziba v. Mephibosheth* in 2 Sam. 16:1–5 and 19:24-30 is beyond the scope of this essay.

40. Note the last stanza of "In Flanders Fields" by John McCrae:

> Take up our quarrel with the foe:
> To you from failing hands we throw
> The torch; be yours to hold it high.
> If ye break faith with us who die
> We shall not sleep, though poppies grow
> In Flanders Fields

41. Shay, *Odysseus in America*, 80.

42. A full literature review on the friendship of David and Jonathan is beyond the scope of this essay. For a good review of recent scholarship see Tull, "Jonathan," 131.

bond between David and Jonathan could not have been stronger—*even* had they been lovers.

The fact that some scholarship has been dedicated to explicating this relationship as homosexual is hardly surprising, since civilians who have never been exposed to combat usually lack the capacity to understand how a relationship that is this close and passionate *cannot* be sexual.[43] Again, my goal here is not to defend the heterosexuality of David and Jonathan, but to suggest that, given their common experiences in war, there may be a more fruitful way to understand their relationship.

"I know it ain't cool, but I cry about him everyday. He was one tough S.O.B. and he ain't ever coming home. Never had a friend like that."[44] Like David's lament for the dead Jonathan,[45] this Marine both weeps and recognizes the uniqueness of the bond formed between him and his comrade during the Iraq War. Relationships forged in combat are different from any other type of human relationship and are exceedingly difficult for the un-initiated, including this writer, to understand. Perhaps the friendship between David and Jonathan was of this type. They were both front-line warriors, bloodied in close-quarters combat. In different ways, they both prioritized their relationship above family and career concerns. They both expressed their relationship in the strongest terms that language allowed. Perhaps theirs was a soldier's friendship.

I have suggested a new tool for understanding warfare and its role in the Hebrew Bible. This is also an attempt to make some sense of what I experienced as a chaplain working with combat veterans, and of the experiences of many young men and women among us now who have "been there and done that," and know things most humans, hopefully, never need to learn.[46] This human phenomenon requires our best understanding. Many questions remain for future study. Perhaps this discussion will be generative not only of new thought concerning war and the biblical text but also the effects of war as we must live with them today.

43. Shay, *Achilles in Vietnam*, 42.

44. Pvt. John Smith [pseud.], Solomon Diary, June 2003.

45. 2 Sam 1:26.

46. "Making sense" of the space between the text and the present world is one part of Hebrew Bible as vocation as Dr. Clines understands it. As a scholar at the beginning of my own vocation, it is my privilege to be asked to participate in this volume.

4

Character Development in the Book of Ruth[1]

David B. Weisberg

IT IS A RARITY FOR WOMEN TO APPEAR AS HEROES IN BIBLICAL TALES. The scroll of Ruth is one exception. Ruth demonstrates that women can be the center of heroic action in the Bible. However, we shall try to show that there is also a subtle lesson in the book illustrating the reverse type of behavior: human beings, women as well as men, may not always act in an appropriate manner. The author presents us with an unspoken question: Whom should we emulate? He leaves us with an eloquent answer: Naomi, Ruth, and Boaz.

The author of the Book of Ruth[2] minces no words in this carefully crafted literary gem. Every word and phrase in the eighty-five verse, four-chapter novella has its place in the narrative. Therefore, I would like to focus on several features pertaining to character development that, in my opinion, reveal an interesting perspective, highlighting the author's skill.[3]

---

1. This article is dedicated to David J. A. Clines, from whose "Notes on the Preliminary Edition" to *Biblia Hebraica Quinta*: (Fasciculus extra seriem: Librum Ruth praeparavit Jan de Waard (Stuttgart: Deutsche Bibelgesellschaft, 1998), as well as his many other important contributions to our field, I have greatly profited. I wish to thank Michael and Jane Fox, Yossi Leshem, Shalom Paul, Gila Rahamim, and Jonathan Weisberg for their kind help. It is also a pleasure to thank the members of Bible seminars given at Hebrew Union College, Jerusalem, in Spring of 2006, for their thought-provoking remarks during our reading of Megillat Ruth.

2. According to the rabbis, the book was authored by Samuel: "Samuel wrote his Book, the Book of Judges and Ruth," *b. Baba Bathra* 14b. A modern view is presented by Edward F. Campbell Jr., "The Hebrew Singer of Tales," in *Ruth*, AB 7 (Garden City, NY: Doubleday, 1975) 18–23.

3. The skillful integration of the Ruth and Abraham stories is touted by Robert Alter, *The World of Biblical Literature* (New York: Basic Books, 1992) 52, as an example

I believe the author wished to contrast the righteous conduct of the three heroes of the story: Naomi, Ruth, and Boaz,[4] who possess unusual and noble characters, with the "run-of-the-mill" persons, whose selfishness prevents them from relating to others except when it is in their interest to do so. All but one (Orpah) are anonymous. In the Book of Ruth, the "ordinary people" are all secondary characters.

Studying the role of "Minor Characters in Biblical Narrative," Uriel Simon, citing S. D. Goitein, refers to the Book of Ruth in the following terms: "Goitein showed that it would have been possible to omit the characters of Orpah and the kinsman, who refuses to redeem Ruth, without doing violence to the plot, and that their sole purpose is to emphasize the merit and praiseworthiness of Ruth and Boaz."[5]

A first example[6] is Orpah, who leaves Naomi.[7] Heading off for Bethlehem, in a foreign land, to an insecure future holds no promise for her, so she turns back. Continuing the line of reasoning set out by Simon and Goitein, the purpose of presenting the person of Orpah is to set off the character of Ruth. A second example is the young men in Boaz' service who might, without a timely warning, "molest" her (2:9). As we listen to the tale, it seems, regrettably, almost an everyday occurrence that these men would seek to take advantage of a young woman who needs to be out in the field in order to collect enough food to eat. Here, too, we have a set-off or foil, the morally indifferent young men contrasted with the character of Boaz. A third example is *ploni almoni* (4:1), who doesn't want to "spoil" his inheritance by accepting Ruth (4:6). This anonymous gentleman possibly had his name deleted from the text due to his inability to get beyond his narrow self-interest to a wider and more compassionate view. As he refused to play a role in perpetuating the name of his deceased relative, it is possible his own

---

of "intertextual play." Alter states that Ruth is set up "as a founding mother, in symmetrical correspondence to Abraham, the founding father."

4. When asked who they thought the hero of the story was, most HUC seminar members answered "Naomi."

5. Uriel Simon, *Reading Prophetic Narratives* (Bloomington: Indiana University Press, 1997) 268, citing S. D. Goitein, *Bible Studies*, 3rd ed. (Tel Aviv: Yavneh, 1967) [Hebrew].

6. We do not consider Elimelek, Mahlon, and Kilyon to be true "secondary characters," as does Yair Zakovitch in "Ruth," *Miqra LeYisrael* (Tel Aviv: Am Oved, 1990) 7, since they do not have a speaking role.

7. MT 1:14; see LXX cited in BHS: "and returned to her people."

name was not included.[8] The anonymous relative is certainly a set-off or foil for Boaz.

Beyond these people we should like to focus upon those whom we consider the most important secondary characters of the book: the women of Bethlehem. We are dealing essentially with classical gossips who do not help, except when they can stand in front of the cameras and pose. What is the role of these women in the story? They bracket the account of Naomi. In 1:19 we read that after Naomi and Ruth make the long trek back from the fields of Moab to Bethlehem, the ladies of Naomi's home town greet her, their long-lost, dust-covered neighbor, with the curt, dismissive phrase: הֲזֹאת נָעֳמִי ("Is this Naomi!"), just the words to cheer up someone who has lost her husband and two sons, and is truly down on her luck![9] Not a single word of kindness or offer of hospitality is extended after a ten-years' absence: "How are you?" "Are you hungry?" "Do you have a place to stay?" "Can we help?" It adds up to a rather rude reception. We hear nothing from the women of Bethlehem until much later.

A further aspect of the book's subtle control of character portrayal is the positive presentation of some secondary characters, as pointed out to the author by Shalom Paul,[10] citing the role of the elders of the city who are sitting by the city gate. These secondary characters are portrayed positively, rather than negatively. Paul cites the speech of the elders:

> All the people at the gate and the elders answered, "We are (wit-nesses). May the Lord make the woman who is coming into your house like Rachel and Leah, both of whom built up the House of Israel! Prosper in Ephrathah and perpetuate your name in Bethlehem! And may your house be like the house of Perez whom Tamar bore to Judah, through the offspring which the Lord will give you by this young woman."[11]

This is a bighearted and unprompted blessing. It shows that not all the secondary characters are "run-of-the mill" and basically uncaring. Not everyone who appears in a story with a minor role is a secondary

8. See the perceptive comment by Feivel Meltzer, "Ruth," *Da'at Miqra* (Jerusalem: Mosad Harav Kook, 1990) 18 n. 49 [Hebrew].

9. Meltzer, "Ruth," cites Lam 2:15 and Isa 14:16 as examples of parallel exclamations of incredulity.

10. Private communication.

11. Ruth 4:11ff., NJPS.

character like the ones being singled out by the author. Obviously, there must be some people who are part of the tale simply to make the plot work. They round out the picture, as opposed to fulfilling a specific literary task. Is it not far more effective to present *some* minor characters in a good light rather than portraying *all* in a bad light? This, it seems to me, strengthens the point of the storyteller.

In 4:17, after a long period of silence, the neighborhood women now reappear, publicly rejoicing in Ruth's happiness and Naomi's good fortune. The wheel has turned, the crowds are gathering around, and Naomi no longer needs their help. Nevertheless, the women press forward and, with regard to the newborn son of Boaz and Ruth, "gave him the name Obed . . ."[12] In other words, when they could have done some good, they held back, and when they were not needed, they offered their advice on the baby-naming.[13] Apparently their unsought advice was graciously accepted!

The author has presented these minor characters in different ways in order to offset the heroes of the book. Yet, though what most of the minor characters do is hurtful, the author does not intend us to think of them as bad people.[14] Like so many "ordinary people," they simply do not rise to the occasion when their help is needed and they barge in where they should be more sensitively quiet. They are, in any case, always situation-inappropriate in the narrative. The true ethical and spiritual pathway is relayed through the actions of Naomi, Ruth and Boaz, the true heroes of the story.

12. It is unprecedented for neighborhood women to name the child of another couple.

13. For "persons other than the immediate parents of a newborn . . . recorded as present during the birth and the naming of a child," see Jack M. Sasson, *Ruth* (Baltimore: Johns Hopkins University Press, 1979) 173 and 239–40. Sasson posits a "political" context for Ruth relating to the activities of "the šekēnôt and to Naomi in 4:16–17."

14. Similarly Jacob Licht, *Storytelling in the Bible,* (Jerusalem: Magnes, 1978) 126, who states: "The hardships of poverty and the selfishness of normal human behaviour appear in the story [of the Book of Ruth] without disguise, but they are not allowed to debase human dignity"; and Yonah Bar Ma'oz, "Adishut HaTsadikim" (*Weekly Circular from Bar-Ilan University* #499, 2003) 2: "The people of Bethlehem are not evil people" (אֵין אַנְשֵׁי בֵּית לֶחֶם אַנְשֵׁי רֶשַׁע; reference courtesy Gila Rahamim).

PART TWO

Analytical Academic Perspectives

5

What Happened to the Yahwist?
Reflections after Thirty Years

A Collegial Conversation between Rolf Rendtorff, David J. A. Clines, Allan Rosengren, and John Van Seters

Rolf Rendtorff

IT WAS IN EDINBURGH IN 1974 THAT I PRESENTED A PAPER TITLED "DER Jahwist als Theologe? Zum Dilemma der Pentateuchkritik" (The Yahwist as Theologian? The Dilemma of Pentateuchal Criticism).[1] In that paper I questioned the validity of the documentary hypothesis, when faced with the new question about the theological intentions of the authors of the Pentateuch, as raised in particular by Gerhard von Rad.[2] Obviously, the time was ripe for that kind of question, since in the following years there appeared, independently from each other, several books dealing with fundamental problems of the methodology in the critical analysis of the Pentateuch.

In 1975 the book by John van Seters, *Abraham in History and Tradition*,[3] appeared in which he dealt briefly with the question of

---

1. Rendtorff, "Der Jahwist als Theologe? Zum Dilemma der Pentateuchkritik," in *Congress Volume: Edinburgh 1974*, VTSup 28 (Leiden: Brill, 1975) 158–66.

2. Von Rad, *Das formgeschichtliche Problem des Hexateuch*, BWANT 4/26 (Stuttgart: Kohlhammer, 1938); reprinted in von Rad, *Gesammelte Studien zum Alten Testament*, 1958, 9–86; English translation, "The Form-Critical Problem of the Hexateuch," in *From Genesis to Chronicles*, edited by K. C. Hanson, translated by E. W. Trueman Dicken, FCBS (Minneapolis: Fortress, 2005) 1–58.

3. Van Seters, *Abraham in History and Tradition* (New Haven: Yale University Press, 1975).

the Yahwist, a matter he later explicated more fully in several books.[4] In 1976 Hans Heinrich Schmid published *Der sogenannte Jahwist: Beobachtungen und Fragen zur Pentateuchforschung.*[5] Finally, in 1977 my own book appeared: *Das überlieferungsgeschichtliche Problem des Pentateuch.*[6] It was later translated into English with the title *The Problem of the Process of Transmission in the Pentateuch.*[7]

The discussion about the whole problem was stimulated in 1977 by a special issue of the *Journal for the Study of the Old Testament* that had recently been founded in Sheffield by David Clines, David Gunn, and Philip Davies. In this issue several authors had been invited to react to my Edinburgh paper. Some of them explicitly asked whether we are "at last witnessing the demise of the Documentary Hypothesis" (to quote R. N. Whybray). Indeed, this was—and still is—my own intention. What happened instead in the following years, however, was a discussion not about an alternative to this hypothesis but about its refinement. In particular a widespread discussion began about the central pillar of the hypothesis, the so-called Yahwist. Indeed, this seemed to be almost unavoidable, because it was a central point in my paper.

I tried to show that the great theologian, whom von Rad saw at work in the Pentateuch, could not be understood as one of several authors of sources, according to the Documentary Hypothesis, but that he was a theological author of a special kind. Von Rad himself had made this quite clear, when he opened the last section of his fundamental study, "Das formgeschichtliche Problem des Hexateuchs," with the following words: "Not that the conflation of E and P with J would now appear to be a simple process, nor one which could be altogether explained to one's satisfaction."[8]

---

4. Van Seters, *Prologue to History: The Yahwist as Historian in Genesis* (Louisville: Westminster John Knox, 1992); *The Life of Moses: The Yahwist as Historian in Exodus-Numbers* (Louisville: Westminster John Knox, 1994); *The Pentateuch: A Social Science Commentary*, Trajectories 1 (Sheffield: Sheffield Academic, 1999).

5. Schmid, *Der sogenannte Jahwist: Beobachtungen und Fragen zur Pentateuchforschung* (Zürich: Theologischer Verlag, 1976).

6. Rendtorff, *Das überlieferungsgeschichtliche Problem des Pentateuch*, BZAW 147 (Berlin: de Gruyter, 1977).

7. Rendtorff, *The Problem of the Process of Transmission in the Pentateuch*, JSOTSup 89 (Sheffield: JSOT Press, 1980).

8. Von Rad, *Das formgeschichtliche Problem*, 68 [reprint, 81] = "The Problem," 55.

At this point I must make a kind of side remark. Unfortunately, in the printed version of my Edinburgh paper there was a mistake. In the just quoted passage two words are left out, including the word "P" for Priestly Code. So the printed text does not speak about the addition of *two* more "sources" to the Yahwist, but only of *one* additional source, namely E. The translation in JSOT tried to make sense of the fragmentary text and spoke about "the conflation of E and J." But this is far from what von Rad himself had written.

Here von Rad explicitly declared that his Yahwist could not be understood by means of the Documentary Hypothesis. He continued saying: "But these problems are generically different from the ones we have been dealing with in our present study." Von Rad did not explicitly reject the Documentary Hypothesis, but he was not interested in dealing with those "purely literary questions." He did not even feel it to be necessary because: "The form of the Hexateuch had already been finally determined by the Yahwist." The writings of the "Elohist" and the priestly writer "are no more than variations upon the massive theme of the Yahwist's conception."

This was written in 1938. Almost forty years later in the mid-seventies the new discussion began, which I mentioned above. It is not my intention to unfold the whole history of research in the last thirty years. But I want to mark some characteristic positions that show the great diversity in the present scholarly debate.

First, there are Old Testament scholars who still adhere to the traditional hypothesis of Pentateuchal sources. In the framework of our discussion it is interesting to see the intention of certain defenders of this theory. One of them, Richard Elliott Friedman, quite recently presented his well known reading of the Pentateuch for a broader public.[9] He named the traditional sources: J, E, RJE, P, D, R. Then he translated a piece of text from Exodus printing the sources in different colors: J in green, E in red, and P in blue. Then he claimed that when the sources are read individually, "each source makes perfectly good sense when read alone." What we now have before us is not *one* Bible but a number of texts, reconstructed by modern scholars, cutting the Bible into pieces by "taking the biblical text apart." But what happened to the Bible itself? What happened to the text as it has been delivered to us through more

9. Friedman, "Taking the Biblical Text Apart," *Bible Review* 21/4 (2005) 19–23 + 48–50.

than two thousand years? It seemed to me to be one of the fundamental mistakes of the modern historical-critical analysis of the biblical texts, that it does not—or at least not sufficiently—ask the question regarding the meaning and significance of the given text.

Of course, this critical question is not only to be addressed to the defenders of the classical documentary hypothesis; but the example just presented shows explicitly that the biblical text itself in its given form is not at all taken as a subject of scholarly interpretation. I believe that this cannot be the last word of scholarly Bible exegesis. I will come back to this question later.

Second, I want to mention a position that could be called a reduced documentary hypothesis. Von Rad, in the above quoted text, saw the Yahwist as a source in the framework of the documentary hypothesis, but he had no concept of how to interpret the relation of his Yahwist to the other sources. So actually his documentary hypothesis remained a fragment. But when in the 1970s the new discussion began, things had changed. First of all, there was almost no mention of the Elohist. That means that the classical documentary hypothesis with four sources did not exist any longer.

Instead, the Yahwist came into the center of the scholarly interest. This is demonstrated by the books by Van Seters and Schmid. Both concentrate on the Yahwist. These two scholars also agree in another important point. They do not believe the Yahwist to be a rather old source, dating from the times of the early Israelite monarchy, as former scholars believed and some still do. Instead, they see the work of the Yahwist in a certain independence from the deuteronomistic tradition. It is obvious that this meant a fundamental change in the understanding of the Yahwist. This is true not only with regard to the dating of the Yahwist, but in particular with regard to the question of an independent Yahwistic work. For Schmid the Yahwist was of a rather elusive character, as expressed already by the title of his book: *The So-called Yahwist*. Therefore, he does not want to speak of the Yahwist as an individual writer but rather of a Yahwistic process of redaction and interpretation. Of course, here we are far from the image of the theological personality of von Rad's Yahwist.

The conception of Van Seters is quite different. In his book *Abraham in History and Tradition*, he presented a concept of a new kind of Yahwist. For him the Yahwist is an individual personality; but he is not a theologian like von Rad's Yahwist. The Yahwist is an historian. He lived and wrote in the period of the Babylonian exile. His message is to be seen in a close relationship to that of Deutero-Isaiah being addressed "to the despairing community of the exile." According to Van Seters, this Yahwist is not one of several pentateuchal sources, but he is *the* one who takes up earlier traditions, forming them into a new whole.

In this sense, Van Seters' concept seemingly could be compared with that of Gerhard von Rad, because there is only one central figure in the literary development of the Pentateuch. However, there is one fundamental difference between the two. While von Rad took the existence of other sources for granted, even if he did not want to deal with them, for Van Seters no other sources exist in the traditional sense of the documentary hypothesis. According to his concept, there are no other authors, but only several levels of tradition. These are taken by Van Seters as either pre-Yahwistic or post-Yahwistic. The Yahwist himself is the only identifiable author. One could call this a reduced documentary hypothesis, namely a one-document hypothesis. Of course, one must ask whether this still can be called a documentary hypothesis. But in any case, this reduced or even fragmentary hypothesis with the Yahwist as its main pillar became a central point in the scholarly debate of the following years.

In 1993 a monograph appeared by Christoph Levin titled *Der Jahwist.*[10] Levin also locates J in the exilic period, later than the book of Deuteronomy, but nevertheless earlier than the Deuteronomistic History. J represents the perspective of a more popular form of religion, as well as the concerns of the diaspora. For this reason Levin argues that J defends the diversity of the cultic places where YHWH may be worshipped, as opposed to the authors of Deuteronomy who wish to limit the location of the cultic site. According to Levin, J is foremost a collector and redactor; he is the first to combine his older sources into a narrative, which covers, more or less, the extent of the Pentateuch. Levin actually combines a fragmentary theory with a supplementary theory, since more than half of the non-Priestly texts of the Pentateuch are supplements, which numerous redactors added to the combined Yahwistic and Priestly narrative.

---

10. Levin, *Der Jahwist*, FRLANT 157 (Göttingen: Vandenhoeck & Ruprecht, 1993).

Now we have before us three different types of understanding of the Yahwist in the framework of the documentary hypothesis. With von Rad, the Yahwist has become not only an author, but above all a theologian.[11] For Van Seters, J is also an author, but he lives five centuries later and is more a historian than a theologian. For Levin, J is a redactor; his Yahwist shares with Van Seters' Yahwist the exilic location, but Van Seters would never agree with the idea of J as a redactor.[12] One could add several variations to these three types held in the recent scholarly debate. There is an almost general agreement that in this framework there is only one narrative source, namely the Yahwist, with the priestly and deuteronomistic elements alongside it. Erich Zenger, in his *Einleitung in das Alte Testament*, calls it JG "Jerusalemer Geschichtswerk."[13]

As mentioned before, the Elohist had almost completely disappeared from this discussion. However, in the meantime a growing number of scholars, who more or less belonged to the second group with a reduced documentary hypothesis, found it difficult to identify the Yahwist. The only clearly identifiable element in the Pentateuch, with the deuteronomistic tradition alongside, seemed to be the priestly texts. Even in this point there is some discussion about details, but in general the existence of a particular P level was taken for granted. So what about the Yahwist? Almost everything came under discussion: his age and dimension, his inner coherence and theological orientation, and finally, his very existence.

In 1999 Professor Christoph Levin, in Munich, invited a number of scholars who shared those critical positions, to engage in a public discussion under the title "Der Jahwist und seine Kritiker" (The Yahwist and His Critics). This group of critics later collected their contributions and invited an additional number of scholars to contribute to a book that appeared in 2002 under the title *Abschied vom Jahwisten: Die*

---

11. See also Hans Walter Wolff, "Das Kerygma des Jahwisten," *EvTh* 24 (1964) 70–98; translated as "The Kerygma of the Yahwist," in *The Vitality of Old Testament Traditions*, 2nd ed., by Walter Brueggemann and Hans Walter Wolff (Atlanta: John Knox, 1982) 41–66.

12. Van Seters, "The Redactor in Biblical Studies: A Nineteenth-Century Anachronism," *JNSL* 29 (2003) 1–19.

13. Zenger, *Einleitung in das Alte Testament*, Kohlhammer Studienbücher Theologie 1/1 (Stuttgart: Kohlhammer, 1995).

Komposition des Hexateuch in der jüngsten Diskussion (A Farewell to the Yahwist: The Composition of the Hexateuch in Recent Discussion).[14]

This book presents a panorama of different approaches to the question of the Yahwist. The predominant impression is that of a great methodological diversity. Jean Louis Ska expresses this by the title of his introductory essay: "The Yahwist, a Hero with a Thousand Faces."[15] Indeed, this collection of essays shows many different faces of J. For many of the authors the Yahwist has no face at all because he does not exist any longer.

The majority of the authors exemplify the problems by individual chapters or smaller corpora of texts. Joseph Blenkinsopp, for example, deals with Genesis 1–11.[16] He criticizes the scholarly world for the fact that these chapters almost never have been investigated with regard to their non-priestly material, neither by the proponents of an early J nor by the revisionist scholars, and that little attention was paid to the relationship between the putative J material and P. Blenkinsopp shows in his essay that the J elements in Genesis 1–11 are added to an earlier priestly text. In his view they are representing a "lay, intellectual milieu of the province of Judah some time during the two centuries of Iranian rule." Blenkinsopp keeps calling this material J or "J supplementary source"; so he remains within the accepted "reduced documentary hypothesis" model, with the two "sources" P and J, the Yahwist being post-priestly.

Several essays in this volume deal with the question of the interrelationship between the main themes of the Pentateuch. One example of this approach might be the essay by Jan Christian Gertz with the title "Abraham, Mose und der Exodus, Beobachtungen zur Redaktionsgeschichte von Gen 15."[17] It is well known, that there is no narrative connection between the story of Abraham and that of the Exodus from Egypt; but in Gen 15:13–16, within the Abraham story, we find a brief prediction of Israel's oppression in Egypt and the Exodus. Gertz investigates the interrelationship between the two themes and

---

14. *Abschied vom Jahwisten: Die Komposition des Hexateuch in der jüngsten Diskussion*, edited by Jan Christian Gertz, Konrad Schmid, and Markus Witte, BZAW 315 (Berlin: de Gruyter, 2002).

15. Ska, "The Yahwist, a Hero with a Thousand Faces," in ibid., 1–23.

16. Blenkinsopp, "A Post-exilic Lay Source in Genesis 1–11," in ibid., 49–61.

17. Gertz, "Abraham, Mose und der Exodus: Beobachtungen zur Redaktionsgeschichte von Gen 15," in ibid., 63–81.

comes to the conclusion that in the time of the formulation of Genesis 15 the two themes were still independent from each other. Genesis 15:13–16 belong to a post-priestly redaction. Hence, it follows that at that time there did not exist a Yahwistic narrative work. The given text is a post-priestly combination of two originally independent traditions. A pre-priestly J does not exist.

Konrad Schmid asks a similar question, using the Joseph story in Genesis 37–50.[18] He accepts the interpretation as "Diaspora Novella," but understands it as referring to the Egyptian diaspora after the end of the Northern Kingdom (720 BC). Here Egypt is seen at least as a temporary *Lebensraum* for Israel. Therefore, the Joseph cycle could be called an "anti-deuteronomistic work." It was originally independent, then it was connected to Genesis 12–36, and later it was expanded as a bridge to the events narrated in Exodus. That means that there was no original text including both the stories of the patriarchs and that of the Exodus. Interesting enough, Schmid does not explicitly mention the consequences for the question of the existence of a Yahwist. Perhaps it is too evident in his view, in particular in the framework of this book of which he is one of the editors. Nevertheless, the question arises: What are the consequences for J and, moreover, for the documentary hypothesis?

Thomas Römer asks a question that is important for this problem, namely: Where do we find the end of the Yahwist?[19] This end is often seen in the book of Numbers. However, Römer shows that even supporters of the traditional documentary hypothesis, such as Martin Noth, had difficulty in finding the traces of J in Numbers. He himself sees Numbers as a post-priestly text. Therefore, it cannot be understood as part of a Yahwist tradition, of whatever kind. However, if Numbers is separated from the first three books of the Pentateuch, the whole documentary hypothesis will have to be re-examined.

Thomas Dozeman asks the question of "Geography and Ideology in the Wilderness Journey."[20] It would go beyond the scope of this paper to enter this interesting question. But Dozeman also raises another

18. Schmid, "Die Josephgeschichte im Pentateuch," in ibid., 83–118.

19. "Das Buch Numeri und das Ende des Jahwisten: Anfragen zur 'Quellenscheidung' im vierten Buch des Pentateuch," in ibid., 215–31.

20. Dozeman, "Geography and Ideology in the Wilderness Journey," in ibid., 173–89.

important question. After a discussion of Van Seters' position, which sees the Yahwist as the author of Numbers 20–21, Dozeman declares: "The Yahwist of Van Seters has nothing to do with the Yahwist of the documentary hypothesis."[21] He continues to speak of "anonymous authors," who appear by new literary hypotheses, and he claims, "They must be named, and their names must be broad enough to embrace distinctive emerging hypotheses."

This is an important point. I raised it already in 1974 in my paper when I said that it was "an historical accident that von Rad ascribed the final formation of the Pentateuch (or Hexateuch) to someone he described as the Yahwist. He could just as well—or better and more appositely—have chosen another, less loaded name." Of course, to choose another name would mean to leave the context of the documentary hypothesis. That, of course, is what von Rad actually did in 1938, unintentionally and without being aware of it. In the meantime, many scholars do the same thing: to argue in a way that is not really compatible with the documentary hypothesis without being aware of it, or at least without being willing to depart explicitly from this hypothesis.

This situation is clearly expressed in the preface of the volume with which we are just dealing. The editors declare with regard to the contributions to this volume: "Gemeinsam ist ihnen, dass sie der Teilthese eines Jahwisten den Abschied geben." (They have in common that they say goodbye to the partial thesis of a Yahwist.) I never heard the word "Teilthese" before. But I understand what it shall express: to say goodbye to the Yahwist while keeping the documentary hypothesis. That would mean to keep the documentary hypothesis with one single document, namely some kind of P; but can that still be called a documentary hypothesis? Some of the contributors to this volume touched this question briefly and rather hesitantly, so that the reader gets the impression that there is a kind of uncertainty.

This brings me to another point in the preface. The editors write that in Old Testament scholarship comprehensive theories of the Pentateuch seem to have a life span of about one century. They mention the Introduction of Johann Gottfried Eichhorn from 1783, then the books of Julius Wellhausen from 1876/77 and 1883, and finally the beginning of the new discussion in the 1970s. Indeed, this rhythm is

---

21. Ibid., 188.

interesting. But there is also a fundamental difference. The first two dates are marking the establishment of a new theory that was more or less accepted within the scholarly community in the next one hundred years. The third date marks only the end of the common acceptance of the Wellhausen theory but not the birth of something new. The editors do not want to call this a crisis. According to them, it only shows that the "source model obviously not always can provide the most fitting interpretation of the findings in a text." But in the next paragraph they continue saying that it became evident that there must be a fundamentally new approach ("dass grundsätzlich neu anzusetzen ist").

At the end of the preface, the contributors declare that this volume would have reached its goal when the Pentateuchal research in the twenty-first century could get along without the Yahwist. But they are leaving open the question whether the research should continue with the old methods, in particular with the documentary hypothesis, or more precisely, with the corpse of this method that would be left after the Yahwist would have passed away?

In my view this book shows very clearly that the end of the Yahwist means at the same time the end of the documentary hypothesis. A documentary hypothesis with just one single document cannot work like a hypothesis, which originally was established and developed with four or at least three documents or sources whose interrelationships are a basic element of the method of working in the framework of this theory. As I mentioned before, only a few of the essays in this volume deal with this question, and they just touch it briefly and rather hesitantly. Instead, the question is raised regarding the interrelations between certain blocks such as patriarchal stories and Exodus traditions or Genesis and the following books. These are questions beyond the documentary hypothesis. By the way, this was already the key point in my paper of 1974. Other scholars developed this approach more deeply and broadly, first of all Erhard Blum in his two books from 1984 and 1990.[22]

It is highly interesting now to meet Blum among the contributors to a volume about the farewell to the Yahwist.[23] He does not need to say

22. Blum, *Die Komposition der Vätergeschichte*, WMANT 57 (Neukirchen-Vluyn: Neukirchener, 1984); and *Studien zur Komposition des Pentateuch*, BZAW 189 (Berlin: de Gruyter, 1990).

23. Blum, "Die literarische Verbindung von Erzvätern und Exodus: Ein Gespräch mit neueren Endredaktionshypothesen," in *Abschied vom Jahwisten*, 119–56.

goodbye because he did it very explicitly more than twenty years ago. In the introduction to his first book, he spoke about the need to free oneself from the "Systemzwang der Urkundenhypothese" (the pressure of the system of the documentary hypothesis). It seems that several of the contributors of this volume did free themselves from that pressure, if even inexplicitly and perhaps unconsciously. Anyhow, the discussion in their book comes about mainly in a methodological world outside of or beyond the documentary hypothesis.

What happened to the Yahwist? The answer is: He faded away, and he took with him the building he had lived in, because there are no inhabitants any longer.

David J. A. Clines—Response to Rolf Rendtorff

I was invited to make this response to Rolf Rendtorff's paper, not, I suppose, because of my own modest contributions to Pentateuch studies, but because I was, with my Sheffield colleagues, the initiator of an interesting and perhaps even significant discussion we organized for the third issue of the *Journal for the Study of the Old Testament* in July 1977. It seemed to us then that one of the rather few areas in Old Testament studies where a mould was being broken and some shaking of foundations could be anticipated was in Pentateuch Studies. We evidently had been attracted by the readiness of Rolf Rendtorff, in his Edinburgh paper to the IOSOT in 1974, to question the consensus that had for a century provided not only the foundation for the scholarly understanding of the Pentateuch but also a framework for conceiving the history of the literature of the Hebrew Bible as a whole.

The roll call of the contributors makes fascinating reading, thirty years on. In response to Rendtorff there were R. Norman Whybray, John Van Seters, Norman Wagner, George W. Coats, and H. H. Schmid, all of whom proved sympathetic in one way or another to Rendtorff's project. What none of us could have anticipated was that thirty years later the Pentateuch would still be a hot issue, and that despite all the dissatisfaction with the Wellhausen theory, it would still be perfectly respectable, and in some places still obligatory, to admit adherence to it—even after the radical questioning of it by Schmid's *Der sogenannte Jahwist: Beobachtungen und Fragen zur Pentateuchforschung* (1976), Whybray's *The Making of the Pentateuch: A Methodological Study* (1987), Van Seters's

Prologue to History: The Yahwist as Historian in Genesis (1992), and *The Life of Moses: The Yahwist as Historian in Exodus-Numbers* (1994), to name only the books of our 1977 contributors. Moreover, no one would have guessed, those thirty years ago, that on a summer evening of 2006 in Edinburgh, a city of many alternative cultural attractions, 150 of us would, of our own free will, make our way to a distant lecture theatre to hear Rendtorff bridge those years with his own inimitable update on the Pentateuchal landscape.

This is not the place for me to attempt to enter into an *Ausein-andersetzung* with the intricacies and evaluations of Rendtorff's paper, but I can at least unburden myself of three thoughts that kept forming in my mind as I read and reread his paper.

First, a distinction between truth and value.

The question above all others about the Pentateuch has long been the question about its origin, usually in this form: Is the documentary theory of Pentateuchal origins, or some other such theory, *true*? However, there is another set of questions we should also be asking, not so much about *truth* as about *value*, such as: Is such a theory useful?, Should I be interested in it? How important is it to have a theory of Pentateuchal origins?

These two questions are often collapsed into one another, and wrongly so, to my mind. At fault on the one side are those who are very enthusiastic about Pentateuchal origins and are, therefore, tempted to think that a theory about them is foundational for Hebrew Bible studies generally, and that nothing serious can be said about the Hebrew Bible if one does not have a good theory about the Pentateuch. At fault on the other side are those who are occupied with one or the other of thousands of current topics in Hebrew Bible studies and have little time to devote to Pentateuchal origins; their temptation is to think that because they are managing quite well without the documentary theory that the theory is actually wrong.

Rendtorff's paper itself, at one point, collapses the two questions, I believe. In commenting on Richard Elliott Friedman's representation of the documentary theory, he complains that Friedman is "cutting the Bible into pieces . . . What happened to the Bible itself? . . . The modern historical-critical analysis of the biblical texts . . . does not—or at least not sufficiently—ask the question, [W]hat is the meaning and significance of the given text[?]." I agree wholeheartedly with that as a criticism of the practice of biblical scholars, but it is not an argument against theories of Pentateuchal origins. If the Bible was indeed formed from bits and pieces, there is nothing wrong to cut it in pieces. Indeed it is a scholarly necessity. If in so doing people neglect the perhaps weightier question of its meaning and significance that may be an error, but it does not undercut the value of their project.

If we can distinguish between the truth and the value of a theory of Pentateuchal origins, we could find it possible to say, the theory, though true, is not useful or important. That is to say, even if it were established that the classic JEDP formulation was indubitable, it could nevertheless happen that scholars in a certain period might value more highly completely different questions and answers: about the ideology of the biblical texts, for example, or about their theological value, or about their literary character. To such questions the history of the formation of the Pentateuch may have very little to contribute. Even if the Pentateuch were composed from pre-existing sources, some scholars might say, do in fact say, "It is not those sources that one is studying when answering questions about the text that now exists, and that has indeed been the only text that has existed for the last two thousand years."

So here is an issue we need to come clean about. Leaving aside for the moment the debate over the origins of the Pentateuch, may we hear some views on how important, or perhaps unimportant, such a matter is? One of our external examiners for our undergraduate degree, a personage from a famous medieval university, let me note, reproached us in Sheffield a few years ago because our graduating students seemed to have a very hazy notion of the documentary theory of the Pentateuch, or perhaps no notion at all. How could we let students do three years of biblical studies and not be proficient in Pentateuchal origins? "Very easily," we answered; "We were busy doing lots of other things with them, and, in a word, we forgot!" There was no conspiracy to exclude JEDP from the course; it just didn't manage to impose itself sufficiently upon us to ensure its place in the curriculum. Maybe we were wrong to let our intuitive answer to the *value* question obliterate the *truth* question, but at least the value question was raised.

Second: The Role of Power in the Perpetuation of Theory

Shocking though it may sound, I believe that the time has long gone when we can discuss questions of Pentateuchal origins as academic questions in their own right. No longer is it the truth or falsity of a particular theory that determines whether it will find favor in the guild. Bad arguments will not be driven out by good arguments. Reason will not be the arbiter.

Rational debate still happens in the academy, I allow, and issues are sometimes settled purely on their merits. But when it comes to grand theories like the documentary hypothesis there is too much investment in the power that worldviews and grand theories accumulate to them selves for that to happen. I do not mean that there is no longer any place for rational argument, but only that rationality is subordinate to the exercise of power. It is naïve to think otherwise, or to act as if our decisions on such matters were not bound up with where we stand in a world of power.

In speaking of power I have in mind two separable kinds of power. In the first place, there is the power of persons and institutions who im- plement the adoption of a certain point of view, and in the second place there is the power of theories, explanations, and worldviews themselves to convince large numbers of adherents.

In the first case, certain important and influential scholars, in cer- tain important and influential institutions, have supported, and contin- ue to support, the classical Documentary Hypothesis. Those who do not adopt that position will find it difficult to get jobs in those institutions; they will not be invited to give seminar papers; they will not be so likely to be recommended for publication. Scholars in those institutions will, not surprisingly, often feel an affinity with their predecessors and de- velop an interest in preserving their legacy. Rolf Rendtorff is one of the most notable exceptions that proves the rule: located for four decades in what must be classified as a centre of academic power in Hebrew Bible studies (Heidelberg), he has gone against type; at the same time, he has no doubt paid a price for his refusal to accept the dominant ideology: among insiders he must be the most of an outsider! Not surprisingly, resistance to the classical Documentary Hypothesis has typically arisen from outside the centers of power, often from younger scholars in insti- tutions of the second and third rank.

The second sense of power is that of the power of the theory itself. It stands to reason that the classical Documentary Hypothesis would never have emerged or attracted such support if it had not had a lot of evidence in its favor. But it is not the existence of supporting data that gave the Wellhausen theory such a long shelf-life: it was its explanatory power and its comprehensiveness. It became a matrix into which all matters of Israelite history and literature were slotted, a truly foundational worldview that can best be called a paradigm. Generations of students internalized this worldview and carried out all their thinking about ancient Israel within its framework. To do so was necessary in order to become part of the scholarly community. The intrinsic power of the theory gave authority to the community that adopted the theory, but in so doing made every new member of the scholarly commentary a victim of its power.

In short, although the question of Pentateuchal origins will continue to be debated by papers on the Yahwist and the Priestly Work, for example, I would suggest that the debate belongs equally in the field of the sociology of knowledge—or perhaps rather in the realm of the protest rally—and it would be a mistake to think that we can arrive at a satisfactory conclusion of our current debates purely on the merits of the case.

Third: What is the Future for a Paradigm of Pentateuchal Origins?

Thinking of the Documentary Hypothesis as a "paradigm" drove me to reread the classic work of Thomas Kuhn, *The Structure of Scientific Revolutions,*[24] a little hackneyed by now, and sometimes controverted, but relevant to our issue. Paradigm change, Kuhn pointed out, is a complex business at the best of times. It results, he said, from the invention of new theories brought about by the failure of existing theory to solve the problems defined by that theory, a failure perceived as a *crisis* by the scientific community. Such failures have generally been long recognized. That is why crises are seldom surprising.

In responding to such crises, scholars generally do *not* renounce the paradigm that has led them into crisis. They may lose faith and con-

24. Kuhn, *The Structure of Scientific Revolutions* (Chicago: University of Chicago Press, 1962; 3rd ed., 1996).

sider alternatives, but typically they devise numerous articulations and *ad hoc* modifications of their theory in order to eliminate any apparent conflict, and save their familiar paradigm. Kuhn might have been listening to Rendtorff's paper on the current state of Pentateuchal criticism.

All crises come to an end in one of three ways, suggests Kuhn:

> 1. The original paradigm proves able to handle the crisis-provoking problem and all returns to normal.
>
> 2. The problem persists and is labeled a problem, but it is perceived as resulting from the field's lack of the necessary tools with which to solve it, and so scholars set it aside for a future generation with more developed tools.
>
> 3. A new candidate for the required paradigm emerges, and a battle over its acceptance ensues—these are the *paradigm wars.*[25]

None of these depictions rings true for our current situation in Pentateuchal studies. We can hardly speak of the emergence of a new candidate for paradigm. Rendtorff has amusingly deflated the pretensions of a new candidate that propounds a source-critical theory of Pentateuchal origins but can find only one source. We are still, are we not, in the phase of exploring the problems of the standard paradigm? Rather than being confronted by a more attractive paradigm than the Documentary Hypothesis, we are still in the process of losing faith in the old paradigm—as we have been for the last three or four decades at least. Inevitably, we must expect to be stuck with that old paradigm for a long time; for a paradigm, says Kuhn, is declared invalid *only if an alternative candidate is available to take its place.*[26] For us, it seems as if the present state of uncertainty is fated to persist.

And yet it may be that a shifting of the paradigm is already silently and almost invisibly under way. To quote a further aphorism of Kuhn: "Because paradigm shifts are generally viewed not as revolutions but as additions to scientific knowledge . . . a scientific revolution seems invisible."[27] We are far from the invalidating of the old paradigm. However, the invisible revolution that is raising issues of value rather than truth, that is insisting on focusing on meaning, textuality, ethics,

25. Ibid., 84.

26. Ibid., 77.

27. Ibid., 198.

and the ideology of the biblical texts—all of them irrelevant to questions of the origins of the literature—may be simply displacing, rather than resolving, the questions of Pentateuchal origins. We can, if we choose, see these new interests as merely additions to the traditional scope of biblical criticism, no more than a broadening out of the field, and thus no threat to the standard paradigm; but a longer perspective may regard their infiltration into the discipline as truly revolutionary.

Will such gestures towards a new paradigm win out? The physicist Max Planck said: "A new scientific truth does not triumph by convincing its opponents and making them see the light, but rather because its opponents eventually die, and a new generation grows up that is familiar with it."[28] My forecast is that the new generation in Hebrew Bible studies will, in some parts of the world at least, grow up with other interests in the forefront of their attention, and lose interest in questions of origins. However, that will not be the end of the Documentary Hypothesis, only its marginalization. The question, How did the Pentateuch, in fact, come into being? will persist, as a minority interest, for a much smaller audience than this.

Allan Rosengren—Why is There a Documentary Hypothesis and What Does it Do to You if You Use It?[29]

The year 1753 was an important one in the history of Old Testament scholarship. It was the year that saw the appearance of two scholarly works, both of which—each in their respective area—were to be hailed as inaugurators of important traditions of scholarship that even today continue to govern our way of thinking. The one book is Jean Astruc's *Conjectures sur les mémoires originaux dont il paroit que Moyse s'est servi, pour composer le Livre de la Genese*,[30] the other Robert Lowth's

---

28. Quoted in ibid., 150.

29. This section is a revised version of my response to David J. A. Clines's "Response to Rolf Rendtorff's 'What Happened to the Yahwist? Reflections after Thirty Years'" (SBL Forum, August 2006, www.sbl-site.org/Article.aspx?ArticleId=551) and was originally published in the SBL Forum, September 2006 (www.sbl-site.org/Article .aspx?ArticleId=566). I am grateful to Dr. J. Harold Ellens for having invited me to contribute to this volume and to Leonard Greenspoon, editor of the SBL Forum, for permission to publish the article here. Also many thanks to Flemming Gorm Andersen from the Royal Library in Copenhagen for valuable assistance.

30. Jean Astruc, *Conjectures sur les mémoires originaux dont il paroit que Moyse s'est servi, pour composer le Livre de la Genese. Avec des Remarques, qui appuient ou*

De Sacra Poesi Hebræorum Prælectiones Academicæ Oxonii Habitæ.[31]
Astruc became known as the father of the Documentary Hypothesis;
Lowth as the discoverer of the nature of Hebrew poetry and the first
systematiser of the phenomenon called parallelism.

The fact that the two books appeared in the same year is, of course,
a coincidence. In many respects, the two works and their authors are
diametrical oppositions: Astruc's book was published anonymously
and even with false indication of place of publication; Lowth's book was
based on public lectures and published at the Clarendon Press. Astruc
wrote his treatise in his past time; Lowth during his professorship at
Oxford. Astruc was in his late 60s and could look back on a brilliant
career as a professor of medicine and as the personal physician of Louis
XV. Lowth was in his early 40s and still in the middle of his career. The
publication of his lectures was only his first major scholarly contribution. Astruc's *Conjectures* appeared as a handsome duodecimo; Lowth's
Prælectiones as an impressive quarto. The former is written in elegant
French; the latter in learned Latin.

But above all, the two books treat two very different subjects.
Astruc's *Conjectures* deal with the composition of a prose text. We can
safely designate the text of the Book of Genesis as prose in this context.
It was only after Lowth that the quest for poetic passages in prose narratives began. Lowth's lectures are on the nature of Hebrew poetry. There is
no reason to believe that the authors knew of each other. Even if Lowth
later read Astruc's *Conjectures*, the reading would not have induced him
to modify his theories in any way, or quote Astruc in his footnotes. Why
not? The answer is that the two scholars were thought to be working in
two completely different areas of literature, prose and poetry.[32]

---

qui éclaircissent ces Conjectures (Bruxelles: Fricx, 1753). [Published without name of
the author and with a false indication of place of publishing. Apparently published by
Cavelier in Paris]. Now available as Jean Astruc, *Conjectures sur la Genèse: Introduction
et notes de Pierre Gibert* (Paris: Noèsis, 1999).

31. Robert Lowth, *De Sacra Poesi Hebræorum: Prælectiones Academicæ Oxonii
Habitæ* (Oxford: Clarendon, 1753). The English translation is quoted from *Lectures on
the Sacred Poetry of the Hebrews . . . to which are added, the principal notes of Professor
Michaelis, and notes by the Translator and others,* 2 vols., translated by G. Gregory
(London: Johnson, 1787). Reprinted in two volumes in the series Robert Lowth
(1710–1787): The Major Works, 8 vols. (London: Routledge, 1995).

32. John Jarick, ed., *Sacred Conjectures: The Context and Legacy of Robert Lowth and
Jean Astruc,* Library of Hebrew Bible/Old Testament Studies 457 (New York: T. & T.

It is my contention that the two books and the two scholarly traditions they engendered are not quite as unrelated as it would seem. Though completely unintended, the two hypotheses in the long run reinforced each other. One example: When the author of Proverbs 30 four times mentions "three things, nay four things," thus:

> Three things there are which will never be satisfied,
> four which never say, "Enough!" (Prov 30:15 REB)

> Three things there are which are too wonderful for me,
> four which are beyond my understanding. (Prov 30:18 REB)

> Under three things the earth shakes,
> four things it cannot bear. (Prov 30:21 REB)

> Three things there are which are stately in their stride,
> four which are stately as they move. (Prov 30:29 REB)

and consistently gives a list of four in each case, this is not a problem for us. No one, as far as I know, has undertaken a documentary-hypothesis-kind-of-analysis of these verses, arguing that there is an older אלעה-source, which has been combined with a later, and more systematic (since the list always contains four elements), ארבעה-source. Why? Because the Book of Proverbs is a book of poetry! And since it is poetry, which is characterized by the widespread use of parallelisms, we have to grant its author poetic licence! And therefore the peculiar and repeated talk of "three things, nay four things" does not confuse us. Examples of this kind could easily be multiplied.

In the Flood Story, however, God commands Noah to bring one pair of all the animals into the ark, and a few verses later Yahweh commands Noah to bring *seven* pairs of all the clean animals and of the birds into the ark. This kind of inconsistency is usually solved through the documentary hypothesis leaving aside the question of whether this is a kind of parallelism. It is surely not a parallelism of members, *parallelismus membrorum*, of the kind that Lowth identified. However, paral-

---

Clark, 2007)—forthcoming when this article was revised—will probably shed new light on this. On Astruc and Lowth in general, cf. Pierre Gibert's "Introduction," in Astruc, *Conjectures sur la Genèse*; Adolphe Lods, *Jean Astruc et la critique biblique au XVIIIe siècle*, Cahiers de la Revue d'histoire et de philosophie religieuses publiés par la Faculté de Théologie protestante de l'Université de Strasbourg (Strasbourg: Istra, 1924); and Brian Hepworth, *Robert Lowth*, Twayne's English Authors Series 224 (Boston: Twayne, 1978).

lelisms are not only of members, but exist on other levels of language as well: two words, two compound expressions, two paragraphs, or two chapters can constitute a parallelism. Parallelism is a much more complex phenomenon than it is often thought to be.[33] Moreover, parallelisms occur in prose both on the level of the line (the traditional parallelism) and on other levels, as well. Genesis 1 and Genesis 2 could be viewed as a parallelism, which is what Mark G. Brett does in his reading of Genesis, though he does not explicitly use the term parallelism. Brett's parallelistic reading is carried out on the level of chapters (the anthropocentric view of Genesis 1:1—2:4a is paralleled with the geocentric view of Genesis 2:4b–25) and on the level of words (hdr, to rule, in Gen 1:26 is contrasted with db(, to work as a slave, to till, in Gen 2:15).[34] Maybe the doublets of the Flood-story could be read as parallelisms.[35] However, very few scholars would read this way, because we are used to thinking not only in terms of the documentary hypothesis, but also in terms of the notions of prose inherent in this hypothesis. A prose-author will strive to obtain clarity and to avoid conflicting statements. This ideal of prose was reinforced by Lowth's pre-romantic description of Poetry:

> The language of Reason is cool, temperate, rather humble than elevated, well arranged and perspicuous, with an evident care and anxiety lest any thing should escape which might appear perplexed or obscure. The language of the Passions is totally different: the conceptions burst out in a turbid stream, expressive in a manner of the internal conflict; the more vehement break out in hasty confusion; they catch (without search or study) what ever is impetuous, vivid, or energetic. In a word, Reason speaks literally, the Passions poetically. (Lowth 1753, *Praelectiones* XIV, quoted from the translation of G. Gregory.)

33. Adele Berlin, *The Dynamics of Biblical Parallelism* (Bloomington: Indiana University Press, 1985).

34. Mark G. Brett, *Genesis: Procreation and the Politics of Identity*, OTR (New York: Routledge, 2000) 30.

35. Allan Rosengren, "Petersen, Prose and Parallelisms: The Beginning and the End of the Documentary Hypothesis" (Ph.D. dissertation, University of Copenhagen, 1998) 162–88.

The Latin runs thus:

> *Loquitur Ratio remisse, temperate, leniter; res ordinate disponit, aperte signat, distincte explicat; studet imprimis perspicuitati, ne quid confusum, ne quid obscurum, ne quid involutum relinquatur. Affectionibus vero nihil horum admodum curæ est: turbide confluunt, intus luctantur, conceptus; ex iis vehementiores temere, qua licet, erumpunt; quod vividum, ardens, incitatum, non quærunt, sed arripiunt: ut verbo dicam, mero sermone utitur Ratio, Affectus loquuntur poetice.*

Prose as the language of reason and poetry as the language of the passions! We may, with Lowth, retain the singular of reason and the plural of the passions, since reason speaks uni-vocally, whereas the passions are many and confused and speak accordingly. This perspective is a notion that we have inherited from the Romantic Movement (Herder was very fond of Lowth). Though we do not speak of it in the same way as did Lowth, it underlies much exegetical work on the Pentateuch. In very general terms, the scholarly preconception could be phrased thus:

> What in a poetic text are perceived as *couplets*,
> which must be appreciated for their poetic qualities,
> are in a prose text regarded as *doublets*,
> which must be explained for their lack of consistency.

This does not mean that documentary-hypothesis-kind-of-work has not been done on poetic texts. Isaiah, Jeremiah, and the Book of Psalms have all been subject to redactional theories. However, at least on one level of the poetic text, namely that of the parallelism of members, repetitions and inconsistencies are admitted in a way that scholars would normally not allow in prose:

> Once God has spoken;
> twice have I heard this:
> that power belongs to God,
> and steadfast love belongs to you, O Lord. (Ps 62:12–13 [ET 11–12])

An obvious prose-question would be, "If God spoke once, who said the other thing that the I of the text heard?" But, thank God, this is poetry! It stands in contrast to the prose passage in which Noah obeys a deity with two different names and who says two different things, and that, therefore, must be accounted for in a different manner.

Why Is There a Documentary Hypothesis?

"Why is There a Documentary Hypothesis, and What Does it Do to You if You Use it?" is a Clinesean kind of question. Clines uses the formula in connection with books of the Hebrew Bible,[36] but the power that texts exercise over our minds is comparable to the influence that hypotheses have over our way of seeing things. Therefore, I have adopted the question and addressed it to the present subject. Properly speaking, the latter part of the question should be "What Do You Do to Yourself, if You Use it?" Hypotheses and texts are only alive in a figurative sense; it is people who use them that are alive and responsible, but I will let that be understood in the following.

I would like to link the first part of the question to one of the questions that Clines raises in his Response to Rolf Rendtorff, namely the question of value: Is such a theory useful? The value or usefulness of the documentary hypothesis lies in its ability to create consistency, and this, I suggest, is also the answer to the question, Why is There a Documentary Hypothesis? The hypothesis readily accounts for the repetitions, doublets, and the alternating names of the deity in the book of Genesis, and thus satisfies our need for consistency.

In the Wellhausen form, the documentary hypothesis was coupled with a historical project, or history-of-religion project. The historian needs consistent sources for his project, and the historian of religion needs unmixed literary specimens of literature pertaining to the various levels of the religion he is about to describe. Again, the documentary hypothesis proved to be a *valuable* tool to create the kind of consistency needed.

Very generally speaking, the text of the Pentateuch, which is mostly prose, was regarded first and foremost as an historical source, and for that reason it had to be consistent. If it was not, scholars had the tools to make it consistent!

---

36. David J. A. Clines, "Why is There a Song of Songs, and What Does It Do to You If You Read It?" in *Interested Parties: The Ideology of Writers and Readers of the Hebrew Bible*, JSOTSup 205 (Sheffield: Sheffield Academic, 1995) 94–121; and "Why Is There a Book of Job, and What Does It Do to You If You Read It?" in *Interested Parties*, 122–44.

What Does the Documentary Hypothesis Do to You, If You Use It?

In positive terms, the documentary hypothesis enables you to create consistency, nay more than that, to create *consistencies* on various levels, and to explain the text in a highly detailed and sophisticated way, which usually is highly regarded and admired in academic circles, and which continues to give power to the theory (see Clines' response, second paragraph). The documentary hypothesis gives you power, if you use it well!

In negative terms, it turns the attention away from the possible meaningfulness of a text containing conflicting voices. Let us for the moment substitute *voice* for *source*. The documentary hypothesis brings about a certain perspective on the text, which inevitably, it seems, high-lights portions of the text that you happen to like or dislike. Note how the Yahwist is often a hero of the scholar who created him.[37] In this respect, the Yahwist resembles the Jesus of scholarly reconstruction. No one dislikes the Jesus they find. Jesus has been misrepresented, it is claimed, especially by the church, but the original Jesus that the scholar reconstructs is always - ideal! And note how P has traditionally been regarded as a late, uninspiring and uninspired level of Israelite religion (Wellhausen), a view that has been challenged in the latter half of the twentieth century by scholars using the same tool![38] The documentary hypothesis helps the scholar to focus on likes and dislikes; it's a tool for theological, ideological, or aesthetic upgrading and downgrading.

This does not mean that the personal bias of the scholar is not visible in final-form exegetical analyses. The question of bias is always

---

37. Jean Louis Ska, "The Yahwist, a Hero with a Thousand Faces: A Chapter in the History of Modern Exegesis," in *Abschied vom Jahwisten*, 1–23. Thomas Christian Römer, "The Elusive Yahwist: A Short History of Research," in *A Farewell to the Yahwist? The Composition of the Pentateuch in Recent European Interpretation*, edited by Thomas B. Dozeman and Konrad Schmid, SBLSymSer 34 (Atlanta: Society of Biblical Literature, 2006) 9–27.

38. E.g., Klaus Koch, *Die Priesterschrift von Exodus 25 bis Leviticus 16: Eine über-lieferungsgeschichtliche und literarkritische Untersuchung*, FRLANT 71 (Göttingen: Vandenhoeck & Ruprecht, 1959); Claus Westermann, "Die Herrlichkeit Gottes in der Priesterschrift," in *Forschungen am Alten Testament: Gesammelte Schriften II*, ThBü 55 (Munich: Kaiser, 1974) 115–37; Jacob Milgrom, *Leviticus 1–16*, AB 3 (New York: Doubleday, 1991); Milgrom, *Leviticus 17–22*, AB 3A (New York: Doubleday, 2000); Milgrom, *Leviticus 23–27*, AB 3B (New York: Doubleday, 2001).

crucial in interpretation. I just want to focus on the blind spot, or one of the blind angles, of the documentary hypothesis.

What Shall We Do with the Drunken Sailor?

Terminology, to some extent, reflects our perspective on a text. The emergence of new perspectives or paradigms only gradually causes a new terminology to appear and replace the older terminology. Perhaps it is time that we change the way we speak of things.

The style and content of Gen 1:1—2:4a is markedly different from Gen 2:4b–25. However, rather than speaking of different *sources*, we should, I suggest, find a different term that implies a different perspective. Perhaps we could speak of *voices* rather than *sources*. The term, *voices*, maintains the differences of style, vocabulary, and so on, that have been identified since Astruc, but does not point to one particular redactional solution. Rather than excluding the possibility of source-hypotheses, it opens the door to other kinds of analyses, for instance a Bakhtinian reading. It also opens the door for the identification of other modes of speaking than what has hitherto been recognized as sources, for instance the voice of particularism, which is often juxtaposed to the voice of universalism, as in Genesis 12:1–3b // Genesis 12:3c or Psalm 149 // 150.[39]

John Van Seters—The Yahwist and the Debate

I was not able to attend the Edinburgh international meeting and to respond directly to Professor Rendtorff's paper so I will take the opportunity to do so here. I will make only some brief comments since I have already anticipated the content of this paper in other places, in particular in my paper, "The Pentateuch as Torah *and* History: In Defense of G. von Rad," given at the symposium held in honor of the one hundredth anniversary of von Rad's birthday, in October, 2001. It was published four years later in *Das Alte Testament—Ein Geschichtsbuch?*[40] A revised version also appeared in my book, *The Edited Bible.*[41]

39. Cf. my forthcoming book, *Parallelism in Interpretation* (working title).

40. Van Seters, "The Pentateuch as Torah *and* History: In Defense of G. von Rad," in *Das Alte Testament—Ein Geschichtsbuch?*, edited by Erhard Blum et al., ATM 10 (Münster: Lit, 2005).

41. Van Seters, *The Edited Bible: The Curious History of the "Editor" in Biblical Studies* (Winona Lake, IN: Eisenbrauns, 2006) 244–97.

In these presentations I strongly protested against what I regard as Rendtorff's misrepresentation of von Rad's position by his dismissal of the Yahwist as an author and historian. Anyone reading through von Rad's corpus cannot be in doubt regarding how strongly von Rad felt about the Yahwist as author and historian. His study, "Das formgeschichtliche Problem des Hexateuch," was primarily to dispute Gunkel's treatment of the Yahwist as merely a random and accidental collection of old traditions, and to argue that the work is that of an *historian*. He says very little about the Yahwist as theologian. It was Noth, in his study of the Pentateuch, who preferred to follow Gunkel and who also spoke of the process of tradition accumulation as theological, and Rendtorff has followed this line, not that of von Rad.

In the now famous quotation of von Rad, Rendtorff interprets the statement as von Rad's way of dismissing the Documentary Hypothesis, but of course von Rad did no such thing. What von Rad seems to have had a problem with is not the notion of multiple authors in the Pentateuch, but how they were combined, namely, the matter of the redactors: "Not that the conflation of E and P with J would now appear to be a simple process, nor one which could be altogether explained to one's satisfaction." It is the theory that redactors were responsible for the combining of the sources or traditions about which von Rad expresses doubt. What has happened, however, is that those who have followed Rendtorff's lead have done away with the authors, or at least the Yahwist, and replaced him with redactors! Nothing could be further from von Rad's intention. Ironically, Noth received his own inspiration, for identifying the Deuteronomist as an historian and not a mere editor, from von Rad's identification of the Yahwist as an historian, as Noth says at the beginning of his own study. Nonetheless, the followers of Noth have turned his Deuteronomist historian into an elaborate redactional process as well.

When it comes to characterizing my own work on the Yahwist, Rendtorff tries to represent me as creating "a new kind of Yahwist . . . an individual personality; he is not a theologian like von Rad's Yahwist, but a historian." As suggested above, this misrepresents both von Rad and me. I have simply followed von Rad's suggestion that J is a historian, but I do not deny that within J's history there is a theology, and I have written on the subject. Rendtorff has constructed a completely false dicotomy here, a false choice.

What is even more puzzling is Rendtorff's assertion that for me there is only one source or author in the Pentateuch and that my views represent a "reduced documentary hypothesis, namely a one-document hypothesis." That bears no resemblance to my views at all. I have rejected the traditional E source, but there were a number of scholars before me who did that so there is nothing new there. I retain Deuteronomy and P as separate sources in the largely traditional sense so that there remain for me three major sources. Where I part from the Documentary Hypothesis is in the rejection of the role of redactor or editor (see my book noted above) as the one who combined these sources. Instead, I advocate the theory of a successive supplementation of one source or author by another. I have even characterized my work as the "New Supplementary Hypothesis," but Rendtorff has ignored all of this. It is also curious to see that Rendtorff's own student, Erhard Blum, also advocated what amounts to three sources, KD (=J?), KP (=P) and Deuteronomy, with a very similar dating to my J, P, and D.

A number of those scholars who have followed Rendtorff's lead in getting rid of the Yahwist as author are reflected in the book *Abschied vom Jahwisten*, which is reviewed by Rendtorff in his paper. I heard that such a book was in the works but I was not asked to contribute or respond to it. However, in a second volume on this same theme, "Farewell to the Yahwist," I have contributed a paper, "The Report of the Yahwist's Demise has been Greatly Exaggerated!" in which I seek to respond to this movement to get rid of the Yahwist.[42] See also my paper, "The Patriarchs and the Exodus: Bridging the Gap between Two Origin Traditions."[43]

I will not comment here on any of these scholars cited by Rendtorff in his support, except to say that they have largely replaced the Yahwist by a series of redactors. They retained the source P, for some strange reason, although large chunks of it have also become the work of the ubiquitous *redactor*. It was the Documentary Hypothesis that created the redactor as a literary devise, a *deus ex machina*, to make the whole theory work. That is the only really distinctive feature of the Documentary Hypothesis and it is this part of the theory that Rendtorff and others

42. Van Seters, "The Report of the Yahwist's Demise has been Greatly Exaggerated!" in *Farewell to the Yahwist?*

43. In *The Interpretation of Exodus: Studies in Honour of Cornelis Houtman*, edited by Reimer Roukema, CBET 44 (Leuven: Peeters, 2006) 1–15.

have retained. Now we supposedly have editors without any authors, which is absurd, and the whole literary process has become known as redaction criticism. It is high time that the redactor takes his leave and the author is restored to his rightful place in literary criticism.

I would make some comments on the "three thoughts" contained in David Clines' remarks. First, regarding his distinction between truth and value, he seems to be setting up a debate between the historical-critical approach to the Bible, on the one hand, and those, on the other hand, who favor approaches that are useful and relevant, whether religious, social, or political, regardless of what the biblical writers meant when they wrote the words in their own social and historical context. He refers to Rendtorff's complaint against the historical-critical analysis of biblical texts as destructive of the meaning and significance of the given text, by which for Rendtorff is meant the canonical text. As Clines admits, Sheffield was more interested in the second of these alternatives, especially with the contemporary denigration of historical studies in post-modernism.

This debate, however, is not new. It came to the fore in the "battle of the books" in the late seventeenth and early eighteenth century in the study of the Greek and Roman classics, especially Homer, which was the secular Bible of the day and the foundation of western education. The historical-critical study of Homer was a threat to the whole educational enterprise. The rise of historical criticism of the Pentateuch in the nineteenth century was perceived as a threat to the religious establishment in the same way. That debate between the two approaches, the historical text of the past and the normative text of the present has been with us ever since.

Second, Clines tries to make the debate about Pentateuchal origins a matter of a power struggle between persons and especially between institutions. This seems to be heavily influenced again by post-modern perspectives in which the contest of views is really a contest of power. Of course, Rendtorff must then be cited as an exception, as professor at Heidelberg, but what about H. H. Schmid at Zurich, and myself at Toronto? Or does Clines consider these second or third rate institutions? As soon as I published *Abraham in History and Tradition* I was promoted to full professor at Toronto and shortly afterwards received an endowed chair at the University of North Carolina. In any case, the academic institutions for which we worked had little to do with what we wrote about the Pentateuch. One could make a better case for the whole issue of biblical archaeology and the historicity of the Patriarchs and Moses and David, but that is another matter.

Third, regarding the notion of paradigm shift, I have been following the discussion in the scientific community as reflected in the *New York Review of Books*, which has leveled some rather serious criticisms at Kuhn's position. In fact, it is most often used as just a cliché to suggest a major shift in thinking and little more. I think that the much greater change that has affected biblical studies is in the historical field, which can hardly return to the old way of doing things. I am much less sanguine about any lasting changes or broad agreements in Pentateuchal studies.

6

Further Reflections on the Yahwist

J. Harold Ellens

NINETEENTH-CENTURY HEBREW BIBLE SCHOLARS IDENTIFIED THE FACT
that the main problem of the Pentateuch arises from the multi-stranded
and multi-layered tradition of ancient Israelite memory contained
within it. A half dozen independent narrative streams or cycles can be
identified as separate traditions:

1. a mythic history narrating the origin of the world and the human race (Genesis 2–11);

2. the story of the patriarchs: Abraham, Isaac, and Jacob (Genesis 12–36);

3. the narrative of Joseph and his extended family (Genesis 37–50);

4. the Moses cycle (Exodus 2–4);

5. the exodus from Egypt and the wilderness wandering (Exodus 12—Numbers 20);

6. the stories of Balaam (Numbers 22–24); and

7. the departure of Moses (Deuteronomy 34).

Linguistic, metaphoric, and religious or cultic features of each stream
or cycle set it apart from the others and suggest for each a different
moment in history.

The issue at stake in the Pentateuchal debate is the matter of how
early in the unfolding of the Israelite national consciousness each of
these strands originated and when they were unified into a somewhat

67

comprehensive whole, more or less as the canonical Torah presents them today. Nineteenth century scholars generally thought that this redactional process took place early, producing edited traditions that represented the Yahwist, Elohist, and other perspectives. Thus, these were thought to have been woven together in a unified national memory, oral or written, at early moments in the formation of the nation's master story.

Early in the twentieth century Gerhard von Rad, Martin Noth, and others began in earnest to modify those earlier assumptions. The suggestion arose that the independent streams of Israelite memory, and the cultic veneration of the cultural *Quelle*, represented separate tribal traditions and the amphictiony of independent cultic centers such as Hazor, Megiddo, Shiloh, Shechem, Bethel, and Gilgal; and perhaps later even Dan and Beersheba.[1] These were thought by some scholars to have been unified by the very early editorial work of a Yahwistic theologian, subsequently streamlined by a Deuteronomist editor, and finalized by a Priestly redactor in the sixth century BCE, during the Babylonian exile.

However, the diversity of the stands of Israelite tradition, even as they are presented today in the canonical Pentateuch (Genesis–Deuteronomy), Hexateuch (Genesis–Joshua), and Enneateuch (Genesis–2 Kings), strongly urges some scholars to suspect that the editorial process by which the strands were woven into a somewhat unified set of narratives took place very late in Israelite history, probably during or after the exile. As debated in the previous chapter, this Pentateuchal problem has given rise to the debate about whether the Yahwist ever existed, if so whether he or she was a creative author of historiography with or without a special theological perspective, or an editor of earlier material that he or she attempted to reduce to a coherent single tradition late in the history of ancient Israel. Rolf Rendtorff and those who see things his way, denies that there ever was a figure to whom we can refer as the Yahwist, whether author or redactor. Van Seters, on the other hand, asserts that we have every reason to conclude that there was such

---

1. See W. F. Albright, *Yahweh and the Gods of Canaan: A Historical Analysis of Two Contrasting Faiths* (Garden City, NY: Doubleday, 1969), 196. This volume was republished by Eisenbrauns (Winona Lake, IN) in a lovely cloth-bound edition, without date, but from the original Jordan Lectures of 1965 delivered by Albright at the School of Oriental and African Studies of the University of London.

a figure in Israelite history and that he or she was the author of the Yahwistic material, not merely an early editor. Indeed, Van Seters is prepared to suggest that a series of authors, over time, each supplemented the work of an earlier Yahwistic author, thus creating a progressively developed Yahwist literary tradition. These two positions represent the extreme poles of the current debate.

It is a most welcome and fortuitous event that Thomas B. Dozeman and Konrad Schmid, recently published their good and timely volume, *A Farewell to the Yahwist? The Composition of the Pentateuch in Recent European Interpretation.*[2] Their book treats the problem of the Yahwist and of the composition of the Pentateuch, particularly as that problem has been debated by European and North American scholars in the Pentateuch Seminar of the Society for Biblical Literature over the last quarter century. The SBL seminar was established in the early 1980s by John Van Seters, Rolf P. Knierim, George W. Coats, Simon J. De Vries, and John G. Gammie. "These scholars were drawn together by a growing uneasiness over the lack of direction in pentateuchal studies, in the wake of the influential synthesis of Martin Noth and Gerhard von Rad."[3] Over the last twenty-five years many scholars contributed to a sturdy discourse on this crucial theme. In *A Farewell to the Yahwist?*, Dozeman and Schmid have presented the essence of the "enormous creativity" that this seminar produced.

Their contribution is launched by an essay from the pen of Thomas Christian Römer, as intriguing as its title: "The Elusive Yahwist: A Short History of Research." Schmid then discusses "The So-Called Yahwist and the Literary Gap between Genesis and Exodus." There follows Albert de Pury's, "The Jacob Story and the Beginning of the Formation of the Pentateuch"; Jan Christian Gertz's, "The Transition between the Books of Genesis and Exodus"; Erhard Blum's, "The Literary Connection between the Books of Genesis and Exodus and the End of the Book of Joshua"; and Dozeman's, "The Commission of Moses and the Book of Genesis." These chapters provide the substantive content and burden of the book. Three responses critique that analysis. These are written by Christoph Levin, "The Yahwist and the Redactional Link between Genesis and

---

2. Thomas B. Dozeman and Konrad Schmid, eds., *A Farewell to the Yahwist? The Composition of the Pentateuch in Recent European Interpretation*, SBLSymSer 34 (Atlanta: Society of Biblical Literature, 2006).

3. Dozeman and Schmid, "Introduction," in ibid., 1.

Exodus"; John Van Seters, "The Report of the Yahwist's Demise Has Been Greatly Exaggerated"; and David M. Carr, "What is Required to Identify Pre-Priestly Narrative Connections between Genesis and Exodus?" Some General Reflections and Specific Cases, round out this report on the quarter century of the SBL Pentateuch Seminar.

In a recent *Review of Biblical Literature*, Eckart Otto reviewed a book by John Van Seters.[4] In that book, Van Seters calls into question the long established, but now variously challenged hypothesis, that the canonical form of the Hebrew Bible was shaped by editors and redactors, making his case that it was creative and imaginative authors that were at work, particularly in forming the Yahwist literary stream. Otto's review focuses this prominent and perplexing issue of OT studies. Van Seters challenges the theories of Wellhausen, von Rad, Martin Noth, and subsequent scholars, pertaining to the Pentateuch, Tetrateuch, Hexateuch, and Enneateuch. As has surely been noted from the debate between Rendtorff, Clines, Rosengren, and Van Seters, in chapter 5 above, the problem has increasingly centered upon the difficulties inherent in the entire Documentary Hypothesis, but more specifically upon the nature and function of the Yahwist.

The Early Research on the Documentary Hypothesis

Julius Wellhausen began his professorial role in 1870 with careful work on 1–2 Samuel. He continued his work following the trajectory of Pentateuchal criticism that had been set by Wilhelm de Wette, Wilhelm Vatke, Eduard Reuss, Karl H. Graf, and A. Kuenen. In 1876–77 his published work on the composition of the Hexateuch employed Hermann Hupfeld's innovative and challenging documentary hypothesis.[5] His perspective came to be known as the Graf–Kuenen–Wellhausen thesis. He largely reversed the accepted theories of the time regarding the dating and sequencing of the sources of the Hexateuch. His new chronology suggested, contrary to previous notions, that the priestly (P) document presupposed the Babylonian exile, and thus constituted the latest layer of the tradition. In 1878 he spelled out the implication of

---

4. Otto, Review of Van Seters, *The Edited Bible: The Curious History of the Editor in Biblical Criticism* by John Van Seters in *RBL* May 12, 2007.

5. Wellhausen, "Die Composition des Hexateuchs," *JDT* 21 (1876) 392–450, 531–602; 22 (1877) 407–79.

this for the historiography of Israel, insisting that P and Chronicles were postexilic rather than preexilic sources.

Wellhausen then concluded that the law formed a divider between the two phases of ancient Israelite history and only took its current shape in the postexilic period. The law arose as a functional element in Deuteronomy and subsequently shaped formative Judaism, making possible the emergence of the formal theocracy of the postexilic period. Wellhausen's perspective was a history of religions approach, rather than the traditional *Heilsgeschichte* emphasis. When he published his definitive work on Israelite and Jewish history in 1894,[6] his reconstruction of history and historiography centered in the maxim, "Yahweh the God of Israel, Israel the people of Yahweh," and claimed this as the grounding *credo* of Israelite national consciousness.

This theme impressed Gerhard von Rad, and his early work emphasized that it is the *motif* that affords the Deuteronomic and Deuteronomistic material their inherent unity. However, he thought P was shaped by three internal cycles: the cycle of the nations of the world (*goyim*), of Noah, and of Abraham. These eventually are unified in the tradition built up around the historical *credo* that celebrated the deliverance from Egypt and the establishment of the people of Yahweh in the Promised Land. That consistent internal theme was therefore thought to be the sustaining and guiding providence of God's *strong arm and outstretched hand.* "The recitation of this credo at the feast of weeks, in combination with the recitation of the Sinai tradition at the feast of booths . . . developed through numerous stages (the most important of which had been the writing down of the story in literary form by the Yahwist)," and thus achieved its final form.[7] Von Rad proposed that a historical and form-critical approach was required to discern the variety of cycles and layers of material, a line of thought and methodology further developed and substantially modified by Rolf P. Knierim and others.[8]

Martin Noth addressed the issues Wellhausen had raised but developed a new and unusual model of ancient Israelite history in which the

6. Wellhausen, *Israelitische und jüdische Geschichte* (Göttingen: Vandenhoeck & Ruprecht, 1894).

7. Rudolf Smend, "Rad, Gerhard von (1901–71)," in *Dictionary of Biblical Interpretation*, edited by John H. Hayes (Nashville, Abingdon, 1999) 2:364.

8. Knierim, *The Task of Old Testament Theology: Substance, Method, and Cases* (Grand Rapids: Eerdmans, 1995).

tribes of Israel developed in Canaan and were later joined by the Joseph group from Egypt, who introduced Yahwism into the region. He was certain that "no documentary connection existed between the material in Deuteronomy–2 Kings and that in Genesis–Numbers (except for a few sections at the end of Deuteronomy), and that Deuteronomy–2 Kings had been put together by a Deuteronomistic historian who employed various forms of source material, writing in Palestine after Jerusalem fell to the Babylonians."[9]

Martin Noth generally accepted the Yahwist (J), Elohist (E), and Priestly (P) sources hypothesis Wellhausen had carried forward from Hupfeld and the Graf–Kuenen school; and spent his scholarly life searching out the origin, transmission, and enrichment of the traditions behind those sources. He accepted as crucial the fact that Israelite traditions were characterized by specific themes such as promises to the patriarchs, exodus, wilderness wanderings, the Sinai theophany, and deliverance into a rich and fruitful land; all of which phases were shaped by divine providence and guidance in Israelite history. These separate phases were originally independent of each other, Noth thought, being individual traditions of specific tribes. Some were oriented on Abraham, some on Moses, some on Joseph, and some on none of the three. The Moses themes were combined with many of the general traditions already in the pre-monarchial era, he thought, and they continued to be enriched by the progressive unification of the tribal system, and thus the individual tribal memories. Ultimately, they were edited into the J and E sources.

William Foxwell Albright erroneously criticized Noth for failing to take a constructive attitude toward the Hebrew Bible as canon and for failing to take into consideration archaeological evidence. Albright himself, however, expended considerable energy trying to reorganize the J, E, and P traditions in the Pentateuch, emphasizing the importance of the variety of tradition cycles rather than simply a unified canon. In fact, Albright's critical allegations regarding Noth are especially unfounded. Moreover, Noth's archaeological, topographical, and geographical studies are noteworthy and still useful. Albright vigorously disagreed with Yehezkel Kaufmann's claim[10] that the ancient Israelites

---

9. John H. Hayes, "Martin Noth (1902–68)," in *Dictionary of Biblical Interpretation*, 2:212.

10. Kaufmann, *Toldot ha-ʾemunah ha-yisreʾelit*, 8 vols. (Tel Aviv: Mosad Byalik ʿal yede Devir, 1937–56); English abridged edition, *The Religion of Israel*, translated by

of the thirteenth or twelfth century BCE developed a monotheism that was unique, uniform, and untrammeled from that point on. However, Albright did hold consistently to the position that Yahwism had been established by Moses, was inherent to the Moses cycle of tradition, and persisted from his day onward as the dominant, though not exclusive, religion of the Israelites.[11]

History of Yahwist Research

The argument of the Dozeman and Schmid volume is illuminating. While scholars in the humanities and social sciences are seldom able to produce empirical certitude in their conclusions, the authors of this work report a surprising level of consensus regarding this very knotty quandary. The recent wave of European biblical research, typified in the debate in chapter five, has produced a rich new analysis of this foundation literature of ancient Israelite religion, thus illumining many facets of the later traditions of both Judaism (Hebrew Bible studies) and Christianity (New Testament studies).

A European consensus argues that the larger blocks of pentateuchal tradition, especially the stories of the patriarchs and Moses, were not redactionally linked before the Priestly Code. They existed side by side as independent rival myths of Israel's origins. This is contrary to the J hypothesis perspective of von Rad and Noth, which suggests that the Yahwist was an early editor, or, in the view of Van Seters, an early and very creative author(s) of historiography. The current dialogue between the proponents of that European hypothesis, on the one hand, and the North American interpreters who raise a critical challenge to that European claim, on the other, is a welcome development.

In the end, the consensus, to which Dozeman and Schmid point, suggests that the traditions of the ancestors, the patriarchs, and the exodus tradition may have been unified to a significant degree in a pre-Priestly document which might be called the Proto-Pentateuch (P), but some difference of opinion persists regarding whether that was an early or late pre-Priestly redaction. Gertz, nonetheless, holds out for a post-Priestly, perhaps post-exilic *Endredaktion* for much of the integration of

---

Moshe Greenberg (Chicago: University of Chicago Press, 1960). See also Albright, *Yahweh and the Gods of Canaan*, 199 and 206–7.

11. Albright, *Yahweh and the Gods of Canaan*, 33, 199, 205–7.

the narratives related to the Patriarchs and those championing Moses. Blum appears to have some sympathy for this notion.

Rendtorff argues for a theory of "complexes of tradition" in the growth of the Pentateuch. However, he challenged Noth[12] and von Rad[13] in their claims about tradition history and source criticism. They judged that the *integration and unification* of the various complexes of tradition, such as those about the ancestors, exodus, Sinai, wilderness wandering, and conquest of the land, *had been achieved* already in the oral formation of the historic Israelite belief system. So Noth and von Rad were primarily interested in the conjoining of the narrative contents of the Israelite memory, rather than the issues of *literary* unity. Noth and von Rad absorbed the sub-units of tradition into the larger narrative fabric, while Rendtorff found this a one-sided focus, raising a methodological problem for which there was not enough research data to support the Noth–von Rad conclusion of a "theory of continuous and unified literary sources."[14]

Rendtorff undertook to fill the methodological gap between the development of oral and literary traditions. He proceeded by analyzing the Genesis ancestor-narratives organized around claims of divine promise. He wished to assess the development and transmission of the literary record of divine promises to discern whether a new methodological model was needed to replace standard source criticism. Then he sought out the theme of promise in other Pentateuchal tradition complexes, other than the narratives of Exodus through Sinai, convinced that the distribution of those occurrences of the promise theme "would provide insight into the organic relationship of the distinct tradition complexes."[15]

On this basis Rendtorff rejected the adequacy of standard source criticism to establish the development of the literary traditions at issue

12. Martin Noth, *Überlieferungsgeschichte des Pentateuch* (Stuttgart: Kohlhammer, 1948); English edition, *A History of Pentateuchal Traditions*, translated by Bernard W. Anderson (Englewood Cliffs: Prentice Hall, 1972); reprinted (Chico, CA: Scholars, 1981).

13. Gerhard von Rad, *The Problem of the Hexateuch and Other Essays*, translated by E. W. Trueman Dicken (London: Oliver and Boyd, 1966); revised as *From Genesis to Chronicles: Explorations in Old Testament Theology*, edited by K. C. Hanson, FCBS (Minneapolis: Fortress, 2005).

14. Dozemann and Schmid, "Introduction," 2.

15. Ibid., 3.

here. He noted 1) that the promise theme reflected a multilayered process of development and composition, 2) that the promise theme was absent from the Exodus–Numbers literature, 3) that the Moses story and ancestors story were each reworked from very different points of view, and 4) that this argued against a source criticism that presupposed an early redactional Yahwistic source for literature from Genesis through Numbers or Joshua.

Schmid raised the question of how discarding the hypothesis of a pre-Priestly Yahwist would alter the way the historiography of Israelite religion is done. He proposed that this would link that historiography more integrally to the influences of the cultures around it. Carr argued, however, that taking such cultural issues into consideration would not obviate the likelihood of a "relatively late combination of ancestral and exodus traditions in a pre-Priestly Pentateuch. Whether one agrees with Schmid, Gertz, and Römer that P was the first to join ancestors and Moses in a literary whole or agrees with" Carr and others "that a late pre-Priestly author-editor created the first proto-Pentateuch, there is agreement that the joining of the ancestral and the Moses traditions came relatively late and—outside the Abraham story—is reflected primarily in insertions such as Gen 46:1–5 or Exod 3:1—4:18." Thus the authors of the Dozeman-Schmid volume largely "agree that the interpretation of the history of the literature and the religion of ancient Israel should presuppose that the ancestral and the exodus traditions were separate most of the preexilic period, if not also through much of the exilic period as well."[16]

Rendtorff and those who follow his equation are convinced that this consensus eliminates a Yahwistic source or tradition in Pentateuchal development. They assume that this stands in contrast to the position that Van Seters continues to champion. However, they are excessively reductionistic in that regard, and have missed the subtlety of Van Seters's position. Moreover, Van Seters thinks that they have misunderstood Wellhausen and von Rad in ruling out a Yahwist. They fail to acknowledge, he believes, that the position of von Rad, in his modification of Wellhausen, did not eliminate the Yahwist but recognized him or her as a creative author of one stream of early Israelite tradition rather than as an editor and unifier of various ancient sources into one later

16. Carr, "What is Required," 179–80.

stream in Israelite development. He asserts that the Yahwist was a wise and imaginative Israelite historiographer.

So it is the case that, while the issues are now vigorously debated regarding the existence of a pre-Priestly Pentateuch, one gets the distinct impression of a strong consensus emerging among most pentateuchal scholars of widely varying methodological backgrounds, specifically regarding the development of the relevant foundational literature of ancient Israelite religion. Dozeman, Schmid, *et alii*, have given us nearly the whole story in a nutshell.

Of course, Van Seters holds out for a distinctive alternative position. In his fine work, *The Edited Bible*, he is sure that the Yahwist cannot be so readily dispatched as Rendtorff and company imagine. Of course, he sees the four hundred years of German scholarly discussion about Pentateuchal editors, redactors, and *Redaktionsgeschichte* to be limited in scope and accuracy. Van Seters is sure that the composers of the Pentateuchal complexes of tradition, to use Rendtorff's phrase, were not redactors at all, but creative authors of ancient historiography; and that the Yahwist was an important one among them. Van Seters has a strong appreciation for the work of von Rad and Noth, as well as that of Klaus Koch and Odil Hannes Steck, under whom he studied at the University of Hamburg. In Van Seters' view, the Enneateuch, Genesis—2 Kings, is not a set of redactions but the product of various serious historians who were on a par with and probably shaped by Greek historiographic traditions and methods. Among these historians, the Yahwist is a shining light and the author of the Covenant Code.

This has consistently been the thrust of Van Seters' scholarly trajectory and argument throughout his career. It is his sense of things that Rendtorff and those associated with him in the elimination of the Yahwist, have really misunderstood von Rad, and that Van Seters' emphasis does justice to him, i.e., that the Yahwist was an historian and author, not a redactor. Eckart Otto[17] takes Van Seters to task here by pointing out that in his famous *Das formgeschichtliche Problem des Hexateuch*, von Rad "demonstrates the Yahwist as a redactor of the Shechem and Gilgal traditions, incorporating a great number of narratives that were until then handed down, independent from the source

---

17. Otto, Review of Van Seters' *The Edited Bible*, 3.

of the Yahwist."[18] Van Seters acknowledges his difference from von Rad on this point, but that does not erase his appreciation for much of von Rad's work. As already noted, he believes Rendtorff does not read von Rad correctly.

Otto thinks Klaus Koch is correct in observing in this regard that von Rad was the one who hatched the idea of redaction criticism as a method for OT scholarship. Otto extrapolates from that in saying that it was this method that von Rad employed in his analysis of "the primeval story in Gen 2–11, which was not invented by the Yahwist but was the outcome of a redaction of older material that was adjusted to its function within the Yahwistic Hexateuch and linked together with the stories of the patriarchs by Gen 12:1–3."[19] So, here the Yahwist is not an author but an editor. Thus, Otto claims that Rendtorff certified the von Rad and Noth perspective when he did away with the Yahwist by insisting that the narrative streams of Israelite memory were separate until the Deuteronomistic or Priestly editors composed the Pentateuch sometime around the era of the exile.

However, Otto acknowledges a problem in this model, namely, that Rendtorff departed from von Rad and Noth on a point of considerable inconsistency in both of them. The Graf–Kuenen–Wellhausen emphasis took a literary-critical approach in which it worked down from the current text to its earliest sources that were assumed to be coherent literary units from which the text was derived and built into a unity. The form-critical method, for example in the work of Hermann Gunkel, started with the most primitive fragments of text or narrative he could identify and then worked up to the current formulation of the finished canonical text.[20] This produced an inconsistency in the scholarly tradition, that was all the more serious because it ultimately proved to be as impossible to identify those original foundational literary components lying at the source level, or make any coherent sense of them; as it has subsequently proven impossible to find the historical Jesus in New Testament studies.

When Rendtorff tried to work out a compromise within this impasse by means of his emphasis upon early narrative cycles that

18. Ibid., 2–3.
19. Ibid., 3.
20. Gunkel, *Genesis*, HKAT 1 (Göttingen: Vandenhoeck & Ruprecht, 1901).

remained independent until the final redaction of the Pentateuch, he thought the Yahwist evaporated. Otto observes that the Yahwist continued to generate some historical interest, but not as an author and historian in Van Seters' sense of the word.

In any case, what led Rolf Rendtorff to the conclusion three decades ago that the Hupfeld–Graf–Keunen–Wellhausen Documentary Hypothesis needed to be abandoned was the hiatus he perceived between the patriarchal cycle of narratives and that of the exodus story. As Römer points out, Rendtorff followed Noth's assumption of independent pentateuchal narrative cycles, but thought that these separate streams were unified at a very late stage and under the influence of Deuteronomistic theological constructs.[21] Rendtorff points out, for example, that in the Moses cycle, a land is promised to Israel but it is never identified as to name and place, moreover no mention is made of any promise to the patriarchs regarding that land, or of any awareness of the fact that they had lived in the land.[22]

Christoph Levin's chapter in Dozeman and Schmid is echoed by his more recent article, "The Yahwist: The Earliest Editor in the Pentateuch."[23] In it he takes issue with Rendtorff's model. He agreed at the outset that the debate about whether the Yahwist existed and whether he was an author-historiographer or a redactor-editor was really a "dispute about the transition between the books of Genesis and Exodus."[24] He wondered whether those two books were separated at a secondary stage. He thought threads of P ran through both Genesis and Exodus, so they must have much in common at some earlier moment in their literary development. He concluded that "To maintain that the transition between the books of Genesis and Exodus is decisive for theories about the Pentateuch goes too far."[25]

---

21. Dozeman and Schmid, 19.

22. Rendtorff, *Das überlieferungsgeschichtliche Problem des Pentateuch*, BZAW 147 (Berlin: de Gruyter, 1976); English edition, *The Problem of the Process of Transmission in the Pentateuch*, trans. by John J. Scullion, JSOTSup 89 (Sheffield: JSOT Press, 1990) 128.

23. Levin, "The Yahwist: The Earliest Editor in the Pentateuch," *JBL* 126 (2007) 209–30.

24. Levin, "The Yahwist and the Redactional Link Between Genesis and Exodus," in *Farewell to the Yahwist?* 131.

25. Ibid.

Nonetheless, he observes that the non-Priestly narratives were not originally a unified, coherent composition. Levin agrees with Römer and de Pury that it has long been correctly recognized that the narrative from creation to the entrance into Canaan is not a coherent unitary composition; and that the patriarchal narratives which connect to the national Israelite history are irreconcilable with the stories related to the Exodus and wilderness phase. Moreover, the complete independence of the Joseph cycle and the Balaam story from each other and from all the other narratives is self-evident from the inherent character of those two traditions. John Greene discusses the story of Balaam in great detail below.

This state of affairs leads Levin to summarize the status of the Yahwist. He or she must be abandoned as a narrator. There was not a storyteller who told this long story from creation to Canaan, because there is no single long story for this long era. There are many different stories, each having its own different character, style, purpose, and language, as narrative. However, Levin insists that this is not a farewell to the Yahwist, as Rendtorff, Schmid, and their colleagues insist. He adduces significant evidence for the claim that the Yahwist is a late editor who composed the non-Priestly narrative into the "literary cohesion" it has today."[26]

For Levin, the dating should be possible to agree upon, since the integration of the various sources of the Tetrateuch cannot predate the Jewish Diaspora, with its global perspective and its uniform Yahwism. "It is emerging ever more clearly that the Yahwist is an editorial collection with a distinctive literary profile that has fused older written sources into a new whole. Editorial compositions of this kind do not stand at the beginning of the history of a literary culture. Numerous indications point to the period after the end of the Judean monarchy, that is to say, the sixth century BCE."[27] If there is a hiatus somewhere in all this, as Rendtorff finds between Genesis and Exodus, it is not to be located at that juncture but at least somewhere after Exodus 14, according to Levin. The enduring importance of the Documentary Hypothesis can no longer be called into question.

Levin disagrees with a number of his colleagues as to how and when the various streams of Pentateuchal tradition were edited into

26. Ibid., 132.
27. Levin, "The Yahwist: The Earliest Editor in the Pentateuch," 212.

uniform and coherent documents, thus he declares that any controversy is merely about the redactional linking of the various cycles. Schmid and Gertz say that the earliest literary grounding of the Pentateuch is in the work of P. The non-P narratives were added later in a separate redaction. Levin says the earliest redaction was a separate one that took place within the non-P material. In his earlier work, Levin insists that the non-P material in Genesis and Exodus, as we have it today, has its own inherent narrative coherence which cannot have been original to it, since it contains so many different strands of independent tradition. However, that coherence cannot be accounted for by the simple mechanism of the cross-references that appear in it. Somebody worked through this material in a pre-P phase and gave it a unified shape. Levin concludes that there is good reason to note that the non-Priestly Pentateuch is a literary unit.[28] This is particularly true with regard to the Yahwist material that "earlier research rightly recognized as providing the basis of the narrative."[29]

Likewise, contra Gertz and others, Levin insists that gaps in or insertions into the P material do not indicate a lack of unity in that document. Its inherent unity hangs on the "well-known correspondence" in the creation narrative and that of the Sinai story, and on the covenant theology evident from Noah through Abraham, Jacob, and Moses. However, there is enough variation in the P document material to indicate that it is not the basic document that unified all the traditions from an early stage. "The fact that the sequence of the whole narrative as we have it today holds together is due to the existence of a second continuous source parallel to P. From Gen 12 it took over the literary lead, just as P took the lead in the primeval history. Besides the document P, the document J also existed. The Tetrateuch thus does not hang on a single thread but on a cord plaited together from two strands."

This confirms the early position of Kuenen, and the current argument of Dozeman. It supports Van Seters' claim in favor of a key role for the Yahwist, but differs from him in that Levin insists upon the Yahwist as redactor and not as author-historiographer. André LaCocque, in his uniquely creative way, emphasizes the crucial anthropological signifi-

28. Levin, *Der Yahwist*, FRLANT 157 (Göttingen: Vandenhoeck & Ruprecht, 1993) 9–35.

29. Levin, "The Yahwist: The Earliest Editor in the Pentateuch," 211.

cance of *humanness* for ancient Israelite models, which mark both the divergences and convergences of J and P.[30]

The debate regarding the Documentary Hypothesis as the key to the structure of the Pentateuch, and so a debate regarding the fate of the Yahwist within that scholarly inquiry, will undoubtedly continue longer than all of us, who enjoy the engagement with these fascinating questions and their somewhat less satisfying answers. Just as the quest for the Historical Jesus has, for two centuries, stimulated rich and urgent inquiry into Second Temple Judaism and New Testament origins, with highly productive rewards, so the quest to sort out the issues of the Pentateuch has been one of the most generative dialogues in Old Testament studies for an equivalent period of time.

30. LaCocque, *The Trial of Innocence: Adam, Eve, and the Yahwist* (Eugene, OR: Cascade Books, 2006) 9–10, 52–53.

7

Yahweh in Jeremiah 1–25

The Canon and Reading Scripture as Text

Dirk Odendaal

Introduction

IN RECENT YEARS CONFLICT ERUPTED IN SOUTH AFRICA BETWEEN SOME theologians and churches about how to read the Christian Canon. The burning issue was finding or isolating texts in the Canon that reflected the original Hebrew Bible sources, or came from the "historical Jesus." For the congregations with which I work in South Africa, those issues have little significance. I work in a church of which a large number of people have to make a living with about a $100 a month. Within that context, there is no luxury for doing "ivory tower theology." Why would one want to undermine the very pillar that gives some reason for living. People find great strength everyday in taking the canon at face value, sometimes in a very fundamentalist or literalist way. To me, one of the ironies of the canon is that although it was originally the product of groups with invested power, in ways never imagined it is a channel of the Spirit of God who makes it work for people without power.

From this small story it becomes clear that the role of the canon cannot be underestimated in the life of Christians and the church. The minimalist history of Jesus does not satisfy the needs of church members as much as the canonical texts about his life. The *story* about Jesus highlights the divide that has come into being between professional theologians and theologians in the direct employ of local churches, together with the members of their congregations. Coming from this background myself, I started looking for another way of interacting

with the texts of the canon without having to choose between funda-
mentalist literalism and criticism. The theories from the world of literary research showed me the way.

Impasse in Hebrew Bible Research?

Brevard S. Childs describes the confusion that has come about in Old
Testament research in recent years, as well as the division between the
Jewish and Christian scholars in the past century, following the popu-
larity of Wellhausen's critical approach.[1] It brought about the independence of Christian scholars from traditional Jewish learning. Although
great achievements were made in the study of the text, there have also
been serious losses. He mentions three.

The first is that it became clear since Eichhorn that there was a
schism between the description of the "development of the critically reconstructed text and the description of the actual canonical text that has
been received and used as authoritative scripture by the community."[2]
The second is an understanding of the dynamics of Israel's religious
literature and its scope, which affected language and imagery, and was
framed by its fixed *historical* parameters, since the focus was on history.
Thirdly, the critical approach missed the important point that the material researched was religious and shaped by the religious community
as it shaped the community(ies) itself, instead of by political, social
and economic factors alone. This misunderstanding led to the friction
that still exists today between "a liberal versus conservative, scientific
versus ecclesiastical, objective versus confessional approach to the Old
Testament." This is a "false dichotomy."[3]

It would seem that the major difference between the traditional
approaches and that of Childs is in the attention that is given to the
text sanctioned by the "faith organization." Of course, this is at the same
time the faith community that, conversely, was and is being built by it.
Critical theologians such as Wellhausen focused more on the reconstruction of the original text or *true texts* that are at the root of the
sanctioned versions or canon. The traditional approaches seem to be

---

1. Childs, *Introduction to the Old Testament as Scripture* (Philadelphia: Fortress,
1979).
2. Ibid.
3. Ibid.

nearing the end of their usefulness for the scholars of the twentieth and twenty-first centuries for many reasons, among them the crucially changed circumstances of the growing church in the third world. That church faces a remarkably different agenda than those addressed by text critics in academic settings. This agenda is dominated by serious operational issues of poverty, violence, war, HIV/AIDS, and the like.

Credible new ways of reading the ancient texts need to be found and taught to young theologians who have to make sense of the texts in these challenging circumstances. It will give new results to old questions, and may even force the scholarship to develop new questions.[4] Childs's proposals make possible new approaches in textual research. The canon bypasses the dualistic arguments from the critical and the conservative perspectives, arguments preoccupied with right or wrong, true or false, historical or mythic. The focus shifts from trying to discover the historical texts, to finding new understanding in the texts we have at present, the transmitted texts.

Ricoeur pointed out that the meaning of a text is construed in terms of its metaphorical character.[5] It is a complete cumulative process that is open to many readings and constructions because the reader is always approaching the text from a perspective, or belief, a one-sided view of that text. The reader starts looking for a reason why action took place in order "to consider the action *as* this or that."[6] In describing reasons for actions, one is already preparing the grounds for arguing about them, being for them or against them. Explanation requires understanding, which exposes the system of oppositions and combinations which make up the text.[7]

Clines and the Literary Criticism of Ancient Texts

There are so many promising results coming from the field of literary theory outside Hebrew Bible (OT) research that it is a loss not to give attention to this larger field of research. The questions remain: whether

4. Martin, *Recent Theories of Narrative* (Ithaca, NY: Cornell University Press, 1986).

5. Paul Ricoeur, *Tragic Wisdom and Beyond*, trans. Stephen Jolin and Peter McCormick (Evanston: Northwestern University Press, 1973).

6. Ibid.

7. Ibid.

one can and how one can apply to the canonical text the theories from this wider field. The contribution that David J. A. Clines has consistently made, in this regard, is in pointing out innovative ways of using modern literary research within biblical studies.

Clines has consistently focused on the important contribution that literary research poses for theological research in general and for Old Testament Studies in particular.[8] This approach he attributes to doing theological research on the periphery of the theological field, thus in a more secular environment.[9] He is engaged in a postmodern way with the Hebrew Bible texts, the Old Testament in the Christian religious context. Post modernism of course assumes a strong connection between language and the creation of texts that empower certain voices and silences others. Clines is critical of the *normalized and accepted* critical approaches adopted in theological research, and allows for the *voices* of other theoretical stances to make a contribution to the reading of these ancient texts.

He distinguishes between three areas of focus in the approach of asking literary questions that are now arising in biblical studies, 1) the focus on the text itself instead of reconstructing the history behind the text, 2) the focus on the role of the reader in the construction of meaning, and 3) the focus on the nature and processes of interpretation, explicating the nature of texts and language. This approach is likely to gain support over the next generation until it gains the same authority as the present historical-critical and form-critical theories.

Newer style critical questions, he imagines, will arise from the literary critical approaches, such us the reader-focused theory, feminist criticism, deconstruction, ideological criticism,[10] and the new hermeneutics.[11] The first asks critical questions about the influence the reader has on the generating of meaning, the second asks about the role of gender in the creation and reading of texts, the third questions whether meaning is carried *in* words and texts or *to* words and texts.

---

8. Clines, *Possibilities and Priorities of Biblical Interpretation in an International Perspective: On the Way to the Postmodern: Old Testament Essays 1967–1998*, 2 vols., JSOTSup 292 (Sheffield: Sheffield Academic, 1998) 1:46–68.

9. Ibid.

10. Clines, *Interested Parties: The Ideology of Writers and Readers of the Hebrew Bible*, JSOTSup 205 (Sheffield: Sheffield Academic, 1995) 9–45.

11. Clines, *Job 1–20*, WBC 17 (Waco, TX: Word, 1990).

This has to do with ideological criticism about the ideological interests that were and are served by the texts. These concern which groups and philosophies would have benefited the most by the particular shape and content of the texts. The last of Clines' emphases, the new hermeneutics, asks critical questions about the meaning of meaning-making in texts.

Although there are points of contact here with Childs' canonical approach, it is clear that Clines takes a more critical approach toward the canon by pointing out that the *canonical texts* are just as much in service of the religious institutions, and portray the ideology of the dominant group and their politics, as they are *creators of meaning* for a community.[12] Canon carries with it an ideological content that legitimizes the power positions of certain parties and delegitimizes those of others. The very texts that we use as *original* texts are creations of the institutions they served, selected from among others and therefore legitimized by those institutions or communities.

Readings from a Text of Jeremiah

It is my purpose in this essay to take my current reader through a sequence of detailed steps in the literary-analytical reading of a specific section of the Hebrew Bible, to demonstrate in detail how this process works and what the fruits of the methodology can be. The passage chosen is intentionally selected because of its complexity and the difficulty it has given to most text critics and commentators employing a great variety of differing methods of biblical critique. It is in the research and discovery of the levels of action in a text that the possibility arises of using a variety of tools or methodologies for reading ancient texts like the canonical text and creating new meaning from that reading.[13] My endeavor here is to hold firmly to Childs' concept of canon while reading the text of Jeremiah methodically several times in several literary-analytical ways, using modern textual theory as the approach. First, I will develop in detail that modern textual theory, and then I will apply it in detail to the biblical text under consideration.

The readings will be restricted to chapters 1–25 of the Hebrew version of Jeremiah.[14] The selected text carries with it many difficul-

---

12. Clines, *Interested Parties*.

13. Ricoeur, *Tragic Wisdom*.

14. The text as constructed in BHS.

ties, for example, there are two sanctioned versions of the text, of which one version is much longer than the other. The main concern will be to show how modern textual theory can assist the reader in discovering threads of meaning that bind the selected texts together as a whole, despite the fact that this has been disputed by several theologians since the early twentieth century. It is my opinion that such a reading will point out that the canonizing of the text preserved a readable version of the text from which the reader can make meaning, even in our day, so long after the original texts were crafted and the Old Testament or Hebrew Bible canon was formulated.

I use a formal reader-response approach in which the reader focuses on several structural layers observed in the text. All of these layers contribute to and support the activity of the telling (narrating) or revealing of the story to its reader. In a prior work I have given more detailed attention to the issue of the layers of this text.[15] Here I wish to work with those layers but focus upon the reader-impact and reader response that the canonical text engenders.

Reading Jeremiah as Literary Text

The canonical text of Jeremiah may be read as a text developed according to certain main and sub-literary themes. At this point, therefore, we shall read it first and foremost as a literary text. In my opinion the historical references in the text are an aid to the literary purpose of the book, not vice versa. Literary techniques are used to create the text and to attract and hold the attention of the reader. If the text is read as a complete unit, everything that is necessary for its proper functioning is included and used to explain all its parts. The text is manipulative in that it manipulates the reader into accepting the truth of the suggested world, characters, and actors.[16]

The text is a dramatic narrative, because it "is the crucial form for the understanding of human action,"[17] and this understanding is that to

15. See Odendaal, "Jeremiah 1–25: A Narratological Analysis" (D.Litt. dissertation, University of Port Elizabeth, 1992), for a more detailed explanation.

16. Ibid.

17. Alister MacIntyre, "Epistemological Crises, Dramatic Narrative, and the Philosophy of Science," in *Why Narrative? Readings in Narrative Theology*, ed. Stanley Hauerwas and L. Gregory Jones (1989; reprinted, Eugene, OR: Wipf & Stock, 1997) 138–57.

which the reader is exposed. We say it is narrated, because the function of the narrator can be identified in the text.[18] It is a narrative, because it is in the process of re-telling the well-known story of the covenant (Old Testament) in a new way, and using well-known conventions (codes) in forming the new narrative.[19] In order to expose these conventions that make it possible to tell the story, a three-fold distinction must be made in the levels of the text, that is, the levels of history, story and text.[20] However, before we can entertain any of those levels, attention must be given to the elements of the text.

First Reading: Elements

One way of describing a narrative text is by making a list of the elements from which it is created.[21] They are the building blocks of the history and story of the text, and the history and story in turn influence the selection of elements. The conditions that regulate the selection are: choice, mimesis, suspense, and repetition.

Choice: The author chooses among an infinite number of possibilities which characters, events, and plots to use; where, when, how, in what place, and at what time.[22]

18. H. P. Van Coller, "Kommunikasie as manipulasie," in *Letterkunde en leser. 'n Inleiding tot lesergerigte literêre ondersoeke*, C. Malan, ed. (Durban: Butterworth, 1983) 113–25; E. C. Britz, "Semantiek van die Poësie: Gids by die Literatuurstudie," in *Gids by die Literatuurstudie*, ed. T. T. Cloete et al., Haum-Literêr Gidsreeks 1 (Pretoria: Haum-Literêre, 1985) 134–39.

19. J. H. Miller, "Narrative," in *Critical Terms for Literary Study*, ed. F. Lentricchia and T. McLaughlin (Chicago: University of Chicago, 1990) 66–79; and Umberto Eco, *The Role of the Reader: Explorations in the Semiotics of Texts*, Advances in Semiotics (Bloomington: Indiana University Press, 1979).

20. H. DuPlooy, *Verhaalteorie in die twintigste eeu* (Durban: Butterworth, 1986).

21. Mieke Bal, *Narratology: Introduction of the Theory of Narrative* (Toronto: University of Toronto Press, 1985).

22. S. Chatman, *Story and Discourse: Narrative Structure in Fiction and Film* (Ithaca, NY: Cornell University Press, 1978); A. P. Brink, *Vertelkunde, 'n Inleiding tot die Lees van Verhalende Tekste* (Pretoria: Academica, 1987).

Mimesis: Elements are selected for their ability to either imitate reality[23] in their structure,[24] or deny or distort of reality.[25]

Suspense: The elements are used in a way that helps create or break suspense, in order to retain the readers' attention and interest.[26]

Repetition: Important elements are highlighted through repetition.[27] The use of repetition makes evident what the author's intentions are at a specific point.[28]

Typically elements are the events, space, time, and actors, which all provide clues to understanding the course and the purpose of the text.[29]

EVENT AS ELEMENT

Event indicates the whole of all the actions in a story of which actors are agents and which are related to each other through causality.[30] There are also categories of action, such as non-verbal action (physical movement of the characters), verbal action (the speech-acts of the characters), and thoughts and sensation (the narrator's report of internal ruminations of the characters).[31] The functions of speech-acts can be divided into (1) locuting sentences, that is, making sentences according to the rules of the grammar; (2) illocuting sentences, namely, performance through non-linguistic means such as signs, and (3) perlocuting sentences, or accomplishing the intention of the illocution.[32] Speech-acts abound in Jeremiah, such as in 2:1ff., "Israel forsakes Yahweh" and in 7:1ff., "The Temple Sermon." There are also many Events, for example, Yahweh touching Jeremiah's mouth (1:9).

23. R. Alan Culpepper, *Anatomy of the Fourth Gospel, A Study in Literary Design*, New Testament Foundations and Facets (Philadelphia: Fortress, 1983).

24. Bal, *Narratology*.

25. J. Van Luxemburg et al., *Inleiding in de Literatuur/Wetenschap*, 3rd ed. (Muiderberg: Coutinho, 1982).

26. Culpepper, *Anatomy*; Alter, *The Art of Biblical Narrative* (New York: Basic Books, 1981); J. H. Miller, "Narrative."

27. Van Luxemburg et al., *Inleiding*.

28. Culpepper, *Anatomy*.

29. Ibid.

30. Bal, *Narratology*.

31. Chatman, *Story and Discourse*; Brink, *Vertelkunde*.

32. Chatman, *Story and Discourse*.

SPACE AS ELEMENT

Space is a dimension of a text that the reader often has to reconstruct or infer from textual codes. Named objects, recorded movement, or observed changes in relationships are ways of creating narrated space.[33] Grouped places may imply space by being associated with psychological, ideological, and moral oppositions, for example, favorable-unfavorable, fortunate-unfortunate, heaven-hell, good-evil, finite-infinite, familiar-strange, safe-unsafe, and accessible-inaccessible.[34] Yahweh is not restricted to physical space (e.g., his reactions to Judah in 1:1; 7:1, Jerusalem in 3:17; 6:1, and in the temple, 7:1ff.). He is everywhere and nowhere. He takes up linguistic space, as he makes himself known in words ("The word of the Lord came to me," 2:1; covenant 11:1) and metaphors (1:9).

TIME AS ELEMENT

The temporal organization of events can differ from the history represented in the text. For example, events can take place earlier or later, or more or less times, than the history indicates.[35] We have such a case in "the word ... in the thirteenth year" (1:1). The repetition of events is called frequency.[36] A time divergence in the text is called an anachrony, of which examples are: analepse, a divergence that refers to the past; prolepse, a divergence referring to the future, and flash-backs or flash-forwards.37

Distance refers to the span of time from now backwards, or forwards, as in "the word ... in the thirteenth year ... when the people went ... exile" (1:1). An external anachrony has a beginning and end that happens before the now. Duration, that is, the speed of an event, refers to the time-span narrated compared to the lines used to present this action, as in an extended description or summary.[38]

33. Brink, *Vertelkunde*.

34. Bal, *Narratology*.

35. Chatman, *Story and Discourse*; Van Luxemburg, et al., *Inleiding*; and Bal, *Narratology*.

36. Brink, *Vertelkunde*.

37. Chatman, *Story and Discourse*.

38. Sometimes the discourse-time is shorter than story-time (summary) or there is no discourse-time, only story-time (ellipsis) or discourse-time and story-time are equal (scene), or discourse-time is longer than story-time (stretch) or when there is

Actors as Element

Actors are agents that perform actions. They are not necessarily human. To act is defined as to cause or to experience an event. What is especially important is the ability of the actors to undergo functional change.[39] Examples of actors in our passage under consideration are: Yahweh, Jeremiah, the fictional narrator, the people, and the nations. Examples of minor actors are: Pashhur, Jehoiakim, Jehoiachin, Zedekiah, and Nebuchadnezzar.

Second Reading: History

The simplest level at which the text can be read coherently is that of history.[40] It is an abstract re-creation of the text in which the narrative elements of the text are arranged in relation to one another by the reader and not in the artistic literary way in which the text is presented. If arranged according to principles of chronology, logic, and causality, it is called the fabula (fable). A following stage of abstraction, the extended fabula, is reached by adding additional material from the text and reality. Other abstracts are made by studying the teleological relationships, as logical structures, between the actors, between the actors and the events, and between the series of actions that exist in the text.

Narrative Elements (Fabula)

Several story lines or histories can be distinguished in this Jeremiah text, but I will focus here on the *history* of Yahweh. In the text, references to Yahweh are numerous,[41] and can be chronologically arranged as follows.

The history starts with Yahweh. He is the eternal King (10:10), God, Creator (10:12, 14) (10:16), and in control (10:13). He made contact with the patriarch of the Jews, who is Jacob. Jacob's clan-name, Israel, becomes the official name of the Jews (2:4; 10:16). Yahweh led the Jews

---

only discourse-time, no story-time (pause). See Chatman, Story and Discourse; Brink, Vertelkunde; Van Luxemburg et al., Inleiding; and Bal, Narratology.

39. Bal, *Narratology*.

40. DuPlooy, *Verhaalteorie*; Van Luxemburg et al., *Inleiding*.

41. 1:5, 7–19; 2:2–13; 3:6–11, 19–22a; 4:1–2, 27–5:2; 5:6–11, 14–19, 22, 29–31; 6:8, 9, 10–23, 25–27; 7:1–2, 27–28; 8:4–6, 10–13, 17; 9:6(7), 14(15)–15(16), 17(18); 11:4–14, 21–22; 12:5–6; 13:1–12; 14:10–12, 14–16; 15:1–2a, 11–14, 19–21; 16:10–11, 16–18, etc.

out of Egypt (2:2, 6) and through the wilderness (2:6). He made a covenant with them (11:3) with promises, dependent on obedience, with punishments announced for cases of disobedience (7:7, 23ff.; 11:3–5, 7–8). He brought them into the promised land (fertile land) (2:7) and made them a nation. When they forgot their allegiance to him (11:1ff.), he used his prophets (5:13; 7:13, 26; 11:7) to call them back to him, but the prophets were persecuted (5:13). Yahweh became angry (4:5ff., 8) and punished the people by using their enemies (4:4ff., 19) to destroy their lands (4:26ff.) and sanctuaries (Shiloh in the days of Samuel, 7:14). With the reign of David a dynasty was started that was looked upon favourably by Yahweh. It is the measure of all subsequent Israelite kings (17:25; 22:2; 23:5). David subdued the surrounding nations and built the kingdom of Judah and Israel into a force to be reckoned with, but did not build a temple of the Lord.

During the time of the Assyrian Empire Israel ceased to exist as a nation (3:8), but Judah managed to survive (2:18, 36), and regained some autonomy during the reign of King Josiah. In Josiah's thirteenth year Yahweh called Jeremiah (1:2) to represent him in Judah (1:5, 10) and among the nations (*goyim*). King Josiah (22:11,15) died at the hand of the Egyptians (2:36), and his successor, Shallum (22:10, 11ff.), was replaced by a corrupt son, Jehoiakim (22:13–19), a vassal of Nebuchadrezzar (25:1–3). Yahweh used Jeremiah to warn Judah (4:5ff.) and also to set his plans for punishment (4:11) in motion. Jeremiah became unpopular (c 15:10; 16:10ff.; 18:19ff.), came into conflict with the leadership, (17:19), was persecuted, and publicly humiliated (20:2). He had to escape to Egypt for safety.

When Nebuchadrezzar attacked and captured the city of Jerusalem (chs. 21, 22), Jehoiakim (22:18) died and was followed by his successor, Jehoiachin, who was replaced by Zedekiah (22:24ff.). Some people, most leaders, and Jehoiachin were deported (22:24–30; 24:1–2). Nebuchadrezzar once more attacked Jerusalem (21:2; 39:1–18) under Zedekiah and destroyed the city (25:15ff.). People and leaders were killed and deported, but after some time the exiles were allowed to return to Judah with a new leadership (3:15; 23:5; 3:15, 17).

The Expanded History

The expanded history is an unconscious creation of the reader who uses narrative elements to form a continuous picture and history of the text. It follows the history closely but fills in the empty spaces between the pinnacles of the living history, within the restrictions and prescriptions of the text.[42] These pinnacles are supported by minor events or satellites of narrative.[43]

The reader of the Jeremiah text is left with the impression of a continuity of Yahweh's involvement with the people and a preoccupation with convincing them to either change their policies or bear the consequences of their actions. The *living history* lies in the progression of sermons, and examples of events from the actual Babylonian attack.[44] The reader is taken on the journey with Yahweh from the time of King Josiah, when the leaders and the people were warned by Jeremiah about the consequences of their moral choices. The poetical or sermonic sections seem to serve the purpose of informing the reader of Yahweh's shift from concern about the dangerous route they have chosen, 1) to a willingness to forgive and protect, 2) to an acceptance of the inevitability of the people of Judah repeating the mistakes of Israel and the inevitable deportation, 3) to devising strategies for picking up the pieces. A few examples follow of how the gaps of the history are filled in the extended history.

1. The kernel or pinnacle about Yahweh as creator (10:12–13) reminds the reader of the Genesis history following from the creation, about the fall of humanity from Eden, about the punishment that followed, and about the start of the covenant history with Noah and Abraham. Noah survives through a period of great destruction wrought by God, and Abraham is called specifically to trust Yahweh.

2. Abraham's grandson Jacob (2:4) becomes the direct ancestor to the Israelite nation and the one through whom the covenant is connected to the people. Jacob serves as reminder to the reader of where their name, Israel, comes from, of the history of slavery and

---

42. DuPlooy, *Verhaalteorie*.
43. Chatman, *Story and Discourse*.
44. DuPlooy, *Verhaalteorie*.

salvation that came through the leadership of Moses and Joshua, of the covenant Yahweh made with them, and of them becoming landowners in Canaan. It is this relationship with Yahweh that is essential to their existence, and not their own leadership, or their idols or political allies. The idols, rather, become a metaphor for the breaking of the covenant with Yahweh (7:9–19; 11:1–17)

3. Another example of a kernel is the reference to the temple's and Shiloh's destruction (7:12–13) which reminds one of the history following the invasion into Canaan. The institutions of government and religion had developed there in the period of the Judges and reached their peak during the time of Samuel and Saul. The leadership was charismatic and represented Yahweh directly. Samuel was an example of how the roles of Yahweh and his prophet intertwined. But even this direct representation of Yahweh amongst the people could not prevent Yahweh from taking action against the sanctuary. The destruction of the sanctuary conversely came at a time when the style of governance changed to that of separation between political and religious leadership, possibly during the reign of David.

4. The final example is found in the words referring to the exile of the "faithless" Israel (3:6ff.). The reader is reminded of the history of the last kings of Israel before the deportation by Assyria took place in 722 BCE. These kings did not heed the warnings of the prophets of Yahweh and did not last long. Their disobedience led to Yahweh taking action against them. The present kings are more in line with those wicked agents than with their ancestor David, from whom they are distinguished in the extended history (24).

The extended history makes it possible for the reader to connect the history of Yahweh's past involvement with the people in the time of the story and to form a continuous picture by using the historical nodes as warning signs about their own situation, but also as signs of seeing some glimmer of hope in a desperate situation.

The Relationship between Actors and Actions

It is important to remind oneself again that at the level of history the relationship between actors and their actions is created artificially and unconsciously by the reader as he or she reads, and can change during the narrative. The acts of the actors are called events and may or may not coincide with the events at the story level.[45] In each history one finds a subject that aspires towards a goal or objective that can be supported or opposed by a power source in the text. The one given the objective is called a receiver or agent. The power may even be abstract, for example, society or fate. Other influences, called *actants*, impact on the function that connects a subject with his goal in an almost incidental way, by aiding or opposing an actor or an action. Actants are concrete, in the foreground and usually one of a number of actants. A power or force manages the whole enterprise. It is often abstract, remains in the background, and occurs singly.[46]

In the text, the actor Yahweh is faced with having to deal with a despoiled land and people. Yahweh is the subject and the power of the expanded history. The word of Yahweh, an agent, creates the reality and the future for the people, just as the creation originates from it his word. The main agent of Yahweh is Jeremiah (1:5; 7:1; 11:1). He feels with Yahweh the pain of rejection, although he longs for friendship and acceptance. He is the messenger who conveys the word of Yahweh to the people. What Yahweh has spoken, will happen, no matter how distant it's time of fulfillment.

Actants that oppose the aspirations of Yahweh, and support the power of opposition to Yahweh, are the acts of apostasy of the people, the faith in idols, and their refusal to listen to Yahweh (3:3, 8; 4:22; 5:28, 31). Their agents are the people and the leadership (3:3, 4; 4:1–4). The king and religious and political leadership play an effective role in opposing Yahweh (5:5, 25ff.; 11:18; 12:4). Actants that support Yahweh's attempts to convince the people to obey Yahweh are, for example, a drought (3:3; chs. 14–15), humiliation in war and its after effects (4:19, 20; 5:16ff.; 6:26ff.; 8:16; 9:16[17]ff.), the enemy from the north (10:22), Nebuchadrezzar and the Babylonians, and exile (9:15[16]; 10:17ff.; 12:14, 15; 20:1–5, 14–18; 21; 25).

As the main actor Yahweh holds the power that controls the destiny and fortunes of Jeremiah, his people, the leaders, the enemy from the north, and the other nations that surround the Jews. It is no impersonal

---

45. DuPlooy, *Verhaalteorie*; Bal, *Narratology*.

46. Bal, *Narratology*.

fate that controls their destinies, but Yahweh, the invisible but present God (10).

SERIES OF EVENTS

The events in a story can be judged according to their place in a logical sequence of events, which makes it possible for the author to pause and to explore a specific situation. This possibility usually allows for development to take place within a story. It means that a possibility can be realized or fail to be realized, and if realized, to be successful or to fail. In this way, three functions together form an elementary series.[47]

Yahweh creates the earth, heaven, and a nation by freeing the Jews from Egypt and leading them through the wilderness to a promised land. He makes a covenant with them and leads them to the promised land. He expects devotion from them after they enter it. However, they defect from him and follow other and false gods as they did in the wilderness. He could choose to ignore their apostasy, or maybe punish them for it, or destroy them completely. He chooses to call them back to him by sending prophets to them to convey this message. In this case, the prophet is Jeremiah. When this fails, Yahweh resorts to using punishment: he allows droughts to ravage the country, he brings destruction on them through their enemies and especially the enemy from the north, and eventually resorts to sending them away into exile, a fate that will also befall the neighboring nations (9:25ff.; 25:15ff.). The land returns to wilderness (8; 9:11–12).

Although he has the ability of destroying them permanently, Yahweh chooses (4:27) differently. This leads to the proclamation of a message of reconciliation (23:7–8); the people will eventually return from exile.

Retelling the Story Once More: The Story

The following level is called (3) the story. Attention is now given to the artistic form in which the material is presented (Du Plooy, 1986). The focus is on the temporal relationships that are found in the presentation of the material. The situation (placement) in history is called space,

---

47. DuPlooy, *Verhaalteorie*; Bremond, "De Logika van de Narratieve Mogelijkheden," in *Teksboek Algemene Literatuurwetenschap*, ed. W. J. M. Bronzwaer et al., 2nd ed. (Baarn: Amboboeken, 1977) 183–207; Bal, *Narratology*; Chatman, *Story and Discourse*.

actors become characters and the fabula becomes a meaningful story line that binds together the text elements into a whole.

The reader can now focus on how the narrative elements were ordered as story by the author. Ordering brings out the distinction between history and story. The history of the text is how the reader rearranges the elements of the text into logical and chronological groups. The story is the result of the author's original perspective on how the elements are arranged. This ordering can make the material either interesting, or boring.[48]

The Ordering Principles in the Story

The reader can consider several ordering principles when reading the story line of the text: (1) the purpose in the structuring (plot), (2) the intertwining of story-lines, (3) and the style of narration, time, rhythm, frequency, characters, space, and motifs.

The Purpose in the Structuring (Plot)

The structuring or plot of the story is as important for the narrative as any of the structures of the text.[49] By discovering the artistic communication, or organizing dynamic, of the narrative, the reader interacts with the text in a way that adds pleasure to the reading of the story.[50] The story in the text starts on a very human note when the reader learns that it is the collection of the words of Jeremiah (1:1). Who Jeremiah was is stressed by briefly giving his genealogical and geographical background. Almost unobtrusively in verse 2 his words are qualified as words of Yahweh. This unobtrusiveness is achieved by putting the emphasis on the names of the kings that reigned during that time. Although they do not figure prominently until chapter 20, it dates the text by giving it a historical setting. In verses 1–3, the reader is introduced to all the

---

48. Bal, *Narratology.*

49. Under the heading "Functions of Rhetorical Features," E. A. Nida et al., *Style and Discourse* (New York: United Bible Societies, 1983) emphasize the functions of rhetorical features and which appear in their relations with other features. This underlines the interrelatedness of textual and rhetorical features.

50. Culler, "Foreword," in Gérard Genette, *Narrative Discourse: An Essay in Method,* trans. Jane E. Lewin (Oxford: Blackwell, 1980) 7–13; Genette, *Narrative Discourse*; DuPlooy, *Verhaalteorie.*

important role players in the text and to the setting against which the story takes place.

In the plot, messenger-formulae that precede important textual sections, are used to structure the story into manageable chapters, not to be confused with the present system of divisions.[51] They are mostly impersonal statements that indicate the presence of the narrator in the text.[52]

The plot of the narrative runs as follows: Jeremiah is called by Yahweh (ch. 1). The explanation of the deportation of Israel and calling follows (chs. 2–3). The warning about the enemy from the north is given (chs. 4–6) to Jerusalem. Because of their sins, the religious activities and presence of the temple will not guarantee them any safety (ch. 7). However, to Yahweh's consternation (chs. 8–10), the people refuse to repent, behavior that can only be attributed to their relationship with Baal and the idols. It means that the covenant is broken (ch. 11). It also leads to enmity with Jeremiah (11:18), and the beginning of his persecution. Yahweh promises to protect Jeremiah and punish Israel and Judah

51. Westermann gives attention to the function of the formula. He makes an unfortunate error when he gives the formula a historical function ("stems from the time before the invention of writing" which is impossible to prove or disprove, and even uses written material to prove this point (!) and misses the formal function that such a formula plays in the text. He, however, gives attention to its important role as "code" to the reader. Claus Westermann, *Basic Forms of Prophetic Speech*, trans. Hugh Clayton White (Philadelphia: Westminster, 1967).

52. Another form is more "personal" in appearance, e.g.: "The word of Yahweh came to me . . ." or as alternative "Thus said the almighty Yahweh of Israel (to me)." In the impersonal grouping one can make even further distinctions, i.e. one can distinguish between those that begin with "that(?)", and those that begin with "word." Those that begin with "that" are found only in 1:2; 14:1; and ch. 46. The reason why the formulae of ch. 14 and ch. 46 start with the relative pronoun is that they all refer back to "the words of Jeremiah" in 1:1.

In 1:2 the "word of Yahweh" is linked to the reported lineage of the kings; in 14:1 they are linked to the "words of drought," which may be a pun on the participle "vintager"; for a discussion of the phrase, see Chapter 2.

In 46:1 it is stated that the word of Yahweh came to Jeremiah "concerning the nations". In both cc 14 and 46 the preposition "concerning, on" is found. This makes these opening statements somewhat different to the other "impersonal" statements. Their presence would then pose the decision to divide the text of Jeremiah as follows: cc 1–13, 14–45 and 46–52.

The other formulae are found in 7:1; 11:1; 18:1; 21:1; and 25:1. What they all have in common, is that they are also "impersonal" and that they start with the words "the words that . . ." They are all subordinate to those formula-like statements that were pointed out in the previous paragraph.

(ch. 13) through the enemies and through nature. No intercession for them will help (chs. 14–15).

Therefore, the time has come for a new beginning which will happen after the destruction (chs. 16; 19) has taken place, consequent to the deceitfulness of people (chs. 17–18). Jeremiah is punished by Pashhur for his outspokenness, but Pashhur is renamed Magor-Missabib (terror on every side). Jeremiah rues the day he is born because of the destructive content of his message (ch. 20). The king's pleas for help will not change anything (ch. 21). Actually, the kings will be held responsible and severely punished. There is hope, however, because another righteous king will be installed after the ordeal (chs. 22–23). It will be to the benefit of those who go into exile rather than those who remain in the land (ch. 24), because the exiled will be protected by Yahweh. Eventually the same fate will befall all the surrounding nations (ch. 25).

In conclusion, it is the Word of Yahweh that functions as an ordering principle of the text. This took the form of a literal warning regarding the consequences of their choices, which is explained to Jeremiah, to the people, the rulers, the nations, and the enemies, at both the textual and experiential levels.

Intertwining of Story-lines

There is a variety of ways in which storylines are intertwined which can vary from very simple to complex. A variety of techniques are used to accomplish this combination of techniques. An event that is described can be the result of an intertwining of a complex series of histories, events, and/or functions that belong together content-wise. The storyline then becomes an even larger unit that includes all the different aspects that belong to that specific line of development. In the *history* of an actor, the chronological and logical order described can converge and intertwine with the histories of other elements.[53]

The text includes material referring to the past, the present and future of the Jews, Yahweh, the nations, the leadership, the enemies, and Jeremiah. The story of Yahweh begins long before that of the people, the nations, and Jeremiah, yet it combines with their stories through his involvement with the patriarchs, the founders, and Israelite nation. The

---

53. DuPlooy, *Verhaalteorie*.

reader becomes aware that this enmeshment also has negative results for the leadership and people when Yahweh acts against them.

Yahweh's story from before the prophet's birth meshes with Jeremiah's actual story, and is an indication of the inseparableness of their stories in the text. This development gets special momentum with the calling of Jeremiah in the thirteenth year of the reign of Josiah, and the unfolding of that development ends in Egypt.[54] Jeremiah is in a position to learn the reasons behind Yahweh's actions and to reveal them to his audience and to prepare them for the consequences of their actions. Jeremiah's story does not have a happy ending in spite of the enmeshment with Yahweh.

The final example presented depicts the interwovenness of Yahweh's story with the stories of the people *and the surrounding nations*, a process that started during the time of the patriarchs and the exodus. There were special moments in this enmeshment, starting with the calling of the enemy from the north and ending with the exile of the people, the leadership, and even Jeremiah. It is ironic that Yahweh appears to develop an affinity for the enemies and a hatred for his own people.

Style of Narration

The style of narration makes a text unique for a reader. Aspects that are usually grouped under this heading are: the input of the narrator, the role of history in the text, the textual style adhered to, the use of repetition, the role of cause, effect, themes and motifs, the use of poetry and narrative, and the way the characters communicate. It is clear that someone other than Jeremiah is telling the story because of his absence in aspects of the story. The *narrator* keeps a low profile in chapters 1–25 of the story. He makes his appearance a few times as an objective presence by introducing either Yahweh or Jeremiah, but does not tell the story from either the perspective of Yahweh or Jeremiah. The characters are left to speak for themselves, and it is left up to the reader to interpret, to deduce from what is said what the character is thinking, for example in the intercession of Jeremiah for the people (8:18).

The narrator, when he does make an appearance, usually sketches the situation, such as the history and background of the text (1:1–3), and

---

54. Sections like 1:4ff. as well as the so-called "Confessions" in 11:18ff.; 12:6ff.; 15:10ff.; 18:19ff.; and 20:10ff.

then allows the characters to act out their roles. This approach gives the characters validity and authenticity. They do not appear to be characters in a story, but to be real. The narrator usually introduces the dialogues of Jeremiah and Yahweh in 1–25. Yahweh is reported indirectly, speaking through the mouth of either Jeremiah and the narrator (1:1, 4; 2:1), or the narrator alone (7:1; 11:1). Yahweh regularly makes long-winded and tedious speeches that are indirectly reported by Jeremiah in 2–9; 22–23; and 25.

The narrator cloaks the story in *history*. The initial setting is historical (The word of Yahweh came . . . in the days of Josiah . . . until Jerusalem was depopulated in the fifth month, 1:2). This historical coloring is found implicitly in all the chapters of the text from 1–25 (1:4ff. recalls the commissioning of Jeremiah in the last days of Josiah). Prominent themes contribute to the historical coloring, for example, themes about the covenant, Shiloh, wars, the exile, and excerpts from historical, prophetical, and psalmic texts.[55] Holladay gives extensive coverage to this topic.[56]

An obvious aspect of the text is the *declamatory or epical* style. Much of the story is rhetoric and gives the impression of being additive, namely, an anthology of sermons consisting of elements added for their own sake without consideration for the story. The style is epic because poetical material is used to recount the deeds of the legendary hero, of Yahweh,[57] or of the saga, depending on whether the emphasis is on the poetry or the prose of the text.[58]

---

55. Odendaal, "Jeremiah 1–25."

56. Holladay, *Jeremiah* 2.

57. The text could therefore be branded as an epic, because it meets so many of the criteria of an epic, i.e. (1) it is based on a great and serious subject, (2) it is centered on a heroic (Jeremiah) and a divine figure (Yahweh) on (3) whose actions depend the fate of the tribe or nation of Judah. It (4) tries to encompass the world of its day and the learning. Some of the conventions of the epic are also employed, e.g. (1) an epic question (1:6–12) is followed by an argument or theme (1:13–19). These are not so clearly distinguished. (2) The narrative starts *in media res*. (3) Although not complete, there is a catalogue of principal characters (1:1,10,14). They are given set speeches, which reveal their diverse temperaments; M. H. Abrams, *A Glossary of Literary Terms*, 3rd ed. (New York: Holt Rinehart & Winston, 1971) 49–51; W. T. MacLeod, *The New Collins Concise Dictionary of the English Language* (London: Collins, 1985).

58. Saga is written prose narrative that bears the marks of oral prose composition, which may well combine prose and poetry without problem. The single-mindedness of the presentation, the neutral point of view of the narrator and author, the use of

Themes or motifs are introduced by key-words and phrases that link them to preceding motifs. "Peace, Peace, while there is no peace!" (6:14), and variants of it, all include the key-word or idea of Peace (4:10; 5:12; 6:14; and 8:11), and are found throughout ch. 7. Alternatives to peace are the concepts temple (7:4), covenant (7:21; 11:1ff.), and words (1:1; 7:3, 4ff.), which in turn lead to alternative linkages.

Repetition is important for telling the story. Scenes are repeated several times in the text: the commissioning of Jeremiah (1:5; 20:14–18) which contains elements that are emphasized: the birth (1:5), the calling (1:5), the refusal (1:6), the promise of support (1:7–8), the commission (1:9–10), and the visions (1:11–13). Other scenes are war, drought, preaching, and opposition.

The use of *causality* shows that actions lead to consequences. The covenant theme highlights the influence of causality in daily life. Blessings or curses follow on keeping or failing to keep basic ethical principles. Taking responsibility for one's actions is an important *ethos*, in the text. It is defended in legal terms. It influences what happens to one. Affiliations with idols and neighboring states are useless (2:11, 16, 36; 10:1), and will lead to judgment (2:35; 17:1).

Although the story has an *overall chronological and causal order*, this line is confused, or made vague by the use of anachronisms,[59] both regarding the past and the future. The order of events is changed and events are presented differently from how they would succeed each other chronologically.[60] This style of narration has confused some commentators and led them to believe that the text is at best but a broken or loose collection of words or lines of the prophet Jeremiah; or even of any number of other prophets, authors, or redactors.[61]

In fairness one must recognize those facts that the present day reader can at best surmise regarding the function of this style. We do not know enough about the rituals and sermons or readings that were

---

chronology and the use of suggestion all seem to support this viewpoint; R. W. Neff, "Saga," in *Saga Legend Tale Novella, Fable: Narrative Forms in Old Testament Literature*, JSOTSup 35 (Sheffield: Sheffield Academic, 1985) 17–32.

59. This term will be explained under the heading 2.4. "Time."

60. Genette, *Narrative Discourse*.

61. John Bright, *Jeremiah*, AB 21 (Garden City, NY: Doubleday, 1965); William McKane, *A Critical and Exegetical Commentary on Jeremiah Volume I*, ICC (Edinburgh: T. & T. Clark, 1986).

held in the temple and sanctuaries; we also know very little about the court (legal) proceedings of those days, and rituals, if any, that were invoked. We also know very little about the proceedings that took place in the royal court and palace of the king. Such knowledge would be valuable for the student of an ancient text to determine the style of narration. Here the reader can only surmise what they are.

Time

In the story the narrator follows conventional guidelines by starting in the middle of the story referring to the start of the exile (1:1–3). He then moves back to the past and tells everything once more, more or less chronologically, from then on to the end (*in media res*).[62] By deviating from the chronology of the history (*fabula*), attention is drawn to certain interpretations of an event and aspects of a complicated history (*fabula*). These deviations are called *anachronies*[63] and, as indicated earlier, can take the form of *analepse*, a divergence to the past, or a *prolepse*, a divergence to the future, thus giving the text it's prophetic quality.[64] Distance then describes the span of time backwards or forwards, from the now of the narrator, from the inception of the anachrony, while amplitude is used to describe the duration of the anachronous event itself.[65]

Chapters 1–25 would be called a mixed anachrony, because the story begins before and ends after the narrators now (chs. 23; 24). Many of the anachronies are repetitive, such as the flash-forwards to the enemy from the north. The story starts with a recapitulation of events in the past - the exile of Israel. The activities of Jeremiah during the reign of the kings Josiah, Jehoiakim, and Zedekiah are recalled, as well as the destruction of Jerusalem. The start of Jeremiah's career is placed more or less in the middle of Josiah's reign. Two analepses are already visible here, the history of the kings that starts before the story-time, and the commission which is given to Jeremiah, which follows just after the start of the reign of King Josiah. As time (reading) goes on, that against

62. Chatman, *Story and Discourse*; Genette, *Narrative Discourse*; Bal, *Narratology*.

63. It is to be clearly distinguished from the word "anachronism," which means "the representation of a event . . . in a historical context in which it could not have occurred; MacLeod, *The New Collins Concise Dictionary*.

64. Bal, *Narratology*.

65. Chatman, *Story and Discourse*.

which Jeremiah warned the people in chs. 2–9, was now coming into effect. Reading chs. 1–11 against the yardstick of anachrony gives the following results.

In Chapter 1 analepses (Jeremiah's calling) and prolepses (the approaching calamity) balance each other. In 2—4:4 this situation changes, so that analepsis dominates (the history of Israel). In 4:5–6 prolepses dominates (a similar fate awaits Judah and Jerusalem). Chapter 7 is mainly dominated by analepses (the role of the covenant and example of Shiloh) with a proleptic goal, namely the destruction of the temple; in 8:4–9 one finds mainly prolepsis (the calamity is near). In ch. 10 analepsis (10:1–16, Yahweh the creator is unique) and prolepsis (10:17–25, the outcome of apostasy) are in balance. From this one can already deduce that analepsis seems to give justification for the action that will be taken in the future, already anticipated by the prolepses.

One can also give attention to how much time is used telling a story and at what pace the presented story proceeds compared with the time suggested in the story. If telling the story is slower than the time the suggested events take, it is called ellipsis, if faster, then summary.[66] Generally one would have to say the text is a summary of the lived time which appeared to have happened over several decades. The sermons are sometimes ellipses.

Rhythm

Another aspect, that is very similar to those discussed above, is rhythm. Rhythm is used to denote the speed of presentation in a text, parallel to the real time suggested. It also makes use of the above-mentioned terms. Rhythm brings into the foreground the element of selection that takes place in a text.[67] The author cannot physically, and does not want to, retell everything that happened, but the story version may be longer or shorter than the selected time, depending on how many events are included.

In this story certain events are chosen to highlight the history that leads to the exile of Judah. The author indicates that the roots of the exile extend far back in the history of the Jews to the founding of the nation (ch. 2). Key ideas serve as building blocks of the story, such as

66. Genette, *Narrative Discourse*; Bal, *Narratology*; Brink, *Vertelkunde*.
67. DuPlooy, *Verhaalteorie*.

destruction, building or planting, enmity, love, and so on. Elements are selected because of their relationship to these motifs. The story covers a period of about forty years and six months (cf. 2 Kings 23–24), during which Jeremiah acted as prophet of Yahweh. The twenty-five chapters discussed, represent only a fraction of all the events of those years. Time is sped up in some sections, through summary or ellipsis, for example, the approach and attack of the enemy is summarized in a few sentences (6:1–3). Time is also slowed down in some sections, namely, the injunction not to pray for the people (7:16ff.), or even the prophecy or sermon against the temple (7). The presence of these devices underlines the point that the material did not just grow together, but was manipulated by the author for the sake of the story.

Frequency

Frequency indicates the numerical relationship between the events in the history (*fabula*) and the story, that is, the number of times an event appears in the history and the number of times it is narrated in the story.[68] Iteration refers to a situation that is repeated often in history (life), but only once in the story-time. It rarely appears in the text.

Frequency, however, as in the use of repetition, is obvious and numerous. Repetition is used to indicate an event that occurs only once, but is presented a number of times in the story.[69] Repetitions occur as key-words, in phrases and also as type-scenes.[70] The purpose of repetition is to build tension and to keep the audience's attention and underline important messages. In this way its use makes reader (listener) participation easier. The enemy from the north is an example of the repetition of a type-scene (1:14–15; 4:6–9, 11–17, 29; 5:6, 10, 14–17; 6:4–6, 19–26; 8:16–17; 10:22; 13:20). Yahweh's utterances repeatedly mention the outcome for the people, which is not peace (8:15; 14:19; 16:5), but mourning (3:21; 4:31; 6:26; 8:19—9:1[2], 13–21[14–22]; 10:19–21; 23:10–12).

---

68. Bal, *Narratology*; Brink, *Vertelkunde*; Shlomith Rimmon-Kenan, *Narrative Fiction: Contemporary Poetics* New Accents (New York: Methuen, 1983); Genette, *Narrative Discourse*.

69. Bal, *Narratology*; Genette, *Narrative Discourse*; and Rimmon-Kenan, *Narrative Fiction*.

70. Alter, *Art of Biblical Narrative*; Culpepper, *Anatomy*.

Characters

From actors performing actions and experiencing events, complicated personalities or characters can arise.[71] The character's existence starts when it is named or mentioned,[72] and forms during the course of the telling of the story.[73]

The purpose of creating or suggesting characters in a literary work is to service the need in such a work to include life-like people, since that makes the narrative more successful in attracting and keeping the interest of the reader, who can then wrestle with a problem from the perspectives of some-one else, namely, the character. When a reader has identified with a character, he becomes involved in interpreting or making meaning of the character's actions.[74] Accepted guidelines for categorizing of characters are: roundness or flatness; lifelikeness, consistency with the roles in the plot, predictability enhanced by the amount of specific data provided about the character. Ironically, too much information limits possibilities,[75] but attention needs to be given to the character's name, descriptions of his or her external lifestyle (profession), and of his or her internal character or strength of character.[76]

Sources of information are repetitions, descriptions, reports of actions, appearance, gestures, posture, costume; their own, as well as actors' comments on one another; the reports of their dialogues (quotes) and their inner speech or ruminations.[77] In the Jeremiah text there appear to be only two characters, Yahweh and Jeremiah. The reader gets to know them through the dialogue, speeches, and descriptions the narrative gives. I will only address the issue of the character of Yahweh at this time.

71. DuPlooy, *Verhaalteorie*; Bal, *Narratology*

72. Brink, *Vertelkunde*.

73. Chatman, *Story and Discourse*.

74. Ryken, *How to Read the Bible as Literature*, Academie Books (Grand Rapids: Zondervan, 1984).

75. Bal, *Narratology*.

76. Brink, *Vertelkunde*.

77. Alter, *Art of Biblical Narrative*; Bal, *Narratology*.

Yahweh

An aspect that has been neglected by commentators is Yahweh's character. None of the commentaries that I examined included any characterization of Yahweh.[78] Only Jeremiah's character received attention.[79] Characterizations of Yahweh received attention in some of the older theologies,[80] and come from the whole Tanach, that is, they are not text bound to this narrative, and are of a theological nature.[81] The later theologies focused mainly on the experience of the people, namely, the ancient Israelites as the chosen people.[82]

One must make a distinction between the YHWH and Yahweh of the text. It must be remembered that the Yahweh of the story is not the real YHWH, but a character based on a presence in a text. A *story* about real people or beings is not necessarily a historical account.[83] The character is an imitation, without flesh and blood,[84] that acts and reacts within the confines of the story. In the case of Yahweh the confines are made vague, and his superiority and authority is never really challenged.

The character of Yahweh is complex. He is addressed by name as Yahweh (1:2, 4), or my Lord Yahweh (Almighty) (2:6, [19]), Yahweh,

78. E.g., G. C. Aalders, *Jeremia*, Korte Verklaring der Heilige Schrift (Kampen: Kok, 1953); Bright, *Jeremiah*; Van Selms *Jeremia*, De Prediking van het Oude Testament, 3 vols. (Nijkerk: Callenbach, 1972); R. K. Harrison, *Jeremiah and Lamentations*, Tyndale Old Testament Commentaries (Downers Grove, IL: InterVarsity, 1973); Childs, *Introduction*; J. A. Thompson, *The Book of Jeremiah*, NICOT (Grand Rapids: Eerdmans, 1980); Robert P. Carroll, *Jeremiah: A Commentary*, OTL (Philadelphia: Westminster, 1986); McKane, *Jeremiah*; Holladay, *Jeremiah 1*, *Jeremiah 2*; R. E. Clements, *Jeremiah*, IBC (Atlanta: John Knox, 1988); Brueggemann, *Jeremiah 1–25: To Pluck Up, To Tear Down*, ITC (Grand Rapids: Eerdmans, 1988).

79. E.g., Bright, *Jeremiah*; Harrison, *Jeremiah and Lamentations*; Thompson, *Jeremiah*; Carroll, *Jeremiah*; Holladay, *Jeremiah 2*.

80. E.g., P. Heinisch-Heid, *Theology of the Old Testament* (Collegeville: Liturgical, 1955), Walther Eichrodt, *Theology of the Old Testament*, 2 vosl., trans. J. A. Baker, OTL (Philadelphia: Westminster, 1961); Th. C. Vriezen, *Hoofdlijnen der Theologie van het Oude Testament* (Wageningen: Veenman en Zonen, 1974); and Gerhard von Rad, *Theology of the Old Testament*, 2 vols., trans. (1975).

81. Alter, *The Art of Biblical Poetry* (New York: Basic Books, 1985).

82. E.g., Walther Zimmerli, *Grundriss der alttestamentlichen Theologie*, Theologische Wissenschaft 3 (Stuttgart: Kohlhammer, 1972); and Claus Westermann, *Theologie des Alten Testament im Grundriss* (Göttingen: Vandenhoeck & Ruprecht, 1978).

83. Robert P. Carroll, *Jeremiah: A Commentary*, OTL (Philadelphia: Westminster, 1986).

84. Bal, *Narratology*.

your God (2:19; 3:13), or impressively Yahweh Almighty, the God of Israel (7:3; 11:3). The name is linked to the creation of earth (chapter 10) and to the Israelites occupying Palestine (2:2–3, 6; 11:3–7). He gives nationality to his people (2:7) but is himself not restricted by it (1:5, 10; 3:17; 16:19). He is creator of Creation (the Universe?), and people (10:10, 12ff.), but is *your* God to Israel. The idols come from his creation (10:5–10).

Because no descriptions of Yahweh's external appearance exist, although he revealed himself to the people (1), he is symbolically described in anthropomorphisms. The symbolic language gives the impression that Yahweh is a male in this text. The people are described as his bride (2:2), and as being divorced by him (3:1, 8). He is also called, My Father, and friend (3:4).

He develops with his people and in his experience of dealing with humans, that is, he moves from a willingness to forgive sins towards a willingness to forgive sins only after punishment (21). The reader becomes aware of humanlike contrasting actions, although far beyond the scope of humans. He knows everything, but is taken by surprise at the apostasy of the people. He is all powerful, but seems strangely inept when he has to start proceedings against the people (11). He is immortal, but not static (2:5; 10:10). He vacillates between forgiving (5:1) and punishing (5:7; 6:8), but is stable and enduring (3:4; 10:10, 12ff.). He experiences emotions of anger (4:26), rejection (2:10, 11), despair (9:1[2]); 13:23), and sorrow. He weeps (8:23 [9:1]) for what is happening and for the destruction that will be wrought in the land (14:17).

Yahweh calls a mortal child or young man (1:6) to do his bidding, and sets him on a par with such leaders as Moses, Joshua, and Samuel. The reader may find it strange that he forces Jeremiah to serve him (20:9), but not the people. Jeremiah has no choice (15:15) but to do Yahweh's bidding, but he *invites* the people to return to him (3:6ff.), and when that fails, he threatens them with destruction and exile (4:6ff.), death (7:33), unrest (8:15ff.), and unhappiness (7:34; 9:17[18]ff.). Nonetheless, he does not force them. He reveals himself to Israel, but also controls the destinies of all people although he is not revered by them (ch. 25). All people are his servants, but he chooses some of them and others he rejects (ch. 20).

The contradictions in the description of Yahweh suggest to the reader the impossibility of understanding him. Yahweh's heart, and his pain at being betrayed, is revealed to the audience by a human author. In this way is conveyed something of the magnitude and incomprehensibility of Yahweh, his unapproachability.

Space

The space in which the story mainly takes place is in and around Jerusalem in the last days of the Kingdom of Judah, although there are references to Israel and some of its counties (2:1—4:4). It has a sort of doomsday setting in which scorching winds blow from the desert (4:11), with quaking mountains and empty charred lands, with enemies approaching on the roads and cross roads around the city (chs. 6; 9). It is also a landscape of forests where trees are cut for idols (10:3ff.). The city is portrayed with bustling streets and plains filled with crooked, lusty people (ch. 5), living and marrying, backstabbing and deceitful (9:4; 11:18–23). There are Zion and the temple in which people are worshipping Yahweh, but also oppressing the powerless (ch. 7); and bringing offerings to foreign gods in another religious space, the Valley of Ben Hinnom. It is a city with a graveyard for its people and kings.

Space in the story is created by setting several places against each other. On the one hand it is the place in which Jeremiah is persecuted, on the other where the temple is located. The point is made that Yahweh is not dependent on the temple, but the temple on him. A reason for this seems to be that Yahweh does not occupy space, although he can if he wishes. He creates it.

The space of the story is more than just a geographical place. The land responds to the changing alliances of Yahweh and the people. The physically observable objects come to suggest the spiritual (hidden) values inside Jeremiah and the people. A person needs wisdom (chs. 10; 17) to make proper choices. The symbol of the choice is being a shrub in the case of the foolish man, or a green tree for a wise man. The morally arid people are running around like a mare donkey or a camel in the desert (2:23–24).

Yahweh chooses the future land, namely, the land the Israelites will occupy after the exile, although it is not yet in existence. It is to be preferred to the land that is now rejected by him (chs. 24; 32). In that sense it is also juxtaposed to the existing and future lands of Egypt, the nations, and Babylonia, which are also in for change.

Motifs

A motif is an element of the story that has meaning by itself and is consistently used with this meaning.[85] An archetype is a form of a motif that occurs in a wide variety of texts in and outside the Canon.[86] One should differentiate between a motif and a leitmotif; the latter carries its meaning over from other texts such as the commissioning of the hero or chosen one (1:5–10; 20:9, 11). The leitmotif appears in different texts of the Old Testament: Moses (Exod 3), Gideon (Judg 6), Samuel (I Sam 3), and even a king such as in the vision of Solomon (1 Kgs 3), and some prophets (Amos: Amos 1; Hosea: Hos 1; Isaiah: Isa 6; and Ezekiel: Ezek 2). The leitmotif of a quest is found in the repeated assurances of Yahweh that Jeremiah is the protected (1:19; 15:20–21; 20:11) and trustworthy receiver of the word of Yahweh (23:9ff.).

Other motifs that occur in the text are: birth, disaster, death and destruction, the enemy from the north, peace, love, and prostitution. Nature is a motif and goes hand in hand with motifs of animals and plants as representing moral values. Drought and water motifs feature in the text in various ways, such as punishment and attempts at ritual cleansing. The motifs of light, darkness, and fire that are used in the text are used to describe hope and punishment and ritual cleansing. A judicial (court) motif expounds in more detail on that aspect. Finally, the natural, chaotic, uncivilized world and civilization feature as motifs. The radical changes that will occur are to be found in the text in the context of these motifs.

Read Once More as Text

Finally, attention can be given to (4) the text itself, to the formal, existing presentation of the signs, the narrative context, and the various levels of meaning in the text, as well as the roles that the reader and the author play in the formation of the text.[87]

---

85. DuPlooy, *Verhaalteorie*.

86. Abrams, *Glossary*; Northrop Frye, *The Great Code, The Bible and Literature* (New York: Harcourt Brace Jovanovich, 1982).

87. DuPlooy, *Verhaalteorie*.

NARRATION AND FOCALIZATION

Whereas, until now the focus was on how the contents of the text have been presented and arranged and to what effect, attention will now be given to the perspective from which the text is approached, and how it is presented to the presumed listener.[88] The roles of the narrator and focalizor are closely related, but distinguishable. The narrator is an instrument using all narrative techniques, including narration and focalization, to tell a story.[89] The focalizer is a more subvert narrative technique that guides the presentation of the story.

Focalization

Focalization (the focal point of view) introduces the reader to a specific way of viewing narrated events: real, historical, or fictitious.[90] The association of the elements (that which is seen) with the viewpoint from which they are presented, as well as the agent that is seeing it, is called focalization, that is, *A narrates what B sees that C does*. Focalization is the direct objective of the narrated text. Any vision can have a strongly manipulative effect, and focalization helps to keep the focus on the technicalities of the manipulation. An example is photography in which focal point (focalization) is different from point of view. Because of the association involved between the elements presented and the identity of the voice verbalizing the vision, it is necessary to distinguish them clearly.[91]

The point from which the elements are viewed (lens), can lie within a character (internal) or outside it (external). It may be someone anonymous (agent) outside the *fabula*. It can also shift from one character to another in the same story and one can yield focalization to another character focalizor within the encompassing vision of the external focalizor. This is called embedded focalization. In some situations only the story as a whole will show who the focalizor is. If the focalizor is a specific character, that character will have a technical advantage, or power, over other characters. The reader who is watching the narrative through a character-focalizer's eyes will tend to accept that vision as authoritative and as a result be biased and limited. Because of the levels

88. Bal, *Narratology*; Van Luxemburg et al., *Inleiding*.

89. Bal, *Narratology*.

90. Bal, *Narratology*; Van Luxemburg et al., *Inleiding*.

91. Bal, *Narratology*.

of focalization, a personal focalizor cannot be aware of invisible objects (e.g. thought, feeling) outside of him.[92] Focalization assists the reader in identifying ideologies and issues of power.

The reader finds references to external (e.g., 1:1–3; 7:1; 11:1; 14:1; 18:1; 19:1, 14; 20:1–3; 21:1; 25:1) and embedded focalizors in the Jeremiah text. The external focalizor coincides with the external narrator, but yields the focalization to Jeremiah as embedded and personal character-focalizor, who yields to the Yahweh character.

The content focalized by the Yahweh-character is found in the messages of Jeremiah, who introduces Yahweh in the first person and yields the focalizing to him. For example, in verse 1:4: "The word of Yahweh came to me" (see also vv. 7, 9, 11, 13, 14–19). The Yahweh-character is imbedded in the Jeremiah focalizor and in turn focalizes objects and himself. Some objects are persons, for example, the people of Judah (v. 14), other nations (vv. 5–10), and the kingdoms of the north (enemies). Some objects are natural events such as drought. The reader (audience) sees them through the eyes of Yahweh, who offers a limited view of them and there is no getting around that perspective of Yahweh.[93] It implies that the reader (audience) is manipulated to accept Yahweh's view, because none of the groups (objects) can (are allowed to?) respond with their own objective focalization. Even when they do act as focalizors, it is as embedded focalizors of Yahweh speaking from his point of view (2:6, 8).

The Yahweh-character focalizes visible and invisible objects. He knows what people think, do, and say, and where their allegiances lie (2:8, 11, 13, 20, 34). He also knows the disposition of objects that do not exist, or have stopped existing, such as the invisible past,[94] and future glory and hope (3:16, 17; 9:23, 24; 16:14–15; 23:3, 5ff.).

An interesting deviation of the text is that Yahweh focalizes the one who is supposed to focalize him. Although structurally Yahweh is focalized by Jeremiah, he focalizes the thoughts of the object of Jeremiah's focalization (2:8: "did not know me"). This in itself is a peculiar thing for an imbedded focalizor to do, and usually only occurs momentarily

---

92. Ibid.; Van Luxemburg et al., Inleiding.

93. Bal, *Narratology*.

94. E.g., the covenant, c 11; the enemy from the north; the creation of earth and his people (c 10; 5:22; 2:2, 5ff.)

in direct speech.[95] More peculiar is his ability to focalize Jeremiah and even his thoughts (1:5, 17; 12:3; 15:19).

The reader therefore gets a picture through Yahweh's eyes of the ungratefulness (2:7, 13) and defiance of the people and leaders of Israel and Judah (2:10; 22:6ff.; 23:9ff.; 2:16–19, 32). These are seen as evil beyond comparison.[96] The focalization serves to justify the severity of the action that is going to follow, but also to manipulate the reader/audience into an understanding of Yahweh's position. The people's reactions are

95. Bal, *Narratology*.

96. The descriptions include: a prostitute and unfaithful (wife) (3:6, 7); adulteress(or) (3:20; 5:11); backslider (3:22); fools (4:22); breakers of the yoke (5:5); stubborn and rebellious (5:23), animals in rut (2:24, 25; 4:30; 5:7, 8; 13:26). Their sins are engraved (17:1) as if on stone. They are without the law of Yahweh (9:12(13); 11:8–10; 17:19ff.) as he has to remind them. Their numbers include wicked men (5:25,26; 22:6; 23:9) who are rich and powerful, but this lifestyle of oppression is loved by the people (5:25–31); they are lawless (chs. 11; 22). They are compared to a well pouring out wickedness (6:6b-7); as having closed (uncircumcised) ears (6:10,17,19); and that from the least to greatest they are greedy for gain and unashamed about these and other evils (6:13–15; 7:9–10; 8:12) and then they trust falsely in the power of the temple (7:4) and thus in man (17:5) to ensure their safety, instead of trusting in Yahweh. Such a person is foolish (17:11). The people trust idols that are made of wood and metal (ch. 10; 11:13).

They will not only not listen (6:16–17; 7:24, 25–26), but even kill those who warn them of the dire consequences of their actions, e.g. "your sword has devoured your prophets" (2:30). They are called by Yahweh to repent (3:14–16; 4:1, 4), but do not listen (7:13; 8:7, 13). They do not know how to speak what is right (8:6). They lie, deceive; even brothers, friends and neighbours are not exempt from being treated in this way (9:3(4)–4(5),7(8); 11:18; 12:6). They cannot do good even if they want to and cannot change from this course (13:23). They trust in man, not in Yahweh (17:5). Worst of all, they build high places to Baal (19:5) and sacrifice their children.

The present system of kings and prophets are focalized in chs. 22 and 23. The rule of the kings from Jehoiakim onwards is described as evil and worthy of destruction, e.g. 22:13ff. "Woe to him who builds his palace by unrighteousness ... injustice ... work for nothing ..." This message is concluded in ch. 24 with the comparison of the rule of Zedekiah to a basket of poor figs (24:8–10). The prophets are shown to be spreaders of false messages and seers of false dreams (23:9ff.).

focalized by Yahweh,[97] namely, their pleas for mercy[98] and their invisible future destiny, the painful exile (13:18–19; 14:1–6, 18; 15–16).[99] The focalization on the one hand covers the role of the author in the text and on the other arouses guilt feelings in the reader, who when reading the text is invited to compare his own actions with that of the Israelites and their leaders.

NARRATION AND SPEECH REPRESENTATION

In reading a text it is useful to the reader to give attention to how speech is represented, for example, in the roles of the narrator and receiver, and in their functions in the text (Bal, 1985). A story can be told without specifying a place where or date when the story is narrated, but it must be located in time, since the story is told in the present, past, or future

97. E.g., "They did not say: 'Where is Yahweh that led us out of Egypt . . . ?'" (2:6); "The priests did not say: 'Where is Yahweh?'" (2:8); "You said: 'I will not serve you!'" (2:20); "How can you say: 'I am not defiled'" (2:23); "But you said: 'It's no use, I love strangers (strange gods) . . .'" (2:25); "They say to wood: 'You are my father. . .'" (2:27); "Yet . . . you say: 'I am innocent' . . . because you say: 'I have not sinned'" (2:35); "Have you not just called to me: 'My father, my friend from my youth. . . ?' but you do all the evil . . ." (3:4); "Although they say: As surely as Yahweh lives, still they are swearing falsely . . .'" (5:2); "They . . . lied about Yahweh and said: 'He will do nothing'" (5:12); "And when you ask: 'Why has Yahweh . . . done all of this to us?'" (5:19); "They do not say: 'Let us fear Yahweh . . .'" (5:24).
More examples are: "They dress the wounds. . .: 'Peace, peace' they say when there is no peace" (6:14); "but you said, 'We will not walk in it'" (6:16); "Do not trust in deceptive words and say, 'This is the temple of Yahweh . . .'" (7:4); "and say, 'We are safe'" (7:10); "How can you say, 'We are wise for we have the law of Yahweh'" (8:8); "'Peace, peace,' they say . . ." (8:11); "If you ask yourself, 'Why has this happened to me?'" (13:22); "this is what Yahweh says about the prophets . . . saying, 'No sword or famine will touch this land'" (14:15); "and they ask you, 'Why has the Lord decreed such a disaster. . .?'" (16:14). All of these quoted phrases are also quoted by Yahweh when he wants to make a point about the people he is focalizing.
98. E.g., "yet when they are in trouble, they say: Come and save us!" (2:27); "gasping for breath . . . : 'Alas! I am fainting; my life is given over to murderers'" (4:31); "We have heard reports . . . hands hang limp, anguish has gripped us, pain like that of a woman in labor" (6:24); "Why are we sitting here? Gather together! . . . Let us flee" (8:14); "Death has climbed in through or windows" (9:21); "although they cry out to me I will not listen", ". . .will go and cry out to the gods . . . not help them" (11:11, 12); "will be like this belt—completely useless" (13:10); "fill with drunkenness all who live in this land" (13:13).
99. E.g., "what will you say when Yahweh sets over you . . . allies? Will not pain grip . . . ?" (13:21); as well as: "Weep and wail, you shepherds; . . . nowhere to flee . . . laid waste" (25:34–38).

tense. The narrating instance and narrator are placed relative to the story's time. Because the text starts in the middle of the narration and then moves back to the past and from there to the future, it indicates that the narrator already knows what the outcome of the story is.[100] By looking at the introduction (1:1–3) and conclusion (52:34) one realizes that the narration follows the reported events of the story.

The form of the narration corresponds to what we in modern literature would call a journal, or epistolary novel, in which a written letter (or sermon) is at the same time both the medium of narrative and an element of the plot.[101] The style of the various narrators is *diegetic* (telling/reporting), such as in 20:3, but much of the text is *mimetic*,[102] that is, the speeches and dialogues (e.g., 11:18 to the end of ch. 17) imitate dialogue between Jeremiah and Yahweh. The purpose is to slow down the tempo of the story and accomplish something with the narrative, which is why they are arranged in acts of locution (what texts in fact do), illocution (what texts intend to do), and perlocution (their effect on the hearer).[103] They also get arranged according to a character's importance.[104]

The Narrator

The narrator of this Jeremiah text is external. The speaking agent does not mention himself or herself in the process of relating the story, but objectively narrates about others. He or she is still an I-narrator, because all narrators are I-narrators, who narrates the story from his or her point of view about a him or her. Saying: "These are the words of Jeremiah", means "I narrate: I testify. These are the words of Jeremiah."[105]

There are several diegetic levels to narrating a story.[106] The highest diegetic (extra-diegetic) level is that of the external narrator (chs. 1; 7; 14; and 18). The reader finds the diegetic levels of Jeremiah and Yahweh included in the external narrator's level. Jeremiah's level as narrator, is called the meta-diegetic level (from the perspective of Jeremiah) and below the

---

100. Genette, *Narrative Discourse.*

101. Ibid.

102. Rimmon-Kenan, *Narrative Fiction.*

103. Chatman, *Story and Discourse.*

104. Brink, *Vertelkunde.*

105. Bal, *Narratology.*

106. Brink, *Vertelkunde.*

narration of the external narrator. It is introduced by "Thus said Yahweh to me" (chs. 15; 16; 17:19) or something similar. The Yahweh narrator functions at an even lower or intra-diegetic level.[107] Jeremiah and Yahweh are character narrators, because they are introduced by name.[108]

From ch. 26 forwards, an additional character-narrator, Baruch, is added as the narrator of the messages of Jeremiah (chs. 36, 45). He functions at a lower diegetic level than the external narrator, because his inclusion is narrated,[109] indicating that the final narrator of the text was not Baruch. Possibly the narrator and Baruch's roles coincide in some instances.[110]

The causal relationship between the diegetical levels confers on the lower levels an explanatory function for events leading to the present situation of the narrator. The diegetic levels are not watertight. In a narrative metalepsis, controlling a higher level from a lower level, the transition from one level to another can take place through narration.[111] In the text Yahweh can, from his diegetic level, still exert full control over Jeremiah and the people, who are at a higher diegetic level. Usually this is seen as either comical or fantastic. In the case of Yahweh, however, it is natural for him as he is God.

In Yahweh one can actually distinguish two actants (the actors performing actions), the narrating I and the narrated I. The narrating Yahweh does not simply know more than the hero Yahweh, he knows in the absolute sense and understands Truth. Everything that Yahweh says about himself is as the narrating I, for example "I order: Do what is right . . ." (22:3); but when the reader is told about his feelings, anger, actions, plans, and the like, he becomes the narrated I. The hero is in other words not always identified with the narrator, because the actions of the hero still have to be described by the narrator.[112]

107. Genette, *Narrative Discourse*.
108. Bal, *Narratology*.
109. Genette, *Narrative Discourse*.
110. Bal, *Narratology*.
111. Genette, *Narrative Discourse*.
112. Ibid.

The Narratee or Receiver

For every narrator there must be a narratee. Whether he or she is named, he or she functions at the same diegetic level. He or she can be, but is not usually the same as the real or implied reader. The presentation of the story implies that it is being presented to someone, who may be mentioned.[113] The external narrator gives a short introduction in 1:1–3 without naming the narratee, and then hands the role over to Jeremiah, who becomes the narrator of his own calling (1:4ff.). He might be telling this story to Baruch, or the people and leaders who become his narratee. However, this changes a few verses later during the speech of Yahweh (e.g., v. 14) about what will happen, then Jeremiah becomes the narratee. From chs. 2–9 Jeremiah becomes the narratee of Yahweh, but the primary (external) narratee, as well as Jeremiah's narratee remain hidden. The text implies that Jeremiah must tell the story to someone, the people and their leaders perhaps, as is the case with the external narrator, who by implication is telling the story to someone.

The Function of the Narrator/Narratee

The narrator can fulfill several functions; 1) in the story: a narrating function; 2) in the text: a directing function; 3) in the narration: communication (between the two protagonists—the narrator and the narratee); 4) about his own feelings: a testimony and if mentioned, 5) the interventions made: ideological.[114] The functions of the external narrator (chs. 1; 7; 14; and 18) are to introduce the Jeremiah and Yahweh-narrators, to set the historical scene for the story (1:1–3), and to give order to the text between narrative (1:1–3; 19:14–20:3; 36–44; 51:59 to ch. 52), sermon (chs. 2–10; 18–35; 44; 46–51:58), and dialogic sections (chs. 1:4ff.; 11–17; 45). The use of a complete messenger-formula functions as divider, and combined with a formal, neutral, and unemotional style, gives credence to the text as authoritative, or at least persuasive and believable.

Jeremiah is a complex narrator whose narrations (1:4—6:30; 11:18—17:27) are introduced by formulaic sayings. They might be about a vision (1:12), a word (3:6), or to action to cede to a lower narrator

---

113. Ibid.; Chatman, *Story and Discourse.*
114. Genette, *Narrative Discourse.*

or actor (metalepsis, with "So says Yahweh").[115] The metalepses expand until they become dialogues with Yahweh (11:18ff.; 15:10ff.; 17:5ff.; 18:18ff.; 20:7ff.). To describe Yahweh as narrator is more difficult. In his speeches he relates history (2:2–6; 3:6–10) of which he is also narrator; quotes words of his antagonists, the people (2:6,8; 2:20); and also his own thoughts (3:19).

The Author and Audience

Every text has an author and must have a reader, but the real reader is not always the ideal reader. While the narrator can be called the narrative voice of a text, the implied author is voiceless or silent.[116] Just as the narrator is not the real author,[117] so one must also distinguish between the real living author outside the text and the implied author in the text;[118] as well as the real reader outside the text and the implied reader for whom the text is intended, and who is therefore inside the text. The implied author and reader in the text represent the real reader and real author.[119] The author writes the text with an intention or purpose (or fictive author), for which he keeps a specific reader (ideal reader) in mind.

The implied author refers to the governing consciousness of a text as well as the ideological and moral stances of a narrative,[120] namely, the meaning of a text, and not the source of the meaning.[121] He functions as the organizer of the whole text inside the text.[122] He chooses the narrator to present the narrated world to the fictive reader. The narrated world can, however, differ completely from the world of the fictive author.[123] For this purpose it will be necessary to give attention to the whole text.

115. "Oracle of Yahweh" assures the reader of the authority and origin of the message (3:23–25; 4:10; 4:19–20; 5:3–5; 6:11a; 8:18—9:1[2]); see ibid.

116. Rimmon-Kenan, *Narrative Fiction*; Clines, *Interested Parties*.

117. Genette, *Narrative Fiction*.

118. Clines, *Interested Parties*.

119. Rimmon-Kenan, *Narrative Fiction*.

120. Ibid.

121. Bal, *Narratology*.

122. H. P. Van Coller, "Kommunikasie as manipulasie," in *Letterkunde en leser. 'n Inleiding tot lesergerigte literêre ondersoeke*, ed. C. Malan (Durban: Butterworth, 1983) 113–25.

123. Ibid.

To highlight the function of the fictive author in the text attention will be given to the following aspects: the text, the story, the characters, the time, the space, and the purpose.

The Text

It was pointed out above that this account was written after the events occurred and that the author referred to other texts and even quoted from them (e.g., ch. 39), such as the Psalms, other prophetic literature, wisdom literature, and historical literature.[124] The purpose seems to be to evoke strong images from the collective conscience of the reader, and to chide, evoke guilt feelings, and bring insight to the audience of the text. The text can be subdivided into several broad categories. Chapter 1 is the introduction to the main themes, and 51:59–52 is the conclusion. Three main subdivisions follow: chs. 2–20; 21–45; and 46–51:58. In chs. 2–20 the focus is on the rejection of the message and it has two subdivisions: chs. 2–10 the rejection of Yahweh, and chs. 11–20 the rejection of Jeremiah. The purpose of the internal author is to highlight the approaching crisis period. Chapters 21–45 develop the theme that the warnings have become realities.

Chapter 25 expands the thought of 1:10 ("to uproot and to plant"), which is carried further in ch. 45 and points to the intention of including a wider audience than the Judeans. Looking back to ch. 2–20 from this vantage point, the reader can see that the references to the nations have the purpose of having him anticipate something even bigger, that is, the warnings in 46–51, aimed at the nations of the world. The inclusion of these chapters was the aim of the author[125] and as the earlier inferrals point out, it was planned. These chapters are also the cause of much dispute because the LXX excludes much of this material and is significantly shorter than the MT. The textual approach followed here indicates that the two textual traditions each probably had a different purpose and readers in mind.[126] The differences come from legitimate

---

124. Holladay, *Jeremiah* 2.

125. The first number of references to the nations up to ch. 20 are usually only a few lines long, they are followed by the longer reference in ch. 25, which in turn is followed by chs. 46–51. This pattern can also be discerned in the references to the exile and a number of other topics.

126. Brink, *Vertelkunde*.

reasons rather than coincidence, that is, to warn a specific generation of impending danger.

The Story

Much of the story is set against the reign of Josiah, the god-fearing king, to whom some important reforms were attributed. Strong denunciations of political leaders, the king (13:18), the religious leaders, and the people in general, are made in this section, and lead to mounting opposition of Jeremiah. It is the story of the prophet who is the bearer of bad news in the good times of Judah and even worse news during the bad times. The news is opposed by many religious and political leaders and leads to Jeremiah's public humiliation and persecution.

In truth, the news can only be discerned through wisdom. It is a story of the development of a legitimate hermeneutic which can interpret the signs of the times even if it means opposing the popular leadership. Jeremiah knew the word of Yahweh because he was created by this word, but in itself it was also a curse (20:14). The intention of the author is to allow the reader to discover the subtle difference between the unpopular authoritative word of Yahweh, and, what is proclaimed to be authoritative but is not, in order to acquire a listening skill for a newer situation.

The author uses this story to open up a discussion about serious issues, such as, whether an individual's interpretation of the word of Yahweh has the same theological weight as of the official institution's functionaries' words, namely, the messages of the professional theologians' interpretations. A scenario is painted in which specifically the institution's orthodox approach is found wanting, discredited.

No happy ending is described, and no solution given because any solution becomes the doorway to other problems. Jeremiah is vindicated, only to die in ignominy in Egypt, a land which he cursed in ch. 22. The lucky man is the unlucky and cursed Jehoiachin (ch. 22). It is a story about listening to the word, of being on a journey of discovery with it, and discovering hope for the future with it. The story gives clues to the reader about how to start this journey. The purpose for the author is to show the power of the word, either to lead or mislead, to build or destroy. Life is a tragic adventure, even in Yahweh's world!

The Characters

On a smaller scale, the story is about people and their choices. At first glance, the author has written a story about the prophet Jeremiah, but the discerning reader soon discovers that it is more a story about Yahweh. The prophet is called by Yahweh and introduced to Yahweh's work and purposeful plans to destroy the nation of Judah, Jerusalem, the temple, and all nations.

The author describes to the reader the characters of Yahweh, Jeremiah, and others, in order to lead the reader to make a choice. Yahweh is the main character and Jeremiah his mouthpiece. Yahweh, Jeremiah, Baruch, and the enemy are cast as the good guys because they do the bidding of Yahweh. The people, the leaders, and prophets are cast as the villains and antagonists of Yahweh. Even the space they function in is described as dark, dry, and barren, in spite of reports of countless sexual activities. Animals become part of this hostile environment. The idols are described as things that cannot hear, or act (ch. 10).

The reader is subtly manipulated to choose Yahweh's side in the matter. Both Jeremiah and the people become foils for Yahweh. Jeremiah has to attract the readers' attention to Yahweh's just claims, and to inspire the reader to understand and choose his side. The people and the leaders serve to expose Yahweh's tenderness, fairness, justness, and strictness even in bad times. It is through their failures that one is shown the value of obedience to and trust in Yahweh. The author sticks to the strict guidelines within Israelite tradition of not describing Yahweh, but still giving Yahweh a powerful voice in which he describes himself. By not using time and space in a description of Yahweh, the author is able to suggest that Yahweh has supra-human characteristics and that the words in the text were not the author's, narrator's, or Jeremiah's. This suggestive character of the text is supported by the vagueness of the situations in which many of the messages and visions were received and by their strong metaphoric character.

One must make the distinction between YHWH and Yahweh. The first is the living independent GOD, who cannot be known except when it pleases him, and the second is the character Yahweh, who is captured in the text, and tells the story of how he perceives the misdeeds of the people of Judah. YHWH is much more than the character of Yahweh of the text. The author tries to explain within the restrictions of human words something of the invisible YHWH in the character of Yahweh.

Time

The story was told in the classic style of *in media res* and the text was written after the events took place. Are there any other indications of external time, that is, the real time when the author actually wrote the story? The Aramaic sentence in 10:11 could be an indicator, as is the use of the cryptogram Sheshak (25:26). It could refer to (atbash) Babylon but offers no help dating the text;[127] and why use the word Babylon freely in 20, 21, and the like, but encrypted in 25? There are constant referrals to kings and royalty, and to the leaders of the people, and very specific references to the temple, its defilement by its users and its anticipated destruction (chs. 7; 26). The king destroys the text and even tries to kill the author (ch. 36) but the word remains more resilient than the king had thought possible.

Although a number of denouncements of Baalism and the idols appear, one is struck by the emphasis on the role of the believer and membership of the people. Not only is idolatry rejected, but also the use of the canon in a stereotypic way. There are repeated references to a conspiracy against Yahweh and his prophet,[128] as well as to the enemy from the north and the surrounding nations. All these literary markers seem to indicate that the specific reason for the differences between the texts of the LXX and the MT had to do with the audiences for whom they were intended.

Space

It appears that the religious sphere of life is the aim of the text. The numerous references to prophets and priests, offerings, religious prac-

---

127. Thompson, *Jeremiah*; Carroll, *Jeremiah*; Holladay, *Jeremiah 1*; McKane, *Jeremiah*.

128. Smith highlights the interesting fact that no historical work deals with the 250 plus years following on Nehemiah, probably because of the possible censorship applied by the Maccabean leaders; *Palestinian Parties and Politics that Shaped the Old Testament*, 2nd ed. (London: SCM, 1987). A reason for the censorship was the fact that the Maccabean priesthood was illegal. The historical material existing is mostly negative about the legitimate priestly family. A legacy of Nehemiah at the end of his reign, was to leave a "separatist party," which opposed official syncretism and many of the priests.

tices, and the temple support the view. The whole *Umwelt* of the text is imbued with religious issues. The material incorporated into the text indicates that the author had an excellent knowledge of the religious activities and the texts that were used in the temple. An example of the use of texts in the temple is recorded in the book of Nehemiah (ch. 8).

Purpose

The purpose of the (fictive) author was to demonstrate to the listener the power of the word (the word of Yahweh) and to show the danger of misusing the word for one's own purposes. It tries to establish that as a hermeneutical principle for using the word of God. It contains a warning for a group of leaders in a period when the Jews are brought into contact with a great influx of people from surrounding nations. He stresses the importance of remaining faithful to YHWH, even when all other securities fall away, even in the midst of their enemies (when they are in exile). That is the only security the nation has. The text reminds the Israelites of what happened to them when they disregarded the words of Yahweh before: losing everything they had and going into exile.

The Israelites are also shown that they have nothing to fear from the nations coming into the land. The nations are instruments of Yahweh who would come and join the Israelites in serving Yahweh and also in being tested in the same way. The final chapter acts as reminder to them that the true word of YHWH will always survive.

The Fictive Reader/Audience

The one reader that the author never kept in mind when writing the text is the modern theologian that lays excessive emphasis on logic as a way of telling stories.[129] Such a reader is easily confused by the presentation of the text. There is no logical, synchronic development typical of the Western theological style. The lack, however, does not indicate that the story is of inferior quality. Nonetheless, the text has several audiences in mind. One can distinguish between the text-internal readers and the text-external readers. The explicit listener (narratee), the explicit (named) reader, and the implicit (abstract) reader are examples of the first group.[130] The function of the narratee was discussed above.

---

129. Bright, *Jeremiah.*
130. J. Senekal, "Resepsie—'n terreinverkenning," in *Letterkunde*, 1–42.

The implicit reader is indirectly addressed by the text and is invisible. That reader embodies the preconditions for actualizing the text and represents himself or herself in the intention that has to be actualized by the action of the receiver (reader or listener). He or she incorporates the pre-structured meaning of the text and the reader/audience's actualization of this potential by reading the text.[131] The text-external readers/audiences are the real persons who were the audience or readers.[132]

The Explicit Reader/Audience in the Text

The explicit readers or audience are possibly mentioned in the speeches of Yahweh. In ch. 2 he tells Jeremiah to "make the proclamation in the hearing of Jerusalem," in 2:4 to the "people of Jacob, . . . families of Israel" and in 2:9 to "you and your descendants." Other instances of the audience appear to be Judah and Jerusalem (4:3, 5, 11) or the *people of the* "streets of Jerusalem" (5:1), "Israel" (5:15; 10:1), "the people of Jacob," and "Judah" (5:20).[133] The explicit audience/reader is found in the text, and varies according to the circumstances and audience to which it is presented.

The Implicit Reader/Audience

It is difficult if not impossible to pinpoint the implicit reader/audience for the simple reason that he is nowhere clearly named. He is also a text-internal reader just as much as the implicit author is text-internal. The implicit reader/audience refers to the qualities that are needed and called for in order to understand the text or intention of the text. A reader of this text of Jeremiah would be well advised to remember that it is confessional in outlook and would be used in a religious context.[134]

131. Ibid.

132. Ibid.

133. Also "people of Benjamin" (6:1), "inhabitants of the land" (6:12), "all you of Judah who come in through these gates to worship" (7:2), "people of Judah" (7:30), 9:16(17) "the wailing women", "Zion" (9:18[19]), 11:3 "the inhabitants of Judah and the citizens of Jerusalem" (18:11; 19:3); or "towns of Judah and streets of Jerusalem" (11:6), 14:10 and 16:10, 14 "this people"; certain groups 11:21 "people of Anathoth", 14:14; ch. 23 "the prophets", ch. 13:18; 17:19; ch. 22 the royal family, and in ch. 24 the exiles in Babylon, as well as those "who remained behind"; the exiled people of Israel (3:12) or the nations (6:18), "the evil neighbours (of Judah)" (12:4) or the enemy from the north (6:6–10, 27–30).

134. Van Coller, "Kommunikasie."

Obviously the text was intended to be read publicly to certain audiences, as literacy was for a long time restricted to guilds, and therefore not available to the public in general (1 Chron 2:55).[135] The question remains, however: Who would the author have had in mind when he wrote the text? At what religious context is it aimed? What is the result envisaged by this aim? Who would the ideal reader be? In theological commentaries the answer seems to differ from commentator to commentator, indicating that there is no clear-cut agreement, and some openly doubt whether any general design for the text ever existed. They conclude instead that it is diffuse and garbled and inconsistent.[136]

Some commentators see the text as coming from the prophet Jeremiah.[137] It was intended for the pre-exilic Israel, people of his own generation, and preserved by the post-exilic people of Israel. There could be no single audience, because the text is seen as an anthology of texts.[138] There is a general intent indicating the purpose to express opposition against the official religion of the people of Judah,[139] or the pre-exilic, royal-temple establishment.[140] Other commentators see the text as a message prepared for the post-exilic community.[141] The text was shaped over a long period of time.

Some think the purpose at first was repentance and then changed to judgment, because of the Babylonian danger. The targeted audience was the people. After the text as a whole had developed, the aim changed again and the audience became the community of faith.[142] On reading the text the following clues are found that might lead one to

135. Wiseman, "Scribe," in *The New Bible Dictionary*, ed. J. D. Douglas (London: Inter-varsity, 1974) 1150–51.

136. Bright, *Jeremiah*. In a sense this approach has much in common with a deconstructive (-ionist?) approach of interpreting a text, i.e. a text cannot be seen as a storage bin for retaining meaning. Otherwise the approach is structuralist, because meaning of sentences and words seem to retain their original value in spite of having been incorporated into a "new" text.

137. Bright, Holladay, and Thompson.

138. Bright, *Jeremiah*.

139. Ibid.

140. Brueggemann, *Jeremiah 1–25*; Norman K. Gottwald, *The Hebrew Bible: A Socio-Literary Introduction* (Philadelphia: Fortress, 1985).

141. P. R. Ackroyd, *Studies in the Religious Tradition of the Old Testament* (London: SCM, 1987); Carroll, *Jeremiah*; Clements, *Jeremiah*; Gottwald, *The Hebrew Bible*.

142. Aalders, *Jeremia*; Childs, *Introduction*.

pinpoint to what the implicit reader could be like. There is a preoccupation with Yahweh, as was seen in the character analysis, with the temple (3:16ff.; 7:4ff.; 19:14; 26:2; 27:16ff.; 52:13, 18ff.), with the covenant (11:3ff.; 17:19; 31:31; 33:20; 42:5), with cultic observances (33:18), with apostasy, priests (20:2ff.), and prophets (23:9). Other *foci* of the text are: the royalty,[143] the people of Israel and Judah (3; 4:3), the gates of the temple, Jerusalem,[144] the nations (1:10; 6:18; 18:7; 25:15), the political and other threats to the existence of the nation (1:15), the seventy years in Babylon,[145] and exile.[146]

There are also the text units like the meta-text in ch. 36,[147] or the report of Jeremiah's prophecies being burnt and rewritten, the description of Jeremiah as coming from a priestly background, and his constant clashing with the various leaders of the Jewish people, that makes one think that the text was in the first place aimed at the religious and secular leaders of Judah and Jerusalem and was not well received.

It was shown above that this audience cannot come from a pre-exilic period. It also has to be a period in which the temple plays an important role in the cultural life of the Israelites. Another matter that receives attention is the role that the nations play in the story, and because of the references to the surrounding and distant nations, one is led to find a period in which there was such influence on the Israelite peoples. Time periods that come to mind are: the period just after the repatriation (the temple of Nehemiah, Ezra), or the period when the

---

143. 1:2ff.; 3:6; 4:9; 13:18; 15:4; 17:19; 21:1ff., 12; 22:1ff.; 23:5, 6; 24:1ff. 25:1ff.; 33:14.

144. 1:15, 18; 7:2; 14:2; 15:7; 17:19ff.; 19:2ff.; 20:1ff.; 22:2ff.; 26:10; 31:38; 36:10; 37:13; 38:7; 39:3; 52:7.

145. 25:11, 12; 27:22; 29:10.

146. 15:2; 20:6; 22:22; 29:14ff.; 30:3.

147. Next to or underlying the narrated text, the reader sometimes encounters commentary that refers directly to the text. This is called the meta-text. The existence of a meta-text makes the text more complex and dense (Du Plooy, 1988). Chapter 36 also acts as meta-text by giving commentary on how the text was created and in what dangerous situations. That it is the word of Yahweh does not prevent people (e.g. the king) from trying to destroy the message and its bearers. It is the story of an author creating a text as reflection of the process of creating texts and the dangers that go with that within another story. The fact that the king fails, has symbolic implications for the future of the people, and is a "meta-story" (i.e. a story about the story [text] itself) regarding the ability of the text to survive all forms of adversity as it is not a "human text."

Seleucids ruled and the temple was defiled,[148] or even the period of Roman rule (the temple of Herod). The emphasis on the idols indicates a period after the exile when the Yahwist religion was under threat. Although the temple still functioned, the institution had lost its clarity of purpose and had become a burden on the faithful. It also appeared to be a tool in the hands of the powerful, which led to institutionalized opposition to these words coming from the true prophet.

The emphasis on the "true and living" word opposing a theology of an institutionalized word, consisting of the old external covenant, the ark, the temple, and its personnel, seems to support the theory that this text was written as a reaction against a growing legalism and prescriptions for the religious character of Judaism.[149]

The Real (External) Readers

There have been and there still are many real readers of the text. Some do so with a scholarly approach, others as lay persons. Many have written about the results of their reading over the long period of time that the Jeremiah text has existed. The comparison of the fictive reader with the real life (explicit) reader of Jewish and Christian perspective is a potentially rich and valuable field of research, as those reports testify to and reflect the life situations of the readers. Such a study could give attention to texts in the Old Testament or Hebrew Canon, that make use of the Jeremiah texts, as well as other texts outside the Canon, such as commentaries, monographs, and testimonies of the Jewish and Christian believer as reader.

Concluding Remarks

The value of this literary-analytical approach to reading the ancient text of Scripture is that it allows the reader (us) to use this text as material for sermons and Bible study and stay true to its tradition as canon. It guides the reader in bypassing the Scylla of Fundamentalism, which places too much emphasis on literalism at the expense of craftsmanship, on the one hand, and the Charybdis of deconstructive criticism, on the other, which places too much emphasis on the historical origin

148. Bright, *A History of History of Israel*, 2nd ed. (Philadelphia: Westminster, 1972).

149. Ibid.

of the "true text," at the expense of reading the existing text as authentic text. The danger of the first is in taking shortcuts to acquiring meaning from or imposing it upon the readings, and of the second, assuming that the original text will reveal the true meaning.[150]

It seems clear that the following conclusions can be drawn.

First, the purpose of the canonical text was probably not to reflect accurately the history it was intended to portray,[151] but more likely to serve the ideological and political aims of the implicit author, whether it was a person or institution, and reflect the accepted societal religious and gender roles of that time. The Hebrew text appears to be aimed at people, Judeans and other national groups, that were in positions of power and were misusing their privileges. The intent of portraying the history in the text was most likely to convince people to make important changes in how emergencies were dealt with.

Second, the Hebrew text has all the necessary elements for constructing and reading a text. Chronological and logical threads running through the text give clues or codes about how the text can be read, as the exercise of constructing the history and extended history has pointed out. The modern reader is invited to join the implicit reader/audience in creating a virtual reality from the text that will challenge his or her own lived reality.

Third, the presentation of Yahweh in the text is, at the same time, complex and sophisticated. The author is doing the impossible in letting the reader know the unknowable Yahweh. The sophistication in that lies in achieving that without breaking Jewish religious and social norms. The technique of focalization explains how it was achieved.

Fourth, the story is told using traditional storytelling techniques that have the intention of keeping the reader's or audience's interest and attention in the story. It has an epic style, in which poetry, sermons, and songs are mixed with historical portrayal. It starts at a time long after the time of the story in ch. 1, and then takes the reader into the story of the last few years of Jerusalem before the Exile. Characterization is restricted mainly to Yahweh and to Jeremiah. The descriptions of them attain the level of fullness because of the many contradictions that are used in the descriptions. The impression is left of complex and rich

---

150. McKane, *Jeremiah*.

151. Clines, *Interested Parties*.

characters. The richness of the description of Yahweh entices the reader into superimposing YHWH, the ethereal extra textual being, onto Yahweh, the character in the text. Therein also lies the source of much of the power of the story, as it is expressed in the voice of Yahweh, most likely never to be doubted.

Fifth, the whole text is focalized directly by Jeremiah and indirectly by Yahweh. It is in fact only late in the reading that the reader realizes that Yahweh is the main focalizer, albeit indirectly, and that the reader is manipulated into choosing for the viewpoint of Yahweh.

Sixth, it was especially the readings at the narrative and internal reader's levels that brought to the fore interesting insights, such as the metalevel purpose for writing the text, or the roles of the focalizers and the narrator. It is at these levels that the reader, living in a time after the Exile, is invited into comparing his or her circumstances with those of the characters of the pre-exilic period, to learn wisdom from that period and to apply it to his or her own period. The period of the implicit reader is more difficult to determine, but there are some clues: 1) it was a period in which the regency came to an end and acted foolishly by contributing to the disastrous situation, in spite of Yahweh's and Jeremiah's attempts at good guidance, 2) when the old Israel was lost forever and the remnant in Judah did not take that history seriously enough, 3) when wise people were seen as enemies and the foolish were followed, 4) when religion was used to bolster folly, and 5) when a theology of the temple played a major part in that false religion. 6) The leadership opposed any opposition with violence, even if it was purportedly the Word of Yahweh and YHWH.

Finally, the discussion above is my contribution to a reflection on reading sacred texts, and is but one among many approaches. The reading itself can learn much from what has been done so far in the field of research on reading. It is in reflection on this reading process that I again become aware, and critical, of the processes that take place in myself in reading scripture analytically. These processes allow me to be persuaded by the communication that takes place when the real reading of the real text happens. Strangely, it is a process that takes place despite the fact that there is a distance of several thousand years between the modern reader and the ancient writer. The value of the canonicity perspective lies in the fact that the text has been more or less preserved over this period of time and still serves to help readers create meaning from it in the present day, whether that is directly related to the original meaning intended.

I think what crystallized for me in this exercise is that the reading had to be structured, possibly because of the danger of reverting to a prescribed way of reading the text through my eyes as a theologian. It also became apparent to me that the text probably has much value for the reader when the reader subscribes to the idea of it being canonical and when the character of Yahweh and YHWH coalesce into each other. A dimension then opens up in the reading that adds to the richness of the reading. A variety of reader-response approaches, such as psycho-narrative, can be employed in rereading the text, with enriching results, as was pointed out by David J. A. Clines in the various publications in which he has used literary critical theory.

8

Favor and Disfavor in Jeremiah 29:1–23

Two Dimensions of the Characterization of God and the Politics of Hope

Mignon R. Jacobs

Introduction

THE BOOK OF JEREMIAH DEPICTS THE PEOPLE OF GOD DURING AND after the demise of Jerusalem in the sixth century BCE. In the midst of the crisis, the prophet Jeremiah posits God's involvement in taking the people to Babylon and keeping them there for an extended duration. Part of the conceptual framework is the portrayal of God's differentiated treatment of people, including God's people and the Babylonians. In particular, Jeremiah 29 extends the perspectives of chs. 24–28 and depicts God's plan, including the wellbeing and *hopeful* future of God's favored people. Yet, the reassurance to this people is immediately juxtaposed to the planned demise of the disfavored others. It is no surprise, then, that some interpreters readily highlight the hopeful future and minimize the promised demise of the disfavored. Even so, the conceptual framework of the text challenges any reconceptualization that ignores its characterization of the multiple dimensions of God's character. It is proposed here that Jeremiah 29:1–23 (MT) represents a theological-political perspective[1] that characterizes God's favor and

1. 'Theological-political' is used to refer to the perspective constituted by the theological and political aspects of the view. It presupposes that God's authorized personnel (e.g., a prophet) uses theological concepts to advance a political agenda and to promote a theocracy where the Deity defines reality and purpose. In such cases, the theological and political dimensions of the view are fused. Cf. Walter Brueggemann, *To Build, to*

disfavor as essential to God's plan and involvement in the repeated selection and de-selection of God's people, as well as the selection and
de-selection of the *goyim*.

First, in order to understand the parameters of God's favor and
disfavor, this paper briefly summaries the conceptual framework of
Jeremiah 29 and then looks at the designated audience and human
agents depicted in the text. Third, it examines the dimensions of God's
character as exemplified in God's choice of whom to favor and disfavor. Fourth, it summarizes hermeneutical questions regarding the text's
theological-political perspective about God.

Conceptual Framework of Jeremiah 29 (MT)

While it is not the focus of this chapter to discuss the macro-structure
of the book of Jeremiah, the significance of the content of chs. 24–28
necessitates a brief note.[2] Building on the perspective in Jeremiah
24–26, ch. 29 belongs to the conceptual framework of 27–29. The latter
unit focuses on Jeremiah's effort to inform and warn the people about
their stance toward Babylon. As seen in Table 1 below, the sequence of
the chapters is not determined by the chronological sequence of the reported events. Chapter 24 is a vision report that Nebuchadnezzar took
the people into exile (24:1).[3] According to the vision, favor and disfavor

---

Plant: A Commentary on Jeremiah 26–52, ITC (Grand Rapids: Eerdmans, 1991) 2; Bob
Becking, *Between Fear and Freedom: Essays on the Interpretation of Jeremiah 30–31*,
OTS 51(Leiden Brill, 2004) 241, regarding identity and the choice of Yahwism in the
Persian period. John Kessler, *The Book of Haggai: Prophecy and Society in Early Persian
Yehud*, VTSup 91 (Leiden: Brill, 2002) 25–30. In his discussion of the approaches to the
study of the book, Kessler notes the "ideological goals" of Haggai as part of the portrait
of the restoration community in the early Persian Period.

2. For discussion of the divisions, see: Robert P. Carroll, *Jeremiah*, OTL (Philadelphia:
Westminster, 1986) 33–50, 86–88; Douglas R. Jones, *Jeremiah*, NCBC (Grand Rapids:
Eerdmans, 1992) 17–37, 51–57. The division of the book is evident in the various
series that propose a two-part structure, for example: William L. Holladay, *Jeremiah
2: A Commentary on the Book of the Prophet Jeremiah, Chapter 26–52*, Hermeneia
(Philadelphia: Fortress, 1989) 1–2, 15–24; Brueggemann, *To Build, to Plant*; Gerald
L. Keown, P. J. Scalise, and T. G. Smothers, *Jeremiah 26–52*, WBC 27 (Dallas: Word,
1995). Others share this perspective, namely, R. E. Clements, *Jeremiah*, IBC (Atlanta:
John Knox, 1988) 7–12; William McKane, *Jeremiah*, vol. 2, ICC (Edinburgh: T. & T.
Clark, 1996) cxxxiii–cxxxiv, clxxii–clxxiv; Louis Stulman, *Jeremiah*, AOTC (Nashville:
Abingdon, 2005) 14–15.

3. The variation of name is noted: Nebuchadrezzar (chs. 24–25) = Nebuchadnezzar
(chs. 27–29). For consistency Nebuchadnezzar is used in this paper.

are manifested in the differentiated futures of two groups of people, the good figs and the bad figs, each designated according to their place in Yahweh's plan.

The good figs are promised restoration as the people of God (24:4–7) while the bad figs are promised destruction (24:8–10). The groups are likewise designated with reference to definitive events: the good figs with the Babylonian exile and the bad figs with the stay in Jerusalem under Zedekiah's reign, or the stay in Egypt. In 24, the place in God's plan is not conditioned upon the people's response to God's prophets. Chapter 25 reports the activities of Jeremiah during the fourth year of Jehoiakim of Judah, and identifies the addressees as all the people of Judah and Jerusalem (605 BCE). It does further condition the level of blessedness of the people in terms of their refusal to heed the prophet, despite the prophet's persistence in communicating God's message (25:3b–4). The twenty-three year duration of the prophetic activity further illustrates that the people's response was neither isolated nor incidental, but as persistent as Jeremiah's and yhwh's efforts to instruct them. Clearly, the indictment is against "all the people of Judah" (כל־עם יהודה) including Jerusalem, lest one endeavor to exculpate the leaders in Jerusalem from the charge.

Chapter 26 reports Jeremiah's receipt of an oracle at the beginning of Jehoiakim's reign (approx. 609 BCE—Jer. 26:1). Like 25, it illustrates the refusal to listen to Jeremiah. All the people (כל־העם), priests, and prophets (הכהנים הנביאים) refused to heed Jeremiah and plotted to kill him (26:8).[4] Interestingly, the officials inquired about the matter and together with the people tried to dissuade the priests and prophets from killing Jeremiah (26:12–19). The portrayal illustrates the people could be swayed if given a voice of reason and discernment. Yet, the competing report is that for decades they did not heed God's word delivered to them through the prophets. In light of 26–28, the lack of response to the prophets is understandable given the competing messages that the people endured.

The officials or princes of Judah (שרי יהודה), political leaders, break the stalemate between Jeremiah and the religious leaders (priests

---

4. See Gen 37–50 for connections to the plot of Joseph's brothers to kill him in order to destroy the dreams. Cf. Mignon R. Jacobs, "The Conceptual Dynamics of Good and Evil in the Joseph Story: An Exegetical and Hermeneutical Inquiry," *JSOT* 27 (2003) 309–38.

Table 1: Framework of Jeremiah 24–29

Text references	Ch. 26	Ch. 25	Chs. 27–28	Ch. 24	Ch. 29
Reported events	Jeremiah receives an oracle—commanding all the people to listen	Jeremiah prophesies	Jeremiah's symbolic act (Babylonian yoke)	Jeremiah's Vision report	Jeremiah sends letter to Babylonian exiles
	Priests, prophets, and people plot to kill Jeremiah / Officials oppose the plot	The people's twenty-three year refusal to heed Yhwh's words through Jeremiah	Competing perspective (short exile) / Jeremiah confronts Hananiah / Hananiah's death	The good figs—promised restoration (Babylonian exiles)	Imperatives regarding the stay in Babylon / Imperative regarding deceitful prophet
	Plot to kill Uriah (the prophet) / Killing of Uriah	70-year Babylonian exile prophesied	Validation of the 70-year Babylonian exile	Bad figs—promised demise (remnant in Jerusalem and Egyptian exiles)	Promised restoration (after 70 years)

Timeline (of the prophetic activities)	609 BCE	605 BCE	594–593 BCE 590–589 BCE	post-597 BCE (594–589 BCE)	post-597 BCE (594–589 BCE)
Reigns of kings	Beginning of Jehoiakim's reign	4th year of Jehoiakim (Judah)	Beginning of Zedekiah's reign*	After Jeconiah's exile	After Jeconiah's exile
		1st year of Nebuchadnezzar (Babylon)	Same year at the beginning of Zedekiah's reign—5th month 4th year	Assumes Zedekiah's reign	Zedekiah sent a messenger to Nebuchadnezzar
			Same year 7th month		

and prophets—see Table 1). In this instance, some elders of the land (זִקְנֵי הָאָרֶץ) put Jeremiah's prophecy into historical perspective with Micah's announcement of judgment (26:16–19; cf. Mic 3:12). For the religious leaders, the concern may have been authority and credibility with the people. On the contrary, for the officials, it may be a matter of diffusing a dispute and facilitating social order to appease an anxious people about their tragedy and potential disenchantment.

The narrative thus indicates that Jeremiah is validated by the political leaders and opposed by the religious leaders. Furthermore, 26 does not distinguish between the good and bad figs in regards to their response to God's prophets; rather, it depicts collective disregard. As a part of the framework of Jeremiah 29, the lack of differentiated responses raises questions about the legitimacy of the rationale for favoring or disfavoring a particular group: Why would refusing to heed God's word be an indictment against those selected for perpetual demise when the favored participated in the same resistance to God?

Chapters 27–28 report Jeremiah's symbolic act regarding the fate of Judah under Babylonian control and Jeremiah's confrontation with Hananiah the prophet, but places the event in Zedekiah's reign (594–593 bce—27:1, 12; 28:1).[5] What is at stake in this confrontation is the validity of two competing ideologies regarding God's people and God's involvement on the world stage. On one side are the prophets and Hananiah, the anti-Babylonian contingent who advocate that God would restore Jerusalem within two years by bringing back the temple vessels, as well as King Jeconiah, and the exiles from Babylon (27:16–22; 28:3–4; cf. 2 Kgs 24:13). This promised restoration of the cultic implements would secure the loyalty of the priests and thus garner support for the agenda. Hananiah broke the wooden yoke that Jeremiah was carrying and declared the Babylonian yoke broken.

---

5. The Hebrew text of Jer. 27:1 reads יְהוֹיָקִם (Jehoiakim—ASV, JSB, KJV), but some modern versions read Zedekiah (צִדְקִיָּה, e.g., NIV, NRSV). Because Jer 27:12 refers to Jeremiah's interaction with Zedekiah, some propose 27:1 may be referring to Zedekiah but may have read Jehoiakim because of the reference in 26:1. Reading the king in 27:1 as Zedekiah would place Jeremiah's symbolic action around 594–593 bce. Cf. Roland K. Harrison, *Jeremiah and Lamentations: An Introduction and Commentary* (Downers Grove, IL: InterVarsity, 1973) 129; Carroll, *Jeremiah*, 525–26; Clements, *Jeremiah*, 160; Holladay, *Jeremiah 26–52*, 112; Brueggemann, *To Build, To Plant*, 13 n. 15; Jones, *Jeremiah*, 349; Marvin A. Sweeney, *The Prophetic Literature*, IBT (Nashville: Abingdon, 2005) 109.

On the other side is Jeremiah, the pro-Babylon advocate who claims to be speaking God's word to the people and priests. He also speaks of restoring the people to Jerusalem but prophesied that God was using Nebuchadnezzar to subdue all the nations, including Judah (27:8–15; 28:14). The closing verse of 28 also defines the ideological lines and perspective. Hananiah is an enemy of the message and he dies as a confirmation of the Jeremiah's prophecy (28:15–17). God validates Jeremiah. Hananiah is characterized as deceitful and as one whom YHWH did not send. This is the same characterization used to invalidate others, including those prophets in Babylon (27:15; 28:15; cf. 29:8–9, 23).

Jeremiah 29 picks up from 24–28 by using almost the same designation to identify those who were exiled from Jerusalem: Jeconiah, the officials, artisans, and craftsmen; reiterating the event of the exile (24:1; 29:2).[6] Chapter 29 continues by addressing the existence in the exile (הגולה—*gola*) in light of the future restoration. The conceptual framework defines the authorized perspective and the advocate of that perspective in several ways: a) it sets up the interpretive context of the historical events (24–25); b) it sets up a scenario between true prophets and the false prophets and people (26); c) it validates one as true prophet, Jeremiah; and the others as false, Hananiah (27–28); and d) it carries forth the pro-Babylonian agenda by advocating the perspective of the true prophet (29). Accordingly, 29 is strategically placed and represents the authorized perspective, while continuing to invalidate and discredit the proponents of the anti-Babylonian and hence anti-YHWH perspective as deceivers and adulterers, i.e., those whom YHWH did not send (29:8, 23).

Human Agents of the Divine Plan

The concept of favor and disfavor is an expression of choice, a choice that by its nature includes and excludes. Consequently, the discussion about the human agent of the divine plan is about identity and the role of identity in God's manifested favor or disfavor. Recognizing the text's focus on human agents, one must also acknowledge the centrality of the Deity's choice to favor, disfavor, select, or reject; and consider that

6. While Jer 24:1 and 29:1 says that Nebuchadnezzar exiled them (הגלה), 29:2 also indicates that they went out (יצא).

rejection is not meta-historical but coincides with particular historical times.[7] The discussion of favor and disfavor regarding the human agents in 29 includes various dimensions, namely, scope (who is involved), temporal extent (how long), and rationale (why).

The Scope: Who Are Involved

The representation of the human agents is facilitated by the literary distinctiveness of a correspondence (the letter, הספר) and the conventions employed to identify the audience, their location, and the circumstances that occasion the communication.[8] Chapter 29 may contain parts of a letter but is not the letter itself. Just as chs. 24–28 are retrospective reports of the events, so ch. 29 is also retrospective, reporting some of the content of that correspondence plus other information.[9]

The genre of 29 has been the focus of many discussions and is mentioned here because of the implication for understanding the agents involved.[10] While it is not the primary task of this chapter to discuss the redaction elements of 29, the task of discerning the conceptuality of the text necessitates a discussion of the text. Fundamentally, the characterization of YHWH is a product of the text's theological-political perspective achieved within the conceptual framework of the book, particularly chs. 24–29. While one cannot be definitive about the intention of any text one can nonetheless investigate the conceptuality and inquire about the ideological aspects. Who will benefit from the perspectives advanced by the text? Who speaks and for whom?

---

7. Cf. Monica J. Melanchthon, *Rejection by God: The History and Significance of the Rejection Motif in the Hebrew Bible*, Studies in Biblical Literature 22 (New York: Lang, 2001) 6.

8. These elements are variously signaled in the text. In particular, the occasion is discerned through the subject matters rather than by a single formulation indicating the purpose of the correspondence.

9. Cf. Klass D. A. Smelik, "Letters to the Exile: Jeremiah 29 in Context," *SJOT* 10 (1996) 285.

10. For discussion regarding the nature of the text see: John Bright, *Jeremiah*, AB 21 (Garden City, NY: Doubleday, 1965); J. A. Thompson, *The Book of Jeremiah*, NICOT (Grand Rapids: Eerdmans, 1980) 545; Holladay, *Jeremiah 26–52*; Brueggemann, *To Build, to Plant*; Smelik, "Letters to the Exile," 283–86; Timothy R. Valentino, "Couriered Hope: The Textual Integrity of Jeremiah's Prophetic Letter to the Exiles in Babylon (Jer. 29:1–23)," *EQ* 19 (2001) 68–73.

The Favored

Perhaps designating a favored group is also a vehicle of compliance and peace. In chs. 24–29 the favored are sent while the disfavored are not. The favored represents boundaries of selection and de-selection. On the one hand, the groups in ch. 29 are part of the selected simply by being in view. On the other hand, the selected is further subdivided into the favored and the disfavored according to the particular role within the divine-human interaction. For ch. 29 one may look at the historically signaled aspects of the scope of favor and disfavor by looking at the roles and events used to identify the human agents.

Regarding the role designations, the text identifies the various groups through their functional identity (priests, prophets, and the like) and with reference to the exile as a decisive event (29:1). The latter provides the temporal timeframe of the exiles from Jerusalem in Babylon (see Table 1).[11] The historical reference also identifies the agents in relation to each other and offers a glimpse into YHWH's relationship with all of the human agents. In this relationship, the favored are always seen in contrast to others.

The addressees of the correspondence. As indicated in the opening of the correspondence and set off by the particle אֶל, the exiles are the primary audience.[12]

> … to the remaining elders among the exiles,[13] and to the priests,
> the prophets, and all the people. (29:1 NRSV)

Set against the backdrop of chs. 24–26, the list of addressees is a salient element in the theological-political perspective. First, in ch. 25 the people are identified as a source of the prophetic opposition to the extent that they do not heed the prophets. Second, in ch. 26, the people, priests, and prophets plot to kill Jeremiah, and the same designation is

---

11. Christopher R. Seitz, *Theology in Conflict: Reactions to the Exile in the Book of Jeremiah*, BZAW 176 (Berlin: de Gruyter, 1989) 25–27. He argues that the date in 29:1 is assumed from 28:17, namely, the seventh month of the fourth year of Zedekiah's reign—approximately 594/93 BCE.

12. The particle indicates the indirect object of the verb שָׁלַח ("to send").

13. Some debate as to whether this is indicting the remnant of the elders *vis-à-vis* the entire group of the other designated persons. Such distinctions are a further function of the delineation of the audience but does not distract from a through understanding of the distinctive group—namely, the favored and disfavored.

used to identify the recipients of the correspondence (29:1; cf. 26:8).[14] In ch. 26, the elders were a voice of reason in the confrontation between Jeremiah and the people, priests, and prophets. Their role was to offer historical perspective and so to validate Jeremiah as the authorized voice among his contemporaries. This group of recipients in ch. 29 represents potential sides in the dispute about God's involvement in the Babylonian Exile. The prophets in Babylonia are not included as supporters of Jeremiah's pro-Babylonian theological-political agenda but as anti-Babylonian opponents.[15]

Because of their influence on the people, the prophets could not be ignored in such a correspondence. As with chs. 26–28, the people would be the focus of the false message and the potential victims of multiple and competing voices. The identification of the addressees then is another way of naming the key players. The recipients are further differentiated from any others who may have received communication from Jerusalem. Jeremiah sends communication by king Zedekiah's messengers Elasah and Gemariah (29:3). Among the Babylonian exiles, the named recipients signal a perception of a continued ideological schism, often depicted by invalidating alternative perspectives as false. Consequently, where one might otherwise expect harmony, namely, among the Judeans, one finds discord, but a semblance of harmony between Babylon and its captives.

Exiles and Babylonians. The intertwined existence of people defines the influence of God's favor or disfavor toward all. As with God's disfavor, the exiles' behaviors influenced, if not regulated, aspects of YHWH's actions and were facilitated by God's disclosure of the favorable behaviors (29:4–7, 14). Notably, God made the exiles the key to the wellbeing of others and the catalysts for God's responsiveness. God's favor toward Babylon would expire with the demise of Babylon as the catalyst for actualizing the promise to the exiles (25:11–14). This paired existence resembles a depiction of Babylon in ch. 27. There one's response to Babylon determines how God treats a nation.

---

14. In Jer 27:9–10 the group advocating a false perspective are the diviners, dreamers, soothsayers, and sorcerers. The people and priests are mentioned in 27:16–22. Cf. Carroll (*Jeremiah*, 534) regarding the prophets as a variation on the "false prophets" tradition.

15. Cf. Harrison, *Jeremiah and Lamentations*, 20; Brueggemann, *To Build, to Plant*, 19.

In both ch. 25 and ch. 27, Babylon is God's authorized instrument, functioning according to God's plan for Babylon and the nations. In this perspective, oppression is disregarded as a reason for resisting Babylon; rather, to resist Babylon is to incur God's punishment. The same fate promised to the people who remained in Judah is promised to those who resist Babylon's yoke. They would be punished with sword, famine, and pestilence and marked for annihilation (27:8; cf. 24:8–10; 29:17–18). Just as the existence of the Babylonian exiles is tied to Babylon (their captor), the existence of the people in Judah is the same as those who resist Babylon. Either way the anti-Babylonian contingency will be destroyed, not because of what they have done but because of their place in the Deity's plan (contrast ch. 38). Even so, the destroyer (favored) and the destroyed (disfavored), along with their descendants, are likewise pawns selected for particular roles in YHWH's plan.

The Disfavored

Disfavor is an active part of the behavior of choosing. Why chose one person and not another? Why design particular selection criteria and not others? Unless one includes the totality of an entity, by its very nature every selection results in a form of rejection. Therefore, to characterize God as selecting and rejecting, favoring and disfavoring, is simply to describe an inevitable part of relationship dynamics. In the conceptual framework of ch. 29, the disfavored were previously part of the covenant community, but are disfavored because of their sin and failure to listen to the prophets (cf. 29:18–19). The indicators of disfavor include punishment in the form of destruction of property, humiliation, and displacement, the reversal of the elements indicating favor and blessing. In particular, disfavor will be manifested in the action of God against the human agents who challenge God's plan and perspectives.

Babylonian exiles vs. Judeans. As in ch. 24, so in ch. 29 the fate of the exiles is contrasted to that of the Jerusalem based Judeans (29:16–19). All the people are selected, but the question is the function for which they are selected. In ch. 29, since the restoration would be actualized within a seventy-year period, the exiles would have to endure the circumstances, but their descendants would experience the restoration. That YHWH orchestrates the exile affirms God's power and refutes any speculated weakness or loss of control. Conversely, those who are left in Judah are left there because of God's purposeful exclusion and disfavor toward them. The disfavored are the negative object lesson of immediate and postponed retribution incurred because of resisting God. Ironically, the Babylonian exiles also resisted but are portrayed as favored.

The actions against the Judeans are itemized using two verbal forms, namely, "I am sending" the sword, hunger, and pestilence against them and "I will make" (ונתתי) them as rotten figs (cf. 27:8, 13). This is the same formulation used in 24:10 to speak of the destruction of Zedekiah, his officials, the remnant in the land and those who live in Egypt. Presumably both 29:17 and 24:10 speak about the same group of people.[16] It is also the announcement of judgment in 25:8–10 used to indicate the plan to annihilate those who do not heed the Deity.[17]

The prophets. Having authorized Jeremiah, the text associates truth with acceptance of YHWH's work. Thus, any who do not advocate God's perspective are disqualified as false (cf. 25:4; 26:5; cf. 14:14; 23:24–32). The portrayal of the prophets is as much a part of the characterization of God as the representation of God's two servants. The text employs consistently the polemical stance against the false prophets by designating them as objects of God's action. Accordingly, YHWH sent the prophet and Nebuchadnezzar, God's servant (25:9; 27:6). On the contrary, the people are warned not to listen to the prophets who oppose compliance with Babylon. These anti-Babylonian prophets do not advocate the authorized perspective because YHWH did not send them (27:15). The sign of being sent is advocating the pro-Babylonian perspective.

All the prophets whom God disfavored are disqualified as "not sent." They speak in YHWH's name (27:14–15; 29:9) but stand in contrast to those whom yhwh sent. Their condemnation coheres with Deuteronomy 18:18–20, which prescribes punishment against those who do not heed the prophets that prophesy in YHWH's name, con-

---

16. In Jer. 24:10 the *waw*-converted perfect form ושלחתי (I will send) is used with the specified objects—the sword, hunger, and pestilence (את־החרב את־הרעב ואת־הדבר) and the indirect object "them" (בם) referring to the disfavored. Other occurrences of the three elements include, Jer 32:24. In Ezek 14:21 identifies four elements that God sent (שלח) as judgment on Jerusalem, namely, "sword, famine, wild animals, and pestilence (חרב ורעב וחיה רעה ודבר).

17. The occurrences of the terms in the book of Jeremiah include: 14:12; 15:2; 18:21; 21:7, 9; 24:10; 27:8, 13; 29:17, 18; 32:24, 36; 34:17; 38:2; 42:7, 22; 44:13. These elements indicate the traditional instruments of destruction. Cf. Mark Roncace, *Jeremiah, Zedekiah, and the Fall of Jerusalem*, LHBOTS 423 (London: T. & T. Clark, 2005) 13.

demning the prophets' claim to speak in the name without receiving a message from God (cf. 14:14, 15; 28:5–9, 15). In Jeremiah 24–29, speaking in God's name is an insufficient criterion for validity. Speaking in the name and being sent together forms the decisive criterion. The false prophets are further disqualified as adulterers, possibly to discredit them on the basis of their character rather than on the validity of their perspective in relation to the perceived historical realities (29:22–23).

Definitive Events

Regarding the events that characterize or identify the human agents, the exile is credited to both the human and divine agents and thus depicted as a deliberate act. The specificity regarding the events further delineates the human agents in God's reassurance and plan for a differentiated future, depending on whether one is perceived as favored or disfavored. The specificity excludes the Samaritans, and both includes and excludes those who may have gone to Egypt, Edom, and surrounding regions.

Further specification of the time frame limits the audience, not everyone who was exiled from 597–586 BCE is in view. Even within the limited time frame, it also designates the addressees with reference to particular exiles, namely, Jeconiah, the queen mother, the eunuchs, princes of Judah and Jerusalem, and men from the crafts and guilds, and smiths (29:2). Surely there were others living in Babylon from other nations subdued by Babylon, but the text does not concern itself with them. In ch. 29, they are non-entities whose place and purpose are not equal to the favored or their disfavored counterpart. The focus itself indicates the status of being selected, and may further indicate the nature of the selection.

Temporal Extent

The focus on the exiles and Babylon is indicative of the selected status. Even so, being selected is governed by temporal constraints. The first part of the temporal aspect is tied to the exiles, not just any exiles but those exiled with Jeconiah; and not just any marked for destruction, but those associated with Zedekiah and remaining in Jerusalem or living in Egypt (29:17; cf. 24:10;). By these designations, the text narrows the focus on a selected group. The association with Zedekiah and the language of the remnant is further significant to the temporal dimension (see Table 1).

The second aspect of the temporal dimension is the link between the exiles in Babylon and the Babylonians. For both the link is temporary and anticipates the differentiated future. Babylon will continue its dominance until it has fulfilled God's plan for it. Then within the 70-years prescribed, other nations will subdue Babylon and punish Babylon for its oppressive practices (25:8–14). For that association of the people, the political situation constitutes the temporal scope of the favor or disfavor.

The third aspect of the temporal dimension is also the people involved. The descendants of the favored and disfavored will also be affected, though not necessarily in the same way. For the favored exiles, their descendants will experience the actualized restoration to Jerusalem. But for the descendants of the once favored Babylonians they will experience postponed retribution, namely, oppression as punishment for subduing the nations (Jer 25:11–14; cf. 50:2, 24, 28–29, 38; 51:6, 15–19, 36–52).[18]

The justification of the demise of the Babylonians is thus fused with the restoration of the exiles to Jerusalem. The destruction becomes the mechanism for advancing YHWH's plan. It is not that Babylon suddenly becomes sinful and oppressive, but that the sinfulness is used as a rationale for punishment once Babylon's usefulness expires. God's de-selection of Babylon as the instrument *de jour* leads to the nation's demise, but Babylon is not vilified as a part of the rationale (contrast Isaiah 46–48).[19] God selects the Persians as the instrument of Babylon's destruction and Judah's restoration.

Noted Reasons/Rationale for the Favor/Disfavor

The expressed rationale for the disfavor toward the Jerusalem-based Judeans begs the question of the nature of disfavor. Are they disfavored because they sinned? The exiles were presumably punished because

18. Cf. Becking, *Between Fear and Freedom*, 232–33; Yair Hoffman, "Jeremiah 50–51 and the Concept of Evil in the Hebrew Bible," in *The Problem of Evil and Its Symbols in Jewish and Christian Tradition*; edited by H. G. Reventlow and Y. Hoffman, JSOTSup 366 (London: T. & T. Clark, 2004) 23.

19. John Hill, *Friend or Foe: The Figure of Babylon in the Book of Jeremiah MT*, BibIntSer 40 (Leiden: Brill, 1999) 135. Cf. Isa 46:1–7; 47:5–7, 10–11.

of their sin. Yet, the retributive aspects of disfavor fail to account for YHWH's different orientation toward the two groups. The people of Judah did not heed Jeremiah and the other prophets whom YHWH sent to them (the favored prophets). On the contrary, they may have listened to the prophets whom YHWH did not send (disfavored prophets) (chs. 25–28).

While the covenant relationship helps to define the rationale for the favor and disfavor in 29, that relationship is not the primary or decisive aspect of God's favor. Rather, God's favor suggests that punishment is regulated by God's plan for all; and the nature of the plan differs from one group to the next. Clearly, there are other instances in the prophetic literature and in Jeremiah where the correspondence between sin and punish defines the rationale for God's rejection and/or punishment of Israel. The punishment may not mean rejection, so when God punishes, God does not necessarily reject.[20] But all rejection may conceivably be a form of punishment (cf. Jer. 12:14–17; 23:1–2; 49:32; 51:2 Ezek. 22:14–15; 29:12; Deut. 28:63).[21]

Summarily, the rationale for favor toward Babylon is its place in God's plan and the ensuing fusion of its wellbeing with the exiles. Regarding the exiles, no specified rationale for favoring them is offered (cf. 24:4–7). By virtue of a different plan for them vis-à-vis their Judean counterpart, a different rationale is implied. Favor is represented by the opportunity to settle and prosper even in the land of their captors. The theological aspects are indicated as a part of the articulated plan of God. The political and social dimension of the articulation constitutes the other aspect. The articulation makes some people a higher priority than others and bases that priority on the will or plan of YHWH.

Dimensions of God's Characterization

While it is not within the scope of this chapter to discuss the principles of characterization, some clarifying comments are in order.[22] Here the

20. Regarding indicators of God's rejection of God's people. Even so rejection does not mean the complete termination of the relationship. Rather it may mean the reconstitution of the relationship under different conditions.

21. S. T. Sohn, *The Divine Election of Israel* (Grand Rapids: Eerdmans, 1991) 235, regarding the language of rejection.

22. For discussion see Robert Alter, *The Art of Biblical Narrative* (New York: Basic Books, 1981); Roncace, *Jeremiah, Zedekiah*, 5–7.

discussion acknowledges that such characterization is inevitably tied to all others of the text. Thus, the representation of God as sending the exiles, commanding them, and designating some people to one future vis-à-vis another future is part of the characterization. Even the text's choice of one type of representation of God, and which prophet is authorized, are also part of the characterization.

Consequently, I propose that the text facilitates ideological perspectives through its presentation of the human and divine agents. By virtue of placing 29 within the literary context that contains competing perspectives, the text already sides with a perspective and thus invites the reader to take a side. Nonetheless, the effort to invalidate the unauthorized perspectives facilitates close inspection of the ideological grounds of the efforts. Jeremiah 29 makes a case for Jeremiah's pro-Babylonian agenda vis-à-vis the pro-Jerusalem agenda of the other prophets. In Jeremiah's perspective and contrary to appearances, God secures the wellbeing of a favored people through their stay in Babylon.

God's Actions Depicted

The responsibility for the exile. Exile is a form of punishment that illustrates God's favor and disfavor toward the exiles. Just as God drove the Canaanites out of the land and gave the land to Israel, so God drove Israel out of the land using Babylon to accomplish the task (cf. Deut 29:25–27 [NRSV 26–28]; Jer 7:15; 8:3; 16:15; 22:28; 27:10; 46:28).[23] Babylon is the instrument used to punish Israel and the exile is simply a mode of punishment.[24] In this representation of the exile, Nebuchadnezzar, God's servant, is the human agent of the exile (cf. Jer. 27:1, 6; 29:1, 4, 7; 43:10).[25] The exile is also seen as a culmination of God's interaction with the people of Judah that followed repeated communication through the prophets (25). They did not respond to God's servants, the prophets, and God opted to use an outsider.

The choice of human agents. God selected the exiles as the agents of the restoration and the Babylonians as the host or homestead for the

---

23. Cf. Sohn, *The Divine Election,* 206–8. Nebuchadnezzar appears as a part f the human agency of the exile. Elsewhere he is designated "the servant of God" (cf. Jer 27:6; 43:10).

24. Hill, *Friend or Foe?* 146.

25. Cf. Sohn, *The Divine Election,* 206–7.

exiles. Likewise, just as God selected the particular group of exiles, God also rejected another group, who like the exiles are a part of the covenant community. In this respect, the choice for one group over against the other is fundamentally a product of the divine choice (27:4–7).

In 29:7 and 14, one sees elements of YHWH's choice to respond to human efforts. God acknowledges a role in exiling the people, bringing them to Babylon, and orchestrating their presence in Babylon. God ties their wellbeing to that of the place where they are and accordingly, would preserve the city or place of their dwelling for the people's sake, at least for the time that it takes to actualize God's plan. Thus, God uses the same setting as the launching place into the plan for each group. For the present, Babylon is God's instrument, but in the future God will effect the destruction of that instrument (25:11–14; 27:6–7). For the present, the exile is punishment and opportunity for recovery, but in the future exile is the stage for the blessing manifested in the restoration of material and land (29:5–7, 10).

Plans as Indicators of the God's Character

SELECTION AND DE-SELECTION

The selection of the exiles represents a reconstitution of the covenant community. All the persons who are chosen are from the Judean community. Jeremiah 29:14 defines the selection to exclude those who remain in the Judean community, to include those scattered in regions other than Babylon and those who departed from Jerusalem by other means than the efforts of Nebuchadnezzar. Finally, those are included who were deported within a particular time frame. While all of these aspects indicate the nature of the selection, they also indicate de-selection by further discriminating among those who were previously part of the selected covenant community group. Consequently, only segments of the sixth century BCE Judean community are part of the future restored community. The temporal aspect of the plan further delimits the selection and de-selection.

Naturally, not all of the audience of the correspondence would be part of the restored community. Those who may be alive to hear/receive the message of the correspondence would have to wait for 70 years for the fulfillment of the plan. Their understanding that they should marry, and allow their children to marry and bear children, is part of the postponed actualization. This aspect functions as a temporal selection and de-selection process, namely, the future generation, and not the immediate one, will experience the actualized promise. In this way, the plan articulated to the exiles resembles the promise to the patriarchs and the deferred actualization of the promise. On the other hand, the nature of the reassurance allows the immediate generation to profit through settlement, marriage, harvest, and peace. In so far as it defines a particular future, the postponed actualization of the promise to the exiles also defines a dimension of selection and a form of determinism.[26]

Elements of the Plan

Indicating the specific aspects of the plan minimizes other aspects making them nonessential and irrelevant. The essential aspects function to delimit the parameters of the plan. As such, each element indicates both the favor and disfavor.

People dimension (scope). The people dimension reflects YHWH's choice and hence the criteria. While the designated audience of the correspondence is the exiled group in Babylon brought there by Nebuchadnezzar and God, the promise of restoration seems to broaden the scope of the favor to include not only those who were exiled in Babylon but all others scattered among the nations (29:14).[27] The people dimension of God's involvement may be further examined by looking at the terminological specificity regarding the people. Although Babylon becomes a metaphor for displacement and exile, one pattern within the book of Jeremiah is the usage of the *hiph'il* (causative) form in reference to deportation. Usually, it is used of those exiled to Babylon (20:4; 27:20; 39:9; 43:3; 52:15, 28, 30).[28] In ch. 29 it is used with God and the human agent (Nebuchadnezzar), each identified as responsible for the presence of the Judeans in Babylon. By comparison, the verb is typically used throughout the book of Jeremiah for banishment to various and usually unnamed nations and is not usually used of the Babylonian exile (cf. 8:3; 16:15; 23:3, 8; 24:9; 27:10, 15; 29:18; 32:37).[29] The usage

---

26. Cf. Becking, *Between Fear and Freedom*, 232–33.

27. Hill, *Friend or Foe*, 156. Here argues that two groups are envisioned within this promise—those who were scattered among the nations and those exiled to Babylon.

28. Ibid., 156. He also notes that while גֹּלָה occurs in Jer 23:12 "the place of exile is unnamed."

29. Ibid., 156.

does not indicate a differentiation between those who will be restored (16:15; 23:3; 32:37). Consistent with 29:14, God will gather the people from all the nations where they are scattered.

God favors Babylon over against a segment of the covenant community. Here another dimension of the favor is evident, namely, those remaining in Judah are disfavored because of their sins (29:16–19). Yet nothing is said of Babylon's sins or the sins of the exiles living in Babylon. The transformation from favor to disfavor is identified in the rationale for Babylon's place in the promised restoration, the fulfillment of its time.[30] Even though it is temporary, God's favor toward Babylon unites the exiles and Babylon's fate in a shared space and purpose. So the two groups are intertwined in their existence; yet, they are differentiated by the very plan that brings them together. Here we see that the favored exiles are dependent on others and must therefore participate in securing the wellbeing of the other if they are to ensure their own wellbeing. The bond is not shared ancestry but shared purpose within God's plan.

Time factor. The element of time represents a criterion for selection and actualization of the plan. Here, as in the people dimension, time also defines the identity of the favored. Jeremiah 29:10 establishes the time frame and the deliverance out of Babylon like the exodus out of Egypt: namely, both are deliberate acts of God. But until the exodus out of Babylon, the exile is to be spent settled in Babylon. The exiles were to begin a new life in a foreign land, presumably an unclean place (cf. Deut 26:5–10).[31]

Accordingly, the audience is admonished to build, plan, marry, and multiply, and seek peace. Some argue that itemized elements of the imperative to settle down are not to be taken literally but as paradigmatic of integration into a society.[32] One sees the similarity of items on this

---

30. The motif of the necessary fulfillment of time as catalyst for actualizing a promise is part of the framework of the Pentateuch, for example, Gen 15:13–15; 46:1–4; Deut 9:4–5.

31. Cf. Samantha Joo, *Provocation and Punishment: The Anger of God in the Book of Jeremiah and Deuteronomistic Theology*, BZAW 361 (Berlin: de Gruyter, 2006) 363.

32. Thus McLane, *Jeremiah*, 743; McKane, "Jeremiah and the Wise," In *Wisdom in Ancient Israel: Essays in Honor of J. A. Emerson*, edited by John Day et al. (Cambridge: Cambridge University Press, 1995) 151.

list to those in Deut 20:5–8.[33] In Deuteronomy, the elements represent the grounds for exemption from military service and by implication the allowance for the exempted to enjoy these elements, the signs of Gods blessing (cf. Isa 65:21–23). To be deprived of these is a curse (cf. Deut 28:30);[34] accordingly, the vision for the restoration includes the image of blessing. In its representation in 29:5–7 the blessing is to be actualized in Babylon, thus indicating a favored existence there. Like Egypt, Babylon represents a dual significance for the people, the favored place for preservation yet the manifestation of subjugation. The significance is further seen through an understanding of the prospective actions articulated in the plan for the exiles.

From another perspective, the advice to settle down may be an admonition to the exiles to refrain from warfare and to embrace the exile as part of the divine plan. This advice would most likely challenge the perspective of those who would advocate resistance (cf. ch. 38). The practical advice is framed theologically, namely, that the exile and any attenuating disruptions are God's actions and that resisting Babylon is futile. Furthermore, such resistance is equal to rebellion against God. Both Gen 15:13–15 and Jer 29:5–10 make subjugation in a foreign land the prelude to deliverance. Jeremiah 29 affirms the Babylonian centered view as the authorized perspective sent by God through Jeremiah.

Prospective actions. Two elements of the prospective actions are indicated. First is the admonition to seek the peace and pray for the city. Second is the promise of restoration. Both of these exemplify the character of God to reveal God's plan and to provide the keys to securing God's favorable response.

The exiles are told to pray for the שלום of the place of exile, having left Jerusalem where there is "no peace and prosperity" (Jer 6:14; 12:12; 16:5; 30:5; cf. Ezek. 13:10, 16).[35] The removal or absence of שלום is indicative of disfavor, conversely *shalom* is indicative of favor. Additionally, favor is manifested in שלום and the reversal of fortunes is clearly depicted. The city of Jerusalem, believed to be inviolable, has no *shalom*, and the city of exile becomes the potential place of שלום.

---

33. E.g., McKane, *Jeremiah*, 743; Adele Berlin, "Jeremiah 29:5-7: A Deuteronomic Allusion," *HAR* 8 (1984) 4, 6–7; Stulman, *Jeremiah*, 251.

34. Hill, *Friend or Foe?*, 148; Berlin, "Jeremiah 29:5–7," 4, 6–7.

35. Jonathan Paige Sisson, "Jeremiah and the Jerusalem Conception of Peace," *JBL* 105 (1986) 440.

The divine prerogative defines favor and disfavor and may even contradict prior manifestations of and articulations about that prerogative. Consequently, any place is subject to destruction or favor based on the divine prerogative (27:4–5).

Furthermore, it seems that the admonition in 29:7 is a plea for intercession on behalf of Babylon that introduces yet another dimension of God's favor.[36] The conceptual challenge is that the exiles are admonished to pray for their captors.[37] That challenge is magnified when 29:7 is juxtaposed to 7:6, which admonishes the prophet not to pray for the people because God will not listen (cf. 11:14; 14:11).

> As for you, do not pray for this people, do not raise a cry or prayer on their behalf, and do not intercede with me, for I will not hear you. (7:6 NRSV)

On the one hand, the exiles, the former people for whom the prophet is told not to intercede, are admonished to pray for their captors because God ties their fates together. This tension has lead some to seek alternative understandings for the text, including the proposal that "the city" refers to every city where exiles live rather than only Babylon, as may be suggested by the designated place of the audience. The reference in 29:7, "seek the peace of the city," raises questions regarding the understanding of the formulation and the city to which it refers. It could be any city but since addressed to those in Babylon (29:4) the introductory formula restricts the audience to Babylon. Even so, 29:14 would indicate the broadened scope of the reassurance.[38]

Clearly whether "the city" refers to the generic city used to indicate wherever exiles dwell, it would include Babylon. Part of the challenge comes out of the discomfort of interpreters with the alignment of Israel and its captors, as favored groups, within the reassurance. Nonetheless, God's reassurance and plan indicates that for whatever duration, God extends favor to both the captor and the captured. The tie with the exiles' wellbeing suggests God's power and responsiveness to their prayer. God

---

36. Ibid.

37. Cf. Stulman, *Jeremiah*, 251–54. "This radical counsel is fraught with political realism, for it concedes that the future of the exiles is tied to the interest of their captors" (251).

38. Hill, (*Friend or Foe?*) argues that the city is Babylon. Contrast Smelik, ("Letters to the Exile," 290–91), who argues for the generic identity of the city.

reveals the keys to obtaining certain aspects of God's favor. Clearly, in this conceptuality, YHWH is characterized by decisive power. Wellbeing lies in God's power regardless of the existence of any other being.[39]

Second, the promise includes the restoration of fortune and place in the land, but does not specify the restoration of the temple vessels (contrast 27:16–22; 28:2–4). In this regard, the perspective re-signifies the elements of favor or blessing by plans to actualize them in Jerusalem. The assurance thus clarifies that while the indicators of favor were to be actualized in Babylon as a temporary incubation phase, the manifested favor in Babylon will be re-actualized in Jerusalem. Like its Babylonian counterpart, the re-actualization will entail a new generation. Here, the command to multiply aims at the pragmatic element of the restoration and the multiplication takes precedence over any anti-foreigner sentiments regarding potential spouses.[40] It would be quite odd in a correspondence that fuses the identity of the captor and captured to discriminate against the captors as disfavored by YHWH. The advice to seek the peace of the city tells the people not to rebel against a powerful nation while the people are in a weak position.[41] The other side of the advice is the re-conceptualization of God's favor and relationship with the nations.

In contrast to Hananiah's perspective that may be an attempt from a perceived center, the admonition in 29:5–10 is about survival and hope offered from the margin (ch. 28). Jeremiah's advice is practical advice about endurance. The articulation is an expression of anxiety about a future whose anticipated reality contradicts the present demise. To envision a captured people in solidarity with its captor makes sense as a means to survival. But these elements leave open the question about their inevitability. Are the particulars of the plan and the plan itself determined and unalterable? If so, what dimensions are inevitable and

39. Cf. Hill, *Friend or Foe?*, 151.

40. Regarding the promise to multiply the people of God in a foreign land see Gen 15:13–15 and 46:1–4.

41. Hill, (*Friend or Foe?*, 152–53), disagrees with the perspective that his is simply pragmatic and argues that the language in Jer. 29:4–7 is more than language of submission. Cf. Stulman, *Jeremiah*, 251–54; Claude Gilbert Romero, "A Hermeneutic of Appropriation: A Case Study of Method in the Prophet Jeremiah and Latin American Liberation Theology" (PhD Dissertation, Princeton, 1982) 56–79.

which are not: people, place, or time?[42] The assurance in 29:11, paired with the portrayal of the Deity's plan in ch. 24, indicates a set plan.

Implications of God's Characterization

Perspective as Definition of the Plan

The plan for the exiles makes sense within Jeremiah's argument concerning God's involvement in all dimensions of the historical situation. Babylon may be a negative and dominate force which no nation can resist, and God's constructed reality makes resistance tantamount to suicide; however, if Babylon is a strong nation without divine authority its aggression is still that of a political powerhouse. While in both perspectives compliance may be necessary to survival, the rationale for the compliance may be different in each case. Perhaps the characterization of God might be best viewed as a political and social strategy for survival, articulated from a theological perspective. God's authority defines Babylon's strength because YHWH's prerogative defines reality, namely:

> It is I who by my great power and my outstretched arm have made the earth, with the people and animals that are on the earth, and I give it to whomever I please. (27:5 NRSV)

IDENTITY AND FAVOR

According to ch. 29, the divine favor is not based on or controlled by the human identity, whether group-defined or functionally defined. Consequently, perhaps the dividing line regarding favor and disfavor is neither between the original covenant community and the Diaspora, nor even between the selected and the disfavored. Rather the distinction and unifying element may be the need for humility in understanding and accepting the dominance of the divine prerogative to favor or disfavor, to select or reject whomever and for what ever reason.

DETERMINISM IN FAVOR AND DISFAVOR

Understanding God's control is decisive to the issue of prediction and fulfillment. Does God guarantee the outcome of the plan? Here it is sug-

---

42. Cf. Becking, *Between Fear and Freedom*, 232–33, regarding tragic fatalism.

gested that the impact of the prediction on the tradition and ideology of the exiles and others, contributes to the orientation toward the plan and its actualization.[43] To the favored, the fulfillment of the plan is positive. To the disfavored the fulfillment is an actualization of their demise and hence something to be avoided. The positive outcome for one group vis-à-vis the negative outcome for the other suggests the inevitability of the outcome.

Particular vis-à-vis Universal Application

All the people have not been replaced as part of the covenant community; however, there is a reconstituted focus defined by favor. This is much like the model seen in Num 14:1–25. The older generation, because of its disobedience, is rejected. That rejection does not negate its prior relationship as the people of the covenant. Likewise, the correspondence in ch. 29 also demonstrates the rejection of one segment of the community in favor of another group and their descendants. As with Numbers 14 which indicates God's rejection of a group of people, in Jeremiah 29 that rejection reconstitutes the relationship with a future generation. In ch. 29 there is both a continuity and discontinuity of the relationship seen in the differentiated present for the Babylonian exiles and their fellow Judeans punished and scattered throughout the nations (29:16) as future restoration community.

Dynamics of favor and disfavor. Both selection and rejection represent God's choices. Some have objected to pairing the exiles and Babylon as favored agents in God's plans because such pairing is believed to suggest a re-conceptualization of the divine presence, no longer in Jerusalem but in the city of the captors.[44] This interpretation of YHWH's dwelling seems to perpetuate the unacceptability of Babylon and hence the shock regarding God's presence there. God's choice to dwell there indicates the fallacy of trying to regulate God's favor. Favor is not universal and its particularity is nebulous. Temporally manifested, the dynamic nature of God's interaction with humanity negates any notion of a static favor. The favor, like the relationship, is subject to

---

43. Tiemeyer, "Prophecy as a Way of Canceling Prophecy," 329.

44. Hill, *Friend or Foe?* 151. "The language from the temple cult adds to the blasphemy. The place now in which Yhwh is to be found is not in the Jerusalem temple, but in the city of the conqueror, an alien and unclean place."

re-conceptualization. Accordingly, some who are favored may in time be disfavored, for various reasons and *vice versa*. This is both the beauty and horror of God's favor and disfavor, they are dynamic and not perpetually guaranteed.

Incidentality of God's favor. YHWH ultimately decides favor and disfavor and both are temporally constrained and non-transferable. The universal aspect is God's choice to deal with people. God's choice transcends the identity of humans and the nature of the circumstances that God orchestrates. Potentially, every human is subject to God's favor and disfavor, selection or rejection. The reassurance to the exiles is only potentially applicable to all depending on the place and identity of the human agents in God's plan.

9

Making a Statement

Rhetorical Questions in the Hebrew Psalter

J. Kenneth Kuntz

In biblical Israel, talented poets transformed thought into discourse in often arresting ways. One of the non-structural devices they enlisted was the rhetorical question. Israel's narrators also used it to their advantage, as is evident when in a moment of crisis the frustrated Moses ventilates his feelings by asking God, "Did *I* conceive all this people or did *I* bear them?" (Num 11:12). While rhetorical questions are crucial in biblical prose narrative, their presence in the poetry of the Psalms is similarly impressive and are the focus of this chapter.

Reflections about Rhetorical Questions

In his masterful study of language, Wallace L. Chafe explains that *question* is "an informal label that embraces sentences of several distinct types."[1] He notes that whereas most imperatives consist of statements that elicit some kind of *nonlinguistic* behavior, questions are spoken to elicit a *linguistic* reaction from the listener. On occasion, *rhetorical* questions are set against so-called *genuine* questions. Perceived as distinguishable speech acts, the former are considered *indirect* and the latter

---

1. Wallace L. Chafe, *Meaning and the Structure of Language* (Chicago: University of Chicago Press, 1970) 309. This is supported by Bruce K. Waltke and Michael O'Connor. Mindful that both English and biblical Hebrew are languages yielding many types of questions, they offer an instructive typology in *An Introduction to Biblical Hebrew Syntax* (Winona Lake, IN: Eisenbrauns, 1990) 315–17.

direct. Moreover, genuine questions are designed to *evoke* information, whereas rhetorical questions *provide* information.[2]

The latter anticipate no answer. To appropriate a term from speech-act theory, the "illocutionary force" of the rhetorical question is not to inquire but to assert.[3] Having generously enriched the literature of English-speaking peoples, some rhetorical questions are well known. Frequently enlisting this device, W. B. Yates closes his poem, "Among School Children," with the question, "How can we know the dancer from the dance?" and Percy B. Shelley's "Ode to the West Wind" concludes, "O, Wind, if Winter comes, can Spring be far behind?"

As a declarative statement in the guise of an interrogative, a rhetorical question takes on what Edwin Black calls "the hue of benign deception." He explains, "It is no more deceptive than other ironies that feint in one direction and move in another, but it has abandoned the beckoning innocence of a real question, one that is seeking an answer rather than sponsoring one."[4]

In numerous dialogic contexts, rhetorical questions serve an appellative purpose. They allow the speaker to capture his or her listeners' attention, making them fully aware of the speaker's presence. This feature fascinates George A. Kennedy who, from his scrutiny of diverse New Testament texts, discovers that in the context of diatribe, rhetorical questions help to maintain "audience contact in strategic locations."[5] The speaker does not anticipate an answer from the other conversation partner. Indeed, in some contexts, social conventions would forbid the addressee from answering.[6]

2. See Jürgen Schmidt-Radefeldt, "On so-called 'Rhetorical Questions,'" *Journal of Pragmatics* 1 (1977) 375, who regards the rhetorical question as "a somewhat hybrid type of utterance."

3. M. H. Abrams, *A Glossary of Literary Terms*, 6th ed. (Fort Worth: Harcourt Brace College, 1993) 183.

4. Edwin Black, *Rhetorical Questions: Studies of Public Discourse* (Chicago: University of Chicago Press, 1992) 2.

5. Kennedy, *New Testament Interpretation through Rhetorical Criticism* (Chapel Hill: University of North Carolina Press, 1984) 115. See Stanley E. Porter ("The Argument of Romans 5: Can a Rhetorical Question Make a Difference?" *JBL* 110 [1991] 655–77), who exposes the rhetorical conventions of diatribe in Paul's discourse.

6. That the addressee shall remain silent is a fundamental convention in the usage of rhetorical questions. See John E. Llewelyn, "What Is a Question?" *Australasian Journal of Philosophy* 42 (1964) 70; and Schmidt-Radefeldt, "On So-called 'Rhetorical Questions,'" 389.

In terms of their potential to persuade, rhetorical questions often outdistance direct assertions. Based on his engagement with rhetorical interrogatives in the Hebrew Bible, C. J. Labuschagne holds that they constitute "one of the most forceful and effective ways employed in speech for driving home some idea or conviction." Given their persuasive force, "the hearer is not merely listener: he is forced to frame the expected answer in his mind, and by doing so he actually becomes a co-expresser of the speaker's conviction."[7] The rhetorical question may induce in the addressee a commitment to the implicit answer that is on par with the speaker's own commitment.[8]

Often capable of unmasking their speakers, rhetorical questions show them to be personally engaged in a given issue. Exposing their propositional attitude, be it one of reproach, wonder, or dismay, a rhetorical question may significantly assist the speaker in rendering a value judgment.[9] If the speaker wishes to evoke, from his or her audience, agreement with a negative position, a deftly framed rhetorical question may carry the day. On occasion, such interrogatives convey an accusatory nuance, as if to say, "Could you have done as well?" Or they may express emphatic denial where the obvious answer is, "No!"

It follows that some rhetorical questions assume the form of exclamatory utterance either for or against something. Consequently, the yes-no type of rhetorical interrogative exhibits a polarity shift between itself and its implied statement. Cornelia Ilie observes that "a question

7. C. J. Labuschagne, *The Incomparability of Yahweh in the Old Testament*, Pretoria Oriental Series 5 (Leiden: Brill, 1966) 23.

8. See Cornelia Ilie, *What Else Can I Tell You? A Pragmatic Study of English Rhetorical Questions as Discursive and Argumentative Acts*, Stockholm Studies in English 82 (Stockholm: Almqvist & Wiksell, 1994) 45. The rhetorical question functions as a challenging statement that will exert "a persuasive effect on the addressee," 25; see also 223. In like vein, Black (*Rhetorical Questions*, 2) holds that a rhetorical question is an interrogative "whose form baits and whose substance hooks, a declaration that solicits assent to a claim by tickling the auditor's social obligation to respond to an interrogative."

9. See Gloria Italiano Anzilotti, "The Rhetorical Question as an Indirect Speech Device in English and Italian," *The Canadian Modern Language Review* 38 (1982) 297. Lénart J. de Regt ("Functions and Implications of Rhetorical Questions in the Book of Job," in *Biblical Hebrew and Discourse Linguistics*, edited by Robert D. Berger [Dallas: Summer Institute of Linguistics, 1994] 365) observes that in general, a yes-no rhetorical question transmits the bias of the questioner: "He does not consider both possible responses to be equally valid but implies or expects that only one of them is right."

in the affirmative usually implies a negative answer and a question in the negative usually implies an affirmative answer."[10] The *negative* rhetorical question, "Don't you want to grow up to be big and strong?" anticipates the *affirmative* answer, "Yes, I do," and the *affirmative* rhetorical question, "Do you want people to think we live in a pigsty?" anticipates the *negative* answer, "No, I don't."[11] Moreover, for the sake of emphasis, rhetorical questions can cluster themselves into a substantial series of interrogatives that highlight the speaker's prevailing concern. Also clustered questions characteristically command a higher level of attention from those who listen.[12]

In the Hebrew Bible, rhetorical questions are prominent in the poetry of Amos, Jeremiah, Deutero-Isaiah, Job, and the Psalms. Jeremiah is well served by these interrogatives as he engages his audience in disputation. In the oracles of Amos, where clan wisdom is reflected, rhetorical questions fulfill a didactic function. That is also the case for Job and his companions as they fervently assert what they believe to be true. As he affirms Yahweh's omniscience, sovereignty, and incomparability, Deutero-Isaiah deftly enlists these interrogatives to intensify the dramatic impact of his oratory as he seeks to gain the assent of his listeners.[13] To be sure, each unit of biblical poetry that hosts one or more rhetorical questions warrants scrutiny on its own terms.

10. Ilie, *What Else Can I Tell You?* 45.

11. These examples are drawn from Emily Norwood Pope, *Questions and Answers in English*, Janua Lingarum (The Hague: Mouton, 1976) 36. Similarly, in *A Glossary of Literary Terms*, 737, Abrams quips, "A common form of rhetorical question is one that won't take 'Yes' for an answer." Nevertheless, some rhetorical interrogatives generate positive answers. "Is the Pope a Catholic?" is a classic example.

12. Karl Beckson and Arthur Ganz refer to the cluster of rhetorical questions in the speech of Shylock in William Shakespeare's *Merchant of Venice*, in which he passionately justifies his conduct: "Hath not a Jew eyes? Hath not a Jew hands, organs, dimensions, senses, affections, passions? . . . If you prick us, do we not bleed? If you tickle us, do we not laugh? If you poison us, do we not die? and if you wrong us, shall we not revenge?" *Literary Terms: A Dictionary*, 3rd ed. (London: Deutsch, 1990) 232.

13. See J. Kenneth Kuntz, "The Form, Location, and Function of Rhetorical Questions in Deutero-Isaiah," in *Writing and Reading the Scroll of Isaiah: Studies of an Interpretive Tradition*, edited by Craig C. Broyles and Craig A. Evans, VTSup 70 (Leiden: Brill, 1997) 2:12–41.

The Presence of Rhetorical Questions in the Hebrew Psalter

Rhetorical interrogatives are an indigenous part of the fabric of discourse in the canonical Psalms. Of course, many questions in the Psalter belong to the genuine rather than rhetorical category. These include the query, "When will you comfort me?" (Ps 119:82b) and the information-seeking interrogative pertaining to temple admission, "Who shall ascend the mountain of Yahweh?" (Ps 24:3a). On the assumption that Psalm 53 should have no part in our calculation, since it virtually replicates Psalm 14, it appears that rhetorical questions are discernible in thirty three different canonical psalms.[14]

Neither the detection of psalmic rhetorical questions nor the demarcation of their boundaries is an exact science. With its disclosure, "What [mâ] are human beings that you are mindful of them, / mortals that you take note of them?" Psalm 8:5 [4] has spent time both on and off my list. Although this couplet may be construed as an exclamation,[15] this does not disqualify it as a rhetorical question, for on occasion such interrogatives facilitate exclamatory speech. When Psalm 118:6, enlisting the interrogative pronoun māh, is rendered, "Yahweh is on my side; I need not fear / what human beings can do to me,"[16] the psalmist is not thought to have posed a rhetorical question. Yet, when the Hebrew māh ya'ăśeh lî 'ādām is more felicitously rendered, "Yahweh is on my side, I have no fear, / what [māh] can human beings do to me?" its status as a rhetorical interrogative is upheld.

The task of discerning the boundaries of a rhetorical question in the Hebrew Psalter ordinarily poses no obstacle, but there are exceptions. I mention two. First, while Psalm 71:19 closes with the interroga-

---

14. The following is a complete listing of psalmic rhetorical questions: Pss 6:6b [5b]; 8:5 [4]; 12:5b [4b]; 14:4 (cf. 53:5); 18:32a [31a], 32b [31b]; 19:13a [12a]; 27:1b, 1d; 30:10ab [9ab], 10c [9c], 10d [9d]; 35:10b; 42:4d [3d], 11d [10d]; 44:21-22a [20-21a]; 49:6-7 [5-6]; 50:13, 16b-17; 56:5c [4c], 9c [8c], 12b [11b]; 58:2 [1]; 64:6c [5c]; 71:19c; 73:11a, 11b, 25a; 76:8bc [7bc]; 77:8 [7], 9a [8a], 9b [8b], 10a [9a], 10b [9b], 14b [13b]; 78:19b, 20cd; 88:11a [10a], 11b [10b], 12 [11], 13 [12]; 89:7-8 [6-7], 9ab [8ab], 49a [48a], 49b [48b]; 94:9a, 9b, 10, 16a, 16b, 20; 106:2; 113:5-6; 114:5-6; 118:6b; 120:3; 130:3; 137:4; 139:7a, 7b, 21a, 21b; 144:3.

15. Hans-Joachim Kraus, *Psalms 1–59*, trans. H. C. Oswald, CC (Minneapolis: Augsburg, 1988) 182.

16. Leslie C. Allen, *Psalms 101–150, Revised*, WBC 21 (Nashville: Nelson, 2002) 160.

tive *mî kāmôkā*, I accept *ʾĕlōhîm*, the divine name in the vocative which immediately precedes it, as part of the rhetorical question: "O God, who is like you?" Second, *māh lĕkā* sharply initiates a rhetorical question in Psalm 50:16b, in which God's word to covenant violators is, "Who are you [*māh lĕkā*] to recite my statutes?" But where does this interrogative cease? If it spans only verse 16bc, then the phrase, "and profess my covenant with your mouth," would be the only other component in the question. In terms of the poetic flow, however, it is more likely that the question only terminates at the end of verse 17. If so, this rhetorical interrogative in its totality may be rendered, "Who are you to recite my statutes, / and profess my covenant with your mouth, / while you hate discipline, / and you cast my words behind you?"

It is also instructive to note that due to the pervasive parallelistic structuring of poetic discourse in the Psalter, a rhetorical question that has as its function the denial of something may stand in a synonymous relationship with a negative statement. The latter is reinforced by the determination of the former not to take "Yes" for an answer. This is aptly illustrated by the suppliant's words to God in Psalm 6:6 [5]. They remind Yahweh, "For in death there is no remembering you; / in Sheol who [*mî*] can praise you?"

The Architecture of Psalmic Rhetorical Questions

Four considerations summon our attention in the remainder of this essay: (1) the architecture of psalmic rhetorical questions; (2) the diverse *Gattungen* in which they are embedded; (3) the issue of who is speaking and who is listening; and (4) the main functions that such questions are capable of fulfilling.

To inquire into the architecture of rhetorical questions in the Psalter is to consider their length, structure, and texture. Rhetorical interrogatives vary widely in length. While many entail a single couplet, some are easily twice as long (Pss 49:6–7 [5–6]; 50:16b–17; 89:7–8 [6–7]; 113:5–6; 114:5–6). A few rhetorical questions are very brief. These include the interrogatives that the psalmist's arrogant enemies voice in Psalms 12:5b [4b]; 42:4d [3d]; and 64:6c [5c], which read respectively, "Who is our master?" (*mî ʾādôn lānû*), "Where is your God?" (*ʾayyēh ʾĕlōheykā*), and "Who will see us?" (*mî yirʾeh lānû*).[17]

---

17. Following the Syriac and Jerome, read *lānû* for *lāmô*.

Moreover, an inspection of Psalms 30:10 [9]; 77:8–10 [7–9]; 88:11–13 [10–12]; and 94:9–10 reveals that psalmic rhetorical questions sometime emerge in clusters containing between three and five discrete entries. Like their non-biblical counterparts, such groupings more fully engage the addressee as a potential co-expresser of the speaker's point of view than is the case with the isolated rhetorical question.

Crafted by numerous psalmists, rhetorical questions strongly resemble genuine questions. In 15 instances, they are activated by the interrogative *hă* particle (Pss 30:10 [2x]; 50:13; 58:2; 77:8, 9, 10; 78:19, 20; 88:11, 12, 13; 94:9, 10, 20). Four of these passages (Pss 77:10; 78:20; 88:11; 94:9) yield a disjunctive interrogative construction involving use of the interrogative *hă* in the first colon plus the *'im* particle in the second, this being what is expected in the framing of double rhetorical questions in Hebrew.

In seven cases, rhetorical questions in the Psalms are initiated by an interrogative *hă* particle prefixed to the negative *lō'* particle (Pss 14:4; 44:22; 56:9; 94:9 [2x], 10; 139:21). In Psalm 58:2 the interrogative *hă* particle is prefixed to the adverb *'umnām* so that the question might commence, "*Do you really* decree what is just, O gods?" Moreover, rhetorical questions in Psalms 73:11b; 77:9b; and 88:12b all begin with the zero element. While this calls to mind the *initial* entry in the double rhetorical question well attested in Ugaritic,[18] the cola in these three verses constitute the *second* component in the double rhetorical question.

Psalmic rhetorical questions also contain their fair share of interrogative pronouns and adverbs. Of highest frequency is the animate interrogative pronoun *mî* ("who/whom") which occurs 21 times (Pss 6:6; 12:5; 18:32 [2x]; 19:13; 27:1 [2x]; 35:10; 64:6; 71:19; 73:25; 76:8; 77:14; 89:7, 9, 49; 94:16 [2x]; 106:2; 113:5; 130:3). For the sake of emphasis, in two cases (Pss 18:32; 89:7) the *mî* entry is prefaced by the deictic *kî* particle ("for, because"). Next in frequency is the variously vocalized inanimate interrogative pronoun *mah* ("what?"), which appears in ten instances (Pss 8:5; 30:10; 50:16; 56:5, 12; 114:5; 118:6; 120:3 [2x]; 144:3).

At three junctures, these two interrogative pronouns are linked by a *maqqeph* to a form of the suffixed preposition *lĕ*. Opening with *mî-lî*, Psalm 73:25a reads, "Whom have I in heaven but you?" Twice

---

18. See H. L. Ginsberg, *The Legend of King Keret*, BASORSup 2–3 (New Haven: American Schools of Oriental Research, 1946) 72.

we encounter the expression *mah lĕkā* in harshly worded texts. In one instance (Ps 50:16), the deity scolds the wicked in the covenant community asking, "Who are you [*mah lĕkā*] to recite my statutes?" In the second (Ps 114:5a), the hymnist poses a rhetorical question that initially taunts certain bodies of water that yielded to Yahweh's dynamic intervention, which ensured the successful passage of the Israelites from Egypt to Canaan: "Why was it [*mah lĕkā*], O sea, that you fled?" Finally, five other interrogatives require cursory mention: *'ayyēh* ("where?") in Psalm 42:4; *'ēk* ("how?") in Psalm 137:4; *'ēkâ* ("how?") in Psalm 73:11; *'ānâ* ("where?") in Psalm 139:7 (2x); and *lāmmâ* ("why?") in Psalm 49:6. Such variation of expression readily supports the assertion of Luis Alonso Schökel that in biblical Hebrew poetry, the rhetorical question is undeniably a "flexible literary device."[19]

Psalmic *Gattungen* Enlisting Rhetorical Questions

A wide range of psalmic *Gattungen* hosts rhetorical questions. They appear in a dozen Individual Laments (Pss 6; 14; 35; 42–43; 56; 64; 71; 77; 88; 120; 130; 139), six Communal Laments (Pss 12; 44; 58; 89:39–52 [38–51]; 94; 137), five Hymns (Pss 8; 89:2–19 [1–18]; 113; 114; and 76 as a Song of Zion), two Historical Psalms (Ps 78 yielding hymnic and wisdom features, and Ps 106 as a Communal Lament), two Royal Songs of Thanksgiving (Pss 18 and 144); and two Wisdom Psalms (Pss 49 and 73). Additionally, rhetorical questions appear in one instance each in five other *Gattungen*: a Torah Psalm (Ps 19); a Song of Trust (Ps 27:1–6); an Individual Song of Thanksgiving (Ps 30); a Covenant Renewal Liturgy (Ps 50); and a Thanksgiving Liturgy (Ps 118).[20]

19. Luis Alonso Schökel, *A Manual of Hebrew Poetics*, trans. Adrian Graffy, Subsidia Biblica 11 (Rome: Biblical Institute Press, 1988) 150.

20. This summary begs for qualifying comment. (1) Although Psalm 73 is intent on rendering thanks to God, its sapiential elements are of sufficient magnitude to warrant our accepting it as the product of a wisdom poet; see J. Kenneth Kuntz, "Wisdom Psalms and the Shaping of the Hebrew Psalter," in *For a Later Generation: The Transformation of Tradition in Israel, Early Judaism and Early Christianity*, edited by Randal A. Argall et al. (Harrisburg, PA: Trinity, 2000) 149. (2) Psalm 94 is a Communal Lament, but vv. 8–15 embody wisdom discourse. (3) Given its emphatic complaint about present tribulation, Psalm 120 better qualifies as an Individual Lament than as an Individual Song of Thanksgiving. (4) Whereas Psalm 139 is laced with hymnic and sapiential features, the suppliant's prayer for divine help against certain antagonists justifies our naming it an Individual Lament. (5) Psalm 144 hosts a plea for deliverance (vv. 5–8) characteristic

In light of their ubiquity in the Psalter and the urgency of their proclamations, it is not surprising that rhetorical interrogatives abound in Individual and Communal Laments. Their poets must have known that by raising poignant rhetorical questions, they were able to generate persuasive discourse that might move God to identify more fully with their own perspective.

Relevant verses in Psalms 8, 76, 89, 113, and 114 disclose that as ancient hymnists sought to celebrate Yahweh's being and interaction with the world in general, and with Israel in particular, they found rhetorical questions to be a promising artifice. At times these interrogatives as exclamatory utterance handsomely served the interests of hymnic rhetoric. Since they tend to "imply more than the face value of the words that make up the question,"[21] such questions were an effective vehicle in the framing of elevated and customarily terse hymnic speech. Whereas rhetorical questions surface in other psalmic *Gattungen*, they are most evident in lament and hymnic discourse.

Speakers and Addressees in Psalmic Rhetorical Questions

If Wilfred G. E. Watson is correct in his supposition that "the use of rhetorical questions (notably by wise men and the preaching prophets) had its origins in oral techniques of composition poetry,"[22] then the issue of who speaks and who listens is scarcely trivial. Although our psalmic texts provide rather few specifics about speakers and addressees, we are not left to grope in the dark.

Eight different situations involving speaker and addressee may be inferred from psalmic rhetorical interrogatives. First, they can disclose someone who speaks with himself or herself.[23] This is especially evident in Psalm 77, an Individual Lament. In verses 7 [6] and 11 [10] a pair

---

of psalmic laments, but its initial expression of gratitude for Yahweh's support and its affinities with Psalm 18 warrant its classification as a Royal Song of Thanksgiving.

21. Anzilotti, "The Rhetorical Question," 293.

22. Watson, *Classical Hebrew Poetry: A Guide to Its Techniques*, JSOTSup 26 (Sheffield: JSOT Press, 1984) 340.

23. Behind this sentence lies my assumption that in biblical times not every psalmist was necessarily a male. That said, in my endeavor to write uncomplicated, smooth-flowing prose, I shall enlist masculine rather than feminine pronouns when it becomes necessary to refer to the psalmist in the third person.

of couplets frames an entire cluster of rhetorical questions. The former yields the first-person disclosure, "I meditate in my heart in the night," and the latter begins, "I say, 'My sorrow is this . . .'" In the intervening verses stand five rhetorical questions that tumble from the psalmist's mouth:

> Will the Lord spurn [us] forever,
> and never again show favor?
> Has his steadfast love ceased forever?
> Are his promises at an end for all generations?
> Has God forgotten to be gracious?
> Has he in anger locked up his compassion? (8–10 [7–9])

Speaker and addressee are one in this graphic text that raises hard questions about Yahweh's love and fidelity. Possibly viewing himself as the representative of his people, the psalmist laments about the deplorable situation that overwhelms them. Fearing that God has abandoned them, the suppliant raises weighty questions that invite "Certainly not!" as the only acceptable answer. Consequently, in verse 12 [11] the psalmist suddenly embarks on hymnic discourse that yields its own rhetorical question in verse 14b [13b], "What god is as great as our God?" The psalmist handles his distress by calling to mind Yahweh's past saving deeds in behalf of his covenant people (vv. 12–14a [11–13a]). In framing a lengthy series of self-directed rhetorical interrogatives, the psalmist is not talking to God, but *about* God. He is both speaker and addressee.[24]

Second, some self-directed rhetorical questions in the Psalter are spoken by several persons speaking among themselves. In Psalm 73:11, within a poem rich in both sapiential and thanksgiving overtones, the wicked, whose prosperity is a monumental issue for the psalmist, are portrayed as scandalously impious persons who express themselves in a pair of rhetorical questions: "And they say, 'How can God know? / Is there knowledge in the Most High?'" In their dual role as speakers *and* addressees, the wicked voice interrogatives that exert greater dramatic impact than would a more conventional statement such as "God is ignorant about our ways." Of course, these questions are intended to invoke a negative conclusion in the mind of the beholder. The blind arrogance

---

24. Two of three rhetorical questions in Psalm 56, another Individual Lament, also show the suppliant engaged in self-directed speech (vv. 5c [4c], 12b [11b]).

of the self-reliant ungodly in believing that the deity will neither discern nor punish them for their malicious deeds is deftly conveyed.[25]

Ordinarily in the Psalter, rhetorical questions are spoken by someone other than the addressee. In our third configuration, the psalmist as the addressee hears a rhetorical question from his adversaries. In Psalm 42–43, an Individual Lament, the assaulted suppliant protests that his opponents regularly ridicule his reliance on the deity by asking, "Where is your God?" (42:4d [3d]). Complaining that "my tears have been my food / day and night" (42:4ab [3ab]), the psalmist depicts his adversaries as those who fling a rhetorical question that is designed to taunt him. Those speaking this question are not seeking information. Rather, as the reviling enemies of the suppliant, their posture toward him is one of derision. As the self-assured speakers of this rhetorical question, the psalmist's opponents deftly convey a propositional attitude of strong reproach.

A fourth configuration, in which the psalmist assumes the role of speaker and his adversaries the role of addressees, is the mirror image of the third. Psalm 58 offers a striking example. This Communal Lament opens with a rhetorical question in which the psalmist and his opponents are respectively speaker and addressees. By asking, "Do you really decree what is just, O gods, / do you judge mortals fairly?" (v. 2 [1]), the psalmist dramatically launches his mediation with a harsh indictment. One might argue that he is calling to account those gods of the nations who are responsible for the justice of humankind but actually support the violent on earth who undermine it. In light of Erhard S. Gerstenberger's comment that this rhetorical interrogative "calls some unidentifiable superiors to account,"[26] we may infer that this disclosure is a harsh invective against those in power who have been derelict in their responsibility to uphold justice. As one who identifies himself with the beleaguered righteous, the psalmist inflicts his rhetorical question against addressees who in their positions of power have sided with injustice.[27]

---

25. For other self-directed rhetorical questions involving several persons in the dual role of speakers and addressees, see Pss 12:5b [4b]; 64:6c [5c]; and 78:19–20.

26. Gerstenberger, *Psalms: Part I, with an Introduction to Cultic Poetry*, FOTL 14 (Grand Rapids: Eerdmans, 1988) 233.

27. For another rhetorical question belonging to this fourth category, see Ps 120:3.

Fifth, the Psalter hosts numerous texts in which the one who raises the rhetorical question is the psalmist and the addressee is God. Psalms 73 and 88 offer two splendid examples. In the former text, the psalmist professes faith in God's supportive presence by asking, "Whom have I in heaven but you?" (v. 25a). At once, this rhetorical question is reinforced by a declarative statement, "None besides you do I desire on earth" (v. 25b). Intending that the first member of this couplet be heard as a question but understood as a statement, the psalmist emphatically declares to his God that despite his having to cope in an outrageously unjust world, his confidence rests solely in God. In Psalm 88, an Individual Lament thick with dark overtones, the suppliant poses in the deity's hearing a compelling series of four rhetorical questions (vv. 11–13 [10–12]), the first of which asks, "Do you work wonders for the dead?" On the brink of death, he mounts the Sheol argument: should the psalmist die, he would be cut off from God's presence and incapable of praising God. In this dire condition, he turns to the efficacy of interrogative rhetoric to induce divine rescue.[28]

In the sixth configuration, the psalmist once more voices rhetorical questions in the hearing of others. But unlike the several cases in which he directs them to his adversaries and the many cases in which he directs them to God, now he voices them to an assembled body of worshipers. As a Song of Trust, Psalm 27 opens with a pair of couplets in which the first member offers an affirmation of faith, and the second a succinct rhetorical question. The initial statement, "Yahweh is my light and my salvation" (v. 1a), evokes the interrogative, "Whom shall I fear?" (v. 1b), and its successor, "Yahweh is the refuge of my life" (v. 1c), evokes the interrogative, "Of whom shall I be afraid?" (v. 1d). The psalmist's protracted confession of trust in the hearing of others spans nearly half of the poem (vv. 1–6). We may infer that he speaks as a temple functionary to the gathered congregation. Envisioning the obvious answer to his rhetorical inquiry to be "Nobody!" the psalmist invites his listeners to assume his propositional attitude as their own.[29]

---

28. Other instances of rhetorical interrogatives in which the psalmist is speaker and God the addressee include Pss 6:6 [5]; 8:5 [4]; 14:4; 19:13a [12a]; 30:10 [9]; 35:10b; 56:9c [8c]; 71:19c; 76:8bc [7bc]; 89:49 [48]; 94:20; 130:3; 139:7, 21; and 144:3.

29. For other examples of this sixth category, see Pss 18:32 [31]; 44:21–22a [20–21a]; 49:6–7 [5–6]; 89:7–9b [6–8b]; 94:9–10, 16; 106:2; 113:5–6; 118:6b; and 137:4.

Seventh, two rhetorical questions, both in Psalm 50, present God as speaker (through the mouth of a cultic prophet) and the misguided covenant people gathered for worship as addressees. The rhetorical interrogative in verse 13 criticizes their worship and its counterpart in verses 16b–17 criticizes their everyday conduct. Enlisting the verbs "to eat" ('kl) and "to drink" (šth) at the extremities of the chiasm, verse 13 yields a rhetorical question intent on correcting the people's misperception of ceremonial sacrifice: "Do I eat the flesh of bulls, / or drink the blood of goats?" This affirmative question just might evoke in the mind of the listeners, "Of course not!" God reproves the congregation that believed him to be a deity requiring food and drink to subsist.

Through artfully crafted language, this psalm instructs that sacrifice is not a mechanism for meeting divine emergency, but a venue for expressing human gratitude. The other rhetorical question in Psalm 50, which we have previously noted, opens, "Who are you to recite my statutes?" (v. 16b). Intent on inflicting rebuke, the deity asks in effect, "What gives you the right to mouth familiar covenant statutes when you are bent on rejecting the discipline they demand?" Both interrogatives place God's case against his people in sharp relief.

One other configuration requires mention. Psalm 114 contains a rhetorical question in which the psalmist and the world of nature respectively function as speaker and addressee. This hymn celebrates Yahweh's awe-inspiring interventions that made possible Israel's successful exodus from Egypt, trek through the wilderness, and crossing of the Jordan. The third of the four superbly balanced line pairs in this psalm yields one protracted interrogative: "Why was it, O sea, that you fled, / O Jordan, that you turned back, / O mountains, that you skipped like rams, / O hills, like lambs?" (vv. 5–6). The first two words of the Hebrew (mah lĕkā) might be rendered, "What was the matter?" Rather than questing for information, this interrogative dramatically rehearses formative moments in Israel's ancient past. Rich in vocatives as it advances toward its goal of vivid personified actualization, this rhetorical question serves as a foil for the final line pair (vv. 7–8) in which an answer *is* forthcoming, one that identifies Yahweh's august presence as the cause of nature's excessive consternation.

The Main Functions of Psalmic Rhetorical Questions

Finally, we shall focus on three main functions that rhetorical questions in the Psalms are capable of fulfilling.

Function One

First, *such interrogatives contribute to the demarcation of certain strophes in which they appear*. By serving as elements that either initiate various strophes or terminate them, rhetorical questions are helpful guideposts as we discern the movement of the poet's thought. Surely, James Muilenburg had this in mind when he observed that diverse rhetorical questions "appear in strategic collocations."[30]

While we cannot claim that biblical scholars have reached consensus in the strophic delineation of psalmic texts, a close reading of the material may give one license to advance a few reasonable suggestions. I would submit that in 13 instances (18:32–37 [31–36]; 44:21–23 [20–22]; 49:6–10 [5–9]; 50:16b–21; 58:2–3 [1–2]; 94:16–19, 20–23; 113:5–9; 120:3–4; 130:3–4; 137:4–6; 139:7–12; and 144:3–4), rhetorical questions may be perceived as the mechanism whereby specific strophes open. In eight other instances (6:5–6 [4–5]; 8:4–5 [3–4]; 12:2–5 [1–4]; 14:3–4; 42:2–4 [1–3]; 56:2–5 [1–4]; 78:17–20; and 89:47–49 [46–48]), strophes achieve closure through rhetorical questions.

Moreover, the Psalter yields two instances in which a strophe consists of nothing but rhetorical interrogative discourse. Forming a strophe of its own, Psalm 88:11–13 [10–12] presents a cluster of four rhetorical questions, which are addressed to Yahweh. This strophe is activated by the interrogative, "Do you work wonders for the dead?" (v. 11a [10a]), and is put to rest with the interrogative, "Are your wonders known in the darkness, / or your beneficent deeds in the land of oblivion?" (v. 13 [12]). In their totality, these questions sharply intensify the suppliant's plea for divine intervention that will rescue him from death's threshold. Rhetorical interrogatives therefore distinguish this strophe from its immediate neighbors (vv. 7–10 [6–9] and 14–19 [13–18]). By contrast, Psalm 114:5–6 consists of solely one rhetorical question that is rich in particulars as it moves across two couplets. With ironic intent,[31] it opens

30. James Muilenburg, "Form Criticism and Beyond," *JBL* 88 (1969) 16.
31. In agreement with Watson, *Classical Hebrew Poetry*, 342.

with a "Why was it?" (*mah lĕkā*) query that is addressed to four entities: the sea, the Jordan, mountains, and hills; all of which were convulsed by Yahweh's intervention on behalf of his people during the Exodus.

In order to reflect more fully on this demarcating function of psalmic rhetorical questions, let us turn to the interrogatives in Psalms 18:32 [31] and 12:5 [4], which respectively open and terminate the strophes in which they appear. As a lengthy poem which conveys a strong note of narrativity, Psalm 18 is an integrated whole richly celebrating what Yahweh has wrought on behalf of his chosen and beleaguered king. That said, this Royal Song of Thanksgiving falls into two halves, verses 2–31 [1–30] and 32–51 [31–50]), each portraying the king's deliverance. Initiating the second half is a strophe (vv. 32–37 [31–36]) describing how God prepared the king for imminent warfare. It opens in a determined manner with its emphatic *kî* particle and pair of rhetorical questions. Both are activated by the animate interrogative pronoun *mî* ("who?"): "For who is God apart from Yahweh? / and who is a rock except our God?" (v. 32 [31]). Both questions glorify the deity by emphasizing his incomparability.

As a "rock" (*sûr*), Yahweh alone is fully able to ensure the king's victory over his enemies. In this strophe, the expression of God's personal concern in equipping his special servant for battle borders on the extravagant. The psalmist crafts a strophe which maintains its focus on Yahweh throughout. As a significant step in that direction, he chooses a rhetorical interrogative boldly opening with the phrase, "For who is God?" (*kî mî 'ĕlôah*). Rhetorical questions in verse 32 [31] deftly initiate a new strophe as Psalm 18 tells its story about Yahweh's gracious way with the king.

The rhetorical question in Psalm 12, a relatively terse Communal Lament, brings closure to its opening strophe (vv. 2–5 [1–4]) that has been set in motion by a paired imperative and vocative, "Help, O Yahweh" (*hôšî'â yhwh*). The strophe which follows (vv. 6–7 [5–6]) is initiated by what is presumably a divine oracle (v. 6 [5]) spoken by a temple functionary. As this psalm opens, the suppliant voices his cry for help, complaining that the faithful seem to have disappeared from the land and that the wicked are rampant. Much of the first strophe highlights the insidious speech of enemy hypocrites whose flattering words lack substance. In his imprecation (vv. 4–5 [3–4]), the psalmist invokes Yahweh to terminate their pernicious use of language. He hopes for the annihilation of "those who say, 'By our tongues we shall prevail; / our lips are our own—who is our master?'" (v. 5 [4]). Mention of the overweening pride of the enemy that is masterfully conveyed by this succinct self-directed rhetorical question brings decisive closure to this strophe. It lends support to Muilenburg's assertion that "questions often provide the climactic line of the strophe."[32] The couplet in verse 5 [4], which depicts the wicked flaunting the power of their own "tongues" and "lips," swiftly reaches a crescendo in its concluding rhetorical interrogative which aptly captures their conviction that they look to no one, not even God, as their master.

Function Two

We turn to a second function. Often presenting themselves as exclamatory utterance that is either for or against something, *rhetorical questions in the Psalms show a proclivity to intensify the discourse in which they appear.* They raise the dramatic and emotional dimensions of the text to a yet higher level. This utilization of rhetorical questions is discernible in diverse contexts that may be categorized under four rubrics: disclosures that convey certain propositional attitudes of the psalmist toward the deity; portrayals of wicked enemies whose behavior threatens the existence of the psalmist; depictions of the psalmist's response toward his enemies; and assertions that impart Yahweh's rebuke of his errant covenant people.

First, rhetorical questions that notably unmask certain propositional attitudes of the psalmist toward God turn on several distinct issues. They candidly convey his confidence that the deity will sustain him during moments of danger. They express his desire to be closely affiliated with God's person and purpose. And they impart his conviction that God stands ready to forgive those who fear him.

That the psalmist is poised to confess his trust in a God to whom he may turn for help in times of acute adversity is obvious in the rhetorical questions set forth in Psalms 27:1; 118:6b; and 56:5c [4c]. Two succinct interrogatives juxtaposed in the parallelism of Psalm 27:1, "whom shall I fear?" and "of whom shall I be afraid?," eloquently convey the poet's

---

32. Muilenburg, "Form Criticism and Beyond," 16.

reliance on God at the outset of this Song of Trust. His declarations in the same verse that "Yahweh is my light and my salvation" and "Yahweh is the refuge of my life" are truly reinforced by this pair of rhetorical questions. In Psalm 118 the poet's statement, "Yahweh is on my side, I have no fear" (v. 6a), is enhanced by the rhetorical question, "What can human beings do to me?" (v. 6b) that completes the couplet. In Psalm 56 the self-directed rhetorical question, "What can flesh [*bāśār*] do to me?" (v. 5c [4c]), as well as its mate, "What can human beings ['*ādām*] do to me?" (v. 12b [11b]) poignantly portray the psalmist's tenacious trust in the word and deed of his saving God.

Psalms 73 and 139 host rhetorical questions that decisively convey the psalmist's wish that he be closely allied with God's person and purpose. Whereas he is perturbed by the prosperity of the wicked, the former text finds the psalmist asking, "Whom have I in heaven but you," and affirming, "None beside you do I desire on earth," to complete the couplet (v. 25). The rhetorical question in verse 25a not only serves as a poignant expression of his confidence in God's presence that he fervently seeks, but it paves the way for his emphatic declaration, "God is the rock of my heart and my portion forever" (v. 26b).

Psalm 139 yields a pair of rhetorical interrogatives that establish the psalmist's desire to be intimately affiliated with the deity's moral purpose. In his address to God, he asks, "Do I not hate those who hate you, O Yahweh? / And those who rise up against you do I not loathe?" (v. 21). The wicked are of profound concern to this poet (v. 19). Still, no personal threat seems to motivate his thinking. Rather, the wicked are perceived as God's own enemies whose conduct betrays their hostility to his purpose. The rhetorical interrogatives in verse 21 poignantly announce the psalmist's loyalty to his God. Embodying a value assessment that God's enemies are in fact his enemies, he voices his fervent desire to identify closely with the divine agenda.

Moreover, the psalmist's propositional attitude toward the deity is forthrightly unmasked by the rhetorical question of Psalm 130. In asking, "If you were to keep account of iniquities, O Yah(weh), / Lord, who could stand?" (v. 3), the psalmist gives poignant utterance to his personal insight that the omniscient deity is prepared to forgive the contrite who pursue a god-fearing existence. The rhetorical question in this Individual Lament superbly conveys the psalmist's assumption that human beings are in no position to celebrate their own righteousness. Yet, the fact that humanity *does* stand testifies to God's readiness to forgive the humble who show him reverence.

Second, several rhetorical questions focused on the psalmist's enemies become emphatic as they depict the behavior of the wicked who threaten his welfare. Two Individual Laments (Pss 42–43 and 64) and one Wisdom Psalm (Ps 73) yield the evidence. In Psalm 42–43 reviling enemies are portrayed as those who inflict upon the sorrowful, suffering supplicant the taunting question, "Where is your God?" (42:4d [3d]). Their ridicule of his reliance on Yahweh is captured there and in 42:11d [10d] where this interrogative is repeated. In Psalm 64 the scheming of the psalmist's self-assured enemies is intensified by their rhetorical inquiry to one another, "Who will see us?" (v. 6c [5c]). Similarly, in Psalm 73 the raw defiance of the psalmist's opponents who contend that God knows not their machinations is dramatically communicated through the medium of paired rhetorical questions. The psalmist reports, "Then they say, 'How can God know? / Is there knowledge with the Most High?'" (v. 11).

Third, the psalmist's response to his enemies in terms of what he says either *to* or *about* them is graphically denoted by rhetorical interrogatives. In Psalm 120, an Individual Lament, the question that is directed to the "deceitful tongue" (v. 3) forcefully expresses the psalmist's disdain for the slanderous speech of hostile opponents who assail him. In Psalm 94, a Communal Lament, the psalmist resorts to a poignant and persuasive rhetorical question as he brings to God's attention the problem which vicious enemies pose for him and like-minded persons in his community. In asking, "Can the seat of injustice be allied with you, / that contrives mischief by statute?" (v. 20), the psalmist, as representative of the faithful, openly complains to Yahweh about the wicked whose oppressive tactics jeopardize communal well-being. With the expectation that the answer, "Of course not!" will be foremost in the divine mind, this interrogative expresses the psalmist's confidence that Yahweh will honor the needs of retributive justice.

Finally, rhetorical questions emphatically portray the way in which God sets about admonishing his errant covenant people. This is evident in the two interrogatives in Psalm 50 that are voiced by a cultic prophet to assembled worshipers. We need not rehearse what has already been stated about the rhetorical questions that God speaks in the hearing of his misguided (v. 13) and deviant (vv. 16–17) people. Suffice it to say that the deity is keen to correct their flawed perception of cultic sacrifice that is grounded in what Kraus labels "naïve, anthropomorphic concepts."[33] Through this literary device, God's rebuke of the blatant hypocrisy of the wicked is brilliantly expressed. In sum, diverse situations and issues in the Hebrew Psalter are portrayed in a decidedly more compelling manner than would otherwise have been possible if rhetorical questions had not entered the scene.

Function Three

A third main function of rhetorical interrogatives in the Psalms is informed by thematic concerns. With some regularity, *these questions serve to focus Yahweh's mind on dire human need and humanity's mind on Yahweh's incomparability*. As such, they are the vehicles of serious theological statement.

No psalmic rhetorical questions outdistance those in Psalms 6:6b [5b]; 30:10 [9]; and 88:11–13 [10–12] in their ability to call God's attention to extreme human plight. With the first text alluding to Sheol, the second to the Pit, and the third to the grave, they all portray the supplicant on the brink of death. When precarious human existence succumbs to forces of such magnitude that they threaten to extinguish not only life itself but any continuing communication with Yahweh, the psalmic quest for deliverance escalates to its greatest intensity.

Psalm 6 yields a couplet fusing a sobering negative statement with an arresting rhetorical question. The supplicant pleads, "For in death there is no remembering you [*zikrekā*]; / in Sheol who can praise you?" (v. 6 [5]). Yahweh is urged to prevent his untimely entry into Sheol. That region distances itself from any interaction with Yahweh. James L. Mays cogently asserts that "the point in the appeal is not so much that God loses the praise of the psalmist but that the psalmist loses God."[34] Thus, intended to motivate Yahweh to bar the supplicant's sinking into that sphere of non-life where the deity is unmistakably absent, this rhetorical interrogative is a poignant expression of human need.

---

33. Hans-Joachim Kraus, *Theology of the Psalms*, trans. Keith Crim, CC (Minneapolis: Augsburg, 1986) 96.

34. James L. Mays, *Psalms*, IBC, (Louisville: Westminster John Knox, 1994) 61.

As an Individual Song of Thanksgiving, Psalm 30 rehearses Yahweh's rescue of the psalmist from severe distress. He admits that he had been thrust from a position of security, in which he was too inclined toward self-satisfaction (v. 7 [6]), to one of extreme adversity in which his foes delighted (v. 2b [1b]). Earnestly seeking divine deliverance, the suppliant directed a triad of rhetorical questions to Yahweh: "What gain is there from my lifeblood, / from my going down to the Pit? // Will the dust praise you? / Will it declare your faithfulness?" (v. 10 [9]). The suppliant's argument resembles that advanced in Psalm 6. Should the psalmist die, the praise that is due God will be aborted. To descend into the "Pit" (*šaḥat*) is to enter a sphere in which contact with God is impossible and no praise of God conceivable. That the final strophe of the psalm opens with the joyful declaration, "You have turned my mourning into dancing" (v. 12a [11a]) denotes that these rhetorical interrogatives served their purpose. Yahweh did intervene, making possible the psalmist's Song of Thanksgiving.

With its cluster of four rhetorical questions forming a discrete strophe, Psalm 88 is especially fervent in its appeal for God's deliverance. Mortally ill, the psalmist has been forsaken by friends (v. 9 [8]) and God alike (v. 15 [14]). Courageously he makes his case to the deity:

> Do you work wonders for the dead?
> Do the shades rise to praise you?
> Is your steadfast love recounted in the grave,
> or your faithfulness in the deadly abode?
> Are your wonders known in the darkness,
> or your beneficent deeds in the land of oblivion? (vv. 11–13
> [10–12]

Already on the edge of Sheol, the psalmist pleads for Yahweh's swift intervention. He is keen to distance himself from this realm that knows nothing of God's wondrous deeds and is incapable of proclaiming his praise. As this strophe terminates, another opens with the psalmist declaring; "But I cry out to you, O Yahweh" (v. 14a [13a]). The suppliant renews his plea to be delivered from Sheol's clutches. Tellingly, this extraordinary psalm offers no clue that his plea was in fact heard. Psalm 88 joins Psalms 6 and 30 in depicting suppliants, who in their dread of an early check-in option into the nether world, enlist rhetorical questions to activate imminent divine intervention.

Function Four

Rhetorical interrogatives in the Psalms often highlight another crucial theme, *God's incomparability.* These appear in Psalms 18:32 [31];
35:10b; 71:19c; 77:14b [13b]; 89:7–9b [6–8b]; and 113:5.6. We shall first
consider two instances in which Yahweh's incomparability is less fully
obvious before taking up the four that are more explicit.

At a strategic collocation, Royal Psalm 18 enlists a pair of rhetorical questions: "For who is God apart from Yahweh? / and who is a rock
except our God?" (v. 32 [31]). Yahweh is affirmed as the sole agent that
is fully able to ensure the king's triumph over his enemies. Yahweh alone
turns the king's hope for victory into reality. Labuschagne submits that
"without being hailed explicitly as the incomparable One, His [Yahweh's]
incomparable position is manifested throughout the Psalm."[35] Then in
Psalm 77, an Individual Lament, a rhetorical query forges a comparison
implying the incomparability of Israel's God. Framed as statement and
question, a couplet in verse 14 [13] affirms God's nature: "O God, your
way is holy. / What god is as great as our God?" While an entire cluster
of rhetorical questions in verses 8–10 [7–9] finds the sorrowful psalmist
coping with adversity, one rhetorical question in verse 14b [13b] finds
him hopeful that a deity, whose past deeds on Israel's behalf have been
extraordinary (v. 12 [11]), will deliver him, and others in whose name he
speaks, from adversity. Acclaiming the excellence of his God, this interrogative presents the psalmist ruminating about Yahweh's uniqueness.

Four psalmic rhetorical questions *explicitly* affirm Yahweh's incomparability. Once the suppliant in Psalm 35 has petitioned God to
render his enemies powerless (vv. 1–8), he looks ahead to that moment
when, having been rescued, he can voice thankful praise (vv. 9–10). As
he expresses confidence in his imminent rescue, not only does he affirm
God as the champion of the weak whom the mighty victimize (v. 10cd),
but he also extols God's incomparability: "O Yahweh, who is like you
[*mî kāmôkā*]?" (v. 10b).

The rhetorical interrogative in Psalm 71 conveys the suppliant's
certainty that God, to whom he has voiced his pleas for help, will deliver him from the adversity that persecution, physical weakness, and
old age have brought upon him (vv. 4, 9, 18). Having petitioned Yahweh
to be his "rock" and "fortress" (v. 3), the psalmist in due course voices

---

35. Labuschagne, *Incomparability*, 117.

his resolve to extol his God as the author of "just deeds" (v. 15a), "acts of deliverance" (v. 15b), and "mighty works" (v. 16a). A climax is reached in verse 19bc when the suppliant jubilantly declares, "You who have done great things, / O God, who is like you [*mî kāmôkā*]." Yahweh's saving work is highlighted as that which discloses his incomparability and is celebrated through the persuasive force of a rhetorical question.

As two hymnic texts that utilize rhetorical questions to proclaim Yahweh's incomparability, Psalms 89 and 113 differ in the extensiveness of their discourse. Whereas Psalm 113 yields one rhetorical question spanning two terse lines (vv. 5–6), Psalm 89 yields a pair of rhetorical questions that fill two lengthy lines plus a portion of a third (vv. 7–9a [6–8a]). Once its opening strophe in Psalm 113, inviting the congregation to sing Yahweh's praise, has run its course (vv. 1–4), a rhetorical question inaugurates the other strophe that brings this rather short hymn to rest.

Assuming that his auditors will infer the answer to be "No one!" the psalmist asks: "Who is like Yahweh our God, / who is enthroned on high, // who looks far down / on the heavens and the earth?" (vv. 5–6). Two factors support this hymnist's claim about Yahweh's uniqueness. He is exalted in glory "above the heavens" (v. 4b) and in raising "the needy from the dust" (v. 7a) he manifests compassion. Convinced that the coexistence of divine majesty and mercy establish Yahweh's incomparability, the psalmist enlists a rhetorical interrogative in order to intensify hymnic speech.

Psalm 89 opens with a hymnic unit (vv. 2–19 [1–18]) that hosts two consecutive rhetorical questions that proclaim Yahweh's singularity. The first is indeed lengthy:

> For who in the skies can be likened [*ya'ărōk*] to Yahweh,
> Can resemble [*yidmeh*] Yahweh among the sons of God,
> A God dreaded in the council of the holy ones,
> Great and awesome above all that are around him?" (vv. 7–8 [6–7])

The second reads,

> O Yahweh, God of hosts,
> who is mighty like you [*mî kāmôkā*], O Yahweh?" (v. 9ab [8ab])

Jointly these interrogatives richly proclaim the uniqueness of the God whom the psalmist celebrates. Through this type of rhetorical question voiced by ancient Israelite psalmists and by the like-minded Deutero-Isaiah,[36] Yahweh's incomparability achieved noble expression. This artifice proved extraordinary in endorsing a monotheistic faith. Perhaps it is here that we encounter the biblical rhetorical question at its best.

36. See especially Isa 40:18, 25; 44:6–8; and 46:5.

10

Proselytes and God's Name in the Septuagint

James LaGrand

IN THE SIXTEENTH-CENTURY RENAISSANCE AND REFORMATION, THE idea of *Hebraica Veritas* energized and reshaped biblical studies and Christian worship. Careful attention to the Hebrew text of the Bible, and reflection on the Hebrew "name of the LORD"[1] have reshaped and expanded Biblical Studies, as especially indicated with the appearance of Mogens Müller's, *The First Bible of the Church: A Plea for the Septuagint* (1996).[2]

The provocative title of Professor Müller's book is a reminder that the very existence of an ancient Greek translation of the Hebrew Bible raises radical questions for biblical studies. Some of these questions have been brought to everyone's attention recently by publications such as Dan Brown's 2003 mystery, *The Da Vinci Code*, and *National Geographic*'s ancient, but newly discovered and translated, "Gospel of Judas" (2006). The *Book of Mormon* is not a new publication, but for social and political reasons it, too, has become newly prominent. So it is that after having lain dormant for decades, the Jewish and Christian (Orthodox, Catholic, and Protestant) understanding of canon is suddenly a hot-button issue.

"Canon" has also become a technical term in university departments besides biblical studies, but it is mainly the older, theological, use of the term that concerns us. One fundamental idea determining the

---

1. David J. A. Clines, "Yahweh and the God of Christian Theology," *Theology* 83 (1980) 323–30.

2. Müller, *The First Bible of the Church: A Plea for the Septuagint*, JSOTSup 206 (Sheffield: Sheffield Academic, 1996).

biblical canon is identified in the title of a 1951 essay by Pierre Benoit: "The Inspiration of the Septuagint."[3] God can be revealed through inspired translators, as well as through the inspired prophets and sages who wrote the original Hebrew text of the Bible. Professor Müller emphasizes this idea from various Jewish and Christian perspectives in *The First Bible of the Church.*

Before the Maccabees

Recognizing the story in the "Letter to Aristeas" as fiction, we can accept as fact, nevertheless, that the Torah was translated in Alexandria in the third century BCE. More specifically, we also accept John Wevers' judgment that "Genesis . . . was the first attempt by the Alexandrians to translate parts of the Torah."[4] The date of the translated Pentateuch relative to other texts that have become part of the expanded Septuagint canon is important, especially for tracing the development of the word and the emerging concept *proselutos*. Also important, but easily disregarded, is the relative dating of the Septuagint translation (third century BCE) and the fixed consonantal Hebrew text (first century CE).[5]

Before the translation of the first five books of the Bible, the Greek word *proselutos* was not frequently used. In classical Greek literature there is no extant example listed in the *Thesaurus Linguae Greacae* (*TLG*) before 200 BCE, except in the Septuagint, where the word is used very many times, especially in the Pentateuch. The Septuagint, it seems, set the stage for the classical meaning ("one that has arrived at a place, stranger, sojourner," Liddell-Scott-Jones). It is also in the Septuagint that the word underwent a transformation. A new, secondary meaning was established and is recorded in LSJ: "one who has come over to Judaism, convert, proselyte." This secondary meaning of the word, once established, became dominant and has been stable for more than 2,000 years in Greek, Latin, English and other successor languages.[6]

3. Benoit, *Jesus and the Gospel*, trans. Benet Weatherhead (London: Darton, Longman & Todd, 1961) 1:1–10.

4. J. Wevers, *Notes on the Greek Text of Genesis*, Septuagint and Cognate Studies 35 (Atlanta: Scholars, 1993) ix.

5. "The date of the 'Synod of Jabnah' (90 C.E.) is conventionally given as that from which the form of the consonantal text can be regarded as fixed." E. J. Revell, "Masoretic Text," in *ABD*, 4:597–601.

6. See the standard dictionaries including Liddell-Scott-Jones, E. A. Sophocles, Lampe, Bauer (*DBAG*), A. Souter's *A Glossary of Later Latin*, *The Middle English*

Since no two words in different languages have exactly the same meaning or exactly the same semantic range, it is not necessarily a linguistic virtue to translate a Hebrew word with the same Greek word every time. It is notable, however, that in Exodus, Leviticus, Numbers, and Deuteronomy one Hebrew word (גֵּר) is translated seventy times as προσήλυτος. For the modern reader and translator of the Septuagint it is difficult to avoid simply reading, proselyte, but such an instinctive short-cut gives a false sense of the original text and of the then-current state of play in Greek. We know that etymology often gives false leads to current meaning; so, too, can knowledge of future meanings. The still-future meaning of the Greek word seems to have begun its definitive development in the Septuagint. The fact that προσήλυτος does not appear at all in Genesis may indicate just when the word was coined: after the translators of Genesis completed their work.[7]

Paul Stuehrenberg suggests that the translation of Greek προσή λυτος for the Hebrew גֵּר was made in the Septuagint only "where the context suggested a religious meaning,"[8] but this test does not seem to explain the absence of the word in Genesis 15:13 where, after the telling of Abraham's encounter with Melchizedek, God speaks to Abraham in a dream and tells him that his offspring will be *aliens* in the land. Similarly, after the death of Sarah, Abraham emphasizes his state in Genesis 23:4 with two Greek words where προσήλυτος in its then-current meaning would have served for one or both. Later rabbis often noted the link between Abraham and proselytes. Indeed, Philo of Alexandria, for whom the Septuagint was ancient holy writ, considered Abraham "the standard of nobility for all proselytes."[9]

Dictionary, and the *OED*. Karl Georg Kuhn's article Proselyte in *TDNT* 6 attempts to trace the concept or "technical term" (tt) from the Hebrew word rg.

7. The one early example of the word cited in *DBAG* "(the word is found in Apollon. Rhod. 1, 834 [μετοίκους καὶ προσηλύτους]" appears to be a reference, not to *Argonautica* but to a commentary two hundred years later. (See Kuhn's identification of the error in an early edition of Bauer, in *TDNT*, 6:728 n. 2.) For the first meaning in the LXX see *A Greek –English Lexicon of the Septuagint*, ed. J. Lust, E. Eynnikel, K. Haupie (Stuttgart: Deutsche Bibelgesellshaft, 1996), and *A Greek-English Lexicon* of *the Septuagint Chiefly of the Pentateuch and the Twelve Prophets*. T. Muraoka (Louvain: Peters, 2002).

8. Paul F. Stuehrenberg, "Proselyte," in *ABD*, 5:503.

9. Samuel Sandmel, *Philo of Alexandria* (New York: Oxford, 1979) 72.

The Hebrew word for resident alien or immigrant (גֵּר) certainly refers to Abraham in significant theological situations, so, as already suggested, it seems best to explain the absence of the Greek word προσήλυτος from the Septuagint Genesis simply in terms of date of translation. In the other four books of the Torah, each appearance of the then-new Greek word seems to be a lightening rod for high-powered theological meaning. The list of Scripture passages under προσήλυτος in the Hatch-Redpath concordance is itself a remarkable theological commentary on immigration in ancient Israel.

The very first appearance of the term προσήλυτος in the Septuagint is paradigmatic, giving directions for the reception of immigrants to participation in "the Passover of the Lord" (Exod 12:48). As though to emphasize the *coming in*, the verb virtually spells out the noun, immigrant. Since this passage follows closely on the description of Israel being formed from "a great mixed multitude" (Exod 12:38) it seems no exaggeration to say that the Greek translators characterized the people of God as "a nation of immigrants." To be sure, a distinction is made between resident aliens (or immigrants), on the one side, and wayfarers and temporary workers, on the other (Exod 12:45), but, for those who had *come in*, circumcision was a guarantee of equal treatment under the law (Exod 12:49).

The pointed reference to immigrants in the Sabbath commandment of the Decalogue reaffirms the constitutional standing of resident aliens in Israel (Exod 20:10; see also Deut 5:12–15). Again, in Exodus 22:21, the people of Israel are reminded that they had been aliens in Egypt and so should identify with aliens joining them. Finally, in Exodus 23:9, identification with immigrants is projected into the future with provisions for a Sabbath of years.

Leviticus, which might appear to be the most exclusive writing in the Bible, has very many references to resident aliens, beginning with direction for their inclusion in the celebration of the Day of Atonement (Lev 16:29). A theme already noted in Exodus, which is characteristic of Leviticus, is the equal application of the law of God to native Israelite and immigrant (Lev 18:26). Also repeated with some variation is the emphasis on coming in with or joining (προσγενόμενος) God's people. Perhaps the most important text (and translation) referring to those coming in or joining Israel is Leviticus 19:34. According to Samuel

Sandmel, it is this text ("You shall love the immigrant as yourself") that led Philo to the conviction that "proselytes possess equal rank with the native-born."[10]

Of the many uses of the word προσήλυτος in Leviticus, two should be noted for further reference to the mission of the Septuagint: "naming the name of the Lord" as a capital offence with emphasis on equal judgment to the native-born or immigrant (Lev 24:16–22) and the projection of Jubilee (Lev 25:23, 35, 47).

The emphasis in Numbers on themes already noted in Exodus and Leviticus marks these themes as more notable, not less. Numbers 9:14 gives direction for keeping "the Passover of the Lord" according to "one law." Unity in the *synagogue of the Lord* for the newcomer and the established member of the congregation is insisted upon (Num 15:13–14). So again, regarding atonement for unintended sin, there is the same procedure for immigrants and for established children of Israel (Num 15:28–29). As for blatant, intentional sin, the newcomer is treated just as harshly as the established member (Num 15:30–31). What is said specifically of the red heifer ceremony, that it is an immutable or eternal law (Num 9:10), indicates that the translators did not see the references to immigrants or "those coming in to join Israel," as a temporary phenomenon associated only with the time of Israel's preparation for entering the promised land after the Exodus.

Although the translators of Numbers faithfully carried forward the celebration of the individualistic disciplinary violence of Phinehas in Numbers 25 (esp. vv. 7–8), a later chapter also documents the equal access to "a place of refuge" guaranteed for the children of Israel and for immigrants, and even for temporary residents, guilty of capital crime of unintentional manslaughter.

When we survey the last of the five books of the Torah, it seems that the use of the word προσήλυτος in Deuteronomy covers much of the same territory as in Exodus, Leviticus, and Numbers, but the style of the narrative seems subtly changed. Whether because of the nature of the original Hebrew text or the understanding of the Septuagint translators, the term προσήλυτος seems closer to the stranger of the King James translation (or to the second meaning of LSJ) than to the immigrant inside Israel who can claim equal rights at law. Nevertheless, the

10. Ibid., 107.

first appearance of the immigrant or stranger in Deuteronomy (1:16) is reminiscent of Leviticus 17:8–9, 10, suggesting that the dispute between brothers is at once complicated and clarified by adding a resident alien to the mix.

Deuteronomy 5:12–15 (following the *Shema'* in 5:4–6) has already been noted here in conjunction with Exodus 20:8–12. Although the text of the Sabbath commandment is remarkably varied in Exodus and Deuteronomy, we should note that the προσήλυτος "who lives next door" is central to both forms. Without asking which form is older, we should observe that both texts (in both the LXX and MT) refer to Egypt as "the house of slavery" in the prologue, but only Deuteronomy demands that the slave-master in Israel identify with his slaves (Deut 5:15). Perhaps an unintended consequence of the Deuteronomy text and the Septuagint translation is that "the immigrant who sojourns with you" is too easily assumed to be a servant boy or maid. This stereotype is clearly defined in a verbal overflow of inclusiveness where "all" standing before the Lord includes the immigrant or resident alien: everyone "from your hewer of wood to your drawer of water" (Deut 29:10–15).

Despite the stunning condescension in that verse near the end of the book, the inclusive language stakes out serious claims for social justice, as in Deuteronomy 10:13, where immigrants are classed with orphans and widows; and Israel is reminded that they were immigrants in Egypt. Levites are added to the list of those subject to deprivation (14:29), and sharp business practices are condemned: holding back wages of the immigrants, and other forms of bullying by established employers with the power to gain additional marginal advantages for themselves in the marketplace (24:14, 17, 19; 27:19).

Such Israelites deserve the reversals with which their imaginations terrify them: "the immigrants are going to take everything so that they will be very high and you will be very low" (Deut 28:43).

Deuteronomy began with Moses addressing "all Israel" (Deut 1:1) and these words appear again, notably in 31:12 and as the last words in the book: παντὸς Ἰσραηλ (Deut 34:12). Those who had entered in seem to have become familiar strangers. As proselytes, in the new, second meaning recorded in LSJ, there is some indication that they are always seeking entry, never fully accepted. The vision projected by the Septuagint is clear, however, whether or not προσήλυτος had become a defined concept by the time the Septuagint Deuteronomy was complete. The fundamental position was already declared in Leviticus 19.34 and is repeated in Deuteronomy 10:19: "Love the immigrant!" (ἀγαπήσετε τὸν προσήλυτον).

Turning from the sentences and paragraphs that incorporate the then-new Greek word προσήλυτος to the word itself, we should recognize that the history of words and concepts is often mysterious and sometimes involves irony and contradictions. No linguistic transition is more remarkable than the transformation of "the Hittites, the Girgashites, the Amorites, the Canaanites, the Perizzites, the Hivites and the Jebusites" (Deut 7:1 NRSV) into children of Israel.

How are the heathen transformed into God's people?[11] That question has been answered in very many ways in different times. In our own time, the Septuagint can provide clues in the development of the word προσήλυτος. The first thing to notice is that the Septuagint translation of the Torah was from before the common era, not only before Bar Kokhba's revolt against the Romans in 135 CE and before the earlier revolt of 66–74 CE, but also before the Maccabean revolt of 168 BCE. The translation followed, we might even say it was a consequence of, Alexander's spectacular conquest. Also an important clue is the time of the narratives' setting when, to use W. F. Albright's description, "Mosaic Yahwehism was a missionary religion, still in its first and most active phase."[12]

Hans-Joachim Schoeps addresses "the piety of the Septuagint" and especially what he understands to be "the missionary purpose of the LXX," in his book, *Paul: The Theology of the Apostle in the Light of Jewish Religious History*. "Propaganda and the mission to the Gentiles appears in the LXX as a specific task incumbent on Jewish piety."[13] Accordingly, in Schoeps' analysis, many crucial texts such as Isaiah 54:14 "are made to yield such a meaning." Schoeps' translation of *proselutoi* is reasonable in this Greek Isaiah which is later than Torah translations: "Proselytes will join themselves unto you for my sake, will seek refuge with you."

11. See Caleb and Ruth in James LaGrand, *The Earliest Christian Mission to 'All Nations' in the Light of Matthew's Gospel* (Grand Rapids: Eerdmans, 1999) 59–62.

12. W. F. Albright, *Archeology and the Religion of Israel* (Baltimore: Johns Hopkins University Press, 1953 [1942]) 99.

13. Hans Joachim Schoeps, *Paul: The Theology of the Apostle in Light of Jewish Religious History*, trans. Harold Knight (Philadelphia: Westminster, 1961) 28, "mission to the Gentiles" is the ET of Schoeps' term *Heidenmission*.

We have already noted the Septuagint translators' use of "all" in Deuteronomy. Schoeps picks this up in "many expressions in the LXX" and, in turn, in the Apostle Paul's writings.[14] Earlier, we also noted two puzzling "immigrant" texts in Leviticus that deserve further consideration in terms of "the missionary purpose of the LXX": one relates to "the Lord's name" (Lev 24:16, 22), the other to Jubilee (Lev 25).

It is not hard to imagine the impact of Leviticus 24:16 in a mission context: "Whoever names the name of the Lord, let him be put to death." The text in context makes clear that this "naming" is blasphemous. The narrative context points to a heathen influence: the blasphemer is the son of an Egyptian man (and an Israelite mother). A main point is made in verse 16 about equal justice: the penalty is the same for immigrant as for an indigenous person. The stark repetition of the judgment ("let him die for naming the name of the Lord") seems likely to persuade most missionaries to hold off giving instruction using the name, Yahweh. Despite the strong impulse to teach the name, as, for example, to enable obedience to texts such as Deuteronomy 6:13 commanding Israelites to swear in the name of Yahweh "and by his name you shall swear." Whatever other texts say and imply, the fact remains that knowledge of the name, Yahweh, could be literally life-threatening to a careless or impudent youth.

Another subtler missionary purpose has often been inferred from the change of the tetragrammaton to κύριος. The replacement of the name "Yahweh" for a title has been thought to be ethnic friendly. Writing for the NRSV Committee "To the Reader" in our own time, Bruce M. Metzger alludes to ancient precedent and confidently declares that "The use of any proper name for the one and only God . . . began to be discontinued in Judaism before the Christian era and is inappropriate for the universal faith of Christians." Whether the change was made on purpose or by accident, God's name being somehow lost in translation, the switch has been carried forward by virtually all subsequent translators.[15]

---

14. Ibid., 29.

15. In English translations, only the American Standard Version (ASV, also known as "the Jehovah Bible") and the first English edition of the Jerusalem Bible (which printed Yahweh where the Hebrew text has the tetragrammaton) identified God's name and encouraged its pronunciation in prayers and worship. Many older hymns include Jehovah and some hymns from the 1960s and 1970s include Yahweh.

Mogens Müller reminds us that "Origen and Jerome are adamant that the best Septuagint manuscripts do not render the Hebrew Yahweh by *Kurios*, but use the tetragrammaton in some form or other."[16] Albert Pietersma has demonstrated that it is more difficult to explain the time and motive for the switch than has sometimes been supposed, but his analysis of "revisionist rescensions" leads him to suppose that the *Kurios* substitution is in the "original LXX."[17] A curious development in our own culture may provide insight for the original move and also provide support for the change, against David J. A. Clines' proposal to bring back the Lord's name to our worship and theological discussions.

The jubilee declared in Leviticus 25 is remarkable for its inclusion of the immigrant and wayfarer not only in the commonwealth (Lev 25:35), but as models from whom the established Israelites must learn their right relations to God and his land (Lev 25:23). It is the immigrants and the wayfarers, those who have no land to call their own, who are parables in place. "The Israelites were to regard their status before God as analogous to that of their own residential dependents to themselves."[18]

Schoeps' challenging and rewarding analysis of "the missionary purpose of the LXX" goes beyond the initial translation of the Torah to the time of the Apostle Paul and the New Testament writings. By suggesting, on the one hand, that the Septuagint translators shaped the text into alignment with their theological convictions, Schoeps opens the possibility that, on the other hand, the still fluid Hebrew text was subsequently fixed in congruence with different and sometimes opposite theological positions from those already established in the Septuagint.

Israel and the Nations

The Hebrew Bible famously divides the world into "Israel and the nations." Many interpretations of various texts, such as Deuteronomy

---

16. *The First Bible of the Church*, 118; see also Joseph A. Fitzmyer, "The Semitic Background of the New Testament *Kurios*-Title," in *A Wandering Aramaean* (Missoula, MT: Scholars, 1979) 137.

17. Albert Pietersma, "*Kurios* or *Tetragram*: A Renewed Quest for the Original Septuagint," in *Septuaginta: Studies in Honour of John Williams Wevers on His Sixty-fifth Birthday*, ed. Albert Pietersma and Claude Cox (Missassauga: Benben, 1984) 85–101.

18. C. J. H. Wright, "Jubilee, Year of," in *ABD*, 3:126.

26:18-19,[19] accept this division as divinely ordained. Whether we take it to be divinely revealed or simply an Israelite idea, what Claude Levi-Straus calls "the ethnocentric attitude,"[20] there is evidence for this attitude in the biblical writings and later in the Talmud. In short, at least some Jews reciprocated the Greek idea: *all others* (including the Greeks) *were barbarians* or heathen; but from the beginning it was not so.

Balaam's prophecy refers to Israel as "a unique people, not numbered among the nations" (Num 23:9). This could mean that they were not ranked. They would never make it in the playoff of nations.[21] N. P. Lemche in his reflection on "'Hebrew' as a National Name for Israel" concludes that "There must have been in the later Israel a historical remembrance that their own society, during the first days of its existence, was interpreted by its neighbors and opponents as a society of *habiru*."[22]

Even so, the very idea of translating Holy Scripture into a heathen language must have raised some serious questions in Alexandria at the time the Torah was first published in Greek. Just how the Jewish translators thought of the Greeks[23] in the third century BCE is not easy to determine. Translating to Greek in the wake of Alexander, to be sure, was not the same thing as proposing that every heathen language get its own version of the Bible. That, of course, is the program in our own time, with the Wycliffe Bible Translators and various Bible societies pressing forward with eschatological fervor.

Putting aside the question of how the Hebrew Scriptures became the Bible, we can assume that the first translators of the Torah considered these five books to be divinely inspired or, as we would say, canonical. It might seem unreasonable, then, to imagine that they would consciously put into their translations meanings not in the texts. The same could

19. "And the Lord has chosen you this day that you should be to him a peculiar people, as he said, to keep his commands; and that you should be above all nations, as he has made you renowned, and a boast, and glorious, that you should be a holy people to the Lord your God, as he has spoken." See also Deut 7:17-18, Num 23:9 (Balaam's prophecy) and many other texts.

20. Claude Levi-Strauss, *Race and History* (Paris: UNESCO, 1958) 12-13.

21. See James LaGrand, "'Hebrews' in the TANAK," in *Proceedings of the Midwest Section of the Society of Biblical Literature* (1991).

22. Niels Peter Lemche, "'Hebrew' as a National Name for Israel," *ST* 33 (1979) 21.

23. No ethnic Greeks appear in the Torah or elsewhere in the TANAK except in one variant reading: *Codex Vaticanus* (B) IV Kings 21:6. Apparently this reading identifies Greeks with human sacrifice (kai\ eopoi/hsen Hellen).

certainly be said of the edition of the Masoretes who transmitted the fixed Hebrew text three centuries later. Nevertheless, there certainly is divergence between the Septuagint translation and the Masoretic text. Some of this divergence can be explained in terms of honest mistakes in translation to Greek or unintentional errors in the transmission of the Hebrew text. There is, in any case, a wide range of possibilities for interpretation even with the same text in the same language. Disputes between Jews and Christians in the first centuries CE focus on some tendentious translations, however, that can hardly be called honest. Some translators and editors in ancient times, it seems, were ready to lie to defend what they saw as threatened truth, just as in our own time.[24]

Sometimes a single word can represent an idea or even a social movement. This seems to have been true of the label, Hebrew, and also the divine name, Yahweh. It also seems to have been true of the Greek word προσήλυτος in relating Israel to the nations.

The word itself hardly changed in terms of morphology and phonetics. Nonetheless, it seems to have been a neologism, or at least a rare word in the third century BCE. After work began on translating the Hebrew Bible into Greek, the focus on outsiders coming into Israel gained importance. Then the word, immigrant, was read as "convert to Judaism." Later, in the New Testament, it came to mean, "a seeker on the way to becoming a Christian." The word itself has become indispensable, at once flexible and controversial. The word's earliest uses in the Torah, and in the subsequent history of its use, are as instructive today as before the Maccabees. The key to its historic and modern usage is the manner in which it proliferated in the Septuagint and in that process developed dramatically, correlating with the developments in the name of Yahweh and in Yahweh's relationship to Israel and all humankind.

---

24. Christian interpolations were sometimes accepted in good faith and brought forward as proofs of the Christian truth, as the "the Lord reigns from a tree" reading, which Justin Martyr accused his Jewish interlocutor of deleting. Cited by Karen H. Jobes and Moisés Silva, *Invitation to the Septuagint* (Grand Rapids: Baker, 2000) 83.

PART THREE

Ancient Intercultural Perspectives

11

The Balaam Figure and Type before, during, and after the Period of the Pseudepigrapha

Hebrew Bible, Deir 'Alla, and Qumran

John T. Greene

Introduction

AT FIRST THOUGHT, BALAAM IS NOT A NAME THAT LEAPS READILY to mind when one considers pseudepigraphical literature or the literature produced in its shadow. Extensive studies of the Balaam traditions reveal, however, that they extend from the tenth century BCE to the present.[1]

1. In two published papers entitled "Balaam: Prophet, Diviner, and Priest In Selected Ancient Israelite and Hellenistic Jewish Sources"(1989), and "Balaam as Figure and Type in Ancient Semitic Literature to the First Century BCE, with a Survey of Post-Philo Applications of the Balaam Figure and Type"(1990), both in the *SBL Seminar Papers* volumes, I explored uses of the Balaam traditions both within and without ancient Israel. I shall refer to them below as "Balaam, '89," and Balaam, '90." The majority of the '89 work is devoted to a critical and exegetical essay on the text of Numbers 22–24, which I term the Balaam cycle of texts. Therein, I concluded that:

   a. The Numbers 22–24 cycle was a literary mosaic.

   b. That mosaic could be subdivided into three distinct parts: a narrative framework, a fable, and a collection of *logia* or *meshalim*.

   c. The "glue" which held these three components together was the wars of Yahweh itinerary.

   d. Balaam was probably a famous priest-king who also demonstrated mantic traits of the "seer," the "gazer," the "*nab/vi*," and the "wizard."

   e. Numbers 22–24 shows signs of having undergone four major rescensions:

   1) a tenth century version wherein the Balaam figure was presented as a type of acceptable, formerly non-Israelite priest who was now accepted as a legitimate priestly

As a *figure*, Balaam was utilized by competing, warring, ancient Israelite priesthoods to support or deny sacerdotal claims for hegemony.[2] He has

colleague by the official national priesthood under either David or Solomon. He might well have been typed as the local Yahweh-loyal prophet/priest/diviner (*prodriediv*, This term is explained in Note #28 below.) in the territories conquered or controlled by David. Thus, a Judean version. A Balaam within the J source stratum was proposed. (pp. 70–71)

2) a later than 922 BCE, but earlier than 722 BCE version which concentrates on a northern homeland Balaam. This northern work is the most nebulous of the discernible recensions. This recension was probably produced by the Shiloh priests. Had we more information, the Balaam type would most certainly have been cast in a negative light. These priests were known to have been rigid in their fierce zealousness and jealousness for Yahweh. Outsider mantics would not have been welcomed by these insiders. A Balaam within the E source stratum was proposed. (72–75)

3) a post-722 BCE recension which was conciliatory in intent. Therein, Balaam once again served as the type *par excellence* of the priesthood member in Judah after the destruction of Israel the northern kingdom. It was a time when refugee priests appeared in large numbers in Jerusalem. Once again outsiders were absorbed into the body of the Judean state priesthood and given legitimacy. A combination of the above two strata was proposed which resulted in a JE proposition. (75–76)

4) a post JE response to JE identified as the P source stratum. This recension is characterized by its anti outsider priest stand, as well as its preoccupation with inefficacious sacrifices offered by other than *bona fide* priests of Yahweh. Its concerns with Assyria as an agent of Yahweh war, or on the one hand, while stating confidently that Assyria shall be trodden down by the Kittim, betray its production during the period of King Hezekiah of Judah. This was the most anti Balaam of the source strata. (76–81)

5) a very subtle response to the P recension. Linguistic analysis provided the program of this last recension writer. Balaam of his product is made to ask questions which marked the major thrust of the deuteronomistic reform movement. Thus, Balaam is made to ask Balak in Numbers 23:19–20 about Yahweh's actions in the following way: "Would he speak and not act (*y'sh*), promise and not fulfill (*dbr wl' ygymynh*)." Truly, my message was to bless: and when he blesses, I cannot reverse it (*wl' 'sybynh*)." This recension bore a treatment of a Balaam with all of the characteristics of the D source stratum.

In neither case did those who produced the recensions I have proposed see a need to change the war setting in which the story about Balaam appears. In fact, it appears that Balaam apart from a war setting was quite unknown to those who employed the story. These recensions were produced over a period ranging from the tenth century (the first recension) to the sixth century (the fifth recension) BCE. Other than the nebulous E recension (2), three of the others correspond to periods of war in which the southern kingdom of Judah was embroiled (1, 4, and 5). Only one of these war periods was offensive: the tenth century (holy/Yahweh) wars of conquest under David (1). Recension 3 was produced during the aftermath of a war that resulted in the total destruction of the kingdom of Israel in 722/1 BCE.

2. Cf. the extended, critical exegetical essay of Numbers 22–24 in Greene, "Balaam '89," 59–92, and a terse summary in Greene, "Balaam '90," 92–94, as well as the studies by Marcus David, *From Balaam to Jonah: Anti-Prophetic Satire in the Hebrew Bible*, BJS

also been used by modern writers concerned with literary types or with political scientific issues shaping modern Israel.[3] As a *type* of mantic, Balaam was to be either shunned, as in the case of the Samaritan literature's Pilti, the Egyptian sorcerer-priests,[4] or emulated, as the literature of 1 Enoch implies.[5] Numerous illustrations of type and figure are evident between these examples. Moreover, between the periods stated above, both figure and type pullulate. With such broad, historical coverage and usage, one would be hard pressed to omit Balaam's influence before, during, and after the period during which the literature contained in the Pseudepigrapha was developed.

This chapter demonstrates the above by (1) concentration on a transitional phase of the Balaam traditions from the Semitic communities to the Hellenistic communities, (2) demonstration of a new attempt to breathe new life into the *word* of the past, (3) assessment of the Balaam of the Qumran Community to show one aspect of Hellenistic influence on the use of Balaam, (4) examination of the recent discovery and reconstruction of a Balaam ben Beor at Deir 'Alla reflecting a non-Israelite view of a polytheistic seer/diviner/king.[6] The following chapter will (5) offer a review of 1 Enoch, which thrusts the Balaam type into the heart of pseudepigraphical writings, and (6) include an analysis of the Middle Platonic, Philonic utilization of Balaam,[7] a survey of the New Testament,

---

301 (Atlanta: Scholars, 1995); and W. W. Fereday, *Jonah the Preacher and Balaam the False Prophet* (Kilmarnock, Scotland: Woldridge, 1946).

3. Joel Chandler Harris has written a series of short stories entitled, *Balaam and His Master*, which is the title of one of the short stories. It reflects a perceptive understanding of the several *leitmotifs* contained in the Balaam cycle of texts at Numbers 22–24.

4. Both Pilti and Enoch bear the stamp of how impressive the Balaam figure and type ultimately became to Jewish and/or para-Jewish communities wrestling with issues of mantology long after the uses of each reflected in my earlier studies of Balaam in the biblical material. For the remainder of this study see Greene, "Balaam, '89 & '90," 92–96, and 94–126 respectively, and n. 89 below.

5. The Enochic text is the most transparent in showing its having been crafted around the Balaam type. Its slavish and unabashed introductory formulations reveal an overwhelming dependence on the Numbers Balaam cycle.

6. Literature on the reconstruction and discovery is prodigious. Cf. Jo Ann Hackett, *The Balaam Text from Deir 'Alla*, (Chico, CA: Scholars, 1980); and Andre Lemaire, "Fragments from the Book of Balaam Found at Deir 'Alla," *BAR* 11/5 (1985) 39.

7. Cf. the excellent study by Robert M. Berchman, "*Arcana Mundi*: Between Balaam and Hecate: Prophecy, Divination, and Magic in Later Platonism," in *SBL Seminar Papers* 28 (Atlanta: Scholars, 1989) 114–17, 122–24, 128–30. Berchman also includes

the *Antiquities* of Josephus, medieval Islamic material, and two selections from modern literature. This will round out the study and demonstrate that Balaam proved to be a figure and type for all seasons before, during, and after the period of the Pseudepigrapha. The study invites thought on the part of scholars who do their work on the Pseudepigrapha to make other connections with what is contained herein.

Toward a Transition to Hellenistic Times

Balaam ben Beor was a name in ancient Israel which kept company with names such as Ruth, Rahab, Melchizedek, Jezebel, and (Pharaoh) Neco of 2 Chronicles 35:20–22. By Israelite standards, all of these people were outsiders: figures used by the writers to establish boundary markers between themselves and others. Yet, these were outsiders who could not have been ignored. They either acknowledged Yahweh openly, or were threatened by his covenant with Israel. They fall into two distinct groups for purposes of analysis.

Group 1	Group 2
Ruth	Melchizedek
Rahab	Neco
Jezebel	Balaam

Ruth the Moabitess, a woman reflecting harlot-like qualities (cf. the Boaz at the threshing-floor incident [Ruth 3:6ff.]), accepted the deity of her mother-in-law. This display of courage and zeal earned for her the respect of the insiders; from her came ultimately a great king (Ruth 4:17).

Rahab, a professional harlot at Jericho, facilitated Yahweh's holy war against the inhabitants of that city. It was an action for which she and her household were rewarded and not subjected to the *ḥerem* (i.e., the ban).

---

in his study Clement and Origen of Alexandria's views of Balaam, 124–27, and 130–33 respectively. Middle Platonic era concerns about Balaam are also studied in Judith R. Baskin, "Origen on Balaam: The Dilemma of the Unworthy Prophet," *VC* 37 (1983) 22–35, and *Pharaoh's Counselors: Job, Jethro, and Balaam in Rabbinic and Patristic Tradition*, BJS 47 (Chico, CA: Scholars, 1983).

Jezebel, another "harlot" (but only in the eyes of the anti-Ba'alists in Israel), was a priestess in the religion of the Tyrian Melkart. She acknowledged Yahweh by waging a war to the death against his prophets.

If all three female outsiders were viewed as licentious (accurate or inaccurate) by insiders, the three male outsiders also shared a common trait; they were all monarchs! Melchizedek, the nebulous priest-king of Salem, participated in a religious order which became paradigmatic for the Judean monarchs (Ps 110:4).

Pharaoh Neco (only in the 2 Chronicles account) acknowledged Yahweh as he announced to King Josiah his gross error; an error which cost the king his life at the Battle of Megiddo.

The third monarch, (on the basis of messenger vocabulary studies, and the language of Combination II from the Deir 'Alla Balaam text),[8] Balaam appears to have been the most fascinating and challenging of the outsiders. Along with Ruth and Melchizedek, Balaam, survives to be mentioned even in the New Testament anthology (2 Pet 2:15; Rev 2:14; and Jude 11).

All of these outsiders are depicted as somehow being instruments of Yahweh's punishment or reward, protection or restoration. Clearly, boundary markers were in place which were set in terms of being or not being the people in covenant relationship with Yahweh.[9] But the boundaries could be stepped over in both directions. The concept which allowed this was *ḥesed*, oftentimes rendered grace or covenant love. It worked both ways. Neco and Jezebel were examples of *ḥesed* denied; Ruth, Melchizedek, Rahab, and Balaam were examples of *ḥesed* in force. Balaam was subjected to exegesis in ancient Israel and beyond to an extent that none of the others were. These outsiders are mentioned here because they served some specific function for those insiders who included them in their works and what they mediate to us moderns.

The Balaam figure loomed larger than life; too large to be ignored or expunged as an outsider; but not too large and powerful to be manipulated at the time of various priestly exegetes. The advantage of this

8. These vocabulary studies are contained in John T. Greene, *The Role of the Messenger and Message in the Ancient Near East*, BJS 169 (Atlanta: Scholars, 1989) 81–83.

9. On the significance of these boundary markers, see the volume of published papers titled *Religion, Science, and Magic: In Concert and in Conflict*, ed. Jacob Neusner et al. (Oxford: Oxford University Press, 1989), especially 3–7.

situation was that Balaam, like Sir Thomas More in British history, loomed large in the popular culture of ancient Israel. However, many could not quite remember what exactly he had done. Thus, he could be depicted as fulfilling Yahweh's *dbr* as well as fulfilling the *dbr* of the deities of Deir 'Alla. By the advent of the Hellenistic Period, Balaam had been turned into a truly malleable figure by warring Israelite priesthoods. It had been they who had kept the Balaam figure and type before them as an example and yardstick for gauging acceptable insider deportment.[10]

Breathing More New Life into the Old Word: Balaam for the Hellenistic World

With the overlay of Hellenistic thought being brought to bear on various forms of Jewish outlook and need, mantological exegeses, within the framework of Middle Platonism and the *Weltanschauung* growing out of it, took on a decidedly different form.[11] Exegetes overlaid earlier *strata* of interpretive grids and responded to new challenges to the traditions of ancient Israel. Balaam, like so many former Soviet leaders whose tombs are now located in the Kremlin, was once again taken out of the mausoleum of interpretive tradition, retouched where decay had become evident to those who view such remains, and placed once more on display. He had thus been made useful to a later generation of exegetes, all of whom had different needs, brought on by the challenges of events being refracted through the prism of a new age.

In a chapter entitled The Jewish Exegetical Context, George Brooke sensitizes his readers to a number of controversies concerning the myth of separateness of Hellenistic exegetical methods from Palestinian exegetical methods.[12] He warns that the implied lines of demarcation do

10. Here I refer to the use of Balaam by the Qumran covenanters and the Samaritan creators of Pilti.

11. That form, bracketed by the geographical area in which Jews found themselves, appeared in writings from Qumran, Shechem, Safed/*Tzfat*, Alexandria, Jerusalem, the Decapolis, Damascus, and the Mediterranean Basin.

12. George J. Brooke, *Exegesis at Qumran: 4QFlorilegium in its Jewish Context*, JSOTSup 29 (Sheffield: JSOT Press, 1985) 1–79, especially 17–19. Brooke's work makes it impossible for one to maintain the rigid views of scholarship on exegesis during the Hellenistic period as had been maintained by exponents of *die Wissenschaft des Judentums* on the one hand, and by many Christian scholars touting a particular schol-

not really exist and that the maintenance of a rigid two-camp theory leads to gross error. His work is important because in studying, in its Jewish context, the document from Qumran known as 4Q Florilegium, he paints an involved and intricate picture of just what evidence must be in place before taking on the task of making a transition from what one could term pre-Hellenistic exegesis of the Hebrew Scriptures, and thereby certain figures such as Balaam, on the one hand, and exegesis of those documents during the Hellenistic Period (whether or not by Jews), on the other.

Below, we shall see one major instance in which certain utterances attributed to Balaam (Num 24:8, 17, and 18) became excerpted, appropriated, and employed by writers of documents found in the caves of Qumran (4QM for example).[13] There, Balaam became far less important than his word(s). They, not he, assisted the writers in articulating their view of messianism(s). But would one normally assign the type of mantological exegesis evident at Qumran (and here I also include 1 Enoch which is discussed thoroughly below) to the category of Hellenistic exegesis? Before one attempted to respond to that question, he or she should also be made aware that Greek documents, among them the book of Numbers, were also discovered at, and evidently employed by, the members of Qumran. Adding thereto the fact that the Qumran community was active until its destruction ca. 68 CE, the issue of what constitutes Hellenistic exegesis takes on a truly complex character.

A similar problem is presented by John Bowman who worked with Samaritan texts.[14] Familiarity with the history of the Maccabeans/

---

arly party line on the other. A pure, hermetically-sealed, Palestinian Jewish thought-world was as impossible as was a hypothesized Hellenistic counterpart, with neither the twain meeting.

13. These would include the documents studied by Chaim Rabin, *The Zadokite Documents* (Oxford: Oxford University Press, 1953); Leonhard Rost, *Die Damaskusschrift*, Kleine Texte für Vorlesungen und Übungen 7 (Berlin: de Gruyter, 1933); Solomon Zeitlin, editor, *The Zadokite Fragments*, Jewish Quarterly Review Monograph Series 1 (Philadelphia: Dropsie College, 1952); E. L. Sukenik, editor, *The Dead Sea Scrolls of the Hebrew University* (Jerusalem: Magnes, 1955) Plates xvi-xxxiv; and Yigal Yadin, *Megillath Milhemeth Bne Or bi-Bne Hoshech*, (Jerusalem: Bialik Institute, 1956). Cf. Patrick W. Skehan's list in "The Biblical Scrolls from Qumran and the Text of the Old Testament," in Cross and Talmon, *Qumran and the History of the Biblical Text* (Cambridge: Harvard University Press, 1975) 265 [264–77].

14. John Bowman, *Samaritan Documents Relating to their History, Religion and Life*, Pittsburgh Original Texts and Translation Series 2 (Pittsburgh: Pickwick, 1977).

Hasmoneans will inform the researcher of a family which began as conservative and anti-Hellenistic, that is specifically, against the Hellenization policy of Antiochus IV Epiphanes, and which ended up Hellenized![15] During this Maccabean/Hasmonean period, a period of Hellenization in Palestine, the Samaritan community was exegetically active just as were the Qumranites, their contemporaries. Concerning the Balaam cycle, of the Balaam figure found in Samaritan documents, Bowman holds that chapters 3–4 of the Samaritan Book of Joshua deal with Balaam and the Moabites.[16]

In another Samaritan work, entitled Discourse Concerning The Angels, Numbers 22:31 is quoted.[17] The Samaritans also believed that Balaam and Jethro knew of a Book Of Signs which was reputed to have been one of a number of books that had been inscribed on the rod which Adam had taken out of paradise.[18] These texts further exacerbate the issue of what constitutes Hellenistic exegesis, while simultaneously showing that the Balaam cycle and the Balaam figure continued to play an important role (and with Balaam, an important *Vorbild*) as Israelite literature continued to generate new living traditions.

It is easier to research the Balaam figure and various uses of the Balaam cycle in the ancient Israelite materials than in later materials. The eighth century was a watershed century for materials about Balaam to appear, whether in ancient Judah/Israel or at Deir 'Alla. Although the Deir 'Alla material was badly damaged, one is still able to form a picture of some continuity between the traditions about Balaam, whether they were formed east or west of the Jordan River during that century.[19] With the Qumran and Samaritan materials, however, the picture is not quite so clear. It becomes even less clear when one attempts to assign a specific name to the type of exegesis of a given biblical book or passage

15. Cf. "Hasmoneans," in *IDB*, 2:529–35, for a summary of rulers from Simon to Aristobulus II; Martin Noth, *The History of Israel*, 2nd ed. (New York: Harper & Row, 1960) 346–401, for the period from Alexander the Great to the activity of Pompey at Jerusalem; and Elias Bickerman, *From Ezra to the Last of the Maccabees* (New York: Schocken, 1962).

16. Bowman, *Samaritan Documents*, 63, 291.

17. Ibid., 248–51.

18. Ibid., 291.

19. See the appropriate sections of the works cited in n. 1 above (96–99 of Greene, '89; 128–32 of Greene, '90), and n. 79 below.

engaged in by a writer of the Hellenistic Period, such as, Philo Judaeus. But this saves one from committing the error of attempting to assign the same pan-exegetical approach to all of the works of Philo. Brooke wrote that:

> Burton L. Mack has proposed a thorough examination of the Philonic corpus with the supposition that "Philo used tradition-al exegetical methods and materials. These materials are diverse and may reflect stages of exegetical history of 'schools' of exegesis which are in debate with one another. Philo employed these traditions with various degrees of acceptance and he reworked them with varying degrees of consistency." R.D. Hecht and H. Moehring are amongst those who have tried to work out the implications of Mack's program. Hecht has attempted to analyze Philo's use of scripture in De Specialibus Legibus; Moehring has considered arithmology as an exegetical tool.[20]

What this points away from is the simple minded approach to Philo and other contemporaries as allegorists, and points toward not only one group of exegetes, but to an era also, both of which need to be understood far better than they are understood at present. Once that precondition has been met, scholars will be in a much better position to fathom specifically the implications of either Philo's or Josephus' treatment of Balaam, as well as point up the importance of Hellenistic hermeneutics concerning Balaam in a general way.

Qumran and the Balaam Traditions

All of the literature which contains an account or mention of Balaam ben Beor thus far has one characteristic in common: these accounts are all located within literature which is not intended to be understood as works purporting to "do history"; they are all ahistorical. Most of the literature of the *TaNaK* may be separated into two main camps: 1) historical books, into which would fit 2 Samuel 9–20; 1 Kings 1–2, the first real attempt at historiographical writing in the Hebrew Scriptures;[21] Ezra; Nehemiah; and the Chronicles; and 2) non-historical.

---

20. Brooke, *Exegesis*, 18–19. See also the work on Balaam in Philo by Robert M. Berchman, "*Arcana Mundi*: Between Balaam and Hecate," cited above in n. 7.

21. Cf. R. N. Whybray, *The Succession Narrative: A Study of II Samuel 9–20; 1 Kings 1 and 2*, SBT 2/9 (Napierville, IL: Allenson, 1968).

The non-historical books have essentially theological agenda. Although the Balaam material mentioned to this point purports to depict a Balaam engaging in mantic activities which were to have taken place within a specific time in ancient Israelite history, one fact does not escape us: the literature which enshrines it is essentially non-historical in character, and therefore may not be trusted to present historical fact and sequence.[22] The agenda it does present has a sacerdotal urgency about it. The historical worth of the already surveyed material has come through analysis of the contents of each given piece and that content's program and intended use. We were even able to tentatively identify the author/editor/concerned group on this basis.

The Balaam Materials from Qumran

Turning to extra-Hebrew Scriptures materials concerning or mentioning Balaam, we must subject them to a rigid scrutiny also.

In taking up the issue of the Qumran Balaam here, I depart from what would have had to have been a chronological approach to the Hebrew scriptural material up to this point. The Numbers 22–24 Balaam cycle, with its overlaid recensions, would have been shown to have stretched from the tenth to the sixth centuries BCE in ancient Israel. With this body having served as a core, I would then have taken up the issues of the Balaam of Numbers 31:8 and 31:16. This material was most certainly later than that of the Balaam cycle material, and also differed radically from it with reference to the Peor issue.

The Mican material came from the eighth century BCE, which was followed by, and maybe produced during the same century as, Deuteronomy 23:4–5. The core material of the present book of Deuteronomy was probably produced long before the Deuteronomist pre-and affixed *addenda* to it and made it part of the Deuteronomistic History during the sixth century.[23] The Nehemiah material comes from

22. This division is certainly for purposes of description and nothing more. I am the first to realize that it could and should be subjected to numerous legitimate attacks; the first of which is that it is too simplistic and artificial. The point here is that certain biblical material exhibits certain characteristics that other biblical materials exhibit as both attempt to "tell a story" and how they do it. See below, n. 55.

23. Be reminded that this deuteronomistic body of material was presented in two "editions," Deuteronomistic History version one (designated D1), and a version (designated D2). Cf. the discussions in Richard Elliott Friedman, *Who Wrote the Bible?*

the Post Exilic period somewhere between 444 and 398 BCE, or even later.[24] If the chronological treatment were to have been continued, we should take up next the material from Deir 'Alla, which is generally believed to be eighth century BCE material.[25]

My rationale for departing from my chronology is based in part on the similarity of language and contents between the materials which would have been studied up to this point and the corpus of writings from the Wadi Qumran. The rationale is also based partially on the fact that the language of the War Scroll from Qumran[26] reflects the language characteristics of a particular earlier priesthood which contributed a Balaam recension overlay available in the Numbers 22–24 account: the P overlay.[27] As will be demonstrated below, the Deir 'Alla tradition is *sui generis*. So this is the appropriate point at which to begin our present analyses. Then we shall also be dealing with literature appropriate to such beginning analysis.

The most famous body of extra-Hebrew Scriptures materials is the corpus of writings produced by the Qumran community located near the Dead Sea in the ancient land of Canaan. This community existed between 150–140 BCE to the middle of the first war against Roman domination, 68–70 CE. With the Nehemiah Balaam recension, the reader is still presented with ancient Near Eastern influenced portraiture of this *propriediv*.[28] The Balaam of Qumran appears in material which has

(Englewood Cliffs, NJ: Prentice Hall, 1987) 129, 137–49; and Brian Peckham, *The Composition of the Deuteronomistic History*, HSM 35 (Atlanta: Scholars, 1985) 7–9 (D1); 21–68 (D2).

24. These dates coincide with the twentieth year of the reigns of either King Artaxerxes I or II. Since neither Nehemiah 1:1 nor 2:1 supply more information, we must proceed with caution in dating the Nehemian material.

25. Cf. Greene, "Balaam,'90," 96–99, for a condensed treatment of these extra Hebrew Scriptural texts, and the discussion which follows below.

26. Cf. n. 13 above, and the bibliography in Millar Burrows, *The Dead Sea Scrolls* (New York: Viking, 1955) 420–35. The classic introductory work is by Frank M. Cross Jr. *The Ancient Library of Qumran and Modern Biblical Studies* (Garden City, NY: Doubleday, 1958); B. Jongeling, *A Classified Bibliography of Finds in the Desert of Judah: 1958–1969*, Studies of the Texts of the Judean Desert 7 (Leiden: Brill, 1971); and J. A. Fitzmyer, *The Dead Sea Scrolls. Major Publications and Tools for Study* (Missoula, MT: Scholars, 1975).

27. The distinction between priests and Levites is maintained here also.

28. There are times when Balaam was being critiqued by his detractors as being more than just a prophet, or a diviner. I coined the word *propriediv*, containing the

been influenced by Hellenistic culture. The war Scroll, which mentions Balaam, comes also under the category of non-historical literature.[29] Thus, the type of literature in which Balaam appears continued to be useful for those writers not concerned with historiography. Below, however, I shall fine tune the non-historical types of literature, and demonstrate major differences.

The Qumran community was the product of war, and it was destroyed by war. Between these wars the community became so influenced by the actuality of war that it on one great literary occasion, produced a work employing the genre of the futuristic, cataclysmic war to end all wars. That is, the Qumranites created their own fantastic war between actual wars!

The Actual War(s)

The ideational war created in the minds of the Qumran writers was preceded in actual historical time by the Jewish wars of either independence, conquest, or collusion, on the one hand, and by the first war between the Jews and the Romans on the other. The Qumran community came into being during the reigns of Jonathan Maccabaeus and his brother/successor Simon Maccabaeus, that is, between 153–152 BCE.[30] Jonathan, a non-Zadokite priest, was elevated to the High Priesthood in Jerusalem by Alexander Balas. Balas had usurped the Syrian Greek Seleucid throne, and Jonathan had supported his bid with Jewish troops that formerly had fought against Balas's predecessor.

When Jonathan was assassinated by a Syrian Greek general named Trypho in 143–142 BCE, Simon was elevated by the Jewish government itself to the position of High Priest and leader of the people. So strong

---

beginnings of the words prophet, priest and diviner, to show this triangulation on the Balaam figure by those engaged in interpreting his activities mantologically.

29. Cf. n. 26 above, and Hannelis Schulte, *Die Entstehung der Gerichtsschreibung im Alten Israel*, BZAW 128 (Berlin: de Gruyter, 1972); John Van Seters, "Histories and Historians of the Ancient Near East," *Orientalia* 50 (1981) 137–85; and André Lemaire, "Vers l'historia de la redaction des livres des Rois," *ZAW* 98 (1986) 221–36.

30. Cf. M. Avi-Yonah, "The 'War of the Sons of Light and the Sons of Darkness' and Maccabean Warfare," *IEJ* (1952) 1–5; Flavius Josephus *Antiquities* XIII, and *War* I, 1 Maccabees (which covers the years 167–134 BCE), and 2 Maccabees (which covers the period 175–160 BCE), and Bar Kochba, *The Battles of the Hasmoneans: The Times of Judas Maccabaeus*, (Jerusalem: Ben Zvi Institute, 1980) [Hebrew], which presents a detailed description of these battles.

and confident had the tiny nation of the Jews become since the outbreak of the Maccabean wars against (originally) religious oppression under Antiochus IV Epiphanes (ca. 167 BCE). The successors of Simon the High Priest recouped much territory around the region of Jerusalem and Judah. First under John Hyrcanus I (134–104 BCE) and then Alexander Jannaeus (103–76 BCE), territory that included Samaria, Galilee, and Edom, to mention just three areas, came under Jewish domination and control. Between the reigns of these two regents occurred the short reign of Aristobulus I (104–103 BCE). Aristobulus has the distinction, according to many historians of this period, of being the first ruler of Jerusalem to wear the title *priest-king* after Zedekiah/Mattaniah of Jerusalem, who reigned before the main Babylonian deportation.[31] War, then, was the order of the day: wars of religious freedom under Judas and Jonathan Maccabaeus; wars of collaboration under Jonathan Maccabaeus; and wars of conquest under Simon Maccabaeus, John Hyrcanus I, Aristobulus I, and Alexander Jannaeus of the Hasmonean era.

Upon the death of Alexander Jannaeus, his able and capable widow, Queen Alexandra Salome, mounted the throne in Jerusalem.[32] This move led in a direct way to another series of wars. These wars pitted Jews in a bloody civil war. At the center of the conflict was a war between two brothers, John Hyrcanus II and Aristobulus II, sons of Alexandra Salome. In short, Alexandra could be king without being contested. However, no woman could attain the title of any kind of priest. Since that was impossible, and the High Priesthood was such an important and powerful position, unlike her predecessors, Salome had to appoint a male to this position. She appointed the weaker of her two sons in order to maintain a firm grip on the position, and it angered the stronger son, Aristobulus II.

31. Sources both ancient and modern are undecided on the issue of who was actually acknowledged as priest-king, and who functioned as "high priest-first citizen." Josephus and the author of 1 and 2 Maccabees exercised caution when assigning titles. Norman K. Gottwald, in *A Light to the Nations* (New York: Harper, 1959) 502, assigns titles more liberally in his table. Most agree, however, that Aristobulus I enjoyed the title Priest-King officially. All of this discussion is built ultimately on a practice commencing with David having brought the ark to Jerusalem dressed only in the priestly *ephod*, and followed by Solomon having served in a priestly capacity at the dedication of the new temple of YHWH (1 Kgs 8:1–26). These actions, as well as Josiah's reforming efforts, all mirrored the designation found in the Psalter (Ps 110:4).

32. Josephus *Antiquities* XIII; and *War* I.

206 Probing the Frontiers of Biblical Studies

Factionalism resulted, political lines were drawn, Aristobulus attempted to usurp the High Priesthood, and formed an army willing to help him do so. This filial and familial conflict unleashed hatred and greed that resulted in an adjudication by the Roman general strongman, Pompey.[33] Although, the High Priesthood office would continue for another three decades, Pompey's actions in 63 BCE of turning the heretofore independent Jewish state into a Roman province effectively ended the battle for the High Priesthood. Rome now controlled the office and appointed the High Priest at its pleasure.

It is not difficult to understand how preoccupation with war for so long a period of time (ca. 167–63 BCE) would move even the intelligentsia to incorporate it into their writings. The difference between seasoned military men and scholars viewing war is that the scholar attempts to manipulate war safely in the library through writing about it, and to ultimately find some positive use for it. Within all these local historical wars, the Qumran producers of the War Rule conceived a war of cosmic proportions. Employing a genre of literature borrowed from Persia on the one hand,[34] and from the Hellenists on the other,[35] they crafted a war scenario in which they, as one of the most injured parties in all these armed conflicts, would direct the ultimate war. They wrote of a war that would result in their being restored to what they understood as their rightful place at the head of the Jerusalem priesthood. Thus, on numerous battlefields, both actual and conceptual, Jews were engaged in combat during the Hellenistic Period.

33. Josephus *Antiquities* XIV, *War* Book I, and Martin Noth, *The History of Israel*, 2nd ed. (New York: Harper & Row, 1960) 346–401, which covers the period from Alexander the Great to the Jerusalem victory of Pompey.

34. Zoroastrian influence provided Jewish apocalyptic with a cosmic dualism: a view which allowed the conception of a world as battleground between a good creative principle (*Ormazd*, or *Ahura-Mazda*), and an evil, disturbing principle (named *Angra-Mainyu* or *Ahriman*). These two principles competed for domination of the world. Cf. among others, the treatment of Zoroastrian literature in A. C. Bouquet, *Sacred Books of the World* (Baltimore: Penguin, 1954) 104–18; and also Albert T. Olmstead's, *History of the Persian Empire* (Chicago: University of Chicago Press, 1948); John M. Cook, *The Persian Empire* (London: Dent, 1983); and Richard N. Frye, *The Heritage of Persia* (London: Weidenfeld & Nicholson, 1966).

35. Cf. E. Mary Smallwood, *The Jews Under Roman Rule*, Studies in Judaism in Late Antiquity 20 (Leiden: Brill, 1976); John J. Collins, "Jewish Apocalyptic Against Its Hellenistic Near Eastern Environment," *BASOR* 220 (1975) 27–36, and Erich S. Gruen, *The Hellenistic World and the Coming of The Romans*, 2 vols. (Berkeley: University of California, 1984).

The Imagined War(s)

The war(s) imagined by the writers of Qumran is/are contained in what is known as the War Scroll. The fullest study of this scroll was produced by Yigael Yadin in a work published in Hebrew in 1955.[36] The scroll itself is identified in literature by the siglum 1QM,[37] and is preserved incompletely in nineteen columns. Rarely has a war been so well described, down to the vivid descriptions of vestments of the combatants and horses. Yet, 1QM is not a military manual. It belongs to the genre known as apocalyptic literature: a genre that requires some comment.[38]

The Balaams of the Hebrew Scriptures, as I shall refer to the types of the various recensions and allied literature discussed above, appear in all three divisions of the *TaNaK* or Hebrew Bible (Old Testament): the Law (*Torah*), the Prophets (*Nebi'im*), and the Writings (*Kethuvim*). The chief work, the Balaam cycle, is imbedded in Numbers 22–24, in the *Torah*. The Deuteronomy 23:5 passage belongs both to the Torah as its last book, and the *Nevi'im*, as the first book the prophets. That D recension of the Balaam cycle belongs to the Deuteronomistic outlook. Thus, the *Nevi'im* perspective is also contained in *Torah* material. Micah, as a scroll contained within the Twelve Prophet Scroll, most certainly takes its place within the *Nevi'im* worldview. These *Torah, Torah/Nevi'im,* or *Nevi'im* works represent outlooks that are un-historical. Nehemiah 13:2 is located within the *Kethuvim* section, and is one of the few works purporting to be "doing" history.

The material of the *Nevi'im* section revolves around the view that at the Mountain of Yahweh two parties, Israel and Yahweh, entered into a covenant.[39] No specific date is provided the reader in relation to some known occurrence, and two names have been assigned to the name of the mountain: Sinai in one tradition, and Horeb in another.[40] Without sacri-

36. Cf. Y. Yadin in n. 13 above.

37. Which means that it was retrieved from Cave 1 of the Qumran Caves, and has the title *Milhemeth Bne Or bi-Bne Hoshech* (The War Between the Sons of Light and the Sons of Darkness).

38. Cf. Paul D. Hanson, "Jewish Apocalyptic against Its Near Eastern Environment," *RB* 78 (1971) 31–58; and John J. Collins, "Jewish Apocalyptic against Its Hellenistic Near Eastern Environment."

39. Cf. Klaus Baltzer, *Covenant Formulary*, transl. David E. Green (Philadelphia: Fortress, 1971); and Moshe Weinfeld, "B'rith," in *TDOT*, 2:253–59.

40. J and E respectively.

ficing the importance of the priestly office and its duties of maintaining a ritual relationship between the two covenanted parties, the prophetic stamp of this sacerdotal responsibility focused more on "grass roots" issues equally important to maintaining the covenant relationship. Thus was born a movement of specialization within the priestly ranks.[41]

The "prophetic" priests focused on ethics, i.e., oughtness, as needing serious and omnipresent cultivation. This stance and decision was especially true when wealthy middle classes emerged during periods of prosperity in Israel and Judah, and gave rise to new moralities and concomitant conduct. The prophetic priests gauged all actions of members of the covenant by the laws of the covenant, and made no exceptions in terms of laying blame at the feet of the proper offender, namely, for rebellion against the covenant demands, whether that offender were a priest-king or a simple farmer.

The most obvious body of literature in which to view this prophetic concern about flagrant violation of covenant rules and requirements is the corpus of writings known as *melachim*, (1 and 2 Kings). Therein, each of the kings of Israel and Judah is subjected to criticism of rebellions characterizing their period of tenure, and are assigned a report card grade. Few of these monarchs received a good report. Among those who do are David, Hezekiah, and above all, Josiah. This prophetic view was written during the age of Josiah (ca. 639–609 BCE).[42] Although the subject of each critique is a king, it is not the kingliness of their office which interests the writer of these critiques. Rather, it is the priestly side of their office that receives stinging rebuke.

These kings did not live up to their priestly responsibilities vis-à-vis the covenant they had sworn publicly to uphold. A further litany of rebellions is available in the writings of such prophetic literature as Amos, Hosea, Micah, Isaiah 10, 23, 28–39, and Jeremiah. What the reader must not lose sight of is the fact that the prophetic priest critiques the un-priestly, namely, the irresponsible acts of priest-kings. The reason lies in the fact that most, if not all, of the prophets after whom biblical books have been named, were themselves priests. The term prophetic, unless strictly understood and adhered to, can be most misleading to the average reader. The author/collector of the Books of the Kings refers

41. Cf. Theophile J. Meek, *Hebrew Origins* (New York: Harper & Row, 1960 c. 1936) 148–83.

42. Cf. Friedman, *Who Wrote The Bible?* 135.

his readers to the archives, namely, the Chronicles of the Kings of Israel and of Judah that were located in Jerusalem in the days of this author/collector. If they want to pursue the issue of how these kings functioned as kings, they can look there. He does not clutter up his critique of them in their role as priests by listing their kingly accomplishments, though for some of the kings these were considerable.[43]

The prophetic priests kept company with the kingly and priest-kingly of the community. As soon as the first king of Israel, Saul (ca. 1020 BCE), had been anointed, he combined with a band of prophets.[44] He thereby effected a marriage, as it were, between the two functions and worldviews. That arrangement lasted until the last king of Judah, Mattaniah, was ignominiously carried off in chains to Babylonia about 587/6 BCE.

Although the office of the prophet, and the prophetic view resurfaced during the exilic and post-exilic periods in the writings of Ezekiel and Deutero-Isaiah, on the one hand, and Haggai and Zechariah, on the other, the prophetic characteristics of the participants remained the same. They were still priests. What had changed was the focus of their writings and their critiques. For one thing, there were no more priest-kings to critique. Their role as consumer advocates of Israel was over. The latest glimpse into the prophetic worldview is contained in the book of Deutero-Zechariah 13:2ff. There one reads of the death knell which has been delivered to that worldview and activity.

Most literature on the subject intimates that the prophets should be pitied as having outlived their usefulness, as having fallen prey to their own devices, as being an example of being on top in May, and having been shot down in June.[45] Nothing could be farther from the facts. What probably occurred is that the former, pre-exilic preoccupation of priest and (priest)-prophet under the monarchy, responded

43. The "Chronicles" would have been kept in priestly, scribal repositories near the temple complex in Jerusalem, available to those who possessed "library cards," as it were.

44. Cf. 1 Samuel 10:1–8.

45. Cf. Georg Fohrer, *History of Israelite Religion*, (New York: Abingdon, 1972) 359: "Ezra's reform finally set the mainstream of Yahwism on the course that turned its back on the insights and principles that had previously prevailed, above all on the message of the prophets." And John Bright, *A History of Israel*, 2nd. ed. (Philadelphia: Westminster, 1976) 322: "The official promulgation of a written law, ... elevated the law until it became in post-exilic times ... the first step in the concomitant process whereby the prophetic movement, ... came to an end."

to the post-exilic preoccupation of priests at the center of a theocratic government,[46] sacrificial priests and scribal priests. Prophets, then, did not disappear in ignominy; they merely joined the scribal side of the priestly equation.

This scribal side of post-exilic priestly activity appears to have taken two trajectories. Following one trajectory, one entered the *arcana mundi* of the Torah of the God of Heaven, a *torah*, which under Ezra the Scribe, had become nothing less than a written constitution of the small Jewish government of Jerusalem sometime between 444–398 BCE.[47] This *torah* gave rise to attorneys-at-*torah* whose job it was to constantly update it and make it useful as a constitution in the face of numerous political and social changes.[48] These attorneys-at-*torah* were priests who specialized in scribal functions. Of course, the ruler of Jerusalem, the center of this constitutional government, was the High Priest.

The other trajectory of the post-exilic priestly concern crystallized into what one may term the apocalyptic worldview. It focused on a specific time in a relatively-understood future. They counted themselves among this elect group which had been selected, and which had been vouchsafed certain key, and heretofore unknown-to-the-public-at-large information about coming events of a cosmic nature. It was their unquestioned piety, faithfulness to the (still in force) covenant, and personal deportment which had caused them to be selected by the deity. Their knowledge guaranteed that they would be at the cutting edge of any new theocratic government established in Jerusalem after the pivotal godly intervention established on earth a Jerusalem after God's heart and desires. After this, nothing would ever be as it had been before. Literature expressing such a Second Temple Judaism apocalyptic and eschatological worldview is legion.[49]

46. Thus, the Temple of Jerusalem was rebuilt between 520 and 515/14 BCE and the sacrificial cult resumed.

47. Ezra the priest's duties do not involve him in sacrificial duties.

48. Even this side of the bifurcated priestly function split, apparently, into two concerns. The first, the *scribal*, is summed up, although much later, in Ecclesiasticus: "On the other hand he who devotes himself to the study of the law of the Most High will seek out the wisdom of all the ancients, and will be concerned with prophecies; . . . He will reveal instruction in his teaching, and will glory in the law of the Lord's covenant" (Sir 39:1–4a, 7–8). The second, the *apocalyptic*, is also *learned*, and is understood to be the continuation of and "heir" to the "prophetic" inclination.

49. Cf. Paul D. Hanson, *The Dawn of Apocalyptic*, rev. ed. (Philadephia: Fortress, 1979); and "Apocalypticism," in *IDBS*, 27–34.

The 1QM scroll belongs to this apocalyptic genre. It tells of events which will occur, not of events which have already occurred. That is the first and major characteristic of this apocalyptic material. Specifically, it describes in futuristic terms a spiritual battle between two ongoing adversarial forces: The Sons of Light and the Sons of Darkness.[50] At a time only known to those who have advance knowledge of the *things to be revealed*,[51] the God of Heaven will intervene. This intervention will surely appear to those on the earthly plane as more of the ongoing struggle between the two equally-matched camps, namely, the ongoing life of warfare, as it had been known until the time of the apocalypse.

God will, by his intervention, turn the tide of the battle in favor of his Sons of Light. This will bring an end to the conflict.[52] 1QM quotes three passages from the Balaam cycle: Numbers 24:8 at 1QM 12:11; Numbers 24:17 at 1QM 7:19–20; and Numbers 24:18 at 1QM 11:6–7. This is typical of the whole Qumran literature which employs numerous glosses, expands parallel passages, and excels in editorial-type activity.[53] The Balaam we study here must be understood within the framework of apocalypticism: we encounter the apocalyptic-relevant Balaam.

Red flags should go up immediately when one begins to read the War Scroll, after having read to this point in my work. The first engagement of the Sons of Light in the war is against the troops of Edom, Moab, and the Ammonites, the Philistines and the *Kittim* of Assyria.[54] All have a connection with my study of Balaam interpretations and uses so far. Edom and Moab, and sometimes Amalek, were the scenes of the desired cursing by Balaam, and Balaam arrived in the city of Moab from Ammon, as we know from the Balaam cycle. The Philistines were one of

---

50. Cf. n. 34 above.

51. That is, *apocalypse*, revelatory knowledge.

52. This, however, is only one battle consisting of seven encounters in its present redacted form. See the discussion in Philip R. Davies, *Qumran* (Guilford, UK: Lutterworth, 1982) 118–25.

53. The *pesher* and sectarian commentary, the best example of Qumran editorial activity, is studied by Y. Yadin, "Some Notes on the Newly Published *Pesharim* of Isaiah," *IEJ* 9 (1959) 39–42; J. Carmignac, "Notes sur les Pesharim," *RQ* 3 (1962) 505–38; and David Flusser, "The *Pesher* of Isaiah and the Twelve Apostles," *Eretz Israel* 8 [E. L. Sukenik Memorial Volume] (1967) 52–62 (Hebrew); J. D. Asmusin, "Ephriam et Manasse dans le Pesher de Nahum," *RQ* 4 (1964) 389–96; and G. Lambert, "Traduction de quelques 'psaumes' de Qumran et du 'pesher' d'Habacuc," *NRT* (1952) 284–97.

54. 1QM 1:1.

the first groups, along with the Moabites, to rebel against the Assyrians under whom they labored as vassals during the days of Hezekiah, king of Judah. In fact, both the Philistines and Moabites sent envoys to Hezekiah attempting to lure him into their political schemes.[55]

Hezekiah merely studied the situation from a safe distance. The *Kittim* (cf. Numbers 24:22 and the P recension of the Balaam cycle, n. 1 above and n. 62 below), underwent development in the minds and interpretation schemes of Israelite priestly groups as well. Essentially, the *Kittim* went from meaning a group of Mediterranean, Cyprus-dwelling warriors who reached the shores of the eastern Levant in the seventh-sixth centuries, to any invader of the eastern Levant from lands located to its west, to foreigners in general with hostile intentions toward the Israelites.[56] *Kittim* later even included the Romans.

The various interpreters of the Balaam material and the Qumran writers who penned the War Scroll had much in common, and their concerns about the virtually same set of enemies is not coincidental. It has been demonstrated that the writers of each piece of biblical Balaam material were priests, either Mushite, based at the shrine at Shiloh, or Aaronid/Zadokite, based at the national shrine in Jerusalem.[57] The Balaam cycle recensions demonstrated that each recensionist added to, rather than subtracted from, the basic stump of the story/mosaic. And although two major trajectories can be followed throughout the remainder to the biblical period, enough remains of the "stump" so that one never has to lose sight of it as the anchoring tradition.

Anywhere one reads in the Qumran literature, one encounters the writings of a priest. Since these writers voluntarily established a monastery in the Judean wilderness, due on no small part to their politico-sacerdotal worldview, they were priests who had no stake in the sacrificial cult side of the priestly office in Jerusalem. The most telling evidence, therefore, to suggest that with the first founders of the

55. Cf. Isa 14:29-31 (an oracle against Philistia) and Isa 15–16 (an oracle against Moab), and the discussion in Greene, "Balaam,'89," 90–92.

56. The *Kittim*, the final enemy of the Qumran sect, are discussed in R. Goossens, "Les Kittim du Commentaire d'Habacuc," NC (1952) 137–70; and by Otto Eissfeldt, *The Old Testament: An Introduction*, trans. P. R. Ackroyd (New York: Harper & Row, 1965) 419–20.

57. Greene, "Balaam,'89," 70–92.

Qumran *yahad*[58] we are dealing with essentially scribe/priests of the type described above, is their copious library, and the way it has come to us modern researchers.[59]

The Nehemiah 8 material tells the reader that many of the associates of Ezra the (priest) Scribe were Levites. The job of these Levites on the most important day of their lives, the day on which an assembly had been summoned officially before the Water Gate in Jerusalem to hear and witness the Torah of the God of Heaven read to them, circulated among the assembly, and according to Nehemiah 8:7–9, they themselves "read from the book, from the Law of God, clearly; and they gave the sense,[60] so that the people understood the reading." Verse 9 tells the reader that: ". . . the Levites taught the people . . ." One more piece of information must be supplied before we continue. It is found in Nehemiah 7:73. If one reads uncritically, the fact will escape that four specializations within the post-exilic priestly ranks are enumerated here: priests, Levites, gatekeepers, and temple servants.[61]

The Qumran material reflects the work of two of these four groups: the priests and the Levites. This particular distinction within the priestly ranks was maintained by the producer of the P source stratum of the

---

58. Cf. Y. Baer, "*Serekh ha-Yahad*—The Manual of Discipline: A Jewish-Christian Document from the Beginning of the Second Century CE," *Zion* 29 (1960) 1–60 (Hebrew); and Ralph Marcus, "Philo, Josephus and the Dead Sea *Yahad*," *JBL* 70 (1952) 207–9.

59. Frank M. Cross Jr., *The Ancient Library at Qumran and Modern Biblical Studies* (Garden City, NY: Doubleday, 1961).

60. . . . *mbynym ʾat-hʾam ltwrh . . . wswm skl wybynw bmqrʾa* (Neh 8:7–8) is a bit more active than many translations into English would suggest *mbynym*, for example, is an active participle of a *hifil* (causative *binyan* or conjugation pattern). "They caused them to understand" (=*mbynym*) produces an image of much verbal give and take on the part of both the Levite Scribe/Assistant to Ezra (the Arch scribe), and the person(s) for whom the teaching was intended. "And placing comprehension (on *Torah*), they caused (the audience) to understand."

61. These four ranks (Scribes according to Nehemiah 8:7 and 8:9 come from both the *priest* and *Levites* ranks) producing the "priestly estates" suggest a highly stratified self-view of the priestly office in Jerusalem in the Ezra-Nehemiah and post-Ezra-Nehemiah periods. Gatekeepers and temple servants were priestly groups whose courses would have required their presence physically within the temple precincts. Not so for the groups priest and Levites. These groups appear to have consisted of various specialized substrata groups. See Ezra 7:7 where singers are also mentioned.

Pentateuch.[62] It may be that the priests referred to as Levites did not mind. At any rate, we have available no text containing a complaint by the group designated Levites which suggests that they had an insurmountable problem with this appellation.[63] Ezra, traditionally held to be the redactor of the R source stratum of the Pentateuch, is cast as their Zadokite, not Levite, leader and arch Sribe, who has no problem working with the Levites.[64] Likewise, the intellectual, multilingual Levites appear to support Ezra's arch scribal efforts. After all, all of them were ultimately official agents of the Persian government![65]

Thus, a strong scribal class of priests was responsible for producing the Qumran library. One may add further, that there is evidence of both Zadokite priestly input and Levite priestly input.[66] Whatever the contents of the Qumran library, the contents are a joint Zadokite (Aaronid)–Levite(Mushite) venture and enterprise. Whatever distinctions existed during the days of P appear to have been no longer of concern during the days of the Qumran covenanters.

Qumran, then, provides the reader with a Balaam type figure who is the product of reconciliation between two formerly warring priestly factions, as well as providing other significant data. The Qumran Balaam influence does not reflect factionalism among traditionally warring priests. Rather, his typology is employed to ensure unity. The medium

62. Friedman, *Who Wrote?*, 210, Greene, '89, 76–81, and n. 66 below.

63. There exists no literary complaint, that is, until one reads critically the *Testament of Levi*, a part of the *Testament of the Twelve Patriarchs* contained in the Pseudepigrapha. The literary view contained therein was probably engendered by the success of the Maccabean Revolt and Hasmonean success. *The Testament of Levi* laments the demise of, and looks forward to the restoration of Levite messiahs (=priest/kings). The Maccabee/Hasmoneans were Levites.

64. Friedman, 217–45; 246–54; especially 218–55 for a discussion of Ezra the Aaronid priest.

65. Cf. Erza 7:11–14 (and Neh 2:5–9).

66. My previous study of the Balaam cycle has shown that "Balaam" was a "bat" in the grip of numerous "sluggers"; all attempting to bash out each other's brains, or at least to "bash" one or another group into submission. The most vicious "slugger" was P, and to him is traced the distinction between *priest* (a priest) and *Levite* (priest!). This distinction, or at least dual appellation at Qumran appears to have been most acceptable in light of non-sacrificing priestly self-views expressed in their writings. "Balaam" is no longer the enemy-*typos*. Danger is not presented by the Sons of Darkness and the *Kittim*! Both terms were loaded.

for accomplishing this is the *pesher*,[67] the interpretive commentary on literature, employed to tell another story, or to present another etiology. At Qumran Balaam is not a shaped explosive charge aimed strategically at rival priesthoods, whether within or without Israel. At Qumran, there is the unified assumption of guilt and culpability on the part of Balaam, the ancient prophet; but his influence, nonetheless, had a major part to play in terms of understanding apocalyptic warfare.

Considering the problem as developed to this point, we are ultimately still in the midst of a situation that pits priest against priest. However, we are no longer still embroiled in a situation where it is Israel priest against Israel priest, or Israelite priest against Judaite priest, or even Shilonite priest against both Israel and Judaite priests, as had been the case in ancient Israel. Balaam the type-figure, therefore, is no longer necessary for the type of anti priestly arguments produced at Qumran.

What is significantly different is that we are now witnessing literature which works through the problem of legitimate Jewish priest *versus* illegitimate Jewish priest! What has altered the earlier equations is a radical change in what is understood to be Israel! And the exigencies of the historical situation had brought that about.[68]

1) Numbers 24:17 reads:

> I see him, but not now; I behold him, but not high: a star shall come forth out of Jacob, and a scepter shall rise out of Israel; it shall crush the corners of the head of Moab, and break down all the sons of Sheth.

2) Numbers 24:18 reads:

> Edom shall be dispossessed, Seir also, his enemies, shall be dispossessed, while Israel does valiantly.

3) Numbers 24:8 reads:

> God brings him out of Egypt; he has as it were the horns of the wild ox, he shall eat up the nations his adversaries, and

---

67. See n. 53 above.

68. With the Maccabee/Hasmoneans, specific Levites found themselves enjoying titles such as High Priest and Priest-King; leadership positions in Jerusalem after the death of the high priest Onias III. The *Testament of Levi* mentioned in Note #63 above is sympathetic with his historical situation.

shall break their bones in pieces, and pierce them through with his arrows.

All three selections come from material that comprises the Balaam cycle of Numbers 22–24. The Qumran worldview embraced that material and saw its usefulness in constructing its idealized and ideological war. Looking at the contents of the three, one sees that the material quoted belongs to the *Book of the Wars of Yahweh* material.[69] Qumran used the Numbers 24:8 "footnote" to describe combatants on the side of the Sons of Light. Its bellicose tone is apropos for the purposes of the War Scroll. Qumran employed the Numbers 24:18 material because it once again names one of the archenemies of Israel, as seen from the point of view of the priestly group writing this scroll. Moab and Sheth complete the list of primary archenemies, and link the Qumran tradition to that of the producers of the Numbers 22–24 material concerning Balaam, and to their epigones. This relates the Balaam cycle of Numbers to those who employed the cycle's contents following by one of the two trajectories about Balaam described above.

Other military oriented material certainly existed which could have been employed to make either of the three above points. My task, therefore, is to ascertain why this material and not some other material was employed in the War Scroll at this point. To accomplish this, let us first look at some particular phraseology of the Scroll column by column. Concerning the religious offices during wartime,[70] the producers of the Scroll wrote:

> After this high priest and his deputy they shall appoint an order of major priests, twelve in number, to serve constantly before God. Furthermore, twenty-six major officials duly assigned to service shall serve in their appointed offices; and after them shall be twelve Levites, one for each tribe, to serve constantly.

Concerning the battle signals,[71] they wrote:

---

69. Apparently, this work was greatly expanded, and thus served as the literary vehicle for telling the story of the journey of Moses and his host from the Mountain of YHWH to a position in Trans-Jordan opposite Jericho. It was from there that the Joshua-led group is depicted as having continued across the Jordan.

70. 1QM II (II:1–2).

71. 1QM VI (a) VII: 8, (b) VII:11; (d) VII:12.

When the lines of battle are drawn up to face the foe, line in front of line, then out of the center gap in the ranks there shall come into the lines seven priests of the descendants of Aaron . . . and: (a) And when these priests go out between the lines, seven Levites shall go out with them, . . . and: (b) And three officers selected from the Levites shall walk ahead of these priests and Levites. As well as: (c) And the priests shall sound a blast on [two of the trumpets] for calling to arms . . . and the levitical officers [shall go out with them]. (d)

Of the order of battle, the covenanters wrote:

After the priests have sounded a blast for them (i.e., the warriors) on the trumpets of [memorial], . . . Then the priests shall blow a second time, . . . And the Levites and all the people with ram's horns shall sound a loud blast.[72]

Finally, on thanksgiving for victory (an apocalyptic gross assumption!), one reads:

And when the sun is hastening to set on that day, the high priest shall stand up, and the priests and the Levites that are with him, . . .[73]

Compare the contents of these excerpts with the following one from the *TaNaK*:

And Hezekiah established the divisions of the priests and the Levites, according to their divisions, every man according to his task, for the priests and for the Levites. (2 Chron 31:2)

What all have in common is that an obvious distinction has been made between priests and Levites. The distinction comes from warfare: warfare between the Aaronid priesthood and the Mushite priesthood. The distinction is introduced and maintained in literature belonging to the Aaronid tradition. It is never located in E or D source *stratum* material. Friedman wrote of the situation which brought this division about: "Solomon had removed the Shiloh (Levite/Mushite) priest Abiathar from Jerusalem and had given authority in the Temple entirely to the Aaronid priest Zadok."[74] This had occurred in the tenth century

72. 1QM XVI:2–9.
73. 1QM XVIII:2.
74. Friedman, *Who Wrote?* 211.

BCE (ca. 966). P wrote at the court of Hezekiah during his attempt at religious reform. One major plank in his reform platform was centralizing the priesthood at Jerusalem. Thus, Friedman's statements,: "King Hezekiah was the best thing that ever happened to the Aaronid priests" and "Hezekiah followed Solomon's priestly preferences,"[75] moreover, the 2 Chronicles 31:2 account provided sufficient information about, and reason for the bifurcation within the seventh century and later priestly ranks in Jerusalem in particular. Later material such as the D source *stratum* did not maintain this distinction; at least it did not reflect such a division literarily.

The priest/Levite division is maintained in 1QM. It reveals that a group of descendants of the Aaronid/Zadokite line wrote this material. Thus, the beginning of the *Manual of Discipline for the Future Congregation of Israel* from Qumran should not surprise the reader:

> This is the rule for the whole body of Israel when, in the future, they lead their lives in the manner of the sons of Zadok, the priests, and of those associated with them . . .[76]

Obviously, one of the associated groups was understood and assumed to have been Levites.

The Balaam material quoted within 1QM has a tradition connection with the P recension of the Numbers Balaam cycle. Any entry into the *arcana mundi* of why only these three Numbers passages from the Balaam cycle were employed must be approached from the standpoint of that P trajectory. The three "footnotes" demonstrate how severely the Balaam tradition within the P trajectory had been altered by the time of the writing of the War Scroll. Balaam the figure and Balaam the type no longer served as foils against other priestly outsiders. At Qumran no nebulous outsider was held up as a paradigm, either to be emulated, or to be spurned. The Balaam of the recensions had all but disappeared: had become blended into the background of the Qumran P program.

At Qumran the words ascribed to Balaam in poetically-written *mshlym* "footnotes" of Numbers were severed from the one who supposedly uttered them. Balaam had been demoted: his words had been promoted. Words of a gazer (*tzofeh*/teleologist) had been lifted from one body of literature which depicted a wartime situation (Israel camped

75. Ibid., 211–12.
76. 1QS 1:1.

in the plains of Moab opposite Jericho, following the Yahweh/holy war itinerary), and had been purposefully imbedded by gazers/apocalypticists in another body of literature which depicts another wartime situation. The reputed utterances of the *propriediv* Balaam at Qumran did not become dead letters once they were written down. A new living tradition about Balaam's words was generated among the P tradition participants and contributors, and new life was breathed into the word. The excerpted "footnotes" are written proof of that.

A Discovery at Tell Deir 'Alla: Its Implications and Significance

Much that has been discussed about the Balaam figure thus far grew out of an ancient document which was certainly earlier than the tenth century BCE. That is, the document on which the writer of the J source *stratum* based his or her Balaam figure preceded the ancient Israelite, Jerusalem-based use of Balaam. Although that document is lost to us, perhaps a later copy, or reworking of that earlier document, survived, at least to the eighth century BCE in a separate, non-Israelite tradition. "This inscription, as we have reconstructed it, provides us with what is probably the best example we have of the appearance of an eighth-century BCE Northwest Semitic manuscript in *Aramaic, Phoenician*, or *Hebrew* [emphasis mine]. At that time, the differences among these three scripts were minimal."[77] With these words, André Lemaire described an extra-Israelite text concerning Balaam ben Beor produced by way of archaeological research in present-day Jordan. The text was written on a plastered wall in black and red. Black was used for writing the majority of the text, while red served for writing titles and key words intended by the scribe(s) to stand in relief. The Balaam text occupied one of four columns. The remaining three columns need not distract us, for Balaam was not their subject. This Balaam text, the latest text concerning him to be found (March 1967), describes the activities of a *ḥzh*, a seer/prophet. He is specifically termed *'š ḥzh 'lhn*, the man who was a seer of the gods. It is generally agreed that the text of Deir 'Alla is a copy of a much older text.[78] A reconstructed text follows.

77. André Lemaire, "Fragments from the Book of Balaam Found at Deir 'Alla," *BAR* 11/5 (1985) 39.

78. It has been suggested that the text was located in a scribal school, and that it

The account of [Balaam, son of Beor], who was a seer of the gods. The gods came to him in the night, and he saw a vision (2) like an oracle of El. Then they said to [Balaa] m, son of Beor: "Thus he will do/make [ ] hereafter (?), which [ ]." (3) And Balaam arose the next day [ ] from [ ] but he was not ab[le to] and he wept (4) grievously. And his people came up to him [and said to him, "Balaam, son of Beor why are you fasting and cry-ing?" And he sa(5)id to them: "Sit down! I will tell you what the Šadda[yyin] have done.] Now, come, see the works of the gods! The g[o]ds gathered together; (6) the Šaddayyin took their plac-es in the assembly.[79]

This account depicts Balaam as having much in common with several ninth-century to sixth-century BCE prophets mentioned in the Hebrew Scriptures. 1) He sees visions, which are like oracles. 2) He responds to bad tidings by not eating, and by weeping, because he must retail these tidings to his people, and he, too, is subject to any coming calamity he must proclaim. 3) He (through his vision) gained entry into the assembly of the gods. The superscriptions of the prophetic books of the Hebrew Scriptures may be likened to the first characteristic. Jeremiah 36:24; Isaiah 20:2–4; and Isaiah 37:1–2 show similar respons-es to the second commonality. The third places Balaam in a class with Michaiah the son of Imlah of 1 Kings 22:19–22; Isaiah 6:1–4; Jeremiah 23:18, 23:22; Psalm 82:1, 89:7; Job 15:8 and the picture painted by Job 1:6–12.[80]

The last observation may be expanded. Following the final sen-tence of the above-quoted Balaam text the account continues: "And they said to Š [ ]: "Sew up, bolt up the heavens in your cloud, ordaining

---

possibly served as a text for copying exercises. This is pure speculation, however. The same was proposed for the Gezer Calendar also.

79. This portion of the translation of the reconstructed text is the work of Jo Ann Hackett, *The Balaam Text From Deir 'Alla*, HSM 31 (Atlanta: Scholars, 1980) 29.

80. The Council of Yahweh receives treatment in Frank Moore Cross Jr., "The Council of Yahweh in Second Isaiah," *JNES* 12 (1953) 274–79; W. Hermann, "*Die Goettersoehne*," *ZRRG* 12 (1960) 242–51; Edwin C. Kingsbury, "The Prophets and the Council of Yahweh," *JBL* 88 (1964) 279–86; H. Wheeler Robinson, "The Council of Yahweh," *JTS* 45 (1945) 151–57 in *Inspiration and Revelation in the Old Testament*, (Oxford: Oxford University Press, 1946); and the discussion in Simon J. DeVries, *Prophet against Prophet: The Role of the Michaiah Narrative (I Kings 22) in the Development of Early Prophetic Tradition* (Grand Rapids: Eerdmans, 1978) 5, 7, 40–42.

darkness instead of (7) eternal light!"[81] Apparently, the council of gods gave a directive to one of its members to cause the calamity which was designed to punish Balaam's people. This recalls a similar scene in Job 1:6–12. Through a series of such images as "the deaf hear from afar" and "a fool sees visions" (lines 13 and 14 of the reconstructed text), existence is depicted as topsy-turvy.[82] That this sole deity's name commences with the letter Š, and that deity is depicted as playing a "spoiler's role" opposite humankind, it is very tempting to see a connection with another figure in a similar role in the prologue of the book of Job: the Satan (adversary). However, we need not yield to this temptation.

The Balaam of the Deir 'Alla text is depicted as a seer who has a dream vision at night. The reconstruction contains numerous *lacunae*. What we know, however, is that the Seer is frightened by its contents, for his people are to be chastised by fire as punishment for somehow having rebelled against their gods. This so unnerves the seer that on the day he arose from his sleep he was unable to eat and drink, but spent much time weeping in sorrow. After describing the nature of the punishment which is to befall his people, he states also that it will be meted out on a specific date. Regarding what will happen specifically, the sun god, Shamash—another candidate for the unnamed deity beginning with the consonant cluster *Sh*, will shut the skies with a cloud. This will bring on utter darkness. Mindless terror will result, his people will be thrown into derision, and a plethora of winged creatures will fill the skies signaling their doom. It is at this juncture, unfortunately, that the badly damaged text breaks off and becomes unreadable. Speculating about what possibly followed, one scholar wrote: "Perhaps by execrations or other forms of magic, Balaam attempted to avert the disaster."[83] Thus, one view of Balaam as magician had been intimated by the contents of this find.

---

81. Hackett, *Deir 'Alla*, 29.

82. Cf. the same type of imagery in the complaint of the Egyptian wise man of the Egyptian Early Intermediate Period, Ipuwer. Contemplating the disasters that had befallen Egypt—especially anarchy—he wrote: "The possessor of property is now one who has naught. Behold, servants have become masters of butlers; He who was a messenger now sends another." The example is derived from T. E. Peet, *A Comparative Study of the Literatures of Egypt, Palestine and Mesopotamia: Egypt's Contribution to the Literature of the Ancient World* (London: Oxford University Press, 1931) 118.

83. Lemaire, "Fragments," 37.

The Balaam text from Deir 'Alla, though newly discovered and recent in arrival into scholarly hands, is rooted in images which have long been familiar to the reader of the prophetic and wisdom literature of the Hebrew Scriptures. Rebellion against the gods by humans and the gods' reply by cosmic conflagration allow one to see that the themes of covenant and holy war are combined in the text. The ancient Israelites and Judahites would not have found its contents foreign. Although the Deir 'Alla text of Balaam probably dates to the eighth century, it is argued that this is merely a copy of a text which was considerably older.[84] The Deir 'Alla text suggests strongly that this figure was important and relevant during the eighth century BCE. Moreover, its existence at Deir 'Alla suggests that its writer(s) had inherited an even older text and tradition about a famous prophet, priest, diviner (*propriediv*) who must have been considered quite a phenomenon to his contemporaries, as well as to those beyond his times.

Conclusion

Deir 'Alla presents the interested reader with the latest discovered installment of an interpretation of Balaam's position and role. It takes its place among many, many others already extant which one reads throughout the literature of ancient Israel, employed here in its broadest sense. It can also be demonstrated that interest in the Balaam type *and* character continued to titillate the imagination of various post-Israelite writers and thinkers, even to modern times. The account of a Balaam ben Beor found recently in the Hashemite Kingdom of Jordan will serve as an excellent *Eintritt* into the fascinating and labyrinthine subject of prophecy, divination and magic. The figure and type, *Balaam*, will be shown to have lent itself well to the analytical and hermeneutical needs of several generations of ancient Israelite thinkers who found it both necessary and convenient to group certain problem-solving solutions around him. This we have already witnessed with the Pentateuchal rescensions and with the Qumran writings.

---

84. Lemaire, "Texts," 38.

12

The Balaam Figure and Type, before, during, and after the Period of the Pseudepigrapha

1 Enoch, Philo, NT, Josephus, Rabbinics, Islamics, and Modern Literature

John T. Greene

The Book of Enoch (1 Enoch)

THE INFLUENCE OF ONE BALAAM TRAJECTORY, (P), IS IMMEDIATELY SEEN when one reads the first vision of Enoch.[1] The *Prooimium* and central theme is the great judgment. Because this is the same theme noticed in the Deir 'Alla text, though in fragmented (text) form, it is appropriate to examine the Enochic theme at just this juncture of this study, namely, at the outset of this chapter. The Enochic type brings together a number of strands of interest observed in earlier studies of material in the previous chapter. It also highlights again the groups producing this material in which Balaam the figure or type appears. First Enoch's beginning "(1) The words of blessing, according to which Enoch blessed the righteous elect who, on the day of tribulation, are to destroy all

---

1. The literature on Enoch is prodigious. Cf. Nathaniel Schmidt, "The Original Language of the Parables of Enoch," in *Old Testament and Semitic Studies in Memory of William Rainey Harper*, ed. R. F. Harper et al. (Chicago: University of Chicago Press, 1908) 2:329–49; Edward Ullendorf, "An Aramaic 'Vorlage' of the Ethiopian Text of Enoch," in *Atti del Convegno Internazionale di Studi Etiopici*, Problemi attuali di scienza e di cultura 48, (Rome: Academia Nazionale dei Lincei, 1960) 259–67; and for a most recent exhaustive study which was designed to upgrade the celebrated work of R. H. Charles, Matthew Black, *The Book of Enoch or I Enoch*, Studia In Veteris Testamenti Pseudepigrapha (Leiden: Brill, 1985). All quotes from 1 Enoch are from Black's work.

the godless,"[2] recalls the *Weltanschauung* of the Qumran covenanters. These, one remembers, incorporated three "footnotes," which had been borrowed from the Balaam cycle, into a fleshed out vision of their own which saw them as the righteous elect engaged in a war of wars that would bring on a day of tribulation for their godless enemies, affecting their utter defeat.[3]

Verse (2)'s contents, some of the most relevant for our study here, will be displayed side by side with their Hebrew Scripture counterparts for immediate clarity.

Enoch 1:2	Numbers 23:15–16
And he took up his discourse and said: [Oracle of Enoch], a righteous man whose eyes were opened by God, and who saw a vision of the Holy One in heaven, which the angels showed me, and from the words of the [watchers and] holy ones I heard all; and I understood what I saw; not for this generation, but for a generation remote do I speak.[4]	And he took up his discourse, and said, "The oracle of Balaam the son of Beor, the oracle of the man whose eye is opened, the oracle of him who hears the words of God, and knows the knowledge of the Most High, who sees the vision of the Almighty, falling down, but having his eyes uncovered."

The reaction of the Qumran community to Numbers 23:15–16 was to include the contents of verses 17ff. in its apocalyptic scheme of holy war. The author of 1 Enoch ennobles the Balaam type, as it were, by appropriating characteristics attributed to him, and by boldly casting him in the light of such a credentialed seer/gazer. The enemies of the Numbers text are Moab, Sheth, Edom, and Seir. These, we saw with the Qumran War Scroll, were the same enemies who would be defeated first in that apocalyptic war. The Enoch text which follows 1:2 combines the concerns of both Qumran and Deir 'Alla; Qumran in that the enemies

2. Cf. Black, *Enoch*, 25.

3. See ch. 11 above, nn. 26, 30, and 36 on the War Scroll.

4. Black, *Enoch*, 25.

of the elect will be destroyed, Deir 'Alla in that the destructive conflagration will be meted out to a kind of heretofore elect who had rebelled
against the gods. One can weave in and out of all three texts with facility
and intuit just how easily one text could affect the others as one moves
toward the first century BCE.

The same formula, borrowed from Numbers 24:15, occurs twice
more in the Enochic materials; chs. 93:1–2 and 93:3ff. Chapter 93:1–2 is
short enough to present in its entirety:

> (1) And after he had given over his Epistle (to Methuselah),
> Enoch took up his discourse, saying:
> (2) Concerning the children of righteousness
>   and the eternal elect
> Sprung from the plant of righteousness
>   and uprightness,
> These things will I recount and make
>   known to you, my children:
> I, Enoch, was shown in a heavenly vision,
>   and from the words of the watchers and
>   holy ones I came to know everything,
>   and from the tables of heaven I read
>   and understood everything.

Once more the themes of righteousness, the elect, and upright-
ness connect the Enochic text with themes from Qumran self-concepts
encountered in the War Scroll; while themes of having been shown a
heavenly vision and words from the (multi-meaning) holy ones, directly
connects with the Balaam *propriediv/hozpriediv* type. Only the reading from heavenly tablets with (visionary) comprehension is foreign to
both themes.

Chapters 93:10; 91:11–17 comprise *The Apocalypse of Weeks*. It
(the apocalypse) begins:

> (93:3) And then Enoch took up his discourse and said: I was
> born the seventh in the First Week; And till my time justice was
> delayed.

Thereafter, ten weeks (or ages, epochs) follow during which various
advances and setbacks to human history are laid out briefly. Themes
familiar from the War Scroll are read in 93:10 ("... in the Seventh Week,
a perverse generation shall arise, ... And at its close the elect shall be
chosen ..."); and in 91:11 ("And they [the elect] will uproot the founda-

tions of oppression, And the structure of falsehood therein to destroy it utterly"). The war theme involving the righteousness continues in 91:12 where during the Eighth Week (a week of righteousness) judgment is meted out to the wicked, for "a sword will be given to all of the righteous." The Ninth and Tenth Weeks will be weeks of righteous judgment both on humans and on the *watchers*, at the end of which "the first heaven shall pass away, And a new heaven shall appear," (91:16). "And thereafter there shall be many Weeks; to all their number there shall be no end forever," (91:17). Such, then, is the fruit of the Balaam type's vision.

Enoch as a Balaam type keeps company with Pilti of the Samaritan material.[5] Both types demonstrate the powerful appeal of the Balaam figure, as groups following the trajectories of interpretation of his character and significance continued through ancient Israelite history. The Samaritans, an essentially prophet-hating group, fabricated out of the Balaam figure of their *verarbeitete/euberarbeitete* (over worked, over laid, reworked, recended) Pentateuch, a negative type whose function was to precurse, literally and figuratively, the appearance of a *propriediv* who, during the pilgrimage of Israel, was made to look stupid and ineffective by the power of Yahweh. It was a most negative view of all who engaged in what would have been understood to have been the prophetic consciousness.

The trajectory out of which the Enochic Balaam type emerges is attitudinally more allied with the Qumran covenanters than with the Samaritans. For this apocalyptic trajectory, the Balaam figure served as the perfect type through which the goals of revealed knowledge could be mediated. Whereas the Samaritans manufactured the type and then hurled it into the past to set up the individual responding to any other prophetic impulse than that of Moses their hero, the Enochic trajectory manufactured the type and depicted the figure as "not for this genera-

---

5. "The Birth Story of Moses," a part of the Samaritan materials, contains references to Numbers 24:17 of the Balaam cycle. It refers to the *star* that is to come forth out of Jacob, and the scepter that is to rise out of Israel. More specifically, the reader discovers that "there was with the wicked Pharaoh a sorcerer . . . and he knew the science of divination and omens." The sorcerer/diviner is identified in the text as a man named Pilti. Cf. John Bowman, *Samaritan Documents*, Pittsburgh Original Texts and Translation Series 2 (Pittsburgh: Pickwick, 1977) 63–85.

tion, but for a generation remote do I speak."[6] This figure was hurled into the future.

Whether directly or indirectly influenced, Enoch the book derives two other characteristics from the Balaam figure, type, and materials. Chapters 37–71 are termed the Parables or Similitudes of Enoch, while chs. 83–90 are known as The Dream-Vision of Enoch. Concerning the parables, there are three located at 37–44, 45–57, and 58–69. In the Aramaic version of 1 Enoch found at Qumran and known as 4QEn, the Parables section (37–71) is absent but the Dream-Vision section is present. At 1:2, cited above, the word rendered *mtlh* (*matlah*), by the now standard phenomenon of consonantal shifts in the Semitic languages, is rendered by *mshl* (*mashal*) in Hebrew. I made the decision to employ this term consistently throughout my analysis of the literature that made the Balaam cycle.[7] Rather than employ such terms as parable, gnome, aphorism, oracle, or discourse, I thought it best to render the Hebrew term only. Due to the possibility of an inaccurate rendering of the term now in the Enochic material, I continue to adhere to this decision, now on the basis of the Aramaic *mtlh*. Enoch, like Balaam, delivered *mshlym* (*meshalim*). I leave it to the bean/bead-counters to make more of this.

From Balaam is also borrowed the practice of entering the world of dream-visions. According to Black, they represent "the longest and the most self-consistent part of the book."[8] In a zoomorphic history of the world set within the framework of Enoch's instructions to Methuselah his son, he presents "a series of visions in which the principle protagonists are symbolized by animals . . ."[9] These visions, which Enoch shares typologically with the Balaam of Deir 'Alla, cover a period from the Deluge to a Last Judgment sometime following the period of the Maccabean Revolt. I focus only on the agency of the Balaam type's knowledge, not on the contents. Balaam as figure, type, and actor in the hands and hermeneutic of the Enochic school proved to have been a man for all (their) seasons, indeed.

---

6. Ibid., 25.

7. Cf. Greene, "Balaam '89," 62; 65–67; 68–70; 72–76, and on Enochic material see "*Mashal* in the Similitudes of Enoch," *JBL* 100 (1981) 193–212.

8. Black, *Enoch* 19.

9. Ibid.

Balaam in the New Testament

With the millennium change from BCE to CE, interest in Balaam did not cease, and his figure and type did not receive rest from hermeneutist detractors. Three such detractors contributed the New Testament works of Revelation, Jude, and 2 Peter.

At Revelation 2:14, one of three major apocalyptic works that incorporate the Balaam figure or type, Qumran and Enoch being the other two, in part of a critique to the angel of the church at Pergamum, the writer holds:

> But I have a few things against you:
> you have some there who hold the
> teaching of Balaam, who taught Balak to
> *put a stumbling block before the sons*
> *of Israel, that they might eat food*
> *sacrificed to idols and practice immorality."* (emphases are mine)

These practices were serious enough for the writer to hold that "He who has the sharp two-edged sword" (Rev. 2:12) will "come . . . soon and war against them (the Balaam-like teachers) with the sword of (his) mouth" (Rev 2:16). This indictment contains the same complaints mirrored in Acts 15:20 and 29; that of food sacrificed to idols, and immorality. Balaam here serves as the type who opposed such restrictions and actually reflects the attitude of the writers of Romans 14:14; 20–21; and Acts 10:28. At any rate, this Balaam is fabricated on the loom of those who were embroiled in the issue of requirements for proselytes coming into various Greco-Roman forms of Hellenistic Judaism(s). To be sure, Balaam-of-the-cycle is associated with sacrifices. On more than one occasion, he gives instructions to Balak to sacrifice. But not to idols! Rather, he sacrifices to Yahweh. And even though the writer of Numbers 31:8ff. is thoroughly irate, the charge against Balaam is not immorality. He tempts the males of Israel to rebel against the covenant, not to be immoral! This is Balaam dressed in later hermeneutical garb to be the fall guy for other problems encountered by a later "Israel".

The writer of the little Epistle of Jude 1:11 packs a lot of complaints into one line of text. Reviling heretic and "false teachers of all kinds, he argues that they: "walk in the way of Cain, and abandon themselves for the sake of gain to Balaam's error, and perish with Korah's rebellion." The themes of jealousy/murder/guilt, greed, and rebellion against the Lord's prophet are there. Cain murdered. Balaam accepted fees for mediating Yahweh's word. This made it a commercial venture, quite different from receiving the acceptable tithes as fees for mediating Yahweh's will! Korah rebelled against the proper leadership of the people Israel, namely, Moses. Evidently for him, Balaam's guilt was false teaching as well as greed, and he is viewed by this writer as one of three past archetypes.

The second epistle of Peter is possibly the latest work in the canonical New Testament. In addition to containing all of Jude, and being written by a different author than 1 Peter, it argues against all heresies, especially those that deny the coming of Christ. At 2:15, Balaam is implicated in influencing people to forsake the right way. Specifically: "they have followed the way of Balaam, the son of Beor, who loved gain from wrongdoing, but was rebuked for his own transgression; a dumb ass spoke with human voice and restrained the prophet's madness." Like the writer of Jude, 2 Peter's author understood that Balaam accepted gratuities, and that this had been wrong. In addition, the writer stressed Balaam's humiliation at the mouth of the ass who shares billing with the Balaam-of-the-cycle.

Josephus' *Antiquities* and Balaam

For Josephus, Balaam was the greatest of the prophets, a viewpoint with which the Samaritans would have taken great issue. He was raised to great reputation because of the truth of his predictions (*Ant.* 4.6.2).[10] He added a few twists to the account contained in the Balaam cycle, however, such as:

1. a statement that Balaam was afraid of having incurred God's wrath after the speaking ass incident, and prepared to return to his homeland instead of continuing on to Balak; and

2. a speech by inspiration in 6.4 characteristic of history writing of the Hellenistic period, and certainly characteristic of Josephus' writings.

Other details are shown by way of comparison. In the Balaam cycle, Balaam goes to meet Balak because Yahweh wanted him to go: he goes as Yahweh's agent. Josephus, like the author of the text underly-

10. Cf. William Whiston, trans., *Josephus: Complete Works* (Grand Rapids: Kregel, 1960) 90. The story of Balaam is on 90–92.

ing Balaam-of-the-wall, understood Balaam to have been a partner in a covenant; Balaam-of-the-wall with the gods, Josephus' Balaam with Balak: "But then Balak was displeased, and said he (Balaam) had broken the *contract* he had made . . ." (6.5). Moreover, Josephus' Balaam makes only *two* attempts to fulfill his contract; the second only because he had a sense of professional duty. Then, like Balaam-of-the-wall, Balaam foretells calamities: the former to befall his people, the latter to "befall the several kings of the nations, and the most eminent cities" (6.5). For Josephus, Balaam's predictions had been verified by history up to Josephus' time, and the remainder would come to pass in coming events (6.5).

After failing to curse Israel for Balak and his associates, indeed, blessing Israel at the direction of Yahweh, Balaam-of-the-cycle departs for home (Num 24:25). Josephus' Balaam also departs for home after the second attempt to curse, but just before crossing the Euphrates he summons Balak and his associates and tells them how they may deliver small setbacks to Israel, but can never affect a curse on them. In another speech recalling the Deuteronomist's rehearsal of the ups and downs of Israel's history, Josephus' Balaam reviews the history of Yahweh's people up to the first century CE, that is, up to Josephus' time. The major agent of the setbacks for Balak's time will be the Midianite women. The short account of Balaam's connection with these women in Numbers 31:6; 2 Peter 2; Jude 11; and Revelation 2:14 is extended into a large account in Josephus (6.6–13), a trait which he shares with the writer of the Samaritan Chronicle and with Philo.[11]

Rabbinics: Balaam in the *Talmud Bavli*

At some time later than the mid first-century CE, Balaam was employed to refer to someone else! Here we have the reversal of someone else being employed to refer to Balaam, as in the case of Pilti of the Samaritan material. Without getting lost in the labyrinthine volumes of the Talmud Bavli, I solicit instead the statement concerning early Christianity and its background in the first note on chapter 2 of Samuel Sandmel's, *We Jews and Jesus*. He writes: "There are a few direct mentions of Jesus in

---

11. Balaam is made to wax long and eloquently in these works. It is a trait of Hellenistic era writing.

the Talmud, and a few passages about one Balaam which some have interpreted to be cryptic, and hence indirect, mention."[12]

The Medieval and Muslim Balaam

I have already mentioned above one work on Balaam which is probably datable to the Middle Ages: The Samaritan Book of Joshua wherein chs. 3–4 deal with Balaam and the Moabites.[13] This work is known as Chronicles IV, and is dated by Macdonald to the fourteenth-century CE.[14] The use of Chronicles IV material may reveal another Balaam figure or type. As of this writing, I have been unable to acquire this text.[15]

The work known as *The Tales of the Prophets of al-Kisa'i* contains a story about Balaam.[16] It contains several of the features known from the Balaam-of-the-cycle. It differs from the cycle text(s) in several respects. In my previous work, I summarized the differences in the final note.[17] It suffices to reproduce a portion of that summary here:

The differences are:

3. Balaam's wife, who, after Balaam is refused permission to go the first time, persuades him to ask for permission again;

4. viziers, as opposed to simple messengers, or even princes; a winged angel whose wings block the East and West;

---

12. Samuel Sandmel, *We Jews and Jesus* (New York: Oxford University Press, 1965) 28. While not directly in the *Bavli*, the sages did have a few remarks to contribute about Balaam in the classics of rabbinic Judaism:

- *Eichah Rabbah Pesikta* 2: "There never arose philosophers the likes of Balaam son of Beor."
- *Pirkei Avot* 5:22: "An evil eye, a haughty spirit, and a lusting soul are signs of the disciples of the wicked Balaam."
- *Bereishit Rabbah* 66:4: "Those who bless you are blessed, and those who curse you are cursed" (Numbers 24:9). Since Balaam was an enemy, he began with a blessing and ended with a curse, for the ending is more significant than the beginning."
- *Vayikra Rabbah* 1:12: "Balaam was granted prophecy for the benefit of Israel."

13. Cf. n. 5 above.

14. Cf. Macdonald, *Theology*, 13, 46ff., and 118.

15. Ibid., 46–47.

16. Cf. W. M. Thackston, Jr., *The Tales of the Prophets of al-Kisa'i*, Library of Classical Arabic Literature (Boston: Twayne, 1978) 244–45.

17. Greene, "Balaam,'89," 104.

5. gifts for Balaam's wife;

6. Iblis interpreting the significance of the angel's sudden departure, allowing Balaam to continue his journey;

7. combined stories of how Balaam's counsel included using the Moabite women as bait for the Moses host, stories that are spread over more material than Numbers 22–24;

8. a "certain book" which the "children of Israel" read, the precepts of which if not followed, will cause calamity to befall them;

9. Balak will be established because "Israel" will rebel against the deity;

10. a man of the tribe of Simeon having sexual congress with an especially beautiful Moabitess, both of whom were impaled together on a spear wielded by a faithful man of Judah;

11. routing of Balak's army; and

12. his and Balaam's subsequent death.

It will be remembered that the story of the man of the tribe of Simeon, Phinehas, is contained in Numbers 25:6–18, and Balaam's death is gratuitously included in a list of Midianite kings killed in battle against Moses in Numbers 31:7–8. So although they stand outside the Balaam cycle, they are not totally new features to overall study of Balaam-of-the-Hebrew Scriptures.

Balaam in Modern Literature

Balaam has not escaped the attention of modern writers. The storyteller Joel Chandler Harris, famous for stories about Uncle Remus and Brer Rabbit, authored an anthology of stories under the title *Balaam and His Master*.[18] The Balaam of his story was a Black slave born on the Cozart plantation. The Balaam figure, the theme of war, and a number of hints borrowed from the cycle are evident in the story.

As to the figure, Harris' Balaam is charged with his senior master's orders: "Balaam," said Mr. Cozart, "this baby will be your master. I want

18. Joel Chandler Harris, *Balaam and His Master: And Other Sketches and Stories* (Boston: Houghton Mifflin, 1891).

you to look after him and take care of him."[19] A special relationship develops between Balaam and his younger master which last a short lifetime. Berrien Cozart grows up to become "a wild ass" of a man. He is dismissed from college and returns home to Billville where the family estate is located. His father refuses to allow him to remain at home, but sends him back to college to redeem himself and the family honor. Balaam returns with him. On the high hill beyond the "town branch" Balaam leaned out of the back [of the wagon] and *looked back* at Billville."[20] The image of the *tzofeh* is thus captured. Balaam "sees" something that Berrien Cozart does not. The next time either of them sees Billville, it is the last thing that either sees.

But instead of going back to college, the son takes his father's money (divinations in his hand?) and begins a gambling career in several southern states. Balaam watches over him and protects him at all cost. When the young Cozart loses all, he devises a scheme to "sell" Balaam for a sizable sum. It is all a "skin game" and scam, however, for Balaam, after being sold, is to gain freedom by escaping, and by the aid of a carefully-written letter to be kept in his possession, he is, theoretically, able to travel in the open unhindered and to rejoin his master in a pre-arranged city, only to repeat this scam as often as Berrien Cozart needs the "divination services" of Balaam, namely, more money to bankroll himself after having lost everything in a poker game. Never forgetting his charge, Balaam replied to his master's proposed scheme in *mashal*-like fashion: "you kin sell me, but de man dat buys Balaam will git a mighty bad bargain,"[21] and "I been 'long wid you all de time, an' ole marster done tole me w'en you was a baby dat I got ter stay wid you."[22] These statements may be compared with those made by Balaam-of-the-cycle in reply to Balak's statements and complaints.

After escaping, Balaam, alias someone else, is picked up on the road by a man known as the Judge. Although Balaam thinks that he had made an "ass" of this man by denying that he resembles Berrien Cozart's slave, a statement the Judge continues to make as they travel, the Judge, a gambler himself who knows Balaam's true identity, allows him to ac-

19. Ibid., 11, 26.
20. Ibid., 24.
21. Ibid., 25.
22. Ibid., 26.

company him to a town close to where Balaam is to meet the master. The Judge then allows Balaam to continue on to meet Berrien Cozart. He does this because of a female cousin Cozart likes, and because he admires Cozart's rascality.

Berrien Cozart had paid Balaam fifty dollars (more divinations in the hand) "in specie" in order to get Balaam to go along with the scam.[23] The escape was announced in a local paper called the "Intelligencer" but no response was ever made.[24] Balaam finally was rejoined his master after crossing "the River." In this case it was the Tennessee River.

War characterized the entire life of Berrien Cozart. He was at war with everyone in the world except Balaam. As a professional gambler/college dropout, Cozart waged war by dealing from the bottom of the deck, and engaging in every activity designed to relieve his opponents of their cash. This led often to brawls and to several deaths at Cozart's hands. Once, onboard a river steamer, Cozart was engaged in his incessant war, was accused of cheating, killed a man, and had to run for his life. He hid among a group of barrels on the lower deck of the steamer after having thrown a heavy object into the muddy river to give the impression that he had jumped overboard. Believing this, the dutiful Balaam sprang into the river in search of his charge and master. The master does nothing to make Balaam think otherwise. After a search through several states by legal authorities, Barrien Cozart is chased and finally captured very near Billville.

Having shot a pursuing lawman through the head, he was finally incarcerated in Billville. The last one reads of prisoner Berrien Cozart, he is lying dead on the floor of his cell. A large hole in the outer wall of the jail building, which at first had given the observer the idea that Cozart had attempted to escape, was seen to have been the entryway for someone to have joined Cozart. Balaam had broken into the jail to be with his master, and was also found dead on the floor beside his master. He had not relinquished his charge. He had done nothing that his master had not dictated. Here the Balaam figure was cast as the archetypical faithful man, servant of his master, as in the Balaam cycle. What the slave/gazer had "seen" was a curse on the Cozarts.

23. Ibid., 28.

24. Ibid., 29.

The final modern example of continuing concern with Balaam themes and types is provided by Moshe Leshem.[25] For him the Enlightenment and emancipation, the twin secular godheads that drew the Jews out of the ghetto, forced the Children of Israel to seek an answer to a difficult question: How could they maintain a Jewish identity while assimilating European culture and values that were not merely alien to Rabbinical Judaism but often irreconcilable with its teachings? Many Jews wrestle with the problem to this very day as individuals; so does Israel in its vocation as the Jewish state.[26]

Leshem's main focus is on Israel the Jewish state, and its status as one nation among the nations, but simultaneously separate from them. He argues that since the establishment of Israel as a state, it has sought to be counted among the nations, especially the United Nations, but has not received the same treatment as other charter members. Its major problem is being viewed by other members as being fair to its most immediate neighbors, the Palestinians. The Palestinians are politically in the same situation, as for many years were, the Kurds, the Lithuanians, the Letts, and the Estonians, all national groups that until recently existed without truly free and unquestioned borders. The difference, Leshem maintains, is that until the overthrow of Saddam Hussein nobody cared about the Kurds. And were he writing today, he would know that all three Baltic states have indeed received their national independence once again.

However, at the time of his writing, his assessment, that the international political community did not care about Israel either, was accurate. Of all these groups, however, the Palestinians are unique, because they and Israel came into existence at the same time, and now, as a result of a number of political moves and the fortunes and misfortunes of war, Israel appears strong in the eyes of the world, while the Palestinians are viewed as those who have been pounced upon unfairly by the aggressive Israelis. Thus, holds Leshem, when Israel engages in politico-military activity engaged in by other member nations of the United Nations, such as the former Soviet Union's actions toward the Baltic States, or Libya's occupation of large portions of Chad, no loud voice is raised in the Security Council in outraged protestation. Israel's

25. Moshe Leshem, *Balaam's Curse: How Israel Lost Its Way, and How It Can Find It Again* (New York: Simon & Schuster, 1989).

26. Ibid., 10

acquisition of the West Bank and large portions of Egyptian territory
as a result of the 1967 war (which it has subsequently returned), or the
two ill-fated invasions of Lebanon in 1982 (against Fatah) and in ----
(against Hezbollah) have been met by vitriolic barrages of declamation
by United Nations members. Whether fairly or unfairly, Israel is now in
a situation where it realizes that it stands virtually alone, whether it does
exactly the same thing as other nations or not, whether it reaches out
to other nations or not: Israel is politically cursed if it does, and cursed
if it does not.

For Leshem, this predicament recalls Numbers 23:9, the so called
Blessing of Balaam: "Israel is a people [that] shall dwell alone, and shall
not be reckoned among the nations." It should be remembered that the
shoresh brk, has the double meaning of "cursing" and "blessing." This
Zweideutigkeit or double meaning is evident in the Balaam cycle and
gives the story of Balaam some of its power punch. Leshem's analysis of
modern Israel's political predicament utilizes once more the ambiguity
of this potential *Zweideutigkeit* to raise the questions: Is the *brk* which
Balak originally requested now the *brk* that Israel has brought upon
itself?

One of Leshem's strongest statements concerning Israel's present
situation is summed up thusly: Whatever the correct interpretation of
Balaam's curse, after 1967, it was cited by religious nationalists as proof
that Israel's isolation was preordained, and therefore was not the result
of any sin of commission or omission of which the Jewish state might
be guilty in the eyes of the world. Dwelling alone was thus hailed as
the normal condition for the Jewish state, though it surely was not the
kind of normality/normalcy Zionism's founding fathers had in mind,
nor what the *Yishuv* had worked so hard to create.[27]

Leshem argues that although religious Jews may find solace in
this development, and may increase their ever strong embracing of the
contents of Jewish Scriptures and their traditional interpretations, the
orthodox should be dissuaded from their attempt to move Jewish history in a circular route back to the self-centered security of faith that is
possible only in a ghetto. Such may be a valid route for an individual,
but it is not a road on which the vehicle of the nation-state can travel.
For if Israel were to dwell alone, the danger is that it won't ere long dwell

27. Ibid., 246.

at all. As the American poet Robert Frost reminds us: "Before I'd build a wall I'd ask to know what I was walling in or walling out."[28] At this writing, Israel is, indeed, building a wall.

We have not read or heard the last of the resilient Balaam image.

Conclusion

Semites, chiefly priests, east and west of the Jordan River, between the twelfth and first centuries BCE, employed the figure and type of Balaam the son of Boer to explain their mantologies. Even the various source *strata* of the Pentateuch contained concealed mantological exegeses of the significance of Balaam for raising questions about legitimate mediation of the word and will of the God of Israel.

The text from Deir 'Alla, written on-plaster, demonstrated that during the eighth century BCE a Transjordan community found Balaam important enough to display a text of him on a public wall; a text which pointed to a much earlier one, probably dating to the twelfth century BCE.

During the Hellenistic Period in Palestine, the Qumran and Samaritan communities employed Balaam in special ways. The priestly writers of Qumran severed from their contexts three verses, contained in the Balaam cycle of Numbers 22–24, and embedded them in a different text; a text about an apocalyptic war between the Sons of Light, the Qumranites constituting the army of the righteous faithful, and the Sons of Darkness, namely, all outsiders. The tactic of the Samaritans, inveterate prophet bashers, was to create a Balaam type named Pilti, based on the story of the Egyptian diviners in the Book of Exodus. They pitted Pilti against the parents of Moses, and ultimately against Moses himself, and concluded that if there had ever existed a legitimate prophet, legitimate mediator of the word of the God of Israel, it had been only Moses. For the Samaritans, Pilti precursed the encounter between Balaam and the Moses-led host depicted in the Balaam cycle.

Also, within the Hellenistic Era, the author of 1 Enoch found, like the authors of 1QM from Qumran, among whom this was also read, words attributed to Balaam from the *Logia* section of the cycle. As with the Qumranites, the apocalyptic-oriented author of 1 Enoch employed

28. Ibid., 263.

these words to alert a generation to another coming war between the righteous and their enemies.

The Hellenist, Flavius Josephus, took a different tactic. Employing the Hellenistic literary device of the "Loaded, extended speech/address" in his *Antiquities*, he placed in the mouth of Balaam a rehearsal of the history of Israel's accomplishments and setbacks. "Balaam," for him became a person useful for allowing Israel to "see" its past, its Hellenistic present, and its future.

The negative allusions to Balaam in the New Testament followed the negative trajectory of viewing Balaam inherent to the apocalyptic movements in Second Temple Judaism. Specifically, he was held culpable, by these writers, for enticing or enchanting those faithful to Christ to eat meat which had been ritually sacrificed to other deities, and for idol worship. The Talmud continued this negativity and directed it toward both Balaam *and* Jesus; sometimes employing the names as *circumloqutiae*.

Balaam ibn Beor did not escape the interests of the medieval Muslims either. Al Kisa'i's depiction of him combined characteristics from the Balaam(s) of Deir 'Alla and the Balaam cycle. Moreover, he added issues such as the role played by Balaam's wife, a "book of precepts" to be followed by the faithful, and the "establishment" of Balak due to Israel's breaking of the covenant.

Joel Chandler Harris and Moshe Leshem showed that Balaam could be made just as useful for the needs of modern writers and thinkers. For Harris, Balaam had the right stuff out of which a cleverly-written short story could be crafted, while Leshem asked whether Balaam's curse on modern Israel had merely been delayed some 2000 years.

No other figure has had such an abiding influence on so many types of writers. Like an all-purpose elixir that was expected to cure everything from snakebite to baldness, Balaam has been called upon to address everything from what the ideal Israelite priest should be to the individual who turned out to be a better seer than all of his interpreters had imagined. For Leshem, Balaam's curse had merely delayed efficacy.

13

"Appearing Gloriously, Manifesting Powerfully"

The King in the Pyramid Texts and Jesus in Mark 13:24–26 and Matthew 24:29–30

Edmund S. Meltzer

DECADES AGO, WHEN I FIRST BEGAN TO READ ANCIENT EGYPTIAN TEXTS, I was struck by what seemed to be a strong correspondence between the opening of the so-called "Cannibal Hymn" in the Pyramid Texts and the description of the *Parousia* in Mark 13:24–26. My interest in this tantalizing resemblance has stayed with me over the years.[1] I have been spending my life in ancient Egyptian texts rather than in Bible texts, and I make no claim whatsoever to expertise or competence in the field of New Testament, but have studied and reflected in depth upon this intriguing phenomenon.

The "Cannibal Hymn" describes the posthumous appearance of the divine king in the horizon and proceeds to narrate how he cooks and eats the other deities in order to ingest their supernal power. It has been much discussed by Egyptologists,[2] and recent translations have been offered by J. P. Allen, J. L. Foster and others.[3] My own translation,

---

1. See my review of John L. Foster, *Echoes of Egyptian Voices* in *Journal of the American Research Center in Egypt* 33 (1996) 208–9.

2. E.g., Christopher Eyre, *The Cannibal Hymn: A Cultural and Literary Study* (Liverpool: Liverpool University Press, 2002); see also the review by U. Verhoeven, *Journal of Egyptian Archaeology* 90 (2004): Reviews Supplement, 17–20; J. R. Ogdon, *Un análisis literario del "Himno Canibal" en los Textos de las Pirámides*, (Buenos Aires: Centro de Estudios del Antiguo Egipto, n.d).

3. James P. Allen, *The Ancient Egyptian Pyramid Texts*, Writings from the Ancient World 23(Atlanta: Society of Biblical Literature, 2005) 50–52; John L. Foster, *Ancient Egyptian Literature: An Anthology* (Austin: University of Texas Press, 2001) 64–69.

which I consider provisional, is as follows, utilizing the text in the pyramid of Unas:[4]

> The sky is overcast,
> The stars are darkened,
> The Bows quiver,
> The bones of the Earth-god tremble,
> The ones who move about are still,
> Having seen King Unas
> Appearing gloriously, manifesting powerfully...

The passage in Mark, in the majestic King James translation,[5] reads:

> But in those days, after that tribulation, the sun shall be darkened, and the moon shall not give her light,
>
> And the stars of heaven shall fall, and the powers that are in heaven shall be shaken.
>
> And then shall they see the Son of man coming in the clouds with great power and glory.

One immediate obstacle to any claim of substantive correspondence between the two passages is the extreme disparity in time between

---

Foster conveys a welcome understanding of the non-"primitive" nature of the ingestion of the deities and their power by using the term "communion" to refer to the meal.

4. For the text of Unas, see the photographs in Alexandre Piankoff, *The Pyramid of Unas* (Princeton: Princeton University Press, 1968) pls. 28–30. Erman understood *iHy sbAw* as "the stars rain down (?)"; thus Adolf Erman, ed. William Kelly Simpson, *The Ancient Egyptians: A Sourcebook of Their Writings* (New York: Harper, 1966) 5; also James H. Breasted, *Development of Religion and Thought in Ancient Egypt* (New York: Harper, 1959) 98, 127, without query. In my translation, the renderings "appearing gloriously" and "manifesting powerfully" are chosen to convey both the most essential sense of the roots *xai* and *bA*, and the fact that they are used in the Stative. For *xai*, see Donald B. Redford, "*xay* and Its Derivatives," in *History and Chronology of the Eighteenth Dynasty of Egypt: Seven Studies* (Toronto: University of Toronto, 1967), chap. 1; out of a huge literature on *bA*, see, e.g., Erik Hornung, *Conceptions of God in Ancient Egypt: The One and the Many* (Ithaca, NY: Cornell, 1982) 138.

5. *The Holy Bible containing the Old and New Testaments, King James Version*, Reference Edition (Nashville: Nelson, 1989) 839; for the Greek text, see Kurt Aland, et al., eds., *The Greek New Testament*, 2nd ed. (London: United Bible Societies, 1968) 180. The parallel passage in Matthew 24:29–30 is extremely close to Mark, while Luke 21:25–27 reads to the present writer as if the description of the celestial portents is condensed or lacks details while other interpolations are introduced. Whatever implications this may have for the textual criticism of the New Testament I leave for my better-qualified colleagues.

the Pyramid Texts, first and most prolifically found in pyramids of the late Old Kingdom, and the New Testament, an interval of more than two millennia. This distance is, however, not impossible to bridge. The *Nachleben* of the Pyramid Texts is attested well into the Greco-Roman period. A convenient brief discussion of the persistence of this corpus is found in an article by Daniel Burnham addressing the Pyramid Texts and the origins of alchemy,[6] and much additional literature on contin-ued use of the Pyramid Texts in later periods can be cited.[7]

Another strike against the feasibility of this comparison is the ob-servation that the "Cannibal Hymn" does not occur in the pyramids of Old Kingdom rulers after the first two recensions, those of Unas and Teti. The quaint rationale has even been suggested that it was realized that each king would be devouring his predecessor.[8] This conclusion seems to me a misunderstanding of Egyptian logic; it seems to me that each successive king would assimilate to the sphere of identity of su-preme, dominant deity, along with his predecessors, as each living king did to Horus and each dead king, and eventually commoner as well, to Osiris.[9] Be that as it may, the ostensible obsolescence of the "Cannibal Hymn" does not take cognizance of its survival in two Twelfth Dynasty tombs, as well as the Coffin Texts, where it appears in a reworked but recognizable form as Utterance 573.[10] Although most of the attestations comprise excerpts rather than the complete composition, the pyramids

---

6. Daniel Burnham, "Explorations into the Alchemical Idiom of the Pyramid Texts," *Discussions in Egyptology* 60 (2004) 11–20.

7. Inter alia, M. Patanè, *Les Variantes des Textes des Pyramides à la Basse Époque* (Geneva: Author, 1992); W. Schenkel, "Zur Herakleopolitanischen Tradition der Pyramidentexte," *Göttinger Miszellen* 28 (1978) 35–44; A. Grimm, "Ein Zitat aus den Pyramidentexten in einem ptolemäischen Ritualtext des Horus-Tempels von Edfu: Edfou III, 130.14–15 = Pyr. 376b (Spr. 269). Zur Tradition altägyptischer Texte: Voruntersuchungen zu einer Theorie der Gattungen," *Göttinger Miszellen* 31 (1979) 35–46.

8. Thus Margaret A. Murray, *The Splendour That Was Egypt*, rev. ed. (London: Sidgwick & Jackson, 1964) 201.

9. For "spheres of identity" in the Egyptian concept of divinity, see Edward S. Meltzer, "A Reflection on the Category *ntr* in Ancient Egyptian Religion," *NAOS: Notes and Materials for the Linguistic Study of the Sacred* 12/1–3 (1996) 2–4.

10. Eyre, *The Cannibal Hymn*, 11; chapter 3 deals with "The Textual Transmission of the Cannibal Hymn." See also Ursula Verhoeven, *Journal of Egyptian Archaeology* 90 (2004): Reviews Supplement, 19. The textual sources are compiled in Eyre's Appendix.

of Unas and Teti cannot be regarded as a closed book with respect to sources of this text text.

Yet, another objection is the ostensibly different cultural worlds and textual/linguistic traditions that gave rise to the two texts in question. But is it really the case that "never the twain shall meet"? Major commentators on Egyptian religion such as Hornung and Morenz point out analogies between ancient Egyptian and Christian theology, and, at the very least, do not exclude the possibility of a historical relationship.[11] One of the most striking examples of a shared theme in Egyptian and Greco-Egyptian sources and Christian texts is the imagery connected with major psychopomorphic figures.

In the "Greek Magical Papyri" and other materials of the Greco-Roman period, Anubis appears as the key-bearer (Greek *kleidoukhos*) and is depicted holding a key,[12] while the image of St. Peter, keeper of the keys and the heavenly gates, has become so ubiquitous in our culture that it is the stuff of common figures of speech and political cartoons. This role of Peter derives from the charge given to him by Jesus in Matthew 16:19, again quoting the KJV:[13]

> And I will give unto thee the keys of the kingdom of heaven: and whatsoever thou shalt bind on earth shall be bound in heaven: and whatsoever thou shalt loose on earth shall be loosed in heaven.

Fundamental to the nature of both Anubis and Peter as psychopomps is their interstitial nature, bridging the domains of this and the other world; thus DuQuesne has repeatedly drawn attention to the

---

11. Erik Hornung, *The Secret Lore of Egypt: Its Impact on the West*, translated by David Lorton (Ithaca, NY: Cornell University Press, 2001) 60, 75; Siegfried Morenz, *Egyptian Religion* (Ithaca, NY: Cornell University Press, 1973), "Egypt's significance for Christian theology," 255–57; R. G. Bonnel and V. A. Tobin, "Christ and Osiris: A Comparative Study," in *Pharaonic Egypt: The Bible and Christianity*, ed. Sarah Israelit-Groll (Jerusalem: Magnes, 1985) 1–29. Please note that I do not wish any of my proposals to be taken as supporting or concurring with the pan-Egyptian understanding of Christology presented by Tom Harpur, *The Pagan Christ: Recovering the Lost Light* (Toronto: Thomas Allen, 2004). This work, in which the Egyptian god Horus is identified as the original Christ, is largely not based on current Egyptological materials or understandings, and indeed does not mention the "Cannibal Hymn."

12. Terence DuQuesne, *A Coptic Initiatory Invocation (PGM IV 1–25)*, Oxfordshire Communications in Egyptology 2 (Oxford: Darengo, 1991) cover, 2, 49 with n. 89.

13. *The Holy Bible*, 807; *The Greek New Testament*, 63.

characterization of Anubis as "master of mysteries in heaven, earth and underworld."[14]

The longevity of a theme or *topos* that goes back to the Pyramid Texts and wends its way into a Greek text—although it cannot claim to preserve unique phraseology of a Pyramid Texts passage—can be illustrated by a Greek Magical Papyrus discussed by Jan Bergman.[15] This text, which refers to the birth or appearance of the "Lord of All, Holy Scarabaeus,"[16] is regarded by Bergman as an example of "a pregnant Khepri (Kheprer)-theology"[17] which he identifies in Pyramid Texts section 1587, Coffin Texts 307, Book of the Dead Chapters 85 and 153B, Papyrus Bremner-Rhind, and elsewhere;[18] and which he ultimately compares to "the Word in the Prologue of the Gospel according to St. John."[19] A reference to the shaking of the earth in the Greek Magical Papyrus passage elicits the following comment from Bergman: "A cosmic reaction in the form of an earthquake upon a cosmic event is a common topic in Egyptian texts since the Pyramid Texts, and certainly not only in Egyptian texts (Cf. St. Matthew 27, vv. 51–53)."[20]

Making an actual relationship, rather than merely a resemblance, more feasible in the case of our text passages is the reuse of Pyramid Texts in a ritual scene found in close conjunction with one of the Ptolemaic hieroglyphic hymns to Isis in the temple at Philae, which Zabkar recognizes as sources of the Greek Isis-Aretalogies, as well as

14. E.g., Terence DuQuesne, *Anubis, Wepwawet, and Other Deities: Personal Worship and Official Religion in Ancient Egypt. Catalogue of the Exhibition at the Egyptian Museum, Cairo, March 2007* (Cairo: Supreme Council of Antiquities, 2007); idem, "Guardians of the Gateway, with particular reference to the Egyptian god Anubis," *Seshat* 7 (Summer 2005) 39–61. The author draws attention to the dog-headed depiction of St. Christopher Cynocephalus, 58 with n. 56. The motif of the key is apparently of Greek origin: Siegfried Morenz, "Anubis mit dem Schlüssel," *Wissenschaftliche Zeitschrift der Karl-Marx-Universität Leipzig* 3 (1953/54), Gesellschafts- und Sprachwissenschaftliche Reihe, Heft 1:79–83.

15. Bergman, "Ancient Egyptian Theogony in a Greek Magical Papyrus (PGM VII, ll. 516–521)," in *Studies in Egyptian Religion Dedicated to Professor Jan Zandee*, ed. M. Heerma van Voss et al., Studies in the History of Religions 43 (Leiden: Brill, 1982) 28–37.

16. Ibid., 30.

17. Ibid., 32.

18. Ibid.

19. Ibid.

20. Ibid., 36.

echoes of Pyramid Texts in the phraseology of the hymns themselves.[21] Also of note is the by- now well-accepted relationship between Gnostic and Hermetic materials and Egyptian traditional sources.[22] The Coptic tradition has always maintained that Mark wrote his Gospel in Egypt; the titles of the Coptic Pope include "Patriarch of the See of St. Mark."[23] This reflects, or is part of, a strong tradition more broadly attested in Christian sources at least as early as Eusebius, that Mark was the founder of the earliest Egyptian church,[24] an account which has received a great deal of skepticism from European and American scholars.[25] Birger Pearson sums up the verdict on this tradition judiciously:

> The tradition of the association of St. Mark with earliest Christianity in Egypt is traceable to the second century and may originate even earlier. The historicity of this tradition, though unprovable, should not be ruled out.[26]

21. Louis V. Zabkar, *Hymns to Isis in Her Temple at Philae* (Hanover, NH: University Press of New England, 1988) 43–44; 162, n. 13; 166 n. 10.

22. For Gnosticism, see Daniel R. McBride, "Gnostic and Traditional Egyptian Religious Affinities in the Magical Papyri," *Journal of the Society for the Study of Egyptian Antiquities* 27 (1997 [2000]) 42–59; Douglas M. Parrott, "Gnosticism and Egyptian Religion," *Novum Testamentum* 29 (1987) 73–92; Parrott, "The Thirteen Kingdoms of the Apocalypse of Adam: Origin, Meaning and Significance," *Novum Testamentum* 31 (1989) 67–87. For the Hermetica, see Howard M. Jackson, "*KOPH KOCMOY*: Isis, Pupil of the Eye of the World," *Chronique d'Égypte* 61 (1986) 116–35; Garth Fowden, *The Egyptian Hermes* (Cambridge: Cambridge University Press, 1986); Richard Jasnow and Karl-Theodor Zauzich, *The Ancient Egyptian Book of Thoth: A Demotic Discourse on Knowledge and Pendant to the Classical Hermetica*, 2 vols. (Wiesbaden: Harrassowitz, 2005).

23. The medal commemorating H. H. Pope Shenouda III's visit to the U.S. and other regions of the Coptic diaspora in 1989 has on one side Mark writing his Gospel in Egypt, and on the other, the Holy Family during their flight into Egypt.

24. William L. Petersen, "North African Christianity," in *ABD*, 1:966; Birger A. Pearson, "Earliest Christianity in Egypt: Some Observations: The Mark Legend," in *The Roots of Egyptian Christianity*, ed. Pearson and James E. Goehring, ed. (Philadelphia: Fortress, 1986) 137–45. A mention ostensibly preceding Eusebius is the controversial letter of Clement of Alexandria published by Morton Smith; Petersen, 966, and Pearson, 138 with nn. 27–28. According to the letter, Mark wrote his Gospel in Rome but expanded it in Alexandria, producing the so-called "Secret Gospel of Mark."

25. See the discussions of Petersen and Pearson cited above. The extremely skeptical assessment is exemplified by C. C. Walters, *Monastic Archaeology in Egypt*, Modern Egyptology Series (Warminster: Aris & Phillips, 1974) 2.

26. Pearson, "Mark Legend," 144.

I cannot conclude this study without noting an objection that was immediately registered by one of the few to whom I have confided the textual similarity noted here over the years. My interlocutor—whose identity through the intervening years or decades I cannot remember— pointed out that the Pyramid Text passage refers to the king's ascent to heaven, and the Gospel passage, on the other hand, to Jesus' descent back into the world. It seems to me, however, that both descriptions are essentially of the glorious epiphany of a divine being, and the comparison, whether valid or invalid, is not invalidated because of that distinction.

PART FOUR

Contemporary Cultural Perspectives

14

A Forsythia for Your Thoughts

Reciprocity in Reading J.B. and Job

Anthony J. Petrotta

Time will of course take care of us all, but for those complacent optimists who have not learned to live as we do in the kingdom of despair, that first glimpse of failure seems like a vision of death itself. (Eric Ambler, *The Care of Time*)

"Whether it be the Soul itself, or God in the Soul, that shines by Love, or both, it is difficult to tell: but certainly the love of the Soul is the sweetest thing in the world. I have often admired what should make it so excellent. If it be God that loves, it is the shining of His essence; if it be the Soul, it is His Image: if it be both, it is a double benefit." (Thomas Traherne, *Centuries*, Book 3, Number 83)

J.B. IS NOT A MAN OF FAITH STRUGGLING WITH GOD, BUT A HUMANIST struggling with the meaninglessness of the Universe. So Susan Schreiner says regarding the Pulitzer Prize winning play by Archibald MacLeish.[1] Schreiner is not alone in this assessment of *J.B.*; numerous reviewers after the play's debut at Yale and then on Broadway in the late 1950s came to similar conclusions.[2]

It's a grand conclusion, but perhaps too facile to draw from a poetic work, a play within a play, replete with characters playing characters, and which itself plays off the biblical book of Job. *Job* resists such

---

1. Susan Schreiner, *Where Shall Wisdom Be Found?* (Chicago: University of Chicago Press, 1994) 173–77.

2. A collection of reviews can be found in Ralph E. Hone, ed., *The Voice Out of the Whirlwind: The Book of Job* (San Francisco: Chandler, 1960).

encompassing judgments, as Schreiner's masterful study displays, and *J.B.* likely does as well. More importantly, the conclusion does not treat the play as a *drama*, that is, as a story. "Humanistic" may be a convenient designation but to treat stories as if morals or ideology drive the story and not the situation of the characters, robs stories of their power as stories. *J.B.*, and *Job*, is a story of a person, a good person, who has horrid things happen to him. *Now what happens?* The storyteller is obliged to tell us what unfolds for this character so that we can enter into this story and perhaps emerge with new perspectives. Any numbers of options are open to the teller of tales, but the interactions and the elements of the story keep us reading; or not reading if the story fails as a story.

My interest in reading *J.B.* alongside *Job* comes out of being a priest who speaks from faith to a community of faith, and as an adjunct seminary professor who endeavors to expose students to the best readings I can find in order to encourage the students to become better readers of religious texts, especially biblical texts. Does *J.B.* deepen our understanding of *Job*? Can we appreciate MacLeish not simply as a poet but also as a reader of the biblical text? Is "turn about" fair play, can *Job* speak to our reading of *J.B.*? Is there a helpful reciprocity in reading these works in light of each other?

I want to consider two interpretive problems in Job, that of Job's repentance and his restoration, to see how MacLeish resolves these problems in his retelling. Repentance and restoration force the issue of retributive justice, an ostensive concern of many of the characters in Job, and many who read the story. If Job is guilty of some sin, then retributive justice stands as a principle in the Universe, and God is justified. However, Job asserts his innocence throughout the book, and the narrator and God support this assessment of Job. Job is a man of integrity. If so, what could restoration *mean* for a person in Job's position, an innocent person repenting? These are *dramatic* challenges for a storyteller, and interpretation problems for a reader. Unless one is simply moralistic or didactic, the storyteller will engage us with the characters and their actions.[3]

---

3. Stories that are driven by morals (or ideology) do not involve readers; if we complete reading them at all, we are not likely to go back to them for the pleasure of reading the story. The fact that we return again and again to both *J.B.* and *Job* suggests that they are neither moralistic nor ideologically driven, but story driven.

In the following remarks I will move between repentance and restoration, and MacLeish's dramatic portrayal of each.

In *J.B.* repentance is obviously a problem for Nickles, the satan-
figure, and Mr. Zuss, the god-figure. Scene Ten is devoted to their interaction on the issue; these two less-than-divine, divine beings in the
play, are not pleased with the way Job[4] plays out the scene. Mr. Zuss has
won the test set up between him and Nickles, but he finds little comfort
in that victory. He says:

Mr. Zuss:	he *calmed* me!
	Gentled me the way a farmhand
	Gentles a bulging, bugling bull!
	forgave me! ...
	for the world! ...
Nickles:	Nonsense! He repented ...
Mr. Zuss:	That's just it!
	He repented. It was *him*—
	Not the fear of God but *him!*
	....
	In spite of all he's lost and loved
	He understood and he forgave it! ...

What other victory could God win, Nickles asks, contemptuously
(138–39). That Job *forgave* God with his repentance rankles Mr. Zuss,
though.

Mr. Zuss and Nickles are rankled by this understanding of repentance, if that is what MacLeish has in mind at this point. They even
question the *art* of the play.[5] We don't think of repentance as *forgiving*
God. This view of repentance seems thoroughly humanistic. Indeed,
Schreiner uses this scene to conclude that Job's new insights are not
gained through revelation, but precisely the opposite, there is no external revelation here at all. She supports this view by appealing to
the divine characters, two broken down actors who provide sardonic

4. I will use "Job" to refer to the character of Job in both the play and the book that
bears his name, and *Job* when I intend the book itself and not the character. The context
should make it clear whether I'm speaking of Job in the play or the book.

5. How fun to analyze that little exchange where MacLeish's characters are questioning *his* ability as author of the play!

comments on the play, but offer no truth.[6] The repentance scene in *J.B.* moves without resolution to the restoration scene.[7]

J.B. and *Job*, however, do not end simply with Job's repentance. There is that troublesome last scene, narrative in *Job*, poetic in *J.B.*, where Job is restored. As readers we are left to puzzle that scene out as much as repentance. Schreiner uses this last scene in *J.B.* to reinforce her point that what Job and Sarah learn is the *harsh reality* that suffering only opens our eyes to the "coldness of the universe without providence and without a transcendent God."[8]

As noted above, Schreiner's view is the prevailing one among critics.[9] However, considering some *odd* dramatic details may suggest other possibilities. I am assuming in my following remarks that MacLeish is well-educated, bright, and a gifted poet. Poetic and dramatic choices are not coincidental, but fraught with background and allusive in nature.

At the end of the repentance scene, Nickles urges Job not to take the restoration, but rather take "a window for a door" (metaphor). Then, when Job hears someone at the door (literally), Nickles violently says that Job will not take *it* (the door; restoration); he will "fling it at God's

---

6. Schreiner, *Where Shall Wisdom Be Found?* 175–76. I wonder how much credit we should give the views of these actors in *J.B.* They are broken down actors, at times pretentious, certainly comic figures. In many ways they function like Job's friends in *Job*. If anything, MacLeish seems to be poking fun at "popular" religious notions rather than saying something about revelation.

7. Job repents but offers no "explanation"; there is only speculation and objections by Nickles and Mr. Zuss. However, MacLeish adds dramatic details to the words taken *Job*. Job "cowers" at first when hearing the Distant Voice; he does not answer God's question of whether he would "disannul" his judgment; he raises his bowed head and "gently" begins his repentance; his face is "drawn in agony" when he says the words, "mine eye seeth thee"; then he bows his head and utters his words of repentance. In a play of words, actions must speak rather forcefully. Zuss and Nickles may be misreading the scene as much as any audience (or critic) might. They are divine figures, but far from omniscient or infallible.

8. Schreiner, *Where Shall Wisdom Be Found?* 176. Again, Schreiner is certainly not alone in this conclusion regarding *J.B.*, but stands in a long line of readers who think similarly. I think that a poet might find "transcendence" and "revelation" less problematic than critics or even contemporary theologians.

9. My reading of the critical reviews and articles, surely not exhaustive, seems to favor Schreiner's view. The reviews in Hone, ed., *The Voice Out of the Whirlwind*, are nearly unanimous that *J.B.* is humanistic (Louis Finkelstein keeps open the option that MacLeish is struggling with the "blurred vision" that mortals inevitably have as mortals), are divided on its merits as a play, and are equally critical of the prose sections of *Job* as they are of MacLeish's humanism.

face" and rather "suffocate in dung." At the beginning of the next scene, Job asks, "Who is it." The stage direction says, "There is no answer."

Throughout *J.B.,* MacLeish uses silence, sightless stars, cold and darkness as indicators of God's absence. However, also throughout the play, there is a *Distant Voice* that speaks and nobody seems to know who/what that voice is. At the end of the prologue, as Nickles and Mr. Zuss are preparing for their roles as (the) satan and god, the stage direction reads: *The bulbs go out. Darkness. Silence. In the silence:*

A Distant Voice: *Whence Comest thou?*

Mr. Zuss: That's my line.

Nickles: I didn't speak it.

They banter briefly, then the "Godmask" (Mr. Zuss), says his line:

Whence comest thou?

No explanation of the voice is given. It is simply present. At the end of Scene Two, the crucial scene where Satanmask gets the Godmask to bet on Job, the Distant Voice makes another anonymous appearance "out of the darkness." The Distant Voice shows up again in Scene Seven when Nickles and Mr. Zuss have an exchange after Job *retains* his integrity through all the calamities.[10] Nickles attributes the words to the prompter, and when Nickles asks who is there, there is only silence again.

Perhaps most telling, though, is Scene Nine where Job and his friends have their exchange. The scene ends with Job repenting. The Distant Voice comes again, after much silence, "Out of the rushing sound." The rushing sound dies out and the friends casually brush it off. They leave and the rushing sound comes round again. MacLeish has additional characters to the Joban story, women and a child, "Jolly Adams." Jolly's mother tells her it is "only the wind" but Jolly insists she heard "a word." Her mother persists and Jolly, drowsily, says, "Under the

---

10. The Distant Voice always quotes lines from the book of Job (Job 2:2 in this scene). The stage direction has the Distant Voice "almost" whispering and then "barely audible" as it concludes the lines: ". . . thou movedst me against him . . . without cause . . ." MacLeish is suggesting *something* in this stage direction—reluctance, sorrow, repentance? Readers are left to decide what force to attribute to those words; a director or actor would have to make a choice in delivering these words.

wind there was a word." She will not be denied what she heard. In this scene, the Distant Voice speaks words from Job 38ff.

The Distant Voice is neither identified nor explained; it comes unbidden and leaves when it has said its piece; it is at the beginning of the play, sprinkled throughout, and at the end. MacLeish is not an *innocent* reader/poet. "Rushing sound" and "wind" are evocative of "spirit" as is evident in both biblical Hebrew and Greek, but not in English.

Moreover, when we first meet Sarah in Scene One at a Thanksgiving dinner where the issue of being *thankful* is discussed, she says in a reply to a statement by Job that the children *know* thankfulness and, besides, it's hard to talk about:

> Sarah: *flushed, an edge to her voice*
>   Even if it is hard we have to.
>   We can't just take it, just eat, just—relish!
>   Children aren't animals.
>
> J.B.:   *he goes on with his serving*
>   Sweet Sal! Sweet Sal!
>   Children know the grace of God
>   Better than most of us. They see the world
>   The way the morning brings it back to them.
>   New and born and fresh and wonderful . . .

In these words and in the character of Jolly Adams, is MacLeish evoking something of the imagery of childhood in the Bible, something of the childlike qualities that are necessary for entering the Kingdom of Heaven (Matt 18:3; 19:4; Mark 10:15; Luke 18:16)?[11] After Jesus reproaches Chorazin and Bethsaida for being unrepentant, and the seventy-two disciples return exclaiming that even demons are subject to them "because of your name," Jesus says, "I saw Satan falling like lightening from the sky . . ." and concludes praising God because even though God has hidden these things from the wise, "you have revealed them to the childlike" (Luke 10:13–22).

The Distant Voice and the *testimony* of Jolly Adams deserve some attention by readers. They certainly do not make MacLeish a theist, but unqualified humanism also seems misplaced. It is *distant* to be sure, but it is present nonetheless. It is a character and part of the action; a reader should account for its presence.

---

11. Is the name "Jolly Adams" *innocent*?

None of this explains Job's repentance, though, and we have not yet restored Job. Somebody is at the door at the end of the repentance scene. Job asks who is there; and there is no answer, still. When Job opens the door, Sarah is there, and she is holding a broken twig in her hand. She says:

> Look Job: the forsythia,
> The first few leaves . . .
> > not leaves though . . .
> > > petals . . .

Flowers are conventional for poets. Job uses the image; they also show up throughout *J.B.*[12] George Herbert's "the Flower" weaves images that are present in *Job* and *J.B.*:[13]

> How fresh, Oh Lord, how sweet and clean
> > Are thy returns! ev'n as the flowers in spring;
> To which, besides their own demean,
> > The late-past frosts tributes of pleasure bring.
> Grief melts away Like snow in May,
> > As if there were no such cold thing.
> Who would have thought my shrivel'd heart
> > Could have recover'd greenness? . . .
> These are thy wonders, Lord of Power,
> > Killing and quick'ning, bringing down to hell
> > And up to heaven in an hour;
> Making a chiming of a passing-bell.
> > We say amiss,
> > > This or that is:
> > > > Thy word is all, if we could spell.
>
> > . . .
>
> And now in age I bud again,
> After so many deaths I live and write;
> > I once more smell the dew and rain,
> > And relish versing: . . .
> These are thy wonders, Lord of love,

12. Job 14 in particular uses this image. Job 14 closes the first cycle of dialogue with his friends; Job introduces the language of lawsuit with God but also moves, in the image of the flower, from his personal "tragedy" to the human plight, the frailty of life. Flower as a sign of hope gets picked up by later theologians as a sign of resurrection.

13. I was familiar with this poem, but the associations with *Job* and *J.B.* were brought to my mind after reading an article by Anne Ramirez, "Flowers and Fruit: The Gifts of George Herbert and Emily Dickinson," *Weavings* 17/2 (2002) 29–37.

> To make us see we are but flowers that glide;
> Which when we once can find and prove,
> Thou hast a garden for us, . . .

For Herbert, the poet is likened to a flower who has experienced, inscrutable at times, and yet grows again in sheer dependence upon God, and in "versing." MacLeish need not have this particular poem in mind, but as the knowledgeable and gifted poet he is, it is reasonable that he is familiar with the imagery and uses of flowers in poetry. Herbert's poem speaks to persistent issues in both *Job* and *J.B.*

Still, why *forsythia* out of all the flowers that MacLeish could use? It is such a specific flower and not one that rolls off the tongue like rose or carnation.[14] A student pointed out to me that forsythias are the first flowers that come out after Winter in the Eastern United States. Further enquiry revealed that forsythias are known as *heart medicine*. Sarah says at the very end of the play:

> Blow on the coal of my heart.
> The candles in the churches are out.
> The lights have gone out in the sky.
> Blow on the coal of my heart
> And we'll see by and by . . .

At this point Job joins her in picking up the chairs. Sarah continues:

> We'll see where we are.
> The wit[15] won't burn and the wet soul smoulders.
> Blow on the coal of my heart and we'll know . . .
> We'll know . . .

The light, we are told in the stage direction, increases as they work.

That same student[16] was reminded of the ending of John Bunyan's *Pilgrim's Progress*:

14. Furthermore, is it an accident that in the stage direction she is holding a twig? In Gen 8:11 the dove brings back a plucked "olive leaf" after the catastrophe of the Flood.

15. "Wit" seems odd here. It can refer to the consciousness of the mind; it is also used of poetic skill and imagination; this latter association fits best here. MacLeish seems to be sporting with us in this imagery. A "wick" may burn or smolder, whereas MacLeish laments the loss of poets who speak to us ("wit"), poets like "Job" perhaps? What "blows" but, again, the wind/spirit (*ruach*)? And what would be the "coal of my heart" but the "soul"—that is smoldering?

16. The student is the Rev. Nancy A. Duff. She continues to enlighten me as she reads my sermons and recalls images, poems, stories, and so forth that support or ex-

. . . a glowing Coal at my Heart. I see myself now at the end of my journey, my *toilsome* days are ended. I am going now to see *that* Head that was Crowned with Thorns, and *that* Face that was spit upon for me. I have formerly lived by Hear-say, and Faith, but now I go where I shall live by sight . . .[17]

MacLeish is not using the image with the same intention and force that Bunyan is, but the image of the coal of the heart and Bunyan's allusion to Job ("I formerly lived by hearsay and faith, but now I go where I shall live by sight . . .") place Sarah's words in a completely different perspective than one where faith is unambiguously absent. Furthermore, Sarah's repetition of "we'll know" in the closing lines also brings to mind Job's words of repentance: "I uttered . . . things too wonderful for me, which I did not know . . . but now my eye sees you . . ." (Job 42:3–6).

In this last scene Sarah is inviting Job back into life after all that has gone on. Nickles, at the end of the previous scene, has a hard time thinking that Job will accept the restoration, but Job opens the door nonetheless, not the window. Moreover, in reply to Job's questioning her leaving him, Sarah says:

I love you.
. . .
You wanted justice and there was none—
Only love.

Job replies:

He does not love.
  He Is.

One of MacLeish's most famous poems is *Ars Poetica*. Here is how he describes a poem:

A poem should be palpable and mute
As a globed fruit,
. . . .
A poem should be wordless
As the flight of birds.
. . . .

tend my thoughts on a passage. I relish the thought of saying that Professor Clines' influence extends to the second and third generations, if not the fourth.

17. John Bunyan, *Grace Abounding to the Chief of Sinners* and *The Pilgrim's Progress*, edited by Roger Sharrock (London: Oxford University Press, 1966) 399.

> A poem should be equal to:
> Not true.
>
> . . . .
>
> For all the history of grief
> An empty doorway and a maple leaf.
>
> . . . .
>
> For love
> The leaning grasses and two lights above the sea--
>
> . . . .
>
> A poem should not mean
> But be.

MacLeish speaks of poetry in the same manner that he dramatizes God in *J.B.* In the Distant Voice and in Jolly Adams, in the forsythia and Sarah, God may be mute, but not inconsequential, much like a poem. Raymond Scheindlin says this of Job's poetry:

> All of this poetry was not written merely to decorate the book. Its energy and exuberance, palpable from the beginning and hardly every fading during the work's long course, keep present before us the fact that we are reading the work of a writer who is fascinated with this life, troubled as it is . . . He may rage at injustice . . . but never in his forty-two chapters does he ever come close to saying, "Vanity of vanities, all is vanity."[18]

MacLeish also is filled with poetic pyrotechnics and with a fascination with life. *J.B.* may tongue-lash the numbness and complacency of belief, but Job in *J.B.* does not fall prey to either Nickles or Mr. Zuss. Job's repentance and restoration remain enigmatic.

Is there any "reciprocity" in reading *J.B.* and *Job*?

MacLeish doesn't "solve" the "problems" of repentance and the restoration of *Job*. However, in *dramatizing* Job's repentance with Nickles and Mr. Zuss, and the restoration with Sarah, MacLeish may be doing us a greater service as readers of *Job*. *Job* itself doesn't feel a need to resolve these tensions in the text. With respect to repentance, the very word that the author chooses is not *shuv*, but *nacham*, which can be translated as repent but also comfort. Many of the contexts of *nacham* suggest an *attitude adjustment* or perspective change (e.g., Jer 18:18; Gen 6:6) more than the classic notion of the *turnaround* of the New Testament Greek

---

18. Raymond P. Schneindlin, *The Book of Job* (New York: Norton, 1998) 24–25. He goes on to say that the poetry is an "antidote to its pessimism."

word for repent: *metanoia*. Job, in both *J.B.* and *Job*, sees things differently by the end of the story.[19] Job is neither repenting of a sin nor of
his insignificance.[20] Maybe Job's repentance is not demanding a desired
outcome, but simply receiving the *given*.[21]

In addition to *J.B.*, MacLeish gave a sermon (in 1955) on *Job* in
which he says that God delivering Job, in his innocence, into Satan's
hand, drives the poem dramatically. "God stakes His supremacy as God
upon man's fortitude and love." And further, "Man depends on God for
all things; God depends on man for one . . . It is a free gift or it is nothing. And it is most itself, most free, when it is offered in spite of suffering, of injustice, and of death."[22] The struggle between good and evil is
held together in our ability "to love *in spite of* . . ." MacLeish says, "The
justification of the injustice of the universe is not our blind acceptance
of God's inexplicable will, nor our trust in God's love—His dark and
incomprehensible love—for us, but our human love, notwithstanding
anything, for him."[23]

MacLeish concludes his sermon on Job much as he concludes *J.B.*
God has need of man, not as *quid pro quo* but simply for love's sake.[24]
MacLeish, the dramatist, gives Job's wife a name, Sarah/Sal, and offers
not leviathan and behemoth, but a forsythia. He places love in the particularity of a person and flower. The love portrayed is not idealized;

---

19. Job is no longer offering sacrifices for his children's *possible* misdeeds at the
end of *Job*. Scene One of *J.B.* (at the Thanksgiving table) deserves thorough study as
Sarah and Job share thoughts on luck, deserving, thankfulness, and gratefulness. Sarah
seems to see "owing" in a different way by the end of the play and Job may have learned
something of gratefulness rather than a simple thankfulness.

20. MacLeish, in a sermon he delivered on Job ("God Has Need of Man," in *The
Dimensions of Job*, edited by Nahum N. Glatzer (New York: Schocken, 1969) 278–86,
concludes that Job's insignificance can't be the focus of the poem. He goes on to say
that Job's suffering is unjustified "in any human meaning of the word justice" (283).
Moreover, MacLeish rejects that even this observation justifies a poem of this breadth
and depth. He asks, How can we believe in life if the universe is unjust? *How are we to
live?* "What answer to *that* question does the poet find? What answer does he show us
in the drama of man's agony?" (284).

21. Job in *J.B.* says in the scene at the Thanksgiving table, "Nobody *deserves* it, Sal:
Not the world that God has given us." Job is tested at precisely that point and by the end
receives, tentatively, the forsythia, the smoldering soul, and, especially, "Sal."

22. Similar words occur on the lips of Job in the Thanksgiving scene.

23. MacLeish, "God Has Need of Man," 285.

24. Ibid., 284–85.

neither is trust placed in human institutions such as politics or science. Job and Sarah pick up chairs and straighten things out; they enter back into life with all it's uncertainties. *Job* similarly ends in the particularity of persons; Job prays for his friends, and his daughters are given names and an inheritance.[25] The names are playful: Cinnamon; Dove; and perhaps something like Eye-shadow. In contrast to MacLeish, theologians and critics disembody love in an "ism."

These reflections lead me to think that reciprocity in reading is no more helpful than reciprocity in the moral world.[26] What *J.B.* does is appropriate the past, and by bringing it into the present in this form, opens up the past.[27] *J.B.* invites us to continue considering *Job*. In reconsidering *Job*, we might be persuaded to keep our reading *open* and avoid reductionist tendencies to explain everything in a text, as if explanation is the supreme outcome of reading.

MacLeish makes a similar point in his sermon. He says that Job is more than "language and metaphors"; it is the action and the meaning to which the action moves. It is "the poem as a whole" that we must consider.[28] For all its history and complexity of composition, Job

25. See Ellen F. Davis, "The Sufferer's Wisdom," in *Getting Involved With God: Rediscovering the Old Testament* (Cambridge, MA: Cowley, 2001) 141–43. See also, Davis, "Job and Jacob: The Integrity of Faith," in *The Whirlwind: Essays on Job, Hermeneutics and Theology in Memory of Jane Morse*, edited by Stephen L. Cook et al., JSOTSup 336 (London: Sheffield Academic, 2001) 100–120.

26. David J. A. Clines, "The Wisdom Books," in *Creating the Old Testament: The Emergence of the Hebrew Bible*, edited by Stephen Bigger (Oxford: Blackwell, 1989) says, "Innocent suffering is a hippopotamus." He explains that God expects Job to realize that the natural order and the moral order are analogous (but not reciprocal), and that God's "inscrutable ways" operate in both (287). Reciprocity in reading *J.B.* and *Job* would turn *J.B.* into a treatise on humanism and *Job* a treatise on innocent suffering. They would be stuffed animals, not hippopotami.

27. Stephen Prickett, in *Origins of Narrative: The Romantic Appropriation of the Bible* (Cambridge: Cambridge University Press, 1996), makes this point with respect to eighteenth century appropriations of the Bible. I think MacLeish is doing something similar with *Job* in *J.B.*

28 See Henry P. Van Dusen's review of *J.B.* in *The Voice Out of the Whirlwind*. He is egregious in his criticism of MacLeish on this point of differentiating the poem from the prologue and epilogue: "Dr. MacLeish, following the devout of the ages, has elected to take the book of Job exactly as it stands on the pages of Scripture . . . without benefit of a footnote or hint as to the true dual character of the "book" . . . [Many think] this is the greatest weakness in *J.B.*, qualifying much of the play's power" (294–95).

deserves to be read as a whole.[29] Literary studies have helped to bring those questions to the surface once again, but it is noteworthy that in the mid-1950s, a poet and reader of MacLeish's stature was trying to show us how important that endeavor is in reading. For MacLeish, *Job* is a conversation partner precisely because it speaks of issues *dramatically,* that is, powerfully open, and he receives it as such.[30]

29. The critical questions of composition are important and worthy of pursuit as well, but in the end it is *this* story that we are given, much as Job experienced his circumstances, not other circumstances.

30. Professor Clines expresses many of these thoughts about reading and being engaged by *Job* in his preface to his commentary, *Job 1–20*, WBC 17 (Dallas: Word, 1989).

15

Reading the Book of Job as a Multicultural Case Report[1]

Rafael Chodos

Introduction

WHENCE COMES THE POWER OF THE BOOK OF JOB? ANY ATTEMPT TO paraphrase the book or to sum it up, or even to find some one idea or some single train of thought that we might call its "point," is doomed to fail as a clumsy oversimplification. To see the Book of Job as the story of a pious man who is tested and then rewarded because he passes the test; or as one who is tested and fails the test but then repents and is rewarded; or to see it as a discussion of the problem of evil; or to see it as an essay on the virtue of patience or of obedience; or to see it as a theodicy, a justification of God—to see it in any of these ways is to trivialize it. Such commentaries and interpretations have said much more about their authors than about the Book of Job. For the Book has an ineffable quality about it: like a symphony, or painting, or play, or other work of art, it is not susceptible of paraphrase or of reduction.

One source of the Book's power will become evident to us when we consider its composition from the points of view of *inventio* and *dispositio*: invention referring to the materials—the stories, themes, ideas, and vocabulary—which the author brought into the work; and disposition referring—not as the term did in Quintillian,[2] to the art of

1. This paper is based on a lecture given by the author at the Institute for Antiquity and Christianity, at Claremont Graduate University, in 1995, as part of the Institute's lecture series on multiculturalism and the Alexandrian Age.

2. Quintilian *Institutio Oratoria* Book 3.

arranging the themes—but rather to the way the themes hang or fail to hang together in the Book of Job. The themes and materials come from the Near East and Greece as well as from classical Hebrew sources; and the ways of putting them together also come from those varied sources. In this way the Book of Job is constructed out of elements culled from different cultures and its power stems largely from the way these cultural elements clash in its pages.

This appears most convincingly in a consideration of the form or literary genre of the book. The book's genre is the author's template: the set of expectations he thinks he is fulfilling. Until now, Job's genre has not yet been satisfactorily identified: it appears to be deliberately ambiguous, or hybrid.

The Genre of the Book of Job

Job has often been called a *dialogue*: we might see it as a foreshadowing of Plato's dialogues, since it does record the speeches of various parties who appear, at least superficially, to be discussing a topic and adopting differing points of view; and who seem to be trying to convince each other of their views. But when we read the book more closely we realize that the characters do not adopt consistent differing points of view; instead, each idea comes up in the lips of each speaker sooner or later. For instance, the notion that God will never do wrong is first offered by Eliphaz in ch. 4, and then echoed by Bildad in ch. 8, and again by Zophar in ch. 11. The notion that man has no right to judge God, or to call God to judgment, is expressed by Eliphaz in ch. 4 (v. 17), by Job at ch. 9, by Bildad at ch. 25 and Elihu in ch. 32. In other words, if we see this book as a dialogue, then we must see it as an early form and we must give Plato enormous credit for having had the brilliant idea to ascribe particular conflicting points of view to each of the interlocutors in his dialogues, and for having made their speeches consistent with their points of view.

We might therefore reject dialogue as the genre of the Book, and see Job instead as a developed form of *tragedy*. On such a view, the function of the chorus can be seen as having been taken over by the comforters, the Greek chorus which was never required to have a particular point of view, but which echoed and voiced the sentiment or thought of the playwright at a particular juncture in the action. Indeed, Plato's own dialogues can be seen as a form of drama, and we are in fact told by Diogenes Laertius that Plato began his career as a poet and dramatist who wrote tragedies,[3] but that he heard Socrates speaking in the agora and he stopped writing plays in early adulthood and devoted his life to philosophy. So has the Book of Job been seen as a form of drama, and can we read it that way?

The Book of Job has also been seen as an *aretalogy*, that is, as the life of a righteous man. Such aretalogies became more common in the centuries after Job was probably written, but certainly there are earlier examples of the genre and the author might have been influenced by that form.[4] However, the story-within-a-story format that we have here is out of character with most aretalogies; and the detailed reporting of the speeches of Job and his friends is also out of character with it. Indeed, if the Book of Job had left those speeches out, then it might in fact look like an early aretalogy, but not as it stands today.

Descriptions of the Book generally refer to it as a prose *framework story* surrounding a series of poetic speeches. The presence of frame-work stories in general is a not uncommon literary device: the Arabian nights stories are told by a maiden who needs to hold the interest of the sultan; the Canterbury Tales are narrated by pilgrims on a journey; the Golden Ass is a series of stories inside the main story of a man who attempts to reverse a spell which was cast over him. However, the relationship of the framework story in Job to the poetic speeches in the body of the book is more direct than in those other examples; and the dramatic force of Job is not really centered in the events that occur, but rather in the ideas that are expressed and the characters' reactions to the narrative events. So it would not be satisfying to view the Book of Job as a story-within-a-story in that later-developed narrative style.

Let us indulge ourselves for a moment in a deliberate anachronism, and view the Book of Job as the first recorded *record of a psychotherapy*. We will find the exercise instructive, for here we have a central character who suffers a trauma. On this view of it, the framework story is there to tell us the background, so that we can understand how great

3. Diogenes Laertius *Lives of the Philosophers* Book III.

4. The lists of virtues recited by Egyptian deities, such as Isis, have been called "aretalogies," but the term is best applied to relatively shorter stories of great men—stories whose length prohibits them from being "epics." The genre became particularly popular during the first century.

his pain must have been. He expresses his pain; he then talks through his problem with his friends, who may be seen as projected voices articulating thoughts in Job's own mind. He struggles with various means of resolving his grief and finally he finds some resolution when God allows himself to be seen by Job, albeit in the Whirlwind; and then the matter is in some way resolved.

As in a therapy process, here, too, in the Book of Job, the same ideas keep coming up over and over again, each time with slightly different emotional coloring. The idea that God will never pervert justice, the idea that man can never understand God's motives, the idea that Job is pure or that he must have sinned, the idea that some member of his family must have sinned, all of which appear and reappear in the mouths of all of the speakers.

Deep psychological problems are seldom solved: they are rather *dissolved* through a process of repetition, revisiting, and slow growth. The dissolution or resolution is sometimes intense, and is sometimes centered on a moment or particular experience, as the appearance of God in a whirlwind. The resolution must take place on many levels at once: on the intellectual, emotional, and spiritual levels. We can read the Book of Job in this way very comfortably. The book deals earnestly with its central problems on all three levels: intellectually, with Job resisting the attempts of the comforters to find easy ways out; emotionally, with all the speakers and particularly Job expressing the strongest feeling; and spiritually, through the constant preoccupation with man's relationship to God that runs throughout the book. If we view the Book this way the last part of the framework story can be seen as an externalization of the notion that Job's world improved once his inner problem was resolved.

However, no matter how instructive it may be to view the book as the record of therapy, historically such a reading would be hopelessly anachronistic. While it is true that therapy has precursors in other forms of dialectic, from a historical point of view we can never think of the author of Job as having set out to record the history of Job's therapy. No, to find what the author of the Book of Job thought he was writing, I think we should look to another literary genre that did exist at that time: the report of a lawsuit, a *case report*.

A Tort Case

That the book has a heavily legal orientation has been pointed out many times by the commentators. There are the constant references to litigation: Job's repeated expressions of concern as to whether he is entitled to haul God into court. "Can a man contend with God? Will God be bound by the judgment? Will not God do whatever He pleases, no matter where justice is said to lie?" This thought runs though the book, and reveals a preoccupation with the legal process. But more fundamentally than that, the book can be read as an actual case report: the report of a lawsuit between Job as plaintiff and God as defendant. The framework story that introduces the book and then concludes it can be seen as the reporter's brief account of the facts and disposition of the case.

We find the same pattern in contemporary appellate reports: they begin with a brief statement of the facts and then present a reasoned approach to those facts and finally end with a brief statement of the disposition. "Smith induced Jones to purchase a business by telling him that it produced $50,000 a year of income. Jones paid Smith $1,250,000, but discovered after eight months that there was no income, and that Smith had given him a false set of books. He sues to rescind the purchase agreement, offering to restore the business to Smith. The law is settled that one who is induced to enter into a contract by fraud is entitled to rescind it; but Smith asserts that his statement that the business would produce $50,000 a year in income was merely opinion, and could not form the basis of a fraud . . ." and so on, until the court comes to the disposition: "Judgment against Smith affirmed."

So it is in the Book of Job: the introduction tells us how God gave Satan leave to invade Job and bring him low; and it describes the damage Job suffered. His children, his flocks, all his possessions were taken away from him and then he was smitten with boils. This is the background. Then the book takes us right into a sort of courtroom: Job begins by cursing his day and raising his complaint. The speeches which follow may be seen as fictional records of court speeches: forensic oratory of the sort we see in the early speeches of Gorgias,[5] and which then developed

5. It is said the Athenians were wowed when Gorgias of Leontini, early in the fourth century BCE, invented his florid parallelistic style: "What have these men done that they should not have done? And what have they not done that they should have done?" Early sources tell us that the people who heard that kind of oratory for the first time were overwhelmed by it and loved it.

into the more sophisticated, toned-down speeches of Demosthenes, Lysias, and Socrates (in the *Apology*). The Greeks were the first, so far as we know, to write out their orations before they were delivered; and the speeches of the rhetors were much admired and discussed. Moreover, as every schoolboy knows, the forensic speech became a highly developed *genre* in Greece and Rome.

We have the same kind of forensic oratory in the Book of Job. Each speaker is making a formal argument, an address to the court. This appears from the repeated use of certain legal phrases in the book. Each speech, for instance, is introduced by the phrase, "And so-and-so answered and said . . ." This use of the word "answer" (*vaya'an*) is not used in the sense of answering a question. No, this is the legal word "answer," meaning to speak when it is one's turn, in response to the speech of one who has spoken earlier. What we have is Job's complaint, and then the speeches of the comforters, and finally, of God himself. Just before Elihu delivers his speech, at the beginning of ch. 32, the author records concerning the three older friends, the original comforters, "*vayishb'tu meanot et Iyov*," that is, they stopped talking and had no more to say. The literal meaning of the Hebrew words is, "Then these three men rested from answering Job": this is a legal term, which we still use in our courts today: the term "to rest" in the sense of acknowledging to the court that they have presented their case in full. Apparently, when one put his hand on his mouth in the Near Eastern court of those days, that was a signal to the assemblage that he had no more to say. Job put his hand on his mouth in 50:4: "Behold I have been a fool, how shall I answer you? I have put my hand upon my mouth." In the Near Eastern court, the speeches continued until no one had anything more to say. This was before the Greek water-clock which timed the speeches of litigants. In Job's court, one could speak until he was finished.

The legal oratory here is not later Greek, but rather oriental: florid, passionate, unrestrained; but the structure of the book is still the structure of the report of a fictional lawsuit. In fact, the framework story ends with God restoring to Job not just all that he had before. No, *double* what he had before. This can be seen as the report of God paying double damages, just as would have been required, at various points under the Mosaic law, in cases of theft, battery, or malicious mayhem.[6]

---

6. Exodus 21–22.

So we conclude that the Book of Job is in its fundamental form, a legal document: a case report. However, seeing it as a case report leads us to observe how it straddles cultural fences. The early case reports that we have from the Near East do not include lengthy quotations of the lawyers' speeches. That was done in Greece, but not further east, in the orient. The oriental case report tended to be short and pithy and to the point: "A stole a servant from B, pays 200 coins"; "A killed B's wife, pays 50 coins."[7] Such reports concentrated only on what I have called the framework part of the case report. But in Greece, the background of the orations is hardly preserved at all, and instead, the bulk of the record is merely the report of what the lawyers said and how well they argued.

There is another aspect of the case report that reflects the Greek influence here. The litigation in the book ends with God paying double damages; but the whole process is reminiscent more of a settlement or mediation than of a court trial. In this report, there is no judge, no jury; there are no findings of fact. All that happens is that Job's complaint is aired before a community of elders, and God's response is heard, and then there is a settlement. The notion of "judgment" is missing: people argue for their positions, but no one adjudicates. All that happens is that there is a result that both parties accept. This was characteristic of civil litigation in Greece up to the fifth century: they used what we today would call mediation rather than what we would call litigation.[8] It was only later that more formal court procedures evolved, with the judges deciding who was right and who was wrong. While the adjudication process was more common in Egypt and the Near East, and while the profession of lawyering arose and flourished in Rome,[9] mediation and settlement was the norm in early Greece.

---

7. Hammurabi's Code has been described as a set of case reports; but even if we read it as a "Code" we see how fact-oriented it is. But more to the point are the now-available collections of ancient Babylonian case reports, which "stick to the facts" more than to the arguments or speeches.

8. See generally Michael Gagarin, *Early Greek Law* (Berkeley: University of California Press, 1986) and the many examples he cites.

9. The "judgment" process in the Egyptian Book of the Dead, for instance reflects a court process that adjudicates in order to get to the outcome. So in the Book of Daniel we see stories of a judge skilled in cross-examination and in eliciting truth from conflicting testimony. The judgment of Solomon reflects a tension between "settlement" and adjudication: one woman is lying, and Solomon proposes a "settlement" in order to expose her.

So we see that in the Book of Job, the author has constructed a case report in a new *genre* which is a melding of legal reporting traditions. The overall structure is a report of an early Greek mediation, but the rhetorical style is Near Eastern, and the litigants and their issues are Hebrew.

Other Multicultural Elements in the Book of Job

This brings us to ask ourselves what the cultural background was of the person who authored the Book of Job. The most cursory consideration will make us realize how intensely multicultural his background was.

We ask first what faith the author held: was he a believer in the traditional Hebrew God, in *Yahweh* or *Elohim*, a monotheistic personal God? Or was the author a Greco-Roman polytheist? In the earlier books of the Bible there is but one God, and when he wants to talk to someone, he needs to talk to people. God speaks to Abraham, Isaac, Jacob; he appears to Moses in a burning bush. He has no one else to whom to talk. However, in the early framework story of Job, God is speaking with the sons of *Elohim*, the Sons of God, and has direct conversation with *the* Satan. His interaction with Job is only indirect: he looks down on Job from above, and is proud of him; and then he shows him off to *the* Satan. Like the Greek gods, this God of the early chapters of Job does not seem to encourage I/Thou relationships: he is distant.

Not just distant: he takes actions and makes bargains in heaven which have effects on earth, but the people on earth can never know the origin of their pain and suffering. This is one of the most interesting features of the Book of Job: the fact that we know why Job is suffering, or at least we are encouraged to think we know, but Job and his friends do not know and can never know. The bet with *the* Satan, the offhand permission given by God to *the* Satan to "test" Job, are things Job is never told, even when God appears to him in the whirlwind.

This theology is not just polytheistic: it is Greco-Roman in its view of the relationship between God and Man. In the Garden of Eden episode, Adam and Eve knew perfectly well why they were being punished. In the story of the binding of Isaac, the angel told Abraham, "Because you have done this, because you were willing to sacrifice your son . . ." People knew the motives of God and understood them. In the Greco-Roman world, it was quite different. The Odyssey begins with the story

of the council of the gods. Many human events are explained as the consequences of divine play, or wrath, or love. Men are but the playthings of
the gods! We see this view of things presented in the opening passages
of the Aeneid which every high school student used to memorize:

> *Musa mihi causas memora, quo numine laeso*
> *quidve dolens regina deum tot adire labores*
> *insignem pietate virum, tot volvere casus*
> *impulerit. Tantaene animis caelestibus irae?*

Virgil knew that Aeneas suffered because some God was angry.
The author of Job had the same idea; but this idea would have been
foreign to Abraham, or to Moses. Yet, the Book of Job returns, in the last
chapters, to a scriptural monotheistic mode, where God finally appears
to Job in the whirlwind, reminiscent of the burning bush, and speaks
directly to him. No longer is God speaking to other gods. No, he speaks
to Job. He tells the comforters that their words have not found favor
with him. He is back to his old style of God-man interaction. This shift
in the book is, of course, one of its dramatic themes, and the whirlwind
appearance is a resolution of sorts.

The author was evidently influenced as well by very different
schools of philosophical thought. For example, his conception of the
self, the identity of a man, is something very much intermediate between
a developed Greek conception and a classical Hebrew conception. The
opening narrative describes Job as righteous, and speaks of his family,
his flocks and his riches, as if they were part of himself. Job makes sacrifices on behalf of children, in case they had sinned; and later, in ch. 8,
Bildad suggests to him that his sufferings are attributable to sins: if not
to his own sins, then perhaps, to the sins of his children. This echoes the
Old Testament idea that the sins of the father are visited upon the children; and with the other Old Testament idea that when God rewards
a man, he "multiplies him" and grants him "increase," which is to say,
children, lands and flocks.

However, woven together with this oriental, semitic conception of
the self is an emerging Greek conception of the self as a body and a
soul, and of the soul as the more important, eternal part. This notion is
imported, to be sure, from Near Eastern sources, but developed in Greek
philosophy, so *the* Satan takes two cracks at invading Job: in the first
round, he destroys his family and riches, but does not touch his body.

In the second round, he is given permission to invade the body but is told not to touch his *nefesh*, usually translated as the soul. Maimonides, the twelfth-century Jewish philosopher, in his discussion of the book, interpreted the word to refer to the immortal part of Job, the part which would live after Job died; but this interpretation does not fit well with the story of the book. The words may mean simply that *the* Satan is told to do whatever he will with Job but not to kill him. However, the entire structure of this part of the story strongly suggests that the soul, which *the* Satan is prohibited from destroying, is the Greek *psyche*, which is to be distinguished from the *soma*.

The author's ethical vocabulary also reflects his variegated cultural background. The book uses several different words to refer to moral virtues, and by writing these words down, mapping out, as it were, the word field, we can see an interesting pattern emerge. The book begins with a description of Job as *tam v'yashar viyre Elohim v'sar mera*, whole and straight and God-fearing and one who avoided evil. God refers to Job as "my servant, Job." Job is concerned lest his children *chatu*, sinned; and would never "curse God" or "lay reproach on God." In Chapter 4, when Eliphaz speaks, he introduces the term *naki*, pure. He speaks of the *chorshey aven*, those who cultivate evil. In ch. 8, when Bildad begins to speak, he uses the word *tzedek* for justice, and *pesha* for transgression. In ch. 9 *tam* is opposed to *rasha*, the perfect as against the wicked. All these words are familiar to us from earlier scriptural sources. We can see these words as indicating the author's deep rooting in Old Testament ethics.

However, in ch. 27 Job says "until I die I will not remove my integrity from me" speaking of his *tum'a*, wholeness, integrity. Later, right before Elihu speaks, the author says Job was righteous, *tzadik*, in his own eyes. In these uses of these words we see an interesting shift from the moral vocabulary of the Pentateuch to an almost psychological vocabulary, *tam v'yashar*, which is a hendiadys and appears elsewhere in the Bible.[10] It starts out as an epithet or description of a person but never as a person's own description of himself. In Job *tam* becomes *tum'ati*; and in Job we see the original phrase, which does not appear elsewhere in Scripture, "Job was righteous in his own eyes," a new Greek notion.

10. *Tam* (e.g. Abimelech, justifying his approach to Sarah), *tamim* (e.g. Noah) and *yashar* (Deut 12:25 and 28, what is right in the eyes of the Lord) are often-used terms of moral approbation in the Old Testament. Here the author of the Book of Job uses them as a kind of hendiadys.

Elsewhere, we do find mention of the righteousness of God; but only here do we see the notion of being righteous in one's own eyes, and of clinging to one's integrity. All of a sudden, one's integrity and righteousness are subject to one's own action and to one's own judgment: one can be conscious of his integrity, and may elect to serve it, or preserve it, or to forsake it. This is new, and this is not Hebrew or Old Testament ethics. This shift in diction from a familiar set of words denoting good and evil, to a more psychological use of these words, is another aspect of the book's mixed cultural background.

However, we need not focus on the details to see that the Book of Job is a cauldron of diverse cultural elements. After all, is not the fundamental tension in the Book of Job the tension between the Old Testament view of God as an object of faith, and the developing Greek view of the universe as an object of reason? Is not the whole point of the book, to the extent that it has a point at all, the struggle between these two differing attitudes toward God who, in the book, represents the universe? By adopting the style and format of a series of legal speeches, the author attempts to bring God into some kind of a court, to litigate with him, to subject God to argumentation and to probe God's motives and actions.

Not quite yet, as we have said, does the book come to the level of a dialogue. The speeches are not responsive to each other in the intricate ways they are in Plato's dialogues, nor are the arguments intended to be detailed. Nonetheless, the legal setting provides a forum for reasoned discourse, which is something quite new in biblical theology. This is a major step forward even from the much-cited passage in Genesis 18, when Abraham bargains with God for the salvation of Sodom and Gomorrah. Here, not only will God come into contractual relationship with man, he may actually litigate with man and join with man in argument and disputation.

The word, covenant, is in Job conspicuous by its absence. Only twice does it occur at all: when Job says, "I made a covenant with mine eyes" (31:1), and when God asks of Job, "will the Leviathan make a covenant with thee?" (40:28). Neither of these uses is particularly evocative of the usage of the Pentateuch, or even of that of the prophets. Although covenant theology appears to be the essential preoccupation of the whole Book of Job, still, it is never mentioned as such. Instead, its axioms and maxims are mentioned, and they are either illustrated or flouted, as the reader may decide; but the word, covenant, and the appeal to covenant are not here.

Cultural Conflict and Resolution in Job

The Book of Job must be seen as attempting to resolve and integrate the many themes and styles of thought that flow into it from the different cultural backgrounds I have identified. The book is terrifyingly ambitious, because the themes with which it wrestles are fundamental and basic to the world-view of its author and of the characters in the book.

Resolution in this book takes place, if it takes place at all, at the end when God appears to Job out of the whirlwind, and Job sees God with his eyes. Job then stops talking in court. This is the part of the book towards which the author has been guiding us all the way through; and according as we feel satisfied or disappointed here, the book has succeeded or failed in achieving a resolution.

However, this resolution does not satisfy us, for God's own self-defense is not convincing. It seems to us that Job has wimped out, and has retreated into the obedience which Jehovah always demanded of the Old Testament figures, and which they always delivered on demand. Reading at this point of the book, we become angry at the author. Has he lost his mind? Has he forgotten everything that came before? Can he now yea-say like Eliphaz, Bildad, Zophar, and Elihu? Can he nod his head so comfortably in shallow affirmation?

Perhaps, not quite: for although Job takes a certain position in the text, it is not at all clear what attitude the author has towards Job at this point of the book. Does he share Job's sentiments here? Does the author worship God? Does he even respect God? It is not clear; and this is something brand new in the history of biblical Literature: the author's attitude towards his material is not quite straight, not simple at all. It needs to be thought about in its own right. When we focus on the author's attitude towards his materials, we see finally a conspicuous and essentially multicultural element in this book: irony, the bitterest irony imaginable, Greek, tragic, cosmic irony woven into phrases and narratives which are culturally complete, incongruent with irony.

Irony in the Book of Job

This author of Job is detached from his materials in a way we might not have thought possible before the last half of the twentieth century. He records the events with frightening objectivity; he reports the speeches with full accuracy; but he does not seem to be a player in his own book. He does not take sides. He does not seem to endorse any one point of view. He exhibits in this way, woven into the very fabric of this book, the highest kind of irony.

There is high irony in the fundamental storyline. As Jung has pointed out in *Answer to Job*, whom is *the* Satan able to corrupt, ultimately? Not Job. No, Job maintains his faith. But someone is corrupted by *the* Satan in this book: it is God. He is shown as vain and corrupt, sitting at an assembly of his vassals and feeling proud of his "servant, Job." *The* Satan is able to trick him. If, as we must believe, Justice exists—not in God, and not in man—but in the I/Thou dialogue between God and man, God has certainly betrayed justice here; and this aspect of the book is ironic.

God, in this book, betrays the covenant, betrays his own law and breaks his own rules. In the works of the other prophets, the breach of the covenant is by Israel, by the people. But in this Book of Job, the breach is by God, and that is a high irony for an author who shows himself to be steeped in biblical lore.

There is irony in the constant quotations of the wisdom literature: these quotations come up in strange ways, as if the author is making fun of them. Does not Job remark, *Adonai natan, v'adonai lakach; y'hi shem Adonay m'vorach* ("The Lord hath given, and the Lord hath taken; Blessed be the name of the Lord") surprise us when we read it? It is not just a pious remark: it is a strange remark, for one who has just lost his children and his riches. It does not seem to be an accurate reportage of what Job actually said. Because of its sing-song rhyming, it feels almost as if the author is laughing at it.

So, too, at Job 3:17, "There the wicked cease from troubling, and there the weary are at rest." At this point, Job is wishing that he might have died at birth and come to rest with kings and princes in death. He quotes this strange fragment of wisdom, which also has a sing-song ring in the Hebrew, *Sham r'shaim chadlu rogez, v'sham yanuchu y'giei koach.*

There is irony when Eliphaz, in his first speech to Job, asserts that evil is in fact punished and good is rewarded. Having made his opening argument, he says to Job in 5:1–2, "Call now, if there be any that will answer thee; and to which of the holy men wilt thou turn? For wrath killeth the foolish man, and envy slayeth the silly one!" This is a slight non sequitur, to which Job might well answer, "But a rolling stone gathers no moss!" Job does in fact mock Eliphaz later on, when he begins his answer with "Doth the wild ass bray when he hath grass, or loweth the ox over his fodder? Can that which is unsavory be eaten without salt, or is there any taste in the white of an egg?"

At the opening of his speech, Elihu introduces his remarks by explaining that he kept his silence because he was the youngest. "I said that days would speak, and that a multitude of years would make us know wisdom." referring, obviously, to some proverb which must have gone, "Days will speak, and multitudes of years will make you know wisdom," that is, that the eldest should speak, and younger listeners should learn from them. You can read the whole Book of Job through this way and see that almost every quotation of the wisdom literature it contains is bitter and ironic.

Then, there is irony in God's response from the whirlwind, a total evasion of the accusation Job leveled against God, as I have just pointed out. There is also irony in God's taunts at Job: "Where were you when I created the world? Can you command the mountains, the rains, the clouds? Where were you when the morning stars sang together, and all the sons of God shouted out? Can you draw out Leviathan with a hook? Will he make a covenant with you?" This long *ad hominem* goes much farther than the customary self-praise that orators in Greece customarily indulged in. For God's speech does not introduce an argument: *his self praise is the argument*; and that is a surprise and a bitter irony.

There is irony in Job's "repentance" and in the fact that God tells the comforters that they have not spoken well even though they seem to have been arguing on the side of God all through the book. Yet, he demands a sacrifice from them, not from Job with whose words he is well pleased.

There is irony built into the very narrative style of the book, as well. First, there is the deliberate transition in style and scene in the opening passages. "There was a man in the land of Uz, righteous and perfect and evil-aversive . . ." This is in the style of a standard biblical narrative, comfortable, and familiar. Then the scene shifts to Heaven, which is unusual and jarring. Then we realize that Job cannot know the source of his woes even though we do; and this discomforts us.

Then there is the painful irony in the fact that Job is correct and all his friends are wrong: can we not enter the story ourselves and tell them why Job is suffering? Cannot the author provide an epiphany of some kind? How foolish all these wise men look arguing over the theory of evil, reward and punishment, when we know it was something as trivial as a conversation between God and Satan that is at the root of the whole thing.

There is bitter irony in the way Job's comforters turn into his accusers: they have come from afar to comfort him; when they saw his affliction, they sat silent for seven days, betraying exquisitely delicate sensibilities. But the minute they begin to interact, to argue, to articulate ideas, only accusations come to the surface. Then there are these sing-song quotations from the wisdom literature, always with an overtone of bitter cynicism, as I have explained.

Moreover, there are the deliberately altered uses of legal terms in senses that are intended to surprise. In Job 19:23–25: "Who will grant it that my words be written down somewhere, that they be printed in a book? That they were engraved with an iron pen and in eternal lead written in a rock. I know that my redeemer liveth, and that in the latter day he will rise up above the dust." This statement of Job's is often quoted as referring to God as his redeemer, but it probably does not. No, the redeemer is the person who is going to come and pay off the pledge, and redeem Job *from* God. God is not the redeemer: God holds Job as pledge. Then in 27:5: "Far be it from me," says Job, "to justify you" speaking to the comforters. "Until I die, I will not remove my integrity from me." This use of the term "to justify" is a play on the senses of the term: it means to adjudicate one as correct, to allow one party to win the lawsuit. In another sense, it means to make another righteous, to correct his moral error, to rectify him. So Job here is adopting the role and character of the judge in his own case, as if now he is litigating with his own friends, not with God. He refuses to justify his friends, and it is beyond his ability to rectify them.

At the end of the book, the author returns to the Genesis narrative style. "And it came to pass after God had spoken these words to Job, and God said to Eliphaz the Temanite, "My nostril hath dilated against you and your two friends, because you have not spoken correctly of me as my servant Job did." What a surprise! What a shock! Did Job really speak well of God? And what God is this? Oblivious to the whole development before, he appears just as he did in Genesis, demanding sacrifices, even speaking in the same cadences as in the earlier books. There is something eerie about this return to the opening style, as if the whole discussion before were a dream, a nightmare, perhaps.

Indeed, so ironic is the Book of Job that it seems to bear the relationship to other books of the Old Testament, that the Black Mass bears to the sacred mass. It is remarkable that this book made it into the canon of scripture: it is a testimonial to the liberality of the compilers, or to some access of ecumenicism that overwhelmed them at the time. For the Book of Job is a great and deliberate and sustained blasphemy. Only instead of being deliberately perverse, as the Black Mass is, this Book of Job is earnest, very earnest, and earnestly ironic.

Irony is a barrier to complacency. There is no room in the Book of Job to feel comfortable, no room to nod your head in assent or affirmation. There is nothing for you but pain, doubt, and anguish, if you read this book from the very beginning to the very end.

Litigation as a Form of Prayer

Yet, there is one more manifestation of irony in the Book of Job that we must savor: *litigation* turned out to be a form of *prayer*. For whatever else we may say about the litigation process recorded in the book, the overriding dynamic is that the defendant actually comes to participate in the process. At the end, God made his own forensic speech and he paid the damages he owed. So Job's litigation turned out to be a way of coming into direct contact with God. It was thus after all a form of prayer, a way of bringing God into the circle of human discussion.

The early Greek litigation process itself had some of the aspects of a prayer meeting: the community gathered together to hear the speeches of the litigants and to express themselves in poetic ways about the deep questions raised by the case. The goal of the process was resolution of the dispute, and this was brought about by allowing the parties to say their peace and express their feelings, and then by the offending party's making reparation. A distortion of the social fabric was repaired and peaceful coexistence was restored.[11]

But in Job these elements are ironically distorted. God chastises the "comforters" and Job is required to make a sacrifice for *them*. Yet, were they not Job's antagonists throughout the book, disagreeing with him and telling him that he was a sinner? Is it not unheard-of for a litigant to make a sacrifice on behalf of his adversaries? Yet, God did not require Job to make any sacrifice to him: it was the comforters, whose speech did not please God, who acted as God's proxy to receive the sacrifice. Only after the sacrifice was made did God pay the double damages. It was as if the sacrifice was essential to the restoring of peace and the harmony of the social fabric, necessary but not sufficient.

This blending of the two forms of communal activity, litigation/mediation and prayer, is the last irony in the book, and it is also a deeplying resolution of many of the multicultural tensions which underlie the book.

Conclusion

We must see the Book of Job as a milestone along the path of intellectual and spiritual development that led from the covenant mentality of the Pentateuch to the mystery mentality of the Alexandrian Age. That path led through multicultural encounter, conflict, and resolution at the deepest psychological levels.

Multicultural encounters are always an important part of history. Wars and commerce rupture borders and create encounters between people of differing backgrounds and world views. But with wars and commerce come new and foreign ideas, and different cultures can react quite differently to the influx of such ideas.

Look at us today. Even though the developed nations are preoccupied now with economic and legal issues surrounding immigration, generally we think of ourselves as a proud example of a multicultural society. We have absorbed, in a friendly and even enthusiastic way, cultural ideas from India, China, and Japan. It is not just that we eat *sushi*: no, we have been quite receptive to big ideas such as karma, the Tao, rebirth, holistic medicine, and the martial arts. We are sufficiently comfortable with our own fundamental beliefs today, despite the apparent

---

11. Gegarin, *Early Greek Law*, ch. 2.

breakdown of our societal values, that we can receive these foreign ideas graciously into our homes.

Varying degrees of openness to other cultures is well-documented throughout history. We read in the story of Joseph how the Pharaoh reacted when Joseph's brothers came to his court. They were well received, with hospitality, but the Egyptians would not eat with them at the same table because that was an abomination to them (Gen 43:32). We remember the late Middle Ages and the Elizabethan Era, when English thinkers accepted influences from France, Italy, and the Arab world, and felt themselves enriched, not threatened. The self-confidence of the English in the Victorian Age was so overwhelming that it went everywhere, to Africa and India, spreading empire and discharging the White Man's Burden.

However, when self-doubt begins to gnaw at the center of our hearts, we cannot accept the Other, the Foreign. Then we see it as a danger and we reject it. It does not give us pleasure, it does not give us comfort. No, then we fight it off; when we cannot fight it off, it gives us pain.

This is what happened in Job's day. The clash of Greek ideas with Jewish ideas was cataclysmic and disquieting to the author of this book. He could not reconcile them. He was convinced that the covenant worldview was dead: he no longer believed in it, at least, not naively. He had tasted reason, dialogue, discourse, dialectic. He had thought beyond the covenant to issues of *enforcement* of the covenant. He was troubled; and in this book he articulated all the thoughts and followed all the trains of thought that he could not reconcile. He knew he could not reconcile them but he wove them together in a fabric of sublime irony, and he let them clash against each other and he gave voice to every one of them.

16

A Test of Balaam

Locating Humor in a Biblical Text

Anthony J. Petrotta

Introduction

THE QUESTION OF HUMOR'S LOCATION IN BIBLICAL TEXTS MAY SEEM like work for idle hands. R. P. Carroll exhorts us, "The concept of a humorous biblical prophet is an oxymoron," and goes on to say, "Humor as we know it today is not a feature of the Bible."[1] There are a few scholars, however, who beg to differ and suggest that not only will we miss a laugh, but we may miss the meaning of a text as well: "By missing the humor in a biblical text taken out of context, we do more than miss the laughter; for by viewing a verse of scripture as solemn

---

1. Carroll, "Is Humour Also Among the Prophets?" in *On Humour and the Comic in the Hebrew Bible*, Yehuda T. Radday and Athalya Brenner, JSOTSup 92 (Sheffield: Almond, 1990) 169. I think the operative phrase for Carroll is "as we know it today." I will concede this point: humor as we know it *today* is probably not part of the Bible any more than love (and marriage, etc.) as we know it today is a feature of the Bible. But this is a minor point, maybe even trivial and pedantic. Contemporary British humor and American humor are not "the same" and often does not carry well from one side of the Atlantic to the other, yet, even as an "American," I would be hard pressed to say that the concept of a humorous Brit is an oxymoron. The ancient Hebrews loved and married— and joked—no doubt, in a different idiom than "we" do, but they still engaged in such activities and we can still speak about those activities without being anachronistic or solipsistic. The points of contact are as important as the differences, and both can be taken into account without losing sight of either.

when it is meant to be humorous, we often get the opposite message than that intended."[2]

The presence of humor in the Bible seems to have some question attached to it, hence my title with the verb "locating" is deliberately chosen because of its ambiguity and the further objections that P. R. Davies mounts regarding the presence of humor in the Bible: "Texts do not *have* humour any more than they *have* meaning," and quoting Freud, "Wit is made, while the comical is found."[3] His contention is that we only find humor in the Bible in our *retelling* of the "joke." The reader creates the humor; humor is not a feature of the text itself.[4]

Can we locate humor in the text not only as readers, but in the actual performance of the text?[5] That is, are there shared features in texts

2. Doug Adams, *The Prostitute in the Family Tree: Discovering Humor and Irony in the Bible* (Louisville: Westminster John Knox, 1997) 7. The work of J. William Whedbee, *The Bible and the Comic Vision* (Cambridge: Cambridge University Press, 1998), is an apologetic for viewing the Bible as "comic" (not the same as viewing it as humorous, but there is an obvious overlap). Also worth noting in the insightful work by T. Jemielity, *Satire in the Hebrew Prophets*, LCBI (Louisville: Westminster John Knox, 1992).

3. P. R. Davies, "Joking in Jeremiah 18" in *On Humour and the Comic in the Hebrew Bible*, p. 191. Davies' quote of Freud and his distinction between "wit" and the "comical" need qualification. The terms employed for speaking about humor and the comic are notoriously wide in usage and while distinctions are important and necessary, the most helpful writings on humor are not overly subtle with their definitions. Indeed, the translator of Freud's book cautions the reader about the terminological difficulty in Freud's work. He further notes that the problem is compounded in trying to render the German terms into English (S. Freud, *Jokes and Their Relation to the Unconscious*, translated by J. Strachey, (NY: Norton, 1963) 6–8. Even narrower and more technical terms such as "satire" and "irony" find little agreement and have a wide range of uses; cf., e.g., A Pollard, *Satire*, (London: Methuen, 1970), and M. Gurewitch, *The Ironic Temper and the Comic Imagination* (Detroit, Wayne State University Press, 1994). See also A. Brenner, "On the Semantic Range of Humour, Laughter, and the Comic in the Old Testament," in *On Humour and the Comic in the Hebrew Bible*, 39–58, who says that the words for humor, etc. range from joy to cruel fun.

4. Davies does the retelling with Jer. 18 by writing a "modern Targum" with a "stream-of-consciousness" approach.

5. In answering the question, I draw upon the eminently readable and helpful work of Walter Nash, *The Language of Humour* (London: Longman, 1985), and the other studies on humor cited below. Nash uses the word "performance" mainly, however, in the sense of an actor rather than an author. Denis Donoghue, *The Practice of Reading* (New Haven: Yale University Press, 1998), argues that texts not only communicate, but perform (78). He uses the term perform to indicate the combining of "words, gestures, and actions to the condition of form." We could call this a "poetics of humor" but that sounds far too grand, perhaps, for the study of humor.

that readers generally agree upon as humorous?[6] These questions involve difficult theoretical issues which Carroll, Davies and others raise, but I propose something more modest and narrow: What would have to be present in a text to even consider it as humorous? What are the most simple and obvious elements in a text that would allow readers to discuss the possibility of humor? By focusing on a particular text that many scholars regard as humorous these key elements may emerge more clearly and perhaps can provide critical clues to the more general or universal issues regarding the presence or absence of humor in the Bible.[7]

An Unequivocal Example

Answering simple questions, however, is seldom simple, so I will start with a text that is unequivocal, then proceed with a biblical text that is more complex but which is regarded by many scholars as humorous.

The most obvious feature of Figure 1 is the visual display. This visual display signals a joke. It is known as a cartoon by its framing and by the drawn characters who are caricatures, in bodies and faces drawn somewhat disproportionately. This cartoon is a recognizable genre in our culture. Its intent is to be humorous.[8]

---

6. Texts may not "have" meaning, as Davies contends, but note that Davies tells us that he will "retell" (perform?) Jer. 18 as a "modern Targum." There must be something in Davies' retelling that corresponds to "Targum" and while an author's intention may not always coincide with the actual performance in the text—is Davies "successful" in writing his Targum?—we as readers can say something about the collocation of words and how these words share features of other writings. *Something* in a text allows readers to talk of genre, style, tone, meaning, and other concerns of reading.

7. My comments will, I think, have implications for more general observations regarding the Bible and humor, but my initial concern is to see if we can speak of humor of any sort in a particular text. In the light of the sweeping statements that are made regarding the absence of humor in the Bible—Alfred North Whitehead's oft quoted line, "The total absence of humor from the Bible . . . is one of the most singular things of all literature" is indicative of this camp--requires only a single example to make qualifications necessary.

8. Again, the intent and the performance may not coincide here—a reader may not find this text humorous. In this case the author has assured me that humor was her intention and the performance supports that intent on a *formal* level (the "cartoon" drawing). As a reader I would give Professor Davies the benefit of the doubt when he tells me that he is doing a modern Targum and unless the performance were obviously at odds, I would say that intent and performance coincided in a recognizable way. I could, however, not agree or like his Targum, but that is a different issue than not intending or not performing. In a (ancient) text where an author has not told us

"I no longer believe in a literal millennium, but I'm collecting
Jacob Neusner books just in case."

Figure 1

This visual display, however, is actually part of a more fundamental feature of humor, the derivation in culture. This derivation is the world

---

her intention, we have the performance and any clues that would undermine what that performance suggests. A. J. A. Waldock, *Paradise Lost and Its Critics* (Cambridge: Cambridge University Press, 1966), argues that Milton intends, by his admission, one thing, but undermines that intention at points in his performance (Waldock in turn has been criticized himself for this argument). This observation simply suggests that we cannot move *automatically* or unequivocally from intention to performance or the reverse. It does show, however, what we experience reading texts: the rich and tentative nature of any reading—but certainly not its impossibility. As we compare features in texts and listen to other readers of these texts, we can at least begin to speak of such things as genre, form, style and so forth.

of the joke, the literal and cultural conventions, prejudices, patterns of behavior, attitudes, themes, and so forth, that are indicated in the text. These assumptions surrounding the characters and their actions or words become grist for the joke-mill. Jokes expose the pretensions of a culture, often in the form of defense by those who are hampered or harmed by them; and pretensions that are seen as arbitrary and no longer tenable.[9] What is the world of the joke in Figure 1?

Figure 1 portrays a culture of scholars. The artist, not an academician, was asked to draw two scholars in dialogue.[10] Scholars inhabit a world of books and debate important, if slightly esoteric, questions. This particular world of scholars requires two further pieces of information that get highlighted when considering the other features of humor: the meaning of millennium and the identity of Jacob Neusner. The millennium being discussed by these scholars has nothing do to with digital clocks malfunctioning or bank accounts disappearing, but rather has theological importance, the thousand year reign of God. Jacob Neusner is a notoriously prolific translator and author of religious texts. So figure 1 has a derivation, a place in our culture, and while it is signaled visually by the form,[11] it is more important to recognize the world of the joke. In this case, it is the world of theological scholars.[12]

9. See, e.g., Freud, *Jokes*, 90–116.

10. How do we know this? The bow-tie, glasses, books under the arms, the "ivy-covered" walls, and the language employed point in that direction. Wall Street or Fleet Street would have to be presented differently. To be sure, there are some readers who would not recognize that world and, no doubt, somebody could construe the world portrayed differently, but that is a different statement than saying that the world portrayed is not academic. The artist was asked to draw two scholars in an "academic" setting. (The author of Figure 1 and the artist actually are two different people in this joke.)

11. Forms (in this case, a cartoon) *can* work across cultures or even periods, though often forms are local. The literature on humor suggests that below the surface of jokes are "types" that jokes draw upon. An "Italian" joke in one culture can easily be transformed into an "Albanian" joke in another. In the case of "Italian" jokes, the type is question-answer or text-rejoinder, a recognizable form in our culture. See Nash, *Language*, "It [a joke he cites] shows that we are not required to have the *specific* experience to which the witticism refers, but only to grasp a category, to recognize the *kind* of image that is raised" (13–14), and 38–53 for varieties of joke formulation.

12. A further "material" fact of the scholarly world that could be helpful is that scholars often pride themselves on the number of books they own—and if the books one has authored fill a shelf, then one can boast all the more. Jacob Neusner does not simply have a shelf of his own books, he has an entire wall. (It should be pointed out that the author of the joke has had the wonderful opportunity of studying, briefly, with Professor Neusner and has tremendous respect for his work.)

A second feature of humor is highlighted by asking a rather obvious question: "Why would any person in his or her right mind collect the books of a rather obscure person?"[13] The question puts the whole joke in jeopardy because it subverts what Jerry Palmer calls the "logic of the absurd."[14] As the respondent to the joke, I have to accept that somebody would collect all those books.[15] The fact that scholars do have shelves and rooms of books makes the unlikelihood of the action likely in a convoluted logical way of jokes. As readers who know the culture, we accept the conditions that the author proposes for the sake of the joke. Figure 1 has a likelihood factor that must be accepted for the sake of the joke. As an audience, we have to accept that scholars would collect books by Jacob Neusner.

The specific use of the term, Jacob Neusner's books, is central to the third formal feature of humor. These words are the center of the joke and actually trigger the joke. If the author changes those words for almost any other words, say, "but I'm collecting rocks just in case," or books by A. J. Petrotta, the text would not work as a joke. It would not be absurdly logical, but simply absurd.

Some word or phrase detonates the humorous mass.[16] Often the trigger or locus of the joke is an ambiguous or multivalent term that signals some duplicity in the joke and turns the joke in a direction other than the obvious.[17] In Figure 1 the words Jacob Neusner's books are not multivalent, but seen in collocation with literal millennium they signal

13. "Obscure" to the general public. Of course to those of us in the guild, Jacob Neusner is anything but obscure, and the joke turns on the knowledge "we" have of his prolific output of books, as will be shown.

14. Jerry Palmer, *The Logic of the Absurd* (London: BFI, 1987).

15. Some of the concerns of Carroll and Davies are evident in this aspect of joke recognition. The "reader" does participate in the joke if he or she is to "get" the joke. However, a joke can be signaled, but missed by a reader; I would contend that a joke is still "performed" though perhaps not realized in that particular instance. "Monty Python" and "The Simpsons" have all the formal features of humor, but some people fail to find anything humorous in these shows. Is it the failure of "Monty Python" or the failure of the audience? I always enjoyed the remarks of "Siskel and Ebert" (movie critics) regarding many of the Hollywood comedies: "This movie suffers what too many 'comedies' suffer from—it's not funny." They did recognize, however, that the "form" was humorous even if the execution was not funny.

16. Nash, *Language*, 7.

17. Arthur Koestler calls this duplicity "bisociation"; *The Act of Creation* (London: Picador, 1975).

a turn from a theoretical theological discussion to a practical concern of how to occupy oneself during this prolonged time.

Victor Raskin uses the helpful image of two scripts present in a joke.[18] These scripts intersect at the trigger or locus. I find the term disequilibrium convenient when speaking of the logic, scripts, and the locus of humor, since the reader must be caught off guard by the absurdity of the word(s) in the first, obvious script, then restored by the logic of the second, sublimated script. The locus puts the movement from one script to the other into play. Laughter ensues from the momentary shift and restoration.[19]

Figure 1 has a locus that triggers a move from one script to another within the joke world. Initially, the shift seems odd, but then proves to be quite logical. Collecting Jacob Neusner's books is odd, but in the context of a millennium the reader is asked to reconsider how literal this millennium might be. Indeed, these words shift the world of the joke from metaphor back to literal.

Finally, often a joke fits a type that transcends the particularities of words and culture.[20] Figure 1 fits a classification of false premises

18. V. Raskin, *Semantic Mechanisms of Humor* (Dordrecht: Reidel, 1985).

19. If both scripts are obvious or one script is not at all obvious without explanation, then we do not laugh. Billy Crystal in "Mr. Saturday Night" tells a joke to his brother, and then says, "Did you see what I did?" If you "see it coming" or if you do not see it at all, you will not find it funny. There must be enough of a shift from one script to another to be caught off guard, but the scripts must be close enough to be seen together. Raskin, *Semantic Mechanism*, speaks of the scripts as being "locally opposite" which captures this sense of disequilibrium that must result from the two scripts intersecting at some point and departing in "opposite" directions. If there is no disequilibrium—no "opposite" or no restoration—then we do not laugh (no "dis") or we simply feel discomfort (no "equilibrium"). The "pleasure" of laughter comes from the momentary imbalance and restoration as we see that both scripts were present all the time. On "pleasure" as an aspect of humor, see. J. Morreall, *Taking Laughter Seriously* (Albany: SUNY Press, 1983) and his essay, "Humor and Emotion," in *The Philosophy of Laughter and Humor*, ed. J. Morreall (Albany: SUNY Press, 1987) 212–224.

20. See n. 11 above; Nash cautions, rightly, that classifications are only tentative since the compositional and semantic features overlap, and variations are too readily made to suffer the simplicity of mere pigeon-holing. That caution, however, does not negate that humor has recognizable categories that transcend particular experiences. I would add that this observation further serves to qualify Carroll's remarks that humor "as we know it today" is not a feature of the Bible. If Nash is correct that there are types of humor, however tentative these classifications are because of the diverse ways that authors can use and vary the types, then we ought to be able to find some recognizable type in different cultures or periods.

and flawed inferences. If one no longer believes in a literal millennium, then collecting books is surely nonsensical. The connection between the millennium and collecting books is not strictly logical, but is logic-boggling to borrow one of Nash's phrases.[21]

These considerations, a derivation in culture that requires knowledge of material facts that will get subverted in the text, a likelihood factor of the unlikely that must be accepted as logical, a locus that triggers a shift from one script to another, and a shared pattern that suggests a type, can suggest the presence of humor in a text. These features may not demand humor, but they open the possibility for considering it in ways that readers can discuss based upon our experiences with humorous texts or situations.

A Biblical Example: Balaam

Introduction

With these considerations in mind, I want to examine Numbers 22–24, the story of Balaam, Balak, and the discerning donkey, to test the possibility of humor in a biblical text. The Israelites, fresh from victories over the Amorites, set out to the plains of Moab. King Balak is concerned and warns the elders of Moab, "This horde [the Israelites] will now lick up all that is around us as an ox licks up the grass of the field" (Num 22:4).[22] So, the king does what any self-respecting, but a trifle fearful, leader would do in a similar situation of facing a horde who could well defeat him in open battle. He calls in a mighty diviner to deal with the

21. The observation that Figure 1 is a joke of a certain type can be supported by the fact that the author patterned her joke on a Woody Allen joke: "I don't believe in life after death, but I'm bringing along a pair of underwear just in case." The statement entails a logical flaw *somewhere*, and yet it does make sense *somehow*. Also, a variation on this joke substitutes "Brueggemann" for "Neusner" and the joke still works since Brueggemann is approaching Neusner for the number of books he has in print.

22. The metaphor to "lick" the grass of the field is interesting and, of course, the early rabbis had to find an explanation. Just as an ox uses its tongue to conquer, so does Israel: "As Israel relies on words of prayer and blessing, so Balak wanted Balaam to counteract his foes with words of curses" (*Num. Rab.* 20:14, as noted by W. Gunther Plaut, *The Torah: A Modern Commentary* (New York: Union of American Hebrew Congregations, 1979).

military threat.[23] The story contains three sections, each escalating and reinforcing the central issue of God's control over the destiny of his chosen people and Balaam's ability to "see" and speak the desired word.

Derivation

In the first episode, Numbers 22:1–20, the design begins to take shape as Balak's emissaries come to Balaam twice. The doublet sets forth the theme(s), but is not in itself humorous. The theme is first stated in 22:8, "Stay here tonight, and I will bring back word to you, just as the Lord speaks to me." Yahweh tells Balaam that night not to curse the Israelites for they are blessed (22:12). Balaam sends the emissaries back to Balak. Balak, however, is persistent and sends a more impressive retinue, with more money and promises. Balaam is not swayed by this new offer and reiterates his resolve to follow the divine command: "Although Balak were to give me his house full of silver and gold, I could not go beyond the command of the Lord my God, to do less or more" (22:18). Nevertheless, Balaam leaves open the door that he might come if God should relent and let him go with them to Balak: "You remain here . . . so that I may learn what more the Lord may say to me" (22:19). The Lord does relent after a fashion, with a proviso: "But do only what I tell you to do," the Lord cautions him (22:20). Nothing will be said, implied, or done, to the Israelites without the prior approval of God.

The world of the story is the culture of kings, prophets, and hostility towards God's people. Interpretive concerns abound in this seemingly simple story. Many commentators question the prophetic status of Balaam,[24] but a more pressing question is, Why is Balaam going at all?

---

23. Knowing the outcome of a battle before entering into one is always the safest foreign policy. As a diviner, Balaam can either "see" the outcome of events or, better, he can effect the desired outcome with a word, which is what Balak desires.

24. The text can be viewed as having implicit question or puzzle that can be stated different ways, but take some form of, Is Balaam a "true" prophet (will he do only what the Lord instructs him)? The "puzzle" is that Balaam is not a Hebrew, so can he be a "true" prophet at all (cf. Deut 18:9–15)? Or, as Milgrom puts it (*Numbers*, JPSTC [Philadelphia: Jewish Publication Society, 1990] 469–71), "Balaam: Saint or Sinner?" Balaam is not called a "prophet" (in Josh 13:22 he is called a "diviner"), but the spirit of God comes upon him (Num 24:2), and throughout the story he seeks the Word of God and is consistently obedience (e.g., 22:8, 20; 24:13). The question of Balaam's status, prophet or not, I think, is not a *central* concern of the passage; rather his commitment to obedience is a concern. That obedience is the issue with Balaam is supported by the

We have already been told that Balaam is not to curse the Israelites, for they are blessed (22: 12).[25] Why go to Balak? In the story God relents after a fashion, and not even on Balaam's initiative, but his own: "That night God *came to Balaam* and said to him ..." (22:20). By going, Balaam is not going against a divine decree. Thus, another question arises: Why, then, does the Lord get angry with Balaam (22:22)? This question seems more puzzling than the prophet question, and sets up the famous scene with the donkey. Answering that question is also part of the material facts of the story that contributes to its humor.

Numbers 22:22 has long been a problematic verse. Commentators have precious few options with this enigma of why Balaam is going and the subsequent anger of God. The easiest way through the problem is to draw upon Deuteronomy 23:4–5 and 2 Peter 2:15 (also Philo in *De Vita Mosis* 1: 48 and many others), and ascribe to Balaam the sin of avarice. Numbers 22–24, however, is rather silent on the issue of avarice or any other sin. Indeed, Balaam rejects the offer of money at the outset (22:18), which is reiterated in the climax (24:13). Critical scholarship of the past two centuries solved the problem by saying that Numbers 22–24 is a combination of two stories being brought together. Numbers 22:22ff. comes from a different hand than 22:7–21, hence has a different

---

repeated use of "do only what the Lord tells" and its variations in the pericope. Levine prefers to speak of "subservience" rather than obedience since there is no real option of going against the Lord in this matter; Baruch A. Levine, *Numbers 21–36*, AB 4A (New York: Doubleday, 2000) 215–17. Perhaps, since the relationships throughout the pericope are hierarchical (she-ass/master; prophet/king; prophet/God). However, even given these hierarchical relationships, the she-ass "acts up" in Balaam's eyes, Balaam "disappoints" Balak to say the least; and God is angered at Balaam for some reason. "Choice" and God's sovereignty are constantly acted out in the biblical narrative with no sense that these are contrary. Also, Levine qualifies his remarks on subservience by "extracting" the "jenny" narrative from this discussion (ibid., 236). On the complexity of Balaam's social roles see M. S. Moore, "Another Look at Balaam," *RB* 97 (1990) 359–78. Since jokes entail multiple scripts (bisociation), they are a kind of puzzle to sort out, and the fact that Balaam's role is ambiguous furthers the humor of the passage with bits of misdirection.

25. The use of "bless" here is worth noting because it calls to mind another person and another passage that becomes important in our discussion. God says to Abraham, "I will make of you a great nation, and I will bless you ... I will bless those who bless you, and the one who curses you I will curse ..." (Gen 12:2–3). Balak says to Balaam, "Come now, curse this people for me ... for I know that whomever you bless is blessed, and whomever you curse is cursed" (Num 22:6). Balak, in effect, imbues Balaam with godly powers, which would be a point of contention with God if Balaam accepts that role.

perspective on Balaam and his actions. Numbers 22:22ff. is not a sequel, but a parallel story in which Balaam does not consult the Lord before setting out.[26] Some commentators simply remain silent on the issue, even though it begs to be addressed.[27]

Between 22:20, when God relents and lets Balaam go, with the important proviso to do only what he is told, and 22:22, when God gets angry at Balaam, is an innocuous little verse that may be telling: "And Balaam rose up in the morning, saddled his ass, and went with the princes of Moab" (22:21). This choice of language is striking, being similar to the language used when Abraham is told by God to sacrifice his only son, Isaac: "So Abraham rose early in the morning, saddled his donkey, and took two of his young men with him . . ." (Gen 22:3).

Hasidic interpreters noted this correspondence of language between Abraham and Balaam, and drew this distinction: whereas God did not permit Abraham to carry out his act even though Abraham was instructed to do so, how much less would God be willing to allow Balaam to succeed when Balaam is opposing God's will.[28] But is Balaam really opposing God? Opposition to God is certainly not clear in the

---

26. Milgrom, *Numbers*, says that if we remove the incident with the ass, what remains is a picture of Balaam as a "saint" (469). Levine, *Numbers 21-36*, also sees the pericope as separate, and Timothy R. Ashley, *The Book of Numbers*, NICOT (Grand Rapids: Eerdmans, 1993), goes so far as to say that this pericope could be excised without changing the main thrust of the Balaam narrative (434–35). I think that they are correct that one could excise the pericope from the larger narrative and still have a coherent narrative, but in excising the text we get a totally different story. My comments on the humor of the passage suggest that the she-ass story is central to the redactor's aim in Num 22–24 (and more generally in Numbers as a whole).

27. It may well be that two stories are combined here or that avarice is the bone of contention between God and Balaam, but both lines of reasoning are equally "harmonistic" and are outside the story proper. An inept "editor" is no less "outside" the story than the sin of avarice, which nobody in Num 22–24 ascribes to Balaam. In putting these stories together in this fashion an editor is fulfilling an editorial function to guide a reading of the text. Balaam is neither saint nor sinner (Milgrom), but a prophet who may or may not fulfill his role (obedient to the Word of the Lord). It is in the playing out of Balaam's ambiguous role as obedient or disobedient prophet that the tight construction of the text comes through (and Balaam is seen as dependent solely upon God's word(s) not his own for his "gift" of prophecy). The interjection of the she-ass story precisely at this point changes how we read the larger narrative, not true versus false prophecy, but obedient or disobedient servant.

28. See Plaut, *Torah*, 241.

story unless one sees going to enquire of God twice as disobedience.[29] The *Aqedah*, the Binding of Isaac, is centered on obedience and is a testing of Abraham (and Isaac!). The echoes between the two stories allow the theme of testing to be brought into the Balaam story. Balaam's character,[30] his obedience, is at stake in Numbers 22. Balaam may well be impetuous in his leaving before Balak's emissaries come to him. He set out in the morning, that is, he is intentionally setting out on his own without the further invitation of the emissaries.[31] However, Balaam is setting out on a trek that is fraught with danger for the People of God, and as a prophet, his resolve to follow the Lord, speaking only what the Lord tells him, is crucial.[32]

If Abraham can be tested and Moses, the Lawgiver, can take matters into his own hand and incur the wrath of God (Num 20:2–13), how much more so a pagan prophet?[33] These observations on the first section may seem to have taken us a bit off track, but they are part of the

29. Rosenzweig adopts this position, as noted by Plaut, ibid., 241. Getting an unequivocal answer from God once should suffice; when someone returns with the same question, "God will without fail speak the words of the demon that is within us ('You may go')." Rosenzweig notes that the theme of "resuming" is pervasive in the story. In my opinion, "repetition" is crucial for the humorous effect, not for the anger of God.

30. Not his role as a prophet, which is everywhere assumed in some form or another. In regard to character and the notion of testing; *e.g*, Deut 8:2: "Remember the long way that the Lord your God has lead you these forty years in the wilderness, in order to humble you, *testing you to know what was in your heart, whether or not you would keep his commandments.*"

31. Balaam shows the same "resolve" in 22:13 though in this passage he arises in the morning to tell Balak's emissaries that he will *not* go with them since he had been instructed by the Lord during the night not to go. The issue again seems to be one of obedience.

32. Note Deut 13:1–5, especially 13:3, "... for the Lord God is *testing* you ..." *Being* a prophet may be no less a test than heeding a prophet. See also 1 Kgs 13 where the man of God from Judah is tested by King Jeroboam (and the prophet from Bethel). The man is offered a gift from Jeroboam, but refuses, saying, "If you give me half your kingdom, I will not go with you ..." (1 Kgs 13:8).

33. The testing of a non-Hebrew is not without parallel in the Bible; the story of Job is also one of testing a "pagan" who proves to be faithful. Note that the angel of the Lord in Num. 22 is described as an "adversary" (*satan*) recalling the prologue to Job, and Job "rises early in the morning" to offer sacrifices to God (Job 1:5), thus connecting once again to Abraham. See R. W. L. Moberly on Gen 22 and the connection with Job 1–2, *The Bible, Theology, and Faith* (Cambridge: Cambridge University Press, 2000) 78–107. Moberly does not mention Num 22–24 with these examples, but his focus on testing, seeing, blessings, obedience, etc. fits well with what transpires in the Balaam story.

material facts, the derivation of the culture of the joke.[34] Balaam is an important seer. Emissaries are sent twice with large sums of money. But his resolve could cause trouble. Balaam sets out early. He is an altogether too industrious a chap. So a test is set up. God manifests anger.[35]

Likelihood Factor, Scripts, and a Trigger

The second episode, 22:22–35, is not marked as a joke with a recognizable visual cartoon or verbal opening ("Have you heard the one about . . ."), but has a classic escalating triad structure and a likelihood factor with which a reader must reckon.[36]

First, the structure. Balaam sets off on the she-ass, whether to assist Balak or speak the word of the Lord is not entirely clear, for in his

---

34. Another "material fact" comes from the *Deir ʿAlla* inscription, the "Balaam Inscription." This inscription, together with the biblical references to Balaam, suggest stories of Balaam circulated widely, and were part of the lore of the Levant. Balaam appears to be the "Nostradamus" of the ancient Near East: His *legendary* status makes the "joke" even more effective. His status as a legendary prophet, however, is not *necessary* to understand the joke. Even within the story, Balaam's role as a prophet of repute is evident since Balak seeks him out and goes to great lengths to procure his services. Recall also Balak's words to Balaam in Num 22:6 and see n. 25 above.

35. That a test is not foreign to the story of Balaam finds support in both Pseudo-Philo and *Numbers Rabbah*, though the "test" mentioned there is associated with God's question in Num 22:9: ". . . God came to Balaam and said, 'Who are these men with you?'" Since, obviously, God knows who these people are and what they want, the question must be a test of Balaam's *character*, not a request for information; cf. James L. Kugel, *The Bible as It Was* (Cambridge, MA: Belknap, 1997) 485. I agree that the test is of character, but I place the test itself elsewhere in the story.

36. Is the character of Balaam drawn as a cartoon? It is not clear to me that he is, but Balak certainly seems a caricature of a monarch. Balak is fearful and superstitious to the point of seeking a renowned seer and offering to pay huge sums to procure his services. As for verbal signals of jokes, that is where the cultural differences would be greatest. It is quite likely that we don't have the linguistic and cultural competence to say what a verbal opening would look like to an ancient Israelite (and in that limited sense Carroll's point is well-taken). There is a paucity of material to draw upon with these ancient texts. However, a series, the form of three—three people, three incidents, etc.—that is required for many types of jokes is present: "A prophet, a priest, and a prostitute died on the same day and came before Saint Peter . . ." The third element (or final in a series) "breaks" the pattern of the joke and provides the shift to the second, sublimated, "script." The parable of the Good Samaritan has a similar triad pattern; the Samaritan, the third passer by, "triggers" the sublimated script of who the true neighbor is (Luke 10: 29–37). Three or four works to set up a joke pattern; two is too compact to set the contrast of the pattern and five or more is too lengthy for the concision required of jokes.

setting out he has found displeasure with the Lord.[37] An angel blocks the way for Balaam three times. Initially the angel stands in the road, the ass sees the angel, and turns aside. Balaam, oblivious to the angel, strikes the ass according to the rules of master and beast of burden: Do as I instruct.

The angel next moves to a more advantageous position, blocking the path with a wall on either side. The ass once again tries to avert disaster by attempting to maneuver in the tight place. In doing so, Balaam's foot is scraped on the wall, not a good sign for the poor donkey, who gets struck once again. Finally, the angel blocks the path so no maneuvering will help. The donkey may be an ass, but it is not stupid;[38] it lies down in the road to avoid the armed angel even though she is sure to find further displeasure with her master. This is too much for Balaam, who strikes the ass a third time.

Something must happen at this point, the structure of narratives and of jokes, demands it. A narrator has several options here. The most obvious is that the angel will speak. That is what angels do (cf., e.g., Gen 18:1–15; 19:1). Here the angel does not speak, however. Another character could be introduced at this point, an observer from the field who sees the angel that Balaam, the seer, does not see. No one steps forward. Balaam himself could finally see what is happening or come to some other course of action befitting his vocation. He does not. Or, again, God could intervene; since God has already spoken to Balaam in these stories, his presence here would not be a bad narrative ploy. However, God remains transcendent rather than coming to the aid of the beast. God is not *deus ex machina* here, but *deus absconditus*.

One other option exists: the she-ass could do something. Donkeys are beasts of burden, a further material fact that now becomes important to recognize. What asses do best is cart goods or people from one place to another, and how one treats a donkey is proverbial: "A whip for

---

37. Ashley, *Numbers*, translates Num 22:22, "As (*ki*) he was going . . ." stating that something occurred during the journey, not prior to it.

38. Ellen Frankel, *The Book of Miriam* (San Francisco: HarperCollins, 1998), says, "Our favorite part of this story is the one about Balaam and his ass. Of course it doesn't surprise us that the animal is a *she*-ass. Nor does it surprise us that the *Tsena Urena* [a Yiddish Torah commentary written in the seventeenth-century basically for women who couldn't read Hebrew] saw fit to neuter the ass when she was translated into Yiddish. They couldn't fool us! It's clear that only a female animal would show such wit and wisdom. After all, *she's* not the ass in this story!" (228).

the horse, a bridle for the donkey, and a rod for the back of a fool" (Prov 26:3). This animal that responds best to force, this beast of burden, as Balaam has clearly treated her, is portrayed by the narrator, however, as a beast of perception. She sees more clearly than the prophetic seer. The ass speaks: "What? Why do you treat me thus?" The she-ass makes no reference to the threat of the angel standing, with sword drawn, but rather appeals to her faithful service, her obedience over the years: "Am I not your donkey, which you have ridden all your life to this day? Have I been in the habit of treating you this way?" (Num 22:30).

Is the speech of the donkey a miracle?[39] Balaam is not troubled by its speech and the narrator makes no comment. What is intriguing is the likelihood factor, the logic of the narrative. In the reality of our everyday lives, asses may speak, but donkeys never do. Biblical narrative eschews fable.[40] It is simply absurd to assert that beasts speak. In the narrative world of the story, however, the action of the donkey has a degree of plausibility. Why? On first reading, we might be surprised when the donkey speaks, but actually we have been set up for this action by the narrator. The donkey has shown a degree of perception that the seer has not. If Balaam the seer speaks, part of his role in connection with seeing, why not the donkey also, since the donkey is the one who has seen more and better all along? She has seen the angel.

The logic of the narrative has shown the plausibility of the donkey speaking, but it is from the implausibility of any beast speaking that the narrative gets its effectiveness. Surely one must ask, with Ellen Frankel and many other perceptive readers of this story, who is the ass in the story? The answer is Balaam, the seer: "In truth, Balaam is depicted on a level lower than his ass: more unseeing in his ability to detect the angel, more stupid in being defeated verbally by his ass, and more beastly in subduing it with his stick, whereas it responds with tempered speech."[41]

39. In *Pirke Aboth*, the speech of the donkey is said to belong to the "ten things fashioned at the end of the sixth day of creation" (see, Plaut, *Torah*, 241; and Milgrom, *Numbers*). As such it is not technically a "miracle" but part of Creation itself.

40. Neither this story nor the Garden of Eden story with a snake that talks (Gen 3) are properly fables. Once the beast speaks, it is gone from the stories for all purposes and no moral is espoused in the words of the animal or is drawn from the words. In *Numbers Rabbah* the beast is said to die immediately after the speech so that it could not be made an object of reverence; cf. Plaut, *Torah*, 242.

41. Milgrom, *Numbers*, 469. Note also that if we change the words of the donkey to almost anything else (even something as obvious and natural as "Can't you see the

This tempered speech triggers the move from the world of seers to shortsightedness; from beasts of burden to perception; from arrogance to humility; from autonomy to obedience. There is momentary disequilibrium, but only until the reader sees what has transpired in the narrative. The speech is the locus of the joke, and any other action or words would change the affect of the passage. Balaam's obedience as a prophet is tested,[42] and the appropriate response is to laugh at the unseeing Balaam.[43]

Type

The "jenny" incident follows the general type of false premises and flawed inferences. The donkey has more insight and obedience truly directed, indeed, more authenticity and integrity, than the famous seer. The central section of the Balaam narrative shows a world of principalities and powers, kingship and prophecy, opposing Israel and God. It moves in an incremental pattern, which is broken in the third element, the speech of the donkey. That donkeys speak at all is absurd but seen to be logical in the story, and it triggers the move from one script to another, from beast of burden to perceptive and articulate animal. Premises regarding

---

Angel *with a sword* standing right in front of us?") the speech is either not humorous or hardly humorous at all. It is the tempered speech and the appeal to obedience that makes her remarks so effective (and affective).

42. Moberly, *Bible*, says, ""[T]esting is necessary for human beings to become truly themselves, and so is for human good; testing may be a searching and demanding process; testing is the action of God within human life" (p. 105). See also H. Fisch's remarks on testing in literature generally in *A Remembered Future* (Bloomington: Indiana University Press, 1984) 3ff.

43. P. J. Budd, *Numbers*, WBC 4 (Waco, TX: Word, 1984), notes the satirical portrayal of Balaam in this story but says that ultimately Balaam is depicted in a good light because he receives revelations, is penitent, and receives a commission: "It is fair to add that the ass story does not depict Balaam in a *seriously disadvantageous light*" (264, italics added). Milgrom, as we have seen, similarly sees this episode in contrast to the larger portrayal of Balaam in a "good" light. I would say to Budd that the ass story does not portray Balaam seriously at all! Or, better, to both Budd and Milgrom I would say that it is precisely the positive portrayal of Balaam that makes for the effectiveness of this episode, the move from appearance to reality: The (famous) seer must be tested at his strongest point in order that he knows to speak *only as he is told*. The test of Abraham similarly focuses on obedience (Gen 22:15–18), but also occurs at Abraham's strongest and most vulnerable point, the Promise. Likewise, Job is tested on his integrity (Job 1:1, 9–11).

power are exposed: whose word, which power? Humility, not arrogance triumphs in this world.

Derivation, knowledge critical to seeing the humor, a likelihood factor, locally opposite scripts, a trigger, and type are present in this middle section. None of this demands the presence of humor, but without them humor would not be present.

The Joke Repeated

The third episode, the longest, Numbers 22:41—24:25, has a feel of a joke as well. Balaam has learned his lesson well, but the king needs instruction. If a question is raised concerning Balaam's character, no such question can be entertained with respect to Balak. Balak is a villain, less subtle, and therefore less humorous, than Balaam. Balak is determined to get his curse.[44]

The derivation remains largely unchanged, and the story continues to play with notions of perception and obedience, and the question of wherein power lies. Furthermore, we have the sequential pattern, a triad, a likelihood factor. An incident triggers a move from one script to another, and it follows a recognizable type.

Three times Balak requests of Balaam a curse on this horde that is encamped within the field of view. Three times Balaam utters only the blessing of the Lord, each one escalating in its implications. As Budd recognizes, Balak's response to Balaam's curse similarly escalates with each frustrated blessing: In 23:11, Balak is shocked (Milgrom); in 23:25, he seems very upset (Milgrom); and by 24:10 Balak fires Balaam in a fit of anger (Milgrom): "Then Balak's anger was kindled against Balaam,

---

44. The ambiguity of my phrase and the verbal play comes from Num 23:7 when Balaam "quotes" Balak and at the beginning of his oracle, "Balak has brought me form Aram/the king of Moab from the eastern mountains; Come *curse Jacob for me* [which can be rendered, "Come, curse me Jacob"; Milgrom] /"Come, denounce Israel!" Ah, the force of a comma and a preposition! Being caught in one's words occurs at other notable places in the Bible: Pharaoh seems oblivious to his words in Exod 5:18, "Go, serve" which can be rendered, "Go, worship." Micah "catches" his opponents in their own words in Mic 2:6–11, they will be the "dribblers" with their wine-soaked messages. See A. J. Petrotta, *Lexis Ludens: Wordplay and the Book of Micah*, American University Studies, Series VII: Theology and Religion 105 (Berlin: Lang, 1990.) This "type" of joke is close to what Nash, *Language*, calls "transforming tags" where words are attributed to somebody as seemingly innocent utterances, but which, in fact, say more than the speaker realizes (41–42).

and he struck his hands together . . ." The striking or clapping of the hands is the locus and shifts the script from a monarch negotiating a military advantage, to a frightened and frantic potentate doing damage control.[45] The type corresponds to caption and annotation: the behavior of the king is commented upon by its skillful and graphic portrayal in the story.

Balaam is risible; Balak is pitiful. With Balaam, we can experience a degree of sympathy since his inability to see what is before his eyes, and his impulsive actions may resonate with many of our foibles. Balak, however, is so mechanical that he makes it difficult to respond in any favorable way. Balak is blindly determined. Robert Alter observes that it is precisely this mechanical stance in human affairs, the persistence in pursuing the curse, the elaborate sacrificial designs to procure a favorable hearing, and so forth, that is the primary source of comedy.[46] Ira Clark, I feel, comes closer when he says, "Their ridiculous stance is increasingly absurd with each stupidly unresponsive reaction of the pagan leaders: let's try again."[47]

This second joke is not nearly as effective as the previous one with Balaam because of the predictable nature of Balak, and the fact that we have just heard this joke about Balaam. Balaam is being maneuvered

45. To "clap one's hands" occurs infrequently in the Bible. At Lam 2:15 the "passers-by" clap their hand, "whistle," and shake their heads at the dismal fate of the "daughter of Jerusalem." Those actions, if taken apotropaically, fit well with Balak clapping his hands to ward off the evil of "his curse." With each reading of this verse I picture "Ollie" in Laurel and Hardy movies responding with his frustrated, "Ooh . . ." as the desired outcome of his words and actions are thwarted and undermined, often by Laurel, his partner. The words employed in Numbers might belie this verbal cartoon--the frantic actions of the king lacks decorum and a primary role of a king is to go to battle (cf., e.g., 2 Sam 11:1). There is also the "ironic" twist that Balak is angered by Balaam's "coming" to him but not cursing the Israelites, whereas God was angered by his going to Balak but perhaps not blessing the Israelites. Everybody in the narrative seems mad at poor Balaam—except the judicious "Jenny" who suffers Balaam's wrath unjustly.

46. R. Alter, *The Art of Biblical Narrative*, (New York: Basic Books, 1981), p. 106. The classic formulation of the mechanical in humor comes from H. Bergson in his essay on "Laughter" (reproduced in *Comedy*, W. Sypher, editor, (Baltimore: Johns Hopkins University Press, 1956), pp. 56-190). Bergson says, "The attitudes, gestures and movements of the human body are laughable in exact proportion as that body reminds us of a mere machine" (p. 79).

47. Ira Clark, "Balaam's Ass: Suture or Structure," in *Literary Interpretations of Biblical Narratives*, vol. 2, ed. by R. R. Gros Louis and J. S. Ackerman (Nashville: Abingdon, 1982) 142, italics added.

into position and he is once again not seeing. The maneuvering and the not seeing are for different reasons in each story, but the effect is the similar. Balak's actions are ridiculous and trigger a move between scripts. If the action of the king is changed in any way, he graciously accepts the word from Balaam or he dashes off to fight the horde himself; it is not funny. We can see the joke coming. Also, episode three is not as tight as episode two;[48] it is more expansive and may even be a parody, of sorts, of the first incident. Balak is no Balaam.

Concluding Considerations

I want to end with a quote from Waldock and make a final, general observation on humor: "The method of the cartoon is to allow the villain of the piece to reach a pitch of high confidence and vainglory, and then to dash him down. The whole point is that he is dashed down, the essence of cartoon-technique being to bring your adversary to grief by unfair means, in short, by some sort of practical joke."[49]

Waldock's comment is not on the *form* of humor so much as on its *function*. Carroll begins his essay by dismissing all forms of denigration as not humorous.[50] However, philosophers since Aristotle, and readers across all disciplines, recognize that put down is part and parcel of humor. Morreall calls this the superiority theory of humor, which he lists along with the incongruity and relief theories.[51] His own theory, however, combines aspects of all three theories and though he tries to overcome the negative associations with the superiority theory by broadening it to cognitive shifts and not just affective shifts, as the

---

48. Freud, *Jokes*, 16ff., notes that brevity is essential for jokes, but it is brevity of a certain type, brevity with "substitute-formation." His substitute formation corresponds roughly to the notion of two scripts and "disequilibrium" (bisociation), one obvious, one sublimated until "exposed" (Freud) by the "trigger" (Nash). On comic expansion see Nash, *Humour*, 17–25.

49. Waldock, *Paradise Lost*, 91–92, italics added. Levine makes a similar observation that Balaam is being mocked and ridiculed, though for Levine this portrayal in Num 22:22–35 is not in accord with the preceding and following view of Balaam in the narrative.

50. Carroll, "Humor," 169–70 mentions, among other things, parody, mockery, language of abuse, harangues, sadistic and skeptical remarks.

51. J. Morreall, "A New Theory of Humor," in *Philosophy*, 128–38.

superiority theory maintains in its classical form, it must be kept in mind that he is speaking of laughter here and not jokes in particular.[52]

The Balaam/Balak story fits with Waldock's portrayal of a cartoon. The biblical stories are not afraid of being moralistic, and dashing down both Balaam and Balak is not shied away from. The story shows that any threat to the People of God will not come from an external source, prophet or potentate. This point is highlighted by Israel being camped in the plains below, oblivious to what is taking place just above them.

However, lest the Israelites themselves reach a pitch of confidence and vainglory, the story does not end at Numbers 24.[53] If we turn the page to Numbers 25, we find that the Israelites have brought Balak's curse down upon themselves (Num 25:1–5)! Here is yet another reversal in the story, a shift from a perceived threat that turns out to be not a threat, the powerful prophet and king, to an unperceived threat that threatens all the more so, the real threat that secretly lies within their own actions.[54] We laugh at Balaam for not seeing, but all the time the Israelites have not seen either, both what God has done above, or the consequences of what they are doing below.[55]

52. He uses the example of seeing an old friend on the street and laughing with her, which is obviously a positive response in the situation and not a negative one. His focus is laughter generally, though, not jokes proper and the element of "surprise" in both cases carries the laughter, not the positive or negative affective associations surrounding the encounter. Morreall makes the point that the "surprise" must be pleasant, on some level, or we would not laugh. It seems to me that "pleasant" feelings stem from seeing what the person has done in the joke, how the shift has taken place before our eyes. We seldom laugh at jokes made at our expense, not because they are not humorous, but as the object of the joke, we are shown to be "inferior" in some way (Balaam is bested by an ass, after all; and the king is thwarted by the prophet he hires).

53. The position of this story in the book of Numbers is a problem that source critics address since the ties with what precedes and follows are not obvious. Milgrom, *Numbers*, says, "Indeed, these chapters are totally distinct from the larger context: Neither the personalities nor the events in them appear in the adjoining chapters" (185). From the standpoint of theology—and humor—the links may be closer than usually thought. Clark, "Balaam's Ass," makes this observation: "God's jokes, no less than his potent commands or his sublime visions, inevitably display his all powerful providence" (138).

54. Laurel and Hardy built their careers on something like this: their elaborate schemes not to get caught or to safeguard something are brought down by the very schemes they devised to ensure the results. In humor, we are often our own worst enemy.

55. Jesus' parable of the log and the mote in a person's eye is a similar joke (Matt 7:4–5//Luke 6:41–42). The story of Jonah, the one other story in the Bible that scholars will cite as an example of a humorous story along with Balaam, also shares this feature of "self-critique."

The difficulty of reading the Bible for humor is not that it does not share our sense of what is humorous, but that we may not, as yet, recognize their signals, their particular ways of formulating joke types. Indeed, our particular visual clues and verbal directives ("Have you heard the one about . . .") obscure the more potent clues of humor, those of cultural derivation, logic, the trigger, and bi-sociative scripts. Perhaps by turning our attention to these features in other texts, we can begin to build a picture of what humor looked like in those days.

17
Afterword

J. Harold Ellens and John T. Greene

OUR TWELVE COLLEAGUES AND WE HAVE NOW BROUGHT THIS STURDY
volume to a close. It is with the fond hope that each reader will find the
illumination from, and appreciation for, the Hebrew Bible that we have
learned to expect from any attempt to read or study it with diligent discernment. The Hebrew Bible is the paradigm that shapes all of our lives,
and our whole lives, in detail, whether we know it or like it, or not. We
really ought to have the interest and concern to know it well and discern
clearly what it does to and for us. This volume is our effort to assist that
quest substantially along the road to greater human wisdom, derived
from wrestling with that divine wisdom that we can acquire from both
the great wisdom and gross dumbness, in the testimony of the prophets
and sages of ancient times.